A Timeless People

PHOTO ALBUMS OF AMERICAN JEWISH LIFE

SAUL H. LANDA

gefen
publishing house
JERUSALEM ◆ NEW YORK

Cover Design, Typesetting and Layout by S. Kim Glassman

ISBN: 978-965-229-486-9

1 3 5 7 9 8 6 4 2

Gefen Publishing House, Ltd.   Gefen Books
6 Hatzvi Street   600 Broadway
Jerusalem 94386, Israel   Lynbrook, NY 11563, USA
972-2-538-0247   1-800-477-5257
orders@gefenpublishing.com   orders@gefenpublishing.com

www.gefenpublishing.com
www.atimelesspeople.com

Printed in Israel   *Send for our free catalogue*

To my mom,

Chana bas Elyokim Getzel, a"h,

for her inspiration

And to

Marlene,

my wife of 40 years,

for her support and endurance

To the
Orthodox Union,
whose *Emerging Jewish Communities Fairs,*
promoting Orthodox growth
in communities throughout North America,
inspired the journeys that produced this book.

Contents

Preface

A holy man, Choni Hamaagal, is walking in the land of Israel when he sees an old man laboring to plant a single carob tree. Choni is mystified. This tree will take 70 years to bear its first fruit.

Choni approaches the old man and says, "Old man, why are you planting this tree, when you know you will never see the fruit?"

The old man shows Choni all the carob trees around him and answers, "When I came into this world, all these trees with their beautiful fruit were already here to greet me. My ancestors planted for me, knowing they would never see the fruit. Now I, too, am planting for future generations."

I observe a 98-year-old man take three steps back, with great effort, hunched over, in obvious pain with each step, just prior to reciting the Amidah prayer as Jews have done for thousands of years, and I am speechless with wonder.

A Holocaust survivor puts on his *tefillin* over his tattooed number and I am overflowing with pride.

As a photojournalist of Jewish communities, I ask, "What is the secret behind the timelessness of the Jewish people that has enabled them to persevere?"

As a Jew I ask, "How can I express my deep sense of respect and love for all Jews while, at the same time, hoping to provide the answer?"

The diverse and lively heritage of the Jewish people can be expressed in many ways, but there is none more powerful than photographic images. The goal of this book is to present the rich history, values, and culture of Jews in communities across the USA through photos.

Supported by what I hope you, the reader, will find to be an informative and intriguing narrative, the photos will explore the growth of communities, the people who pioneered in their founding, and those who continue their legacy. This is the story of a four-year state-by-state odyssey, visiting a sampling of Jewish communities that have something fascinating to bring to the table. To create a vivid picture of each selected community's past, present, and likely future, I interview the community's elders, historians, and leaders. Archival photographs of neighborhood beginnings are juxtaposed with current photos of these same communities to round out the story.

Taken together, the collection of images provides a moving look at American Jewish life, emphasizing the common threads that bind American Jews to each other from state to state and from generation to generation. It features holiday observances, lifecycle events and the emotions they evoke, and the institutions of Jewish life – synagogues, cemeteries, schools, and libraries – that have enabled Jews to fulfill the biblical injunction to "be strong and of courage" for more than 350 years on American soil.

"*Es iz shver tzu zein a Yid*" (It's hard to be a Jew) has been a cry of despair through the generations, but it has been matched by the even stronger rallying cry "*Es iz gut tzu zein a Yid*" (It is good to be a Jew). The Jewish people of this post-Holocaust era symbolize not only survival, but a triumph of the human spirit unparalleled in history. American Jews embody this timelessness, representing the struggle of Jews who gravitated to American shores from all over the world. Each group, from Bangor to San Francisco and from Seattle to Charleston, contributed its own specific quality and means of coping with the vast and challenging spiritual terrain of America.

In essence, then, this is a family album. Intimate, yet broad, it is a collage of Jewish faces and stories told by Jews of different backgrounds and climes, united by history and destiny. You will find it immediately familiar, yet striking in its diversity. The featured communities reveal the perseverance, the drive – and sometimes the sheer uncanny providence – that enabled them to strike their roots and grow. I invite you to come along with me; together we'll visit fellow Jews in their homes and synagogues, exploring archives and attics for clues to the past.

There is a verse that is read daily, whose meaning has always intrigued me: "*V'chayei olam nata b'socheinu.*" The simple meaning is, "and planted eternal life in our midst." I heard a different commentary on this same verse, which helps to clarify a possible answer to my question: The life experiences of all Jews who came before us are planted within each and every one of us. These experiences are part of our very soul. In his heart, the old man, while planting his carob tree, certainly felt the experiences of his ancestors.

As the Torah tells us in Numbers 2:17, "as they encamp, so shall they travel." Just as the Israelites camped at Sinai and received the Torah, so shall they travel together, clinging to their Yiddishkeit.

Travel with me. I hope you will find this a most rewarding journey.

Acknowledgments

This book is the culmination of a four-year odyssey, visiting 18 communities, traveling tens of thousands of miles, taking thousands of photographs, reviewing thousands of archival images, and surviving the trauma of one car accident and one traffic violation (neither of which were my fault, of course).

There are certainly many thanks to go around (other than to the police officers, of course), so please bear with me, as this is one of the most important things left for me to do.

I would like to acknowledge, first, the wonderful people who advised me at the beginning and convinced me to trek on.

Charlotte Friedland was my initial editor, advisor, and researcher for the whole project. Her enthusiasm for the project almost exceeded mine!

My deepest thanks to Aaron Shmulewitz, whose legal advice and constant words of encouragement were indispensable. I owe you a large debt of gratitude impossible to describe.

Profound thanks must go out to Michael Svei, Joe Beer, Jeff Moskowitz, and Mitchell Mond for their extraordinary help and expertise in computer science. If not for them, I would have smashed my computer countless times over. My thanks also go out to Rabbi Jay Weinstein, Rabbi Yaakov Wasser, Rabbi Yaakov Weinstein, Milt Heumann, and Gary Balsam for their suggestions and advice.

To my dearest mom, who passed away during the third year of my odyssey, there aren't enough pages to thank you for your ideas, advice, and encouragement to keep me going when I was ready to give up. I know you're reading this book as I write this.

Above all, with love, as always, my deepest thanks to my ever-so-patient wife, Marlene, who listened to my complaints for four years, accompanied me on many of my journeys, and incredibly still remains my wife (of 40 years!).

Special thanks to my publisher, Ilan Greenfield at Gefen Publishing House in Jerusalem. His attention to detail always kept me on my toes. To Smadar Belilty, Gefen's project coordinator, many thanks for successfully juggling all the diverse phases of the project. To Kezia Raffel Pride, my editor at Gefen, and S. Kim Glassman, my graphic designer, thank you both for magically mixing the right ingredients and pulling this book out of a hat!

Finally, I want to thank the hundreds of Jewish friends across the US, whose names will appear at the end of each chapter, for their generous and enthusiastic assistance to a total stranger. You have given me the *chizuk*, the strength, to persevere. You are indeed the true links in the endless chain of continuity. Your priceless stories will live on in perpetuity.

THE
Northeast

Lovingly dedicated in honor of
our terrific daughters and sons-in-law

Sandy and Ilan Katz

Terri Machtiger
and Lawrence Szenes-Strauss

and our delightful grandchildren

Josh, Maya, and Liora Katz

We are so proud that you are
continuing our family's traditions.

May we be privileged to celebrate
many more chagim together.

"And all your children
will be students of Hashem,
and your children will have
abundant peace" –
do not read "your children,"
but "your builders."

Elaine and Neal Machtiger

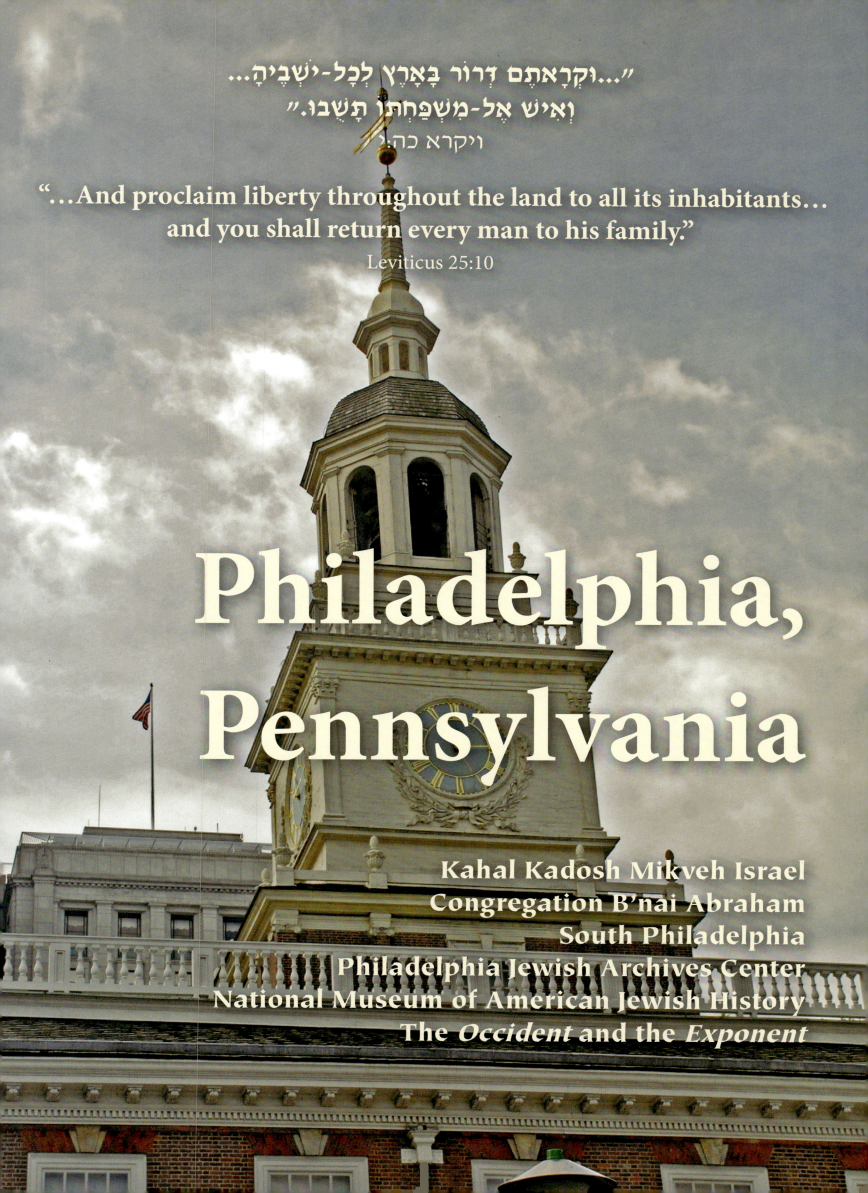

"...וּקְרָאתֶם דְּרוֹר בָּאָרֶץ לְכָל-יֹשְׁבֶיהָ...
וְאִישׁ אֶל-מִשְׁפַּחְתּוֹ תָּשֻׁבוּ."
ויקרא כה,י

"...And proclaim liberty throughout the land to all its inhabitants...
and you shall return every man to his family."
Leviticus 25:10

Philadelphia, Pennsylvania

Kahal Kadosh Mikveh Israel
Congregation B'nai Abraham
South Philadelphia
Philadelphia Jewish Archives Center
National Museum of American Jewish History
The *Occident* and the *Exponent*

Philadelphia, Pennsylvania

Purim and the Liberty Bell in Ir Ahavas Achim, *"the City of Brotherly Love"*

Let me paint you a picture on the canvass of the Past.

It is a cloudless summer day....

Plain red brick the walls...[of] the State House of Philadelphia, in this year of our Lord, 1776...but why do those clusters of citizens, with anxious faces, gather round the State House walls?

...In yonder wooden steeple, which crowns the red brick State House, an old man with white hair and sunburnt face...[gazes]...upon the ponderous outline of the bell, suspended in the steeple.... "Haste you down stairs, [says he to a blue-eyed boy,] and wait in the hall by the big door, until a man shall give you a message for me.... Then, run, out yonder in the street, and shout it up to me...."

The old Bell-keeper was alone. Many minutes passed...yet still he came not. The crowds gathered more darkly along the pavement and over the lawn, yet still the boy came not.

"Ah!" groaned the old man, "he has forgotten me!" ...As the word was on his lips, ...[there] stood the blue-eyed boy, clapping his tiny hands..., and then swelling his little chest, he raised himself on tip-toe, and shouted a single word – "Ring!"

Do you see that old man's eye fire? ...Backward and forward, with sturdy strokes, he swings the Tongue.... Yes, as the old man swung the Iron Tongue, the Bell spoke to all the world....

Under that very Bell, pealing out at noonday, in an old hall, fifty-six traders, farmers, and mechanics, had assembled to shake the shackles of the world....

Look how the names blaze on the Parchment....

And now the Parchment is signed, and now let word go...out to all the earth...let the Bell speak out the great truth.

– Excerpts from *Legends of the American Revolution: or, Washington and His Generals* by George Lippard
(Philadelphia: TB Peterson and Brothers, 1847)

1. The sound that changed the world

2. A *mezuzah* found on the doorpost of an old tenement depicting the Liberty Bell and the inscription from Leviticus

I was standing in a room, alone with the Liberty Bell, in a building called, appropriately enough, Liberty Bell Center. An odyssey on which I was about to embark was on my mind: my goal was to visit Jewish communities throughout the United States and, through my experiences, write a book demonstrating the continuity and

3. A wonderful
sense of pride

perseverance of the Jewish people in a strange new world. Philadelphia was my first stop.

Can one man's journey convey the complex story? I wondered. Would I be able to transmit the admiration I feel for the perseverance of my people through 350 challenging years in America?

In the midst of these thoughts, three young boys entered the room – packs on their backs and *yarmulkes* on their heads – and stood in front of the bell without saying a word to each other for a few minutes. As I watched from afar, a wonderful sense of pride enveloped me, and I knew the answer to my troubling question. I was surely ready to travel.

It is Purim in Philadelphia. As in the Purim story, the story of Philadelphia's Jews is one of struggle and survival in a strange land. And just as the fate of the Jewish nation rested on what was taking place at Queen Esther's banquet in the royal palace of Shushan, the future of Jewish life in America hung in the balance, in a country poised on the cusp of the American Revolution, with freedom for all, freedom of religion and assembly, freedom to enact fair laws applying equitably to Jew and gentile alike.

As I walked through the streets of Philadelphia, the heart and soul of the American Revolution, guided by the omnipresent blue and gold historic signposts, I could sense the deep pride this former colonial city had in its pioneer founders.

The Jewish pioneers of Philadelphia in the eighteenth and nineteenth centuries were revolutionary in their own way. They were largely responsible for the development of a prototypical American Jewish community that would ensure religious continuity in the New World. As they pioneered the formation of American Jewish religious, educational, and welfare institutions, Philadelphia's Jews served Jews from New England to Alabama and taught them to start their own organizations.

The first Jews came from New Amsterdam (later New York) in 1650 to trade in the Delaware Valley, long before William Penn founded the colony of Pennsylvania in 1682. Nathan Levy and David Franks were the first permanent Jewish merchants in Philadelphia. It was on their ship that the Liberty Bell was brought to America.

4. One of many historic signposts found throughout Philadelphia. This one commemorates the contributions of Haym Salomon.

When, in 1737, Levy was granted a plot of land to bury his child in accordance with Jewish law, the first Jewish community took root. Very often, beginnings of communities and synagogues dated from the establishment of the first cemetery. According to Lou Kessler, archivist at the American Museum of Jewish History in Philadelphia, only Sabbath observers were given the privilege of burial there. Kahal Kadosh Mikveh Israel, the second-oldest synagogue in America, was established in 1740

5. Mikveh Israel Cemetery, founded in 1737, when a plot was granted to Nathan Levy by William Penn. Among the prominent persons buried here are Haym Salomon and Rebecca Gratz.

(Shearith Israel, established in 1654 in New York, was the first). Religious services were held first in people's homes and then in a rented building on Sterling Alley (now called Orianna Street).

The first synagogue structure for Mikveh Israel was dedicated in 1773 on Cherry Alley. While the majority of the members were German Jews (Ashkenazim), the original pioneers were of Spanish-Portuguese descent (Sephardim), as in New York. This synagogue has always followed their Sephardic custom in the prayer service, through 200 years of operation in five different buildings, to this day.

6. Orianna St. today, restored to the way it was in the eighteenth century

7. Kahal Kadosh Mikveh Israel: sketch of the original building on Cherry Alley (1782). It housed the school, a home for the *chazzan*, and the *mikveh*.

For more than 80 years, Zev Hoffman has been a member of Mikveh Israel. He remembers, with a smile, going to Shabbos services in the 1920s and '30s at the fourth Mikveh Israel building on Broad Street, where two rabbis – one Sephardic and the other Ashkenazic – were seated on either side of the *bimah*. By then, Mikveh Israel was a very prestigious house of worship; all the VIPs came here.

He told me how all five buildings from 1741 to the present remained Orthodox, no small feat in a country where most Orthodox synagogues eventually ripped out their *mechitzos* (barriers separating the men's and women's sides of the synagogue) to accommodate Reform membership. "As a matter of fact," he told me, "the original congregation was an offshoot of the famous Bevis-Marks Congregation in London. It brings back the common thread of continuity from colonial days."

Permanent ordained rabbis were not to be found in the US until the mid-nineteenth century. A *chazzan* would be hired to serve multiple roles: conductor of marriages and funerals, kashrus supervisor, and interpreter of Jewish law.

8. Zev Hoffman remembers the fourth Mikveh Israel building on Broad St.

The Philadelphia *shul* gained its first *chazzan* in the person of Gershom Mendes Seixas, who fled along with many of his congregants from Shearith Israel in New York when the British invaded in 1780. When the British were defeated in 1788, he and many others returned to New York, leaving Mikveh Israel without leadership and lacking sources of money. The synagogue was in danger of closing its doors at this early point in its history. A call for local funds

9. Gershom Mendes Seixas, first Jewish clergy born in America. He participated in the inauguration ceremonies of George Washington.

went out, and Benjamin Franklin was one of the prominent donors who helped keep the synagogue financially stable.

In 1825, the Board of Adjuntos (managers) voted to build a larger synagogue on the same site. It was one of the most dignified buildings of its kind in the young country. Five hundred Jews were living in Philadelphia back then, and this Jewish community was one of the most innovative and influential in the US throughout the nineteenth century.

Mikveh Israel rose to national prominence under the leadership of arguably the greatest American Jewish leader of the century, Isaac Leeser (1806–1868). Born in Prussia, Leeser was invited to be the *chazzan* of Mikveh Israel in 1829 and was the first to give sermons in English. He founded the first Jewish newspaper in America, the *Occident and American Jewish Advocate*, whose editorials included a plea for the retention of Hebrew as the language of worship, a proposal for a network of Jewish day schools (in the 1830s, truly ahead of his time), and an appeal for Jewish unity in action and opinion.

10. Isaac Leeser, *chazzan*, writer, publisher, and educator

In response to the Damascus affair, a blood libel accusation in Syria where 13 Jews were imprisoned and tortured and 63 Jewish children were held hostage, he said in a speech, "As citizens, we belong in the country we live in; but as believers in one G-d…we hail the Israelite as a brother….oceans may intervene between our dispersed remnants, …mountains may divide us, but…the Israelite is ever alive to the welfare of his distant brother, and sorrows with his sorrow, and rejoices in his joy."

Leeser, a true innovator and major builder, founded the first Jewish publication society (forerunner of today's JPS) and also published the first English translation of the Jewish prayer book and of the Bible. He founded the first Hebrew high school (1849), the first American Jewish defense organization (Board of Delegates of American Israelites, 1859), and the first rabbinical college in America (Maimonides College, 1867). He was also very active in stemming the tide of the Reform movement, at that time seen as the most viable threat to the continuation of Orthodoxy in America.

11. One of the first Hebrew prayer books published with an English translation: a *machzor* for Sukkos (1837)

Perhaps the best-known American Jewess of the early nineteenth century was Rebecca Gratz (1781–1869). She was identified with most of the Jewish charitable organizations in Philadelphia, which were replicated, in turn, throughout the US. She was one of the founders of the Hebrew Benevolent Society (1819), the Hebrew Sunday School Society (1838), and the Jewish Foster Home. Her brother, Hyman, bequeathed money to fund Gratz College (1897), the first Jewish teacher-training

12. Rebecca Gratz, major founder of charitable organizations

institution in the US. Her sister Richea is reputed to have been the first Jewish girl to attend college in the US. Renowned for her beauty, Rebecca Gratz was reputed to have been the model for Rebecca in the classic novel *Ivanhoe* by Sir Walter Scott, who met her through the author Washington Irving.

Isaac Leeser retired from Mikveh Israel in 1850 and was succeeded by Sabato Morais, who also exerted a powerful influence in opposing the Reform movement. He founded the Jewish Theological Seminary to train rabbis and teachers to help preserve traditional Jewish values. (It did not become Conservative until later.)

In 1860, prior to the Civil War, as the Jewish population grew, an elegant Mikveh Israel building (its third) was constructed on 7th Street by the architect who later designed Philadelphia's City Hall. In 1909, its fourth building was constructed on Broad Street, furthest away from its original location.

By 1880, the Jewish population in this city had grown to 12,000. Towards the end of the nineteenth century, and for the next 35 years, Philadelphia was overwhelmed by the eastern European immigration, and the Jewish population soared to 200,000 by 1915.

To accommodate this sudden influx, Congregation B'nai Abraham was founded in 1874 by Russian Jews fleeing the oppressive Czar Alexander II. The present Moorish-style building was erected in 1910; it is the oldest building in Philadelphia built as a synagogue and still in use.

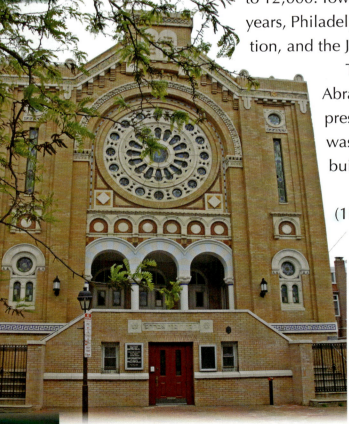

13. B'nai Abraham, founded in 1882 and still flourishing today. The building was constructed with a Moorish architectural style.

During this critical time, Rabbi Bernard Louis Levinthal (1865–1952), who was born in Lithuania and studied at the yeshivos of Vilna and Bialystok, became the rabbi of B'nai Abraham and gave his sermons in Yiddish. As leader and spokesman for the Orthodox community, he was considered the unofficial chief rabbi of Philadelphia and was responsible for the establishment of a number of institutions tending to the religious and social needs of the growing and diverse community. These included the Central Talmud Torah and the Vaad Hakashruth. Rabbi Levinthal was also one of the founders of the Union of Orthodox Rabbis of the US and Canada (1902), the American Jewish Committee, and the Mizrachi Organization of America. He held his position at B'nai Abraham until his death in 1952.

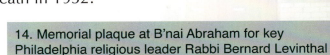

14. Memorial plaque at B'nai Abraham for key Philadelphia religious leader Rabbi Bernard Levinthal

IN MEMORY OF RABBI B. L. LEVINTHAL SEPT. 23RD 1952

הרב דוב אריה בן הרב אברהם הכהן
ד תשרי תשי"ג

15. Regina Rosenblatt in her South Philadelphia shop

Till the middle of the twentieth century, the commercial and Jewish religious center of Philadelphia had been "South Philly." Strawberry Mansion and Marshall Street catered to the immigrant community with its push-carts and shops, pickle barrels, herring with schmaltz, halvah, and horserad-ish, much like the Lower East Side in New York. Comedian David Brenner, who was raised in these neighbor-hoods, called them the largest, friend-liest villages in the world.

Two men whose families have been active in the growth of B'nai Abraham for over 75 years filled me in on local lore. Jerry Zaslow was born in Philly and brought up on South Street in the heart of Jewish Philadelphia. "My father came here from the Ukraine in 1910," he told me. "The ship docked on South Street in Philly, not on Ellis Island as most did. I remember six *shul*s in a three-block radius: the Russian *shul* [B'nai Abraham], the Hungarian *shul*, and the Polish *shul* [Vilna Congregation], among others. We've been members of B'nai Abraham since 1936."

He took Hebrew lessons from the *shamash* (care-taker) of the *shul*, the legendary Pesach Wapner. "He charged us one dollar a week for the lessons. He would speak in Yiddish, and I spoke only English, so it was a heck of a combination!"

His bar mitzvah at B'nai Abraham in 1938 was marked by special gifts from his grandmother – his first *tallis* (prayer shawl) and also a *yarmulke* for the occasion. "I still wear them today on special occasions," he recalls fondly. "My speech was in Yiddish, written by Pesach Wapner, which I had to memorize, as I didn't speak the lan-guage." (Like so many American-born children, Jerry attested, "My parents would speak Yiddish when they didn't want me to understand!") Rabbi Levinthal was in attendance, of course. The reception in the *shul*'s basement fea-tured corned beef sandwiches and the total cost of the affair was twenty dollars!

16. Golden book of Congregation B'nai Abraham, dating back to 1920. This page honors longtime *gabbai* and *shamash* Pesach Wapner.

17. Bar mitzvah photo of Jerry Zaslow, 1938, wearing the gifts from his grandmother, a *tallis* and *yarmulke*

Money was hard to come by, back then. Jerry's father had started a linen business in 1919, closed because of the Depression, and reopened in 1931. "We lived over the store. When I was eight, my father would come up to my room early in the morning and wake me up to help him in the store." Jerry and his brothers have continued working their father's business, but on a larger scale, doing business with the government and the military – selling sheets, pillowcases, and uniforms, as well as furniture, handcuffs, rifle scopes, and even hand grenades!

Jerry has been a marathoner since 1975 and has competed in New York, Boston, Copenhagen, London, Paris, Moscow, Rome, and Tokyo. At age 86, he is training for yet another marathon!

18. Jerry Zaslow's marathon sports card, 1987 (#262). He's still training for one more at age 86!

I also had a chance to chat with Dick Tucker, another active member of the B'nai Abraham community. "My mother was born here in Philly in 1898 and my father came here in the 1890s. I remember my father playing 'cage basketball' [played inside a chicken-wire fence so balls wouldn't go out of bounds] right next to the synagogue building. In the middle of the game, men from the *shul* would come to the cages looking for the tenth man to make a *minyan*."

"I'm a throwback," he confided, "because there are very few people walking around who can remember when 3rd Street was both the Jewish machinist block and the *shmattah* district [where old clothes were sold]. On 4th Street were the shoe dealers." On South 7th were the pushcarts selling fresh produce and fish. And every merchant spoke with a Yiddish accent.

When it came to Purim, Dick had an important job: "My job was to *hock der muhn* – pound the poppy seeds for my grandmother's *hamantaschen*. There was no cookie dough *chazerai* in *her* kitchen as we have today – only 'raised' dough with yeast. I would mix in the honey and the lemon." Her *hamantaschen* must have been out of this world.

As in many communities across the country, the housing trend during the 1960s and '70s shifted away from the original city neighborhoods. In the case of Philadelphia, the shift was to northeast Philly, to the Bala Cynwyd and Wynnewood areas, among others. Synagogues, day schools, restaurants, and shops abound in these newer areas.

Yet central Philadelphia is still thriving with the old *shul*s like the Vilna Congregation and the Society Hill Congregation, as well as, of course, B'nai Abraham and Mikveh Israel. Both are enjoying revitalization in the midst of the city, surviving the movement of many of the Orthodox community to the suburbs.

19. Dick Tucker, Philadelphian all his life, points out the buildings on Vine St. that housed the *mikveh* and the *shul*, which was known as the "machine dealers' *shul*" back in the 1940s. The red bricks seen on these buildings are the original bricks from Civil War days, 160 years ago.

A Tale of Two *Shul*s

I chatted with Rabbi Yochonon Goldman, who became rabbi of B'nai Abraham in 2000 and has been a major factor in its wonderful rebirth. After a devastating flood that closed the building down for over a year, the *shul* (which has been totally renovated and is a true wonder to see) now boasts a preschool program and adult education programs (part of an initiative called the Zaslow Institute of Jewish Learning), as well as classes given by the rabbi.

"Our *shul*," the rabbi explained, "is about to celebrate the 100th anniversary of this building. It was the center of relief efforts for Jews from the 'old country.' People came here to *daven*, to get jobs, to help others, and to celebrate life-cycle events.

"When you bought a seat in this *shul*," he smiles, "you and your family owned it forever. You even received a deed for it proving ownership!"

B'nai Abraham did not have a permanent rabbi for almost fifty years after the passing of Rabbi Levinthal. Rabbi Goldman, a member of Chabad Lubavitch, remembers the first time he ever came to B'nai Abraham – on Purim, of all times. "I was a yeshivah student from New York. When I walked into B'nai Abraham, it seemed like a happening place!" He liked it right away, and the congregants liked him. Two years later, they hired him as their rabbi, and he is going on his tenth year in that position. With Rabbi Goldman at the helm, it has been "a happening place" every day. He heartily approved of my visiting on Purim because it's the best time to see the larger community. Jews of every age and background gather here from all over the city, even from the newer neighborhoods.

20. Rabbi Yochonon Goldman in front of the *aron* in the 100-year-old B'nai Abraham. Now in his tenth year as its spiritual leader, Rabbi Goldman calls his *shul* "a happening place."

> Jews of every age and background gather here from all over…. He has attracted many Jews from Egypt, Iran, and Iraq, and, of course, Israel, to this historic synagogue that started it all.

During the American Bicentennial celebration at Independence Mall in 1976, Mikveh Israel opened its fifth building, only a few blocks from its original location on Cherry Alley.

The venerable old synagogue has played a great part in the revitalization of the city's Jewish neighborhoods. At the forefront of this effort has been Rabbi Albert Gabbai, Mikveh Israel's rabbi for the past twenty years. He has attracted many Jews from Egypt, Iran, and Iraq, and, of course, Israel, to this historic synagogue that started it all.

Rabbi Gabbai was born in Egypt, and during the 1967 Six-Day War with Israel, he was imprisoned by the Egyptian government until his release was gained through the efforts of Spanish and French officials. With the serendipity that seems normal in Jewish history, the rabbi wound up in the United States and ultimately found himself heading this unique Sephardic congregation.

He came to Mikveh Israel first as a *chazzan*, just as Seixas and Leeser had done 200 years earlier. Rabbi Gabbai sees a palpable resurgence in the leadership role of his synagogue for the Jews of Philadelphia – but it is leadership of a different kind from that of the Colonial era.

In the past, the synagogue provided the *mohel* for circumcisions, the matzoh oven for Passover, the *shochet* for kosher meat, the school, and a rabbi to resolve questions of Jewish law. "Now," Rabbi Gabbai intones earnestly, "our leadership role has changed: it involves Ashkenazim and Sephardim growing together with respect, order, and unity. We are growing both in quality and in quantity – more young people, lots of babies. We have plans for a new day school, *mikveh*, and *eruv*." He is glowing with enthusiasm and expectations of a bright future for Philadelphia's Jewry. An apt feeling indeed for the rabbi of a *shul* called Mikveh Israel, the Hope of Israel.

21. Mikveh Israel's fifth building, a centerpiece in downtown Philadelphia, was dedicated, appropriately enough, in 1976, the bicentennial of this country. Four of the five Mikveh Israel structures stood within a few blocks of this structure, in what is now Independence Mall.

The Purim story is one of survival in a foreign land, and the unseen hand of G-d guiding a community through seemingly impossible difficulties. Time and time again, this survival is mirrored in Philadelphia today.

And the Hand of G-d is there too: as in the Megillah, you can see it if you look. Both Rabbi Goldman and Jerry Zaslow told me the following story. A long while back, Jerry had lost touch with the *shul* of his parents, B'nai Abraham. While training for a marathon with a fellow athlete, they "happened" to pass by the Moorish-looking *shul* of old. Jerry wanted to show his friend where he had his bar mitzvah. When they stepped inside, memories came rushing back. He met Rabbi Goldman for the first time, sat and they chatted. That encounter started a process in his mind and heart. Ever since that "chance" meeting, he has been a stalwart in supporting this Jewish community, revitalizing adult education in the form of the Zaslow Institute.

Michael Neff wrote this for a pamphlet about B'nai Abraham, and it succinctly describes not only this early Philadelphia synagogue, but also those that followed in towns across America:

Do you remember the old shul?
A Judaism of warmth, Yiddishkeit, family atmosphere – most likely the very synagogue of your bubbes and zaydes when they came to the new world.

It was here that people met their *landsmen*, found homes and jobs, celebrated weddings, Bar Mitzvahs and bought their burial plots.

And then we moved to new neighborhoods and built new synagogues.

But the old shul remained there for us as an example, a memory of our true home.

B'nai Abraham and Mikveh Israel are more than just a memory. They are living examples of the will, perseverance, and unity that have brought these neighborhoods back.

It is the kind of unity found in our Purim Megillah. Haman knew that if the Jews remained "dispersed and scattered," he could destroy them. In response, Queen Esther commands all Jews to gather together and fast to avert his treacherous plans. And this triumphant unity is forever entrenched in our Jewish consciousness through the Purim *mitzvos* – also the work of Queen Esther and Mordechai – of sending gifts to friends and provisions for the needy.

This lesson was well remembered in the colonial town of Philadelphia and in successive generations of Philadelphia's Jews. They knew that in Exile, the Jew cannot stand alone. He must build a community based on camaraderie and cooperation from within – first in his family, then with his neighbors, then with fellow Jews who share the time and place of his sojourn.

We all know the verse from Leviticus found on the Liberty Bell: "Proclaim liberty throughout the land…" But the end of this verse, not found on the old man's bell, is just as important: "…And you shall return each man to his family."

Welcome to "the City of Brotherly Love."

22. The *heichal* or ark of Mikveh Israel contains nineteen *sifrei Torah* (Torah scrolls) with covers made traditionally by the women of the congregation from their gown material. Some of the *rimonim* (silver finials) were made over 250 years ago, by the famous colonial silversmith Myer Myers.

23. Feeding the tiger! Taking a snack break from the Purim excitement at a local kosher eatery on Castor Ave.

The synagogues

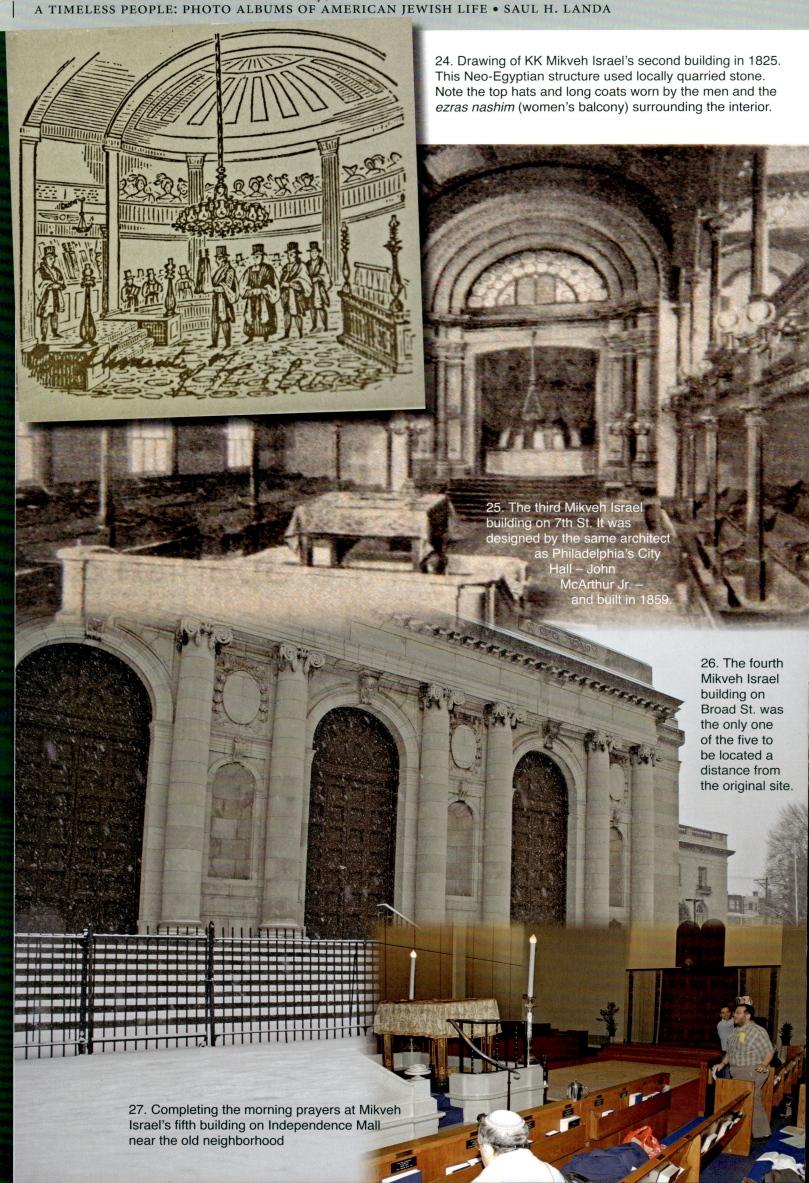

24. Drawing of KK Mikveh Israel's second building in 1825. This Neo-Egyptian structure used locally quarried stone. Note the top hats and long coats worn by the men and the *ezras nashim* (women's balcony) surrounding the interior.

25. The third Mikveh Israel building on 7th St. It was designed by the same architect as Philadelphia's City Hall – John McArthur Jr. – and built in 1859.

26. The fourth Mikveh Israel building on Broad St. was the only one of the five to be located a distance from the original site.

27. Completing the morning prayers at Mikveh Israel's fifth building on Independence Mall near the old neighborhood

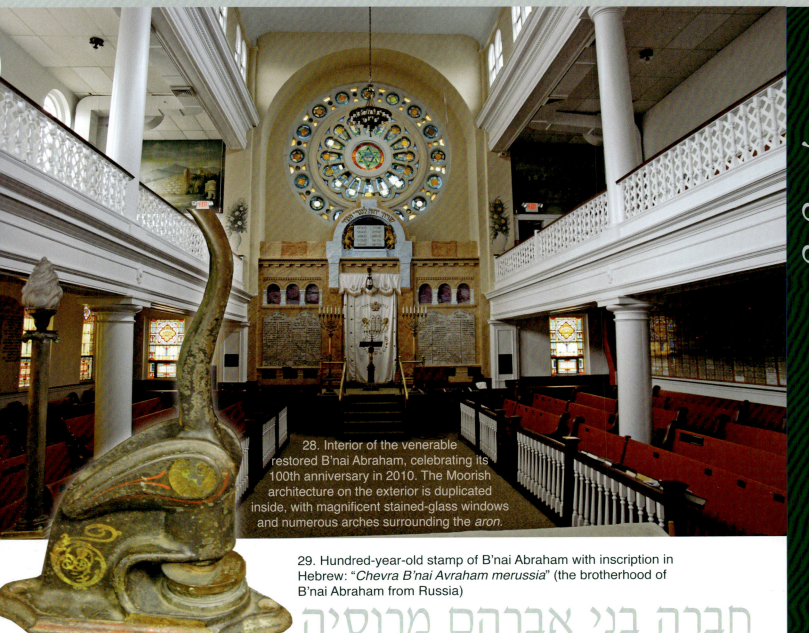

28. Interior of the venerable restored B'nai Abraham, celebrating its 100th anniversary in 2010. The Moorish architecture on the exterior is duplicated inside, with magnificent stained-glass windows and numerous arches surrounding the *aron.*

29. Hundred-year-old stamp of B'nai Abraham with inscription in Hebrew: "*Chevra B'nai Avraham merussia*" (the brotherhood of B'nai Abraham from Russia)

חברה בני אברהם מרוסיה

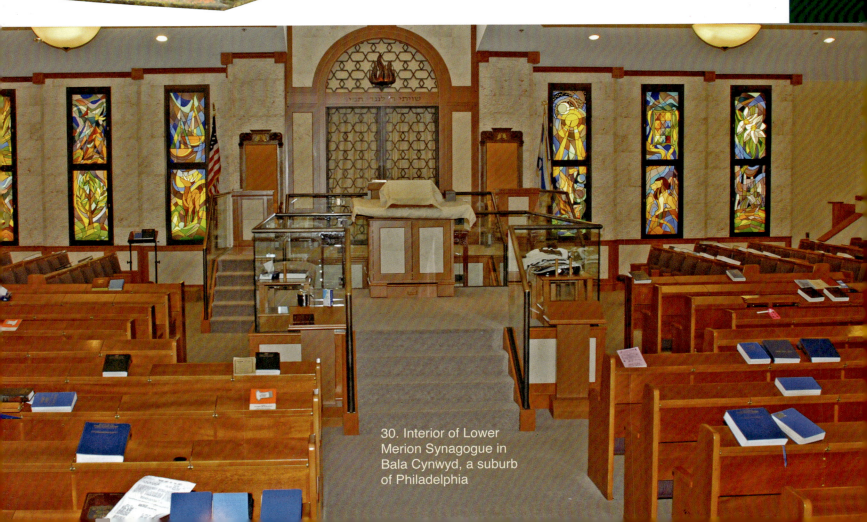

30. Interior of Lower Merion Synagogue in Bala Cynwyd, a suburb of Philadelphia

31. Eight men studying Talmud around the table at the Jewish Sheltering Home, c. 1940s

32. Young rabbinical students studying Talmud in the Talmudical Yeshiva of Philadelphia, founded in 1952 by students of the preeminent Rav Aharon Kotler of Lakewood, NJ. Note the decorations for the Purim holiday.

33. The late Rav Elya Svei, center, dean of the yeshivah

34. Sketch of the first Hebrew Sunday School building on 7th St. It was founded by Rebecca Gratz and others in 1838.

35. The Torah Academy of Greater Philadelphia in the northern suburbs

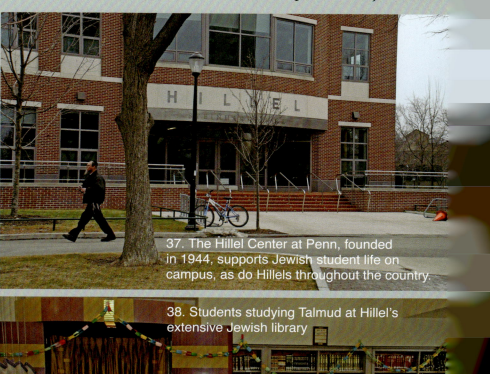

37. The Hillel Center at Penn, founded in 1944, supports Jewish student life on campus, as do Hillels throughout the country.

38. Students studying Talmud at Hillel's extensive Jewish library

36. The Jewish Student House (1919) on the Philadelphia campus of the University of Pennsylvania was the predecessor to the present-day Hillel Center. Note the Torah scroll engraved above the doorway.

39. Rabbi Bernard Levinthal of Congregation B'nai Abraham, key religious figure for the first half of the twentieth century, and great-granddaughter Linda Belkin, c. 1940

40. Father-son *mishmar* or night learning session at the Torah Academy of Philadelphia

41. Elfreth's Alley was a residential and business street dating to colonial times. Many Jewish businessmen lived on this street, now accurately restored to the way it was. Note the *mezuzah* in the first doorway (far left). Some things never change.

42. Vine St., early twentieth century, of which Dick Tucker spoke. Note the baths and *mikveh* to the left. This photo was taken during a garbage strike, c. 1914.

44. Kosher wine store and Judaica in Bala Cynwyd. From the '60s to the present, new neighborhoods have flourished in North Philly.

ROSENBERG Judaica & Wine
610-667-3880

WEST PHILA. OLD ESTABLISHED TAILOR
SUITS MADE TO ORDER AT REASONABLE PRICES. FIT GUARANTEED
SCOURING, DYEING, ALTERING, REPAIRING, DRY CLEANING & PRESSING
LADIES & GENTS GARMENTS DYED, SCOURED, ALTERED, REPAIRED, Dry Cleaned AND PRESSED AT REASONABLE PRICES. GOODS CALLED FOR AND DELIVERED.
B. SNYDER TAILOR

...he old ...borhood ...had ...esses ...tayed in ...mily, like ...ilor shop.

46. Rabbi Moshe Trager (and son). Along with his wife, he owns a local kosher restaurant, Café Shira, in Bala Cynwyd. He is also a certified *mohel* (performs circumcisions).

47. Rally for Soviet Jewry at the Liberty Bell, c. 1970

48. Yeshivah students admiring the Liberty Bell and the freedom that the "Refuseniks" fought for. A great source of inspiration!

50. Combining the two flags has remained a popular way to express support for Israel.

49. *Honor to the Unity of the Zionist Movement and the United States*, watercolor on paper made in Philadelphia, c. 1936

51. Israel always on their mind: father and son at a Purim carnival at the Lower Merion Synagogue

FAMILIES OF ISRAEL'S 'LONE SOLDIERS' WAIT AND WORRY, PAGE 24

Jewish EXPONENT

WWW.JEWISHEXPONENT.COM

Published Weekly Since 1887 • $1

Volume 221, Number 23 • 11 Adar 5767 • March 1, 2007

Illustration by Suzanne Tornquist

Israeli I...
Split Ov...
Peace ...

LESLIE SUSSER
Jewish Telegraphic Agency

JERUSALEM

THE OCCIDENT,
AND
AMERICAN JEWISH ADVOCATE.

Vol. XV.] IYAR 5617, MAY 1857. [No. 2.

THE PRESS AND THE PULPIT.
No. II.

THE PULPIT.

PERHAPS of the two elements which so greatly influence the popular mind, and which we proposed to ourselves as the theme for discussion in our last number, the pulpit is the most effective in its direct action on the spirit, though necessarily more limited in its extent. There is something in the human voice which has in all ages been felt as exceedingly insinuating, and as leaving an effect often much greater than the words employed would warrant one in believing. The inflection given to the uttered phrase, and the intonation of a sentence as it falls from the lips, are quite different in their action on the mind, than when the same are presented to it by written characters laid before the eye. It must not surprise us, therefore, when we learn that certain orators in whom voice and eloquence were of that kind as to captivate the feelings, should have been able to sway the multitude they addressed, as the wind causes the waves to surge to and fro. The people felt themselves identified with those who addressed them, and hence shared every emotion which swayed the others, and felt with a sensation not originally theirs, but enkindled involuntarily within them by the sounds conveyed to their perception, as they dropped one by one into their ear. And though sound is evanescent, and ceases as soon as the organs which pro-

VOL. XV. 5

52. The Purim edition of the present Jewish newspaper, the *Exponent*, founded in 1887

53. The *Exponent*'s immediate predecessor was the *Occident*, the first American Jewish newspaper, founded in 1843 by Isaac Leeser, c. 1857. Apropos of Purim, in response to a discourse by Judge Noah that an Israeli nation should be established through the protection of European countries, Leeser wrote in the 1845 *Occident*: "An independence so feeble…we do not wish our people to establish. They had better remain scattered…rather than expose themselves to an extermination by some modern Haman." How prophetic!

54. The Purim balls of the mid-nineteenth century were a common way to raise money for charities. From *Frank Leslie's Monthly*, 1877.

55. Purim *seudah* or festive meal at Poale Tzedek, c. 1930

56. Purim *seudah* Hawaiian style at Congregation B'nai Abraham

The joy of Purim

57. Purim celebration in costume, Hebrew Sunday School Society, c. 1930

58. Yo ho ho, a pirate's life for them! Purim carnival at Lower Merion Synagogue, in costume.

59. Baking *hamantaschen* is a serious business for the Katz family in Bala Cynwyd.

60. Albert Gabbai, rabbi of Mikveh Israel for the past 19 years, inspects a scroll of Megillas Esther before Purim. This scroll dates back to 1772, four years before the founding of the United States. Rabbi Gabbai foresees a new leadership role for Mikveh Israel in this century.

61. This Megillah found at B'nai Abraham is well over 100 years old and has the special characteristic of being a "Melech Megillah." At the top of every column is the word *melech* (king).

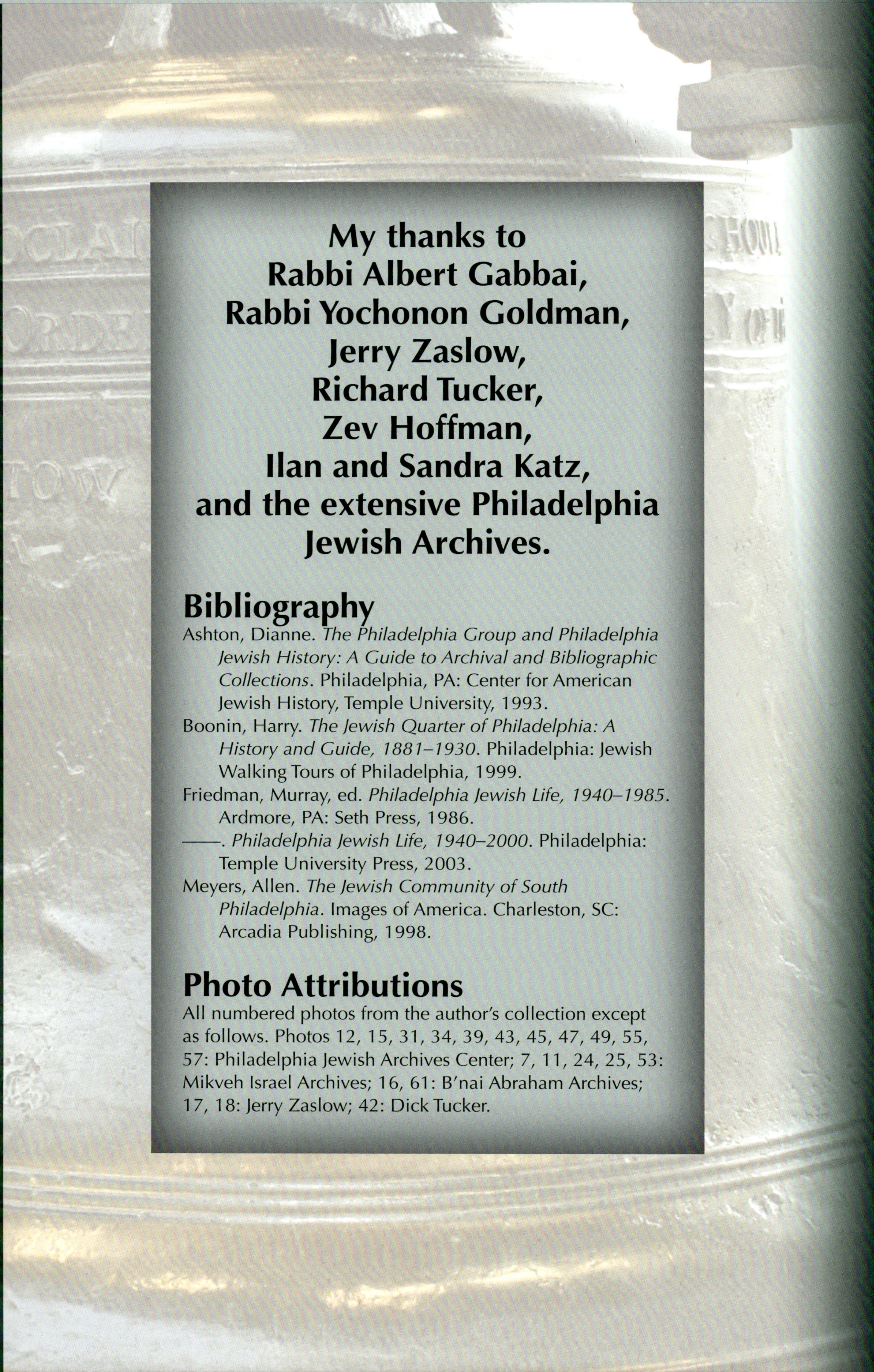

My thanks to
Rabbi Albert Gabbai,
Rabbi Yochonon Goldman,
Jerry Zaslow,
Richard Tucker,
Zev Hoffman,
Ilan and Sandra Katz,
and the extensive Philadelphia
Jewish Archives.

Bibliography

Ashton, Dianne. *The Philadelphia Group and Philadelphia Jewish History: A Guide to Archival and Bibliographic Collections*. Philadelphia, PA: Center for American Jewish History, Temple University, 1993.

Boonin, Harry. *The Jewish Quarter of Philadelphia: A History and Guide, 1881–1930*. Philadelphia: Jewish Walking Tours of Philadelphia, 1999.

Friedman, Murray, ed. *Philadelphia Jewish Life, 1940–1985*. Ardmore, PA: Seth Press, 1986.

——. *Philadelphia Jewish Life, 1940–2000*. Philadelphia: Temple University Press, 2003.

Meyers, Allen. *The Jewish Community of South Philadelphia*. Images of America. Charleston, SC: Arcadia Publishing, 1998.

Photo Attributions

All numbered photos from the author's collection except as follows. Photos 12, 15, 31, 34, 39, 43, 45, 47, 49, 55, 57: Philadelphia Jewish Archives Center; 7, 11, 24, 25, 53: Mikveh Israel Archives; 16, 61: B'nai Abraham Archives; 17, 18: Jerry Zaslow; 42: Dick Tucker.

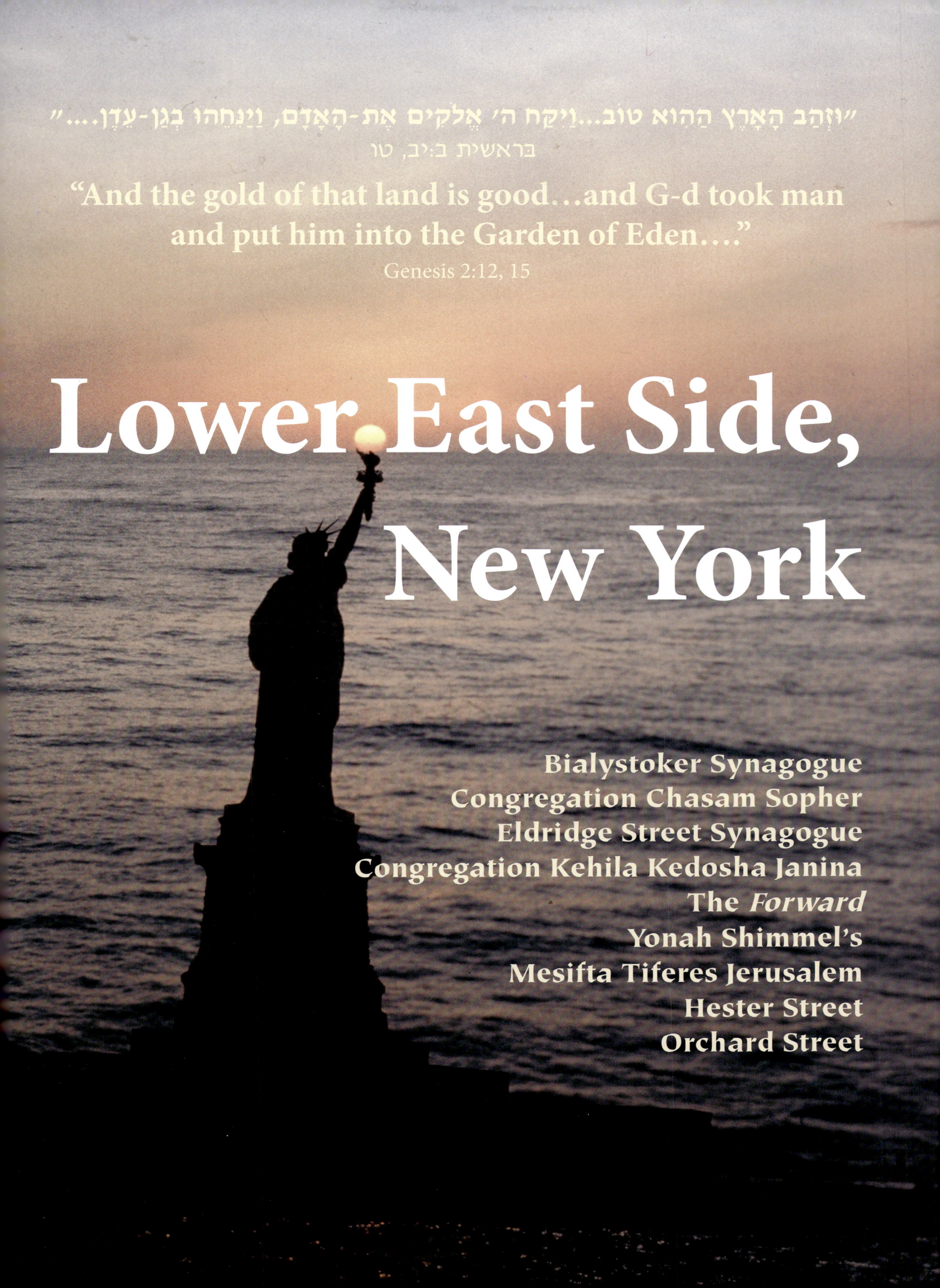

"וְזָהַב הָאָרֶץ הַהִוא טוֹב...וַיִּקַּח ה׳ אֱלֹקִים אֶת-הָאָדָם, וַיַּנִּחֵהוּ בְגַן-עֵדֶן...."
בראשית ב:יב, טו

"And the gold of that land is good…and G-d took man
and put him into the Garden of Eden…."
Genesis 2:12, 15

Lower East Side, New York

Bialystoker Synagogue
Congregation Chasam Sopher
Eldridge Street Synagogue
Congregation Kehila Kedosha Janina
The *Forward*
Yonah Shimmel's
Mesifta Tiferes Jerusalem
Hester Street
Orchard Street

The Lower East Side, New York

Passover, Freedom, and the Classic American Story

The Lower East Side – notice the capital letters! What is it about this small neighborhood at the southern tip of New York City that gives it the distinction of its own proper name? That this locale was the first American neighborhood of numerous immigrant groups over many generations not only gives it a special character, it freezes it in collective memory with an almost hallowed glory. Its importance to American Jews cannot be overstated. As I walk (you must never drive!) through the heart of the Jewish East Side, 45 blocks between streets with legendary names – Division, Clinton, Rivington, and Chrystie – I wonder why it remains so beloved in people's hearts: is it the associations of this neighborhood with turn-of-the-twentieth-century life – pungent smells, chaotic crowds, the innumerable pushcarts? The *Forward* – that renowned Yiddish newspaper known to so many back then as "der Forverts"? Was it the Yiddish theater, or the hundreds of synagogues, large and small?

I'm trekking through the area where it all started for millions of Jews coming out of steerage, weak and lost, with only their immediate families for support. It is just three days before Passover and I can't help thinking that this timing is perfect. I've come to the Lower East Side just when we are about to commemorate the time when our people came out of their bondage in Egypt. In many ways, the story of the immigrants of the Lower East Side mirrors the story of our people's exodus.

While today's generation may regard immigrant images nostalgically, the truth is that wretched, crowded tenements, unbearable sweatshops, crushing poverty, and conflict between Americanized children and their "greenhorn" parents typified life here. Yet precisely because of these conditions and the triumph over them, this historic enclave has created a legacy of Jewish endurance and perseverance that will forever leave its imprint.

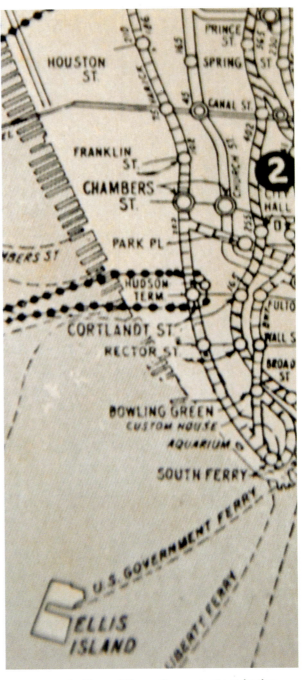

1. Map of the subway system in the Lower East Side area with Ellis Island in the lower left corner, c. 1930s

2. Five-story walk-up tenement typical of the period between 1880 and 1924. There were as many as three or four families living in one room.

In the Beginning…

The tenaciousness that saw Jewish New Yorkers through did not begin in the nineteenth or twentieth centuries, but much earlier than that. In August of 1654, a few Ashkenazic Jews arrived in the Dutch colonial settlement of New Amsterdam (later renamed New York) with documents issued by the Dutch West India Company. But when 23 Sephardic Jews fleeing the Portuguese reconquest of Dutch territory in Brazil arrived in New Amsterdam without the required papers, its governor, Peter Stuyvesant, immediately wanted to turn them away. It took the stern intervention of the Dutch West India Company, which owned and administrated the colony, for permission to be granted for their continued residence. They were not citizens at that point, but they were allowed to stay and pursue their own lifestyle. Land was acquired for a cemetery, the first Jewish cemetery in America, in 1656. The remains from the cemetery were moved in 1682 to a permanent location off Chatham Square, where it stands today on the Lower East Side. Among those

3. The Chatham Square Jewish cemetery is the oldest Jewish cemetery in America, established in 1682. Most of the tombstones have had their engravings worn away by time and the elements. The large stone on the left, which has been partially protected, dates from 1798. The grave is that of a *kohen*, a person from the tribe of Levi, as shown on the top by the hands held together for the priestly blessing.

buried there are members of the Levy family, the first prominent Jewish merchant family in America.

Gershom Mendes Seixas, *chazzan* (religious leader*) of Congregation Shearith Israel in the colonial era, is also buried in the cemetery. An energetic and resourceful leader, Seixas helped build Shearith Israel – known as the Spanish/Portuguese Synagogue (the first synagogue in New York) – at its first location on Mill Street. He was also instrumental in the growth of the synagogue Mikveh Israel in Philadelphia during the Revolutionary War, while the British occupied New York. He is credited with saving the Jewish cemetery from obliteration.

4. Gershom Mendes Seixas, *chazzan* of the first synagogue in New York, Shearith Israel. During the Revolutionary War he fled to Philadelphia, where he helped found Mikveh Israel congregation.

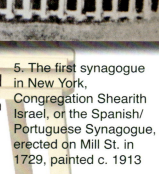

By the 1830s, there were 8,000 Jews in New York. German Jews, running from a populace angered by its subjugation to Napoleon Bonaparte, began emigrating in the 1840s. They started as peddlers and later opened retail clothing stores, the direct predecessors to the well-known department store chains, including B. Altman, Macy's, and Bloomingdales.

5. The first synagogue in New York, Congregation Shearith Israel, or the Spanish/ Portuguese Synagogue, erected on Mill St. in 1729, painted c. 1913

An Eastern European Influx Sets the Tone

The key time period for the development of Jewry in America, especially Orthodox Jewry, was the relatively short span from 1880 to 1924, which saw the mass arrival of the eastern European Jews. Fleeing from political turmoil, oppression, and pogroms in Russia, Poland, Lithuania, Galicia, Romania, and Hungary, 500,000 Jews settled on the Lower East Side. Most could not afford even cabin class on the ships that brought them;

---

* While today the term *chazzan* means cantor, in early American Jewish communities the *chazzan* did much more, serving as the community *mohel*, officiating at all types of life-cycle events, often serving as *shochet* (kosher butcher), and generally performing the jack-of-all-trades functions of a Jewish community's primary spiritual leader. Ordained rabbis did not come to America until the late nineteenth century.

6. Immigrants packed together on a ship heading for the Castle Garden port, trying to get some fresh air before they go back to their steerage quarters in the cargo hold, c. 1890

they traveled in steerage, the cargo holds. Those deemed healthy enough were admitted to the United States, initially through Castle Garden at the Battery from 1880 to 1892, and later through Ellis Island, off the port of New York. For many, there was nowhere to go. They stayed in New York City, where there was a vibrant, teeming Jewish presence. Jews who had come earlier and had acquired some wealth already had moved uptown. The poor stayed on the Lower East Side, side by side with other immigrant groups, notably the Italians and Irish.

They had come from Europe out of desperation, with a vision of *die goldene medinah* – the golden land. Their greatest fear was not the crushing economic conditions, but rather the very real potential loss of their Jewish tradition through assimilation. In the Torah, the slaves from Egypt and their descendants had to prove themselves capable of using freedom in their new land. Similarly, in the American story, Jews had to go through terrible trials while holding on to the ideals and religious practices they held dear.

7. Ellis Island opened its doors in 1892 when Castle Garden, which was a concert hall in the 1850s, could no longer handle the thousands of immigrants on a daily basis. The historic Ellis Island closed its doors in 1954.

What were these trials? Imagine living in a five-story "walk-up" tenement, with 10 people sharing a room, and no windows for air. Imagine working 15 hours a day in a sweatshop in overcrowded, merciless conditions. Imagine the endless cycle of poverty and disease, and the jarring temptations of an unfamiliar slick city environment. And imagine being told that if you don't come to work on Shabbos, you'll be out of a job.

8. The intolerable conditions that existed in tenements such as these that were turned into sweatshops forced the workers into strike after strike, with emotions running high. In the spring of 1911, the Triangle Shirtwaist Company burst into flame and, in 18 minutes, 146 workers were burned to death. The Yiddish poet Morris Rosenfeld wrote a poignant poem about it that ran across the full front page of the Yiddish newspaper the *Jewish Daily Forward*. It talked about the sorrow of the Jewish people, "in darkness and poverty," whose loved ones were lying in graves. Rose Schneiderman, fiery spokeswoman of the Women's Trade Union League, said, "Too much blood has been spilled…. It is up to the working people to save themselves."

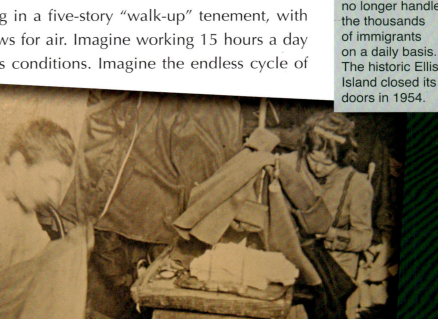

The struggle to survive, both physically and spiritually, gave rise to a remarkable Jewish community solidly based on religious and social institutions. The Jews of the Lower East Side labored to establish yeshivos and synagogues. They organized numerous *landsmanshaftn* (mutual benefit societies). A *landsman* is someone who comes from the same city or *shtetl* (town) as you did, and the term implies a loving bond – here is someone from "the old country" who remembers the same places and people, someone whose experience is like yours and is also struggling to start a new life in this alien environment. *Landsmanshaftn* played an important role in taking care of the newcomers – helping the sick, assisting widows and orphans, and providing loans and burial services. Formed to help their people from within, rather than through government aid, the Hebrew Immigrant Aid Society (HIAS) emerged in the 1880s. It provided kosher food, lawyers, temporary housing, and employment information – anything to give comfort and aid to a new life that started in a ship's steerage.

9. New Americans proudly waving their new country's flag in front of the Hebrew Immigrant Aid Society building, on East Broadway, c. 1912. This structure is now the Young Israel of Manhattan.

The first and only chief rabbi of New York City was appointed in 1888. At that time, Jewish religious life in the city was in a shambles: the kosher meat industry was in the hands of charlatans; there was no halachic authority of note for weddings, divorces, and other complex issues; even those who wished to remain faithful to religion were leaving observance in droves, whether due to the economic pressures or disillusionment with Jewish institutions. In desperation, the rabbis of 18 synagogues formed the Association of American Orthodox Hebrew Congregations and conducted an extensive search in Europe for a rabbi of stature who could save the situation. Rabbi Jacob Joseph, a renowned European scholar, was an excellent choice, and he agreed to come from Lithuania with his family. When his ship docked in the port of Hoboken, 10,000 Orthodox Jews were waiting to greet him.

Though Rabbi Joseph made significant inroads in righting the corrupt kosher meat industry, his leadership was doomed from the start. In the pluralistic Jewish world of America, so foreign to his experience, he was ridiculed in the liberal Yiddish newspapers, vehemently opposed by wealthy German Reform Jews, and was the subject of divisive infighting among Orthodox Jews who would not accept the authority of a "Litvak" (Lithuanian Jew). He died at a relatively young age, an impoverished and broken man. The institution of a chief rabbinate was deemed untenable on American soil, where rabbis were no longer regarded as strong communal leaders, but merely as congregational employees.

Those who cared deeply about Jewish education during this era made several attempts to establish schools. In contrast to a *cheder* (the typical model of a Jewish elementary school run by an administrator with absolute authority), Machzike Talmud Torah was founded in 1883 as a communal school with a board of directors. It was reputedly the pride of the Lower East Side for a long while. Yeshiva Etz Chaim was founded in a building on East Broadway in 1886, while Rabbi Isaac Elchanan Theological Seminary was founded in 1896, the year of the passing of the European scholar Rabbi Yitzchak Elchanan Spektor. These two institutions merged in 1912, forming the root from which Yeshiva University later grew.

10. Founded in 1896, the year of the passing of Rabbi Yitzchak Elchanan Spektor, Rabbi Isaac Elchanan Theological Seminary merged with Yeshiva Etz Chaim in 1912, forming the root from which Yeshiva University later grew. Its first building, shown here, was on the Lower East Side.

11. Rabbi Bernard Dov Revel, early leader of Yeshiva University from 1915 to 1940, c. 1920s or 1930s

The first institution of higher education in America to combine rabbinic studies with a secular college program, the university's core mission was solidified under the direction of Rabbi Bernard Dov Revel, and was guided by prestigious scholars including, among others, Rabbis Moshe Soloveitchik, Joseph B. Soloveitchik, and Shlomo Polachek, all noted rabbinic figures from Europe.

Ironically, though he lived a life of conflict and misery, Rabbi Joseph was venerated by the community upon his death in 1902. His sons founded a yeshivah in his memory and named it for him. Known for several recent decades as RJJ, Rabbi Jacob Joseph School was built in 1913. Mesifta Tiferes Jerusalem, a yeshivah built around 1900 and still functioning today, had the world-famous Torah scholar Rabbi Moshe Feinstein as its dean.

12. Rabbi Moshe Soloveitchik, of the famous Lithuanian rabbinical family which began in the early eighteenth century in Slobodka, was *rosh yeshivah* (dean) of the Rabbi Isaac Elchanan Theological Seminary. The Soloveitchik family had a tradition against publishing writings unless under special circumstances, so we find little in the way of published works from this honored name.

13. Mesifta Tiferes Jerusalem was founded around 1900 and had as its *rosh yeshivah* Rav Moshe Feinstein. His answers to halachic questions covered a wide range of subjects including modern science and technology as it relates to *halachah*. The yeshivah still thrives today in its original location on East Broadway with a second location in Staten Island.

By 1910, the heyday of the Jewish East Side, there were over 600 synagogues clustered in its small expanse. The first major Orthodox building built as a synagogue was the Eldridge Street Synagogue (1886). One of the founding fathers was Rabbi Isaac Gellis, later of hot dog fame. Yossele Rosenblatt was once the cantor of the *shul* and a young Eddie Cantor (who later went on to great popularity as an entertainer) sang in the choir. The oldest existing structure to house a synagogue is the Bialystoker Synagogue, built originally as a Methodist church in 1826. It still has services every day as well as a small Hebrew school.

14. The Eldridge Street Synagogue was built in 1887 and is a National Historic Landmark. It is a true early marker of the mass migration of the Jewish immigrants to the Lower East Side. This drawing of religious services in the Eldridge Street Synagogue was found in *Century Magazine*, c. 1892.

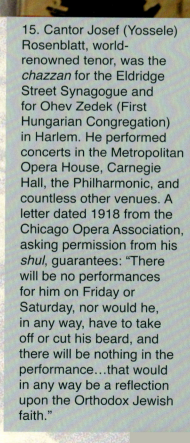

15. Cantor Josef (Yossele) Rosenblatt, world-renowned tenor, was the *chazzan* for the Eldridge Street Synagogue and for Ohev Zedek (First Hungarian Congregation) in Harlem. He performed concerts in the Metropolitan Opera House, Carnegie Hall, the Philharmonic, and countless other venues. A letter dated 1918 from the Chicago Opera Association, asking permission from his *shul*, guarantees: "There will be no performances for him on Friday or Saturday, nor would he, in any way, have to take off or cut his beard, and there will be nothing in the performance…that would in any way be a reflection upon the Orthodox Jewish faith."

Congregation Kehila Kedosha Janina has a unique history that stretches back to antiquity. After the destruction of the Holy Temple by Rome circa 70 CE, the Jews were taken on slave ships to Rome. On the way, one ship was forced to dock, due to a storm, in Greece. The Jews stayed there for the next 2,000 years and developed customs far different from those of Jews in other parts of the Diaspora. When Jews from Janina (Ioannina) wound up in the melting pot of the Lower East Side, they discovered that their practices differed greatly from those of the eastern Europeans. They founded their own synagogue in 1906, where services are still conducted today.

Congregation Shaarey Shamoyim, or the "Roumaniashe Shul" (1890), once heard the voices of Cantors Moshe Koussevitzky, Yossele Rosenblatt, Moishe Oysher, Jan Peerce, and his brother-in-law, Richard Tucker, resounding through its hallowed halls. Crowded along a few blocks, one after the other, were hundreds of *shtieblach,* small *shuls*, each servicing the immigrant families from a particular European *shtetl*. Some of these still exist today.

By 1911, Jews constituted over one-fourth of Manhattan's residents, and on the Lower East Side, Jews outnumbered non-Jews. There were five times as many Jews living there as in all of Chicago or Philadelphia. More than 2,000 *landsman-shaftn* serviced the community. Along with the synagogues and the incredible network of free loan societies, *gemilus chesed* charitable organizations, and Jewish homes for the aged, they became a stabilizing force for the steadily building wave of immigrants.

16. Shtiebl Row. A number of small synagogues still exist from the hundreds that crowded a few blocks in the first decades of the twentieth century.

The Yiddish Theater, which came into existence in the 1880s, and the many eateries such as Ratner's, Feigenbaum and Suss, and Yonah Shimmel's, became places where you could leave your troubles behind, at least for a short while. Characteristic of the era, many establishments carried no kashrus certification, relying on the locals' trust of their owners. So some people would eat in one place, but not another, others would eat at all of them, and some would frequent none of them.

17. Quite a contrast! In the background, the Manhattan Bridge overlooks the tenements of old on Henry Street mixed with the newer apartment buildings.

In 1924, US immigration laws restricted Jewish (and other) immigration to a quota. The Williamsburg and Manhattan Bridges were open, and so were the tunnels and subways, all ways to cross the East River – allowing for a mass migration of Jews from the Lower East Side to Brooklyn and beyond. By the 1940s and '50s, just a small percentage of Jews, mostly the elderly left from its peak years, remained on the Lower East Side. Remarkably, however, over the last 40 years a new influx of young, upscale Orthodox couples have moved into new and renovated apartments in the "*alte heim*" (old home) of their grandparents. How chic!

When we look at the religious community thriving there today, it is hard to imagine the daily struggles that took place on those same streets in the early years. Though many Jews were indeed lost to assimilation, a good percentage held on, despite the hardships. How were these immigrants able to survive test after test? What was in their souls that enabled them to persevere and retain their Torah Judaism?

The Secrets of Endurance – and Revival!

I met with two elderly gentlemen in their *shtiebel*, the Austrian-Hungarian *shul*. It's one small room, maybe 10 feet by 25, five stairs below street level, and it looks exactly as it did all those years ago. Marvin Mayer and Israel (Izzy) Suss have lived on the Lower East Side for over 75 years. According to Izzy, this *shul* has been here for at least 125 years, a product of many consolidations through the years; the Torahs in the Ark come from each *shul*. Both prefer to pray here, rather than in a larger synagogue, because "It's a more *heimish* [homey], warmer *davening*."

18. Marvin Mayer (left) and Israel Suss (right) show the many Torahs in the ark that have come here due to the consolidation of many *shtieblach* over the last 125 years.

We chatted for almost three hours about Jewish East Siders. During that conversation, they revealed much about the spirit that enabled survival and gave me their own personal take on life in this unusual place.

Izzy: "In Europe, my father [Ezra Suss] learned with the Dumbrova Rov, Rav Nachum Weidenfeld, who said in 1932, 'Things don't feel right [in eastern Europe], it's time to go to the US.' It's amazing how he knew that! After my father finished his studies at MTJ [Mesifta Tiferes Jerusalem], he and a partner started their restaurant, Feigenbaum and Suss."

[Ironically, the renowned *gaon*, Rav Nachum, did not himself leave, and was caught by Nazis at the Russian border. When they found his *tefillin* and threw them to the ground, he was gripped with shock and immediately suffered a fatal heart attack.]

I asked about formal kashrus supervision in those days, and Izzy laughed, explaining, "A *mashgiach* [kashrus supervisor] never entered the store in all the years. It was considered an insult! When a stranger came and asked where to eat, the answer was simply, 'Go to Ezra's.' Trust was very important in those days.

"The Lower East Side was a way of life – you had to be here to understand it. There was respect, trust for one another. And it was different from everywhere else, because Jews were everywhere. Years ago, a story went around about a religious Jew who had to work on Sunday, contrary to the 'Blue Laws.' He was brought before the judge [and claimed that he had to work on Sunday because he was Sabbath-observant] and the judge said to him, 'So, you're a Sabbath observer, eh? What *parshah* [Torah portion] did we read this week?' He told him, and the judge dismissed the case. This can only happen on the East Side.

"Even the best gangsters came from the Lower East Side – Meyer Lansky and 'Bugsy' Siegel [in the 1930s]! Let's face it, if you score 100 out of 100, you're not human, you're an angel. The Torah wasn't given for the angels!"

19. The *yahrzeit* plaque (commemorating the anniversary of death) of Benjamin Siegel, better known as "Bugsy," an American gangster whose family seems to have been members of the Bialystoker Synagogue. He was the driving force in developing Las Vegas.

Marvin: "My father came in 1920, after serving eight years in the Austrian army, during World War I. He was a peddler whose customers would pay off items one dollar a week. The *landsmanshaft* helped him to survive initially. The rest of the family came in 1929.

"A man from Boro Park once came to me and said he was told I could help him. I asked him how, and he said, 'I need a *shidduch* [marriage match] for my daughter.' I said, why come here? There are plenty of choices in your neighborhood! He said he wants a girl from the Lower East Side – unpretentious, down-to-earth.

"The Lower East Side, its people and organizations, had a profound influence on many Jewish communities, like a sun shining and giving off its rays. It was their responsibility to keep *Yiddishkeit* [Jewish lifestyle] going during hard times. Poverty brought out the best in people."

So how do we define an East Sider? The secret word is sincerity, they agreed. Izzy added, "Those people, those East Siders – you weren't judged by perception, but by who you really were. Those who had little helped those who had even less. These characteristics, caring for one another, and a little *mazal* [luck] helped us to pass our traditions on for generations."

Rabbi Zvi David Romm of the 160-year-old Bialystoker Shul echoed this sentiment. "Call us an 'out-of-town' community, with no pretensions. Men with *shtreimlach* [fur hats worn by Chassidim] pray together with men who are barely religious. There is a sense of continuity. Many members come from three and even four generations here."

20. Rabbi Zvi David Romm of the Bialystoker Synagogue calls his community an "out-of-town" community with no pretensions.

Sometimes that continuity seems guided by a Heavenly Hand. Rabbi Azriel Siff, of the 150-year-old Congregation Chasam Sopher, told me of a stranger who dropped in looking for directions a few years ago. After helping him, the rabbi urged him to come back for a Shabbos. He eventually did so, liked it, and kept coming back. Recently, he got married at the *shul* and subsequently gave a Kiddush. At that event, he made this shocking announcement: "I was going through some old family papers recently and I came across the marriage document of my great-grandfather. It said he was married in this same *shul* in 1908!"

"I was at a loss for words," said Rabbi Siff, "It sent shivers up and down my spine." I must admit, the story had the same effect on me.

The Lower East Side today is still truly an immigrant neighborhood. I walked through the many Jewish enclaves, which are now interspersed within predominantly Asian neighborhoods. But despite the dispersal of the Jewish community, the feeling that our people had for each other, the concern for an individual's well-being, and the tenacious hold they maintained for spiritual survival, still hovers here. I walked into three Orthodox synagogues, each over a century and a half old, each still holding services every day – some have had daily *minyanim* for 150 years straight! These synagogues have been restored painstakingly to their original grandeur, with the women's section surrounding the men's as a wraparound balcony.

I walked into the venerable yeshivos where the *gedolei hador,* the outstanding rabbinic leaders of the generation, taught, and where children and adults still study. I walked into the *shtieblach* and understood how their survival is no less magnificent

> I walked into three Orthodox synagogues, each over a century and a half old, each still holding services every day – some have had daily *minyanim* for 150 years straight!

or important than the survival of grand synagogue structures. The original Young Israel (synagogue) is still active and the original immigrant association – HIAS – is still helping its people. The pushcarts may be gone, the sweatshops long closed down, the tenements less crowded, but the ageless traditions remain intact.

I couldn't help wondering – after so many other Jewish communities have died, why has the Lower East Side persevered and even seen a recent resurgence? Rabbi Siff told me that when the great Torah scholar Rabbi Moshe Feinstein was asked this question, he answered that in the *zechus* (the spiritual merit) of the residents fulfilling the *mitzvah* of *hachnasas orchim, lifnim mishuras hadin* – welcoming strangers beyond the normal requirements – G-d has seen to it that the Lower East Side survived. In simple terms, the very warmth of Lower East Siders, that highly developed compassion and empathy intrinsic to immigrant survival, is the lifeblood of its endurance.

Yes, this is a story of a people who fled to this country, narrowly escaping tyrants and violent mobs. Weak, impoverished, but with their faith and families intact, they slowly began to build. It was much like their ancestors fleeing the Egyptian tyrant: not in tents, but in tenements, they endured hardship, but the tradition remained alive.

Walk around the Lower East Side. Enter its historic buildings, its kosher eateries, its unbelievable *shul*s; speak to its young rabbis, with their glowing eyes and deep Torah knowledge. You will learn, as I did, how a small community of only 45 city blocks succeeded in preserving the Torah tradition in that vast, surprising, challenging land they called *die goldene medinah*.

21–22. Historic symbols of freedom. The Bialystoker Synagogue has been around for 160 years and for the last 30 years has been thriving with a new life. This could not have occurred without the unprecedented freedom that the Jewish immigrants experienced in their new country 130 years ago. This matzoh (unleavened bread) at the Streit's matzoh factory represents the bread the Jewish people baked as they experienced freedom for the first time in 200 years.

The shuls

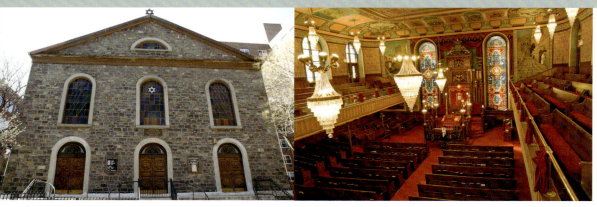

23–24. The Bialystoker Synagogue was first organized in 1865 by a group of Jews from Bialystok, Poland (home of the famous bialy bread). It was begun on Hester and then Orchard Streets. The edifice that houses the synagogue today was built in 1826 as the Willett Street Methodist Church, from fieldstone that was quarried only a few blocks away. Scenes of holy places in Eretz Israel are painted on the walls in the *ezras nashim* (women's section). The three massive crowns that adorn the top of the ark, representing the Torah, priest, and king, were imported from Europe in 1905. An opening in the women's gallery leads to a ladder going up to an attic that acted as a stop on the Underground Railroad where runaway slaves found sanctuary. The synagogue is a national landmark.

25–26. Built in 1853, the Chasam Sopher Synagogue, named after the great German Talmudic scholar (whose real name was Moshe Schreiber), has always been a "free" synagogue; there is no membership fee or charge for High Holy Day seats. In the 1960s, the synagogue was in danger of closing. A couple, Moses and Paula Weiser, kept it going for 40 years, until, in 2003, a man came along to save it. His name? Hank Sopher, who turned out to be a direct descendant of, you guessed it, the Chasam Sopher, the namesake of this *shul*! This synagogue building is one of the oldest still standing in the US.

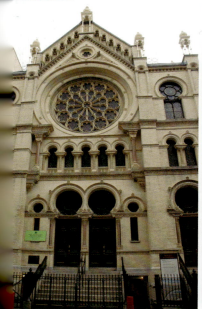

27–28. The Eldridge Street Synagogue, a national landmark, was built in 1887. The yellow brick facade combines elements of Moorish, Gothic, and Romanesque design. It is rich in symbolism: The Rose window, below the central gable, has 12 rondels symbolizing the 12 tribes. The five Moorish-style horseshoe arches symbolize the Five Books of Moses. The four carved central doors represent the four Matriarchs. The first full-time rabbi was Isaac Gellis, of hot dog fame. Some famous congregants were Al Jolson, Jonas Salk and Linus Pauling.

29–30. Austria-Hungary Congregation or Chevra Yeshuas Yaakov Anshei Sfard. One of the few *shtieblach* in existence for over 100 years.

31. The Young Israel of Manhattan, the original Young Israel *shul*. The building once served as the home of HIAS.

32. Immigrants packed together, c. 1890

33. Jewish refugees from Russia passing the Statue of Liberty, c. 1892. Engraving by C.J. Staniland, Bettmann Archive.

4. Eastern European marketplace, late nineteenth century. Peasants and merchants meet here to do business.

5. Hester Street, the home of the peddler's wagon, as it was in eastern Europe, c. 1899

36. Stores today on the corner of Essex and Hester

Education and making a living

37. The Bialystoker Talmud Torah building located to the side of the synagogue. Founded in 1910, along with other similar institutions it was the main source of Jewish education for the early immigrants.

38. At Mesifta Tiferes Jerusalem (MTJ), young adults gather in the principal's office.

39. At MTJ, adult students study in the *beis midrash*, some to acquire *smichah* (rabbinic ordination), as they have here for over a hundred years.

40. Orange vendor, c. 1895

41. A mainstay for a hundred years: Yonah Shimmel's knish bakery

42–43. Yiddish theater productions like *Tevye the Milkman* and, later, *Brothers Ashkenazi* started on the Lower East Side and were exported all over the US.

44. A Walk of Fame for Yiddish theater stars can be found on Second Avenue. It includes 30 stars and was maintained by the famous Second Avenue Deli. Here is the star of Molly Picon and Jacob Kalich, two of the stars who defined Yiddish theater.

45–47. The inside of an 80-year-old Yiddish theater now serving as a movie theater; the intricately designed chandelier with a Jewish star in the center and the walls and ceiling with Moorish/Gothic influences bring back the long-lost years when Yiddish theater offered a small escape, where you could leave your troubles outside. Inset: foundation stone of the theater.

48. The headquarters for over a hundred years of the Yiddish newspaper the *Jewish Daily Forward*

49. Volume one, number one: the first edition in April 1897

50. A Jewish state! The headlin splashed all over this 1948 edi

סדר הגדה של פסח

51. Title page of the first Hebrew-English Haggadah published in New York, c. 1837

52. Rabbis keeping a close watch at Streit's as water is added to the dough for the matzoh, c. 1930s–1940s

53. Rabbi today watching the kneading very carefully at the Streit's bakery

54. After rolling into sheets, dough is cut, c. 1930s

55. Carefully readying the matzoh for packaging

56. Author appointing Rabbi Romm of the Bialystoker Synagogue to sell his *chametz* (leavened foods)

57. The police and fire departments help to set up cans for the burning of the *chametz* at each *shul*. Sign announcing the times of burning at the Bialystoker Synagogue.

58. One of the fire monitors prepares to burn his own *chametz*.

59. Image from the 1940s or 1950s: reading the Haggadah at the Seder table

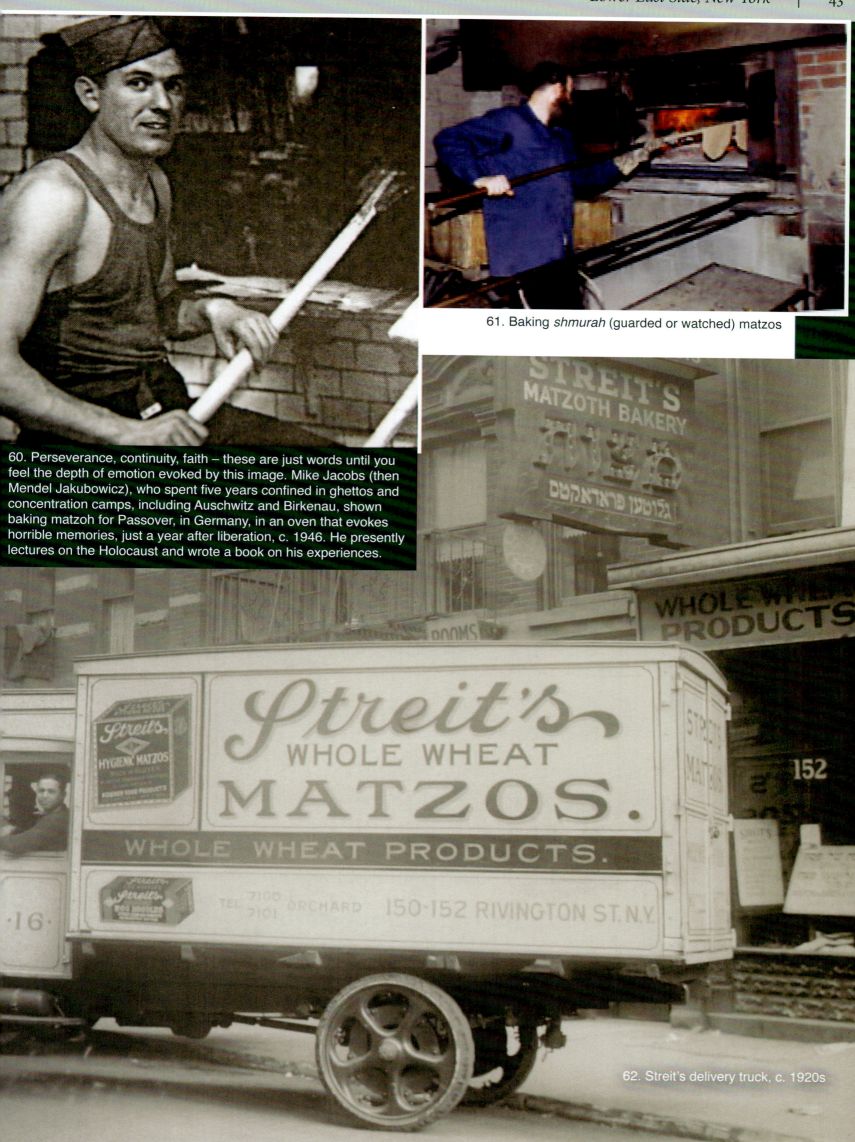

61. Baking *shmurah* (guarded or watched) matzos

60. Perseverance, continuity, faith – these are just words until you feel the depth of emotion evoked by this image. Mike Jacobs (then Mendel Jakubowicz), who spent five years confined in ghettos and concentration camps, including Auschwitz and Birkenau, shown baking matzoh for Passover, in Germany, in an oven that evokes horrible memories, just a year after liberation, c. 1946. He presently lectures on the Holocaust and wrote a book on his experiences.

62. Streit's delivery truck, c. 1920s

My thanks to
Rabbi Azriel Siff, Rabbi Zvi Romm, Marvin Mayer, Israel Suss, and Michele Heilbrun.

Bibliography

Birmingham, Stephen. *Our Crowd: The Great Jewish Families of New York*. New York: Harper and Row, 1967.

Howe, Irving. *World of Our Fathers*. New York: Harcourt, Brace, Jovanovich, 1976.

Diner, Hasia. *Lower East Side Memories: A Jewish Place in America*. Princeton, NJ: Princeton University Press, 2002.

Levinger, Lee. *A History of the Jews in the United States*. New York: Union of American Hebrew Congregations, 1930.

Pessin, Deborah. *History of the Jews in America*. New York: United Synagogue Commission on Jewish Education, 1957.

Elias, Joseph, ed., *The Haggadah*. New York: ArtScroll/Mesorah, 1977.

Zevin, Rabbi Shlomo Yosef. *The Festivals in Halachah: An Analysis of the Development of the Festival Laws*. New York: ArtScroll/Mesorah, 1991.

Attributions

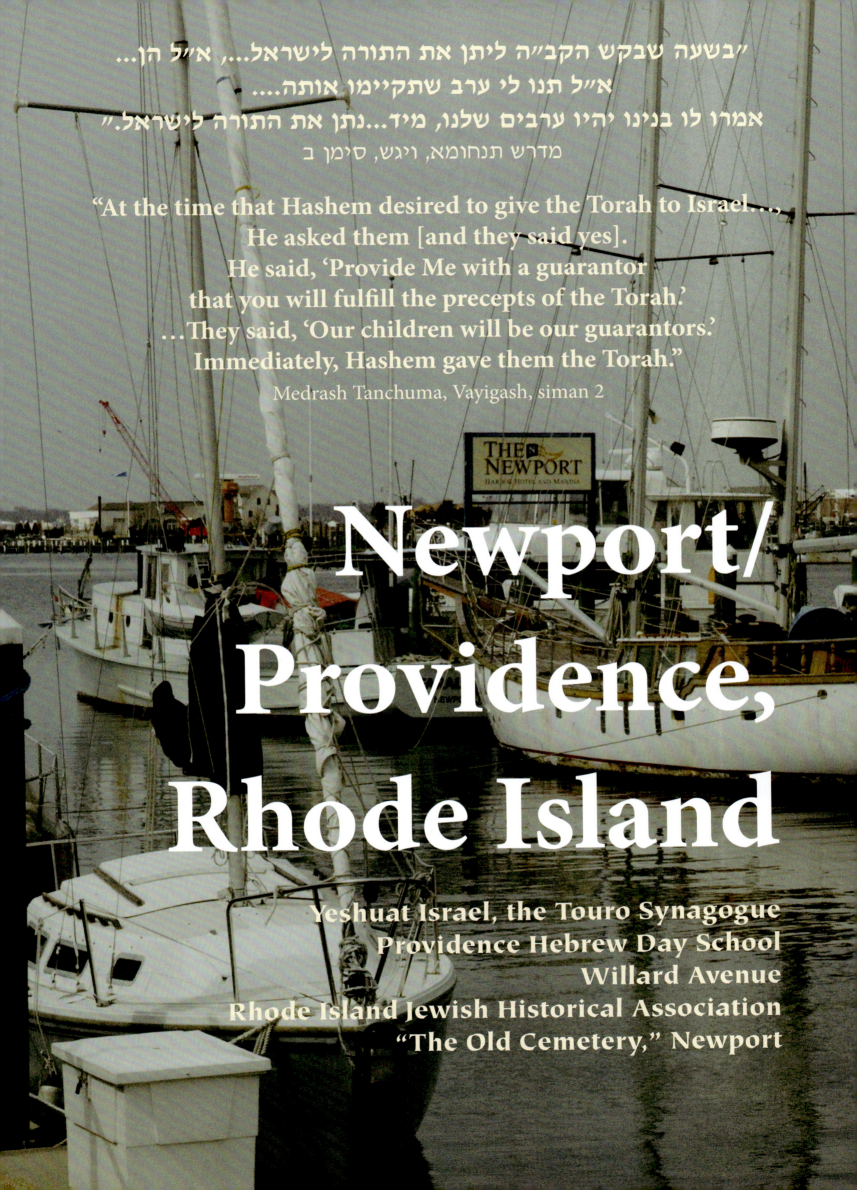

"בשעה שבקש הקב"ה ליתן את התורה לישראל..., א"ל הן...
א"ל תנו לי ערב שתקיימו אותה.....
אמרו לו בנינו יהיו ערבים שלנו, מיד...נתן את התורה לישראל."

מדרש תנחומא, ויגש, סימן ב

"At the time that Hashem desired to give the Torah to Israel…,
He asked them [and they said yes].
He said, 'Provide Me with a guarantor
that you will fulfill the precepts of the Torah.'
…They said, 'Our children will be our guarantors.'
Immediately, Hashem gave them the Torah."

Medrash Tanchuma, Vayigash, siman 2

Newport/ Providence, Rhode Island

Yeshuat Israel, the Touro Synagogue
Providence Hebrew Day School
Willard Avenue
Rhode Island Jewish Historical Association
"The Old Cemetery," Newport

Newport and Providence, Rhode Island

"With Our Elders and Our Children We Shall Journey"

One of the unique and most mystifying of Jewish customs is the *upsherin*, a festivity marking the first haircut of a three-year-old boy. While it faded from observance a few generations ago, it has since made a comeback, giving us another life-cycle event to celebrate, another occasion for plenty of *nachas* and plenty of food. I'm on my way to observe this reemerging custom, accompanied by the boy's great-grandmother from Rhode Island. One of the oldest Jewish enclaves in North America, Rhode Island is a place where the Jewish community took root, then died, then flourished again.

It was no accident that Jews settled in this early American colony; it had everything to do with the colony's founding tenets. Roger Williams, who was an outspoken, independent-minded Christian minister, was banished from Massachusetts Bay Colony for propagating innovative and dangerous opinions. He founded a new colony, which he reverently named Providence, in 1636. So began what we know today as Rhode Island. Another group of dissenters moved to the southern end of the island and founded the city of Newport.

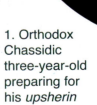

1. Orthodox Chassidic three-year-old preparing for his *upsherin*

Although none of these founders were Jews, the ideals that underlay Rhode Island's establishment would later have a dramatic impact on Jewish migration. Williams had argued for the readmission of the Jews to England (for they had been banished), so it came as no surprise that Rhode Island's charter in the 1660s became the first in North America that provided for religious freedom as part of the colony's new law. The charter stated that "Noe person within the sayd colonye at any tyme hereafter, shall be any wise molested, punished, disquieted or called in question for any differences in opinion in matters of religion…." This unprecedented tolerance was in direct contrast to Maryland's Act of Toleration (1649) – which tolerated various forms of Christianity, but discriminated against Jews and others – as well as Peter Stuyvesant's attempt to keep Jews out of New Amsterdam.

So the Jews arrived in Newport from the tiny island of Barbados in 1677. Several of these Sephardic Jews were descendants of *conversos*, Jews who had converted to

Christianity under duress, but practiced their faith underground, transmitting the teachings of the Torah to their children under constant threat to their lives. When they arrived in Newport, the new charter professing religious liberties was put to the test.

A year later, the Jews purchased land to be used as a cemetery, a sign that they intended to stay permanently. An old map, dated 1712, discloses the existence of "Jew Street" (now part of Bellevue Avenue) opposite this burial site.

2. "The Old Cemetery" in Newport on Bellevue St., whose deed was signed in 1678. The weather-worn lettering on the tombstones has virtually disappeared.

3. The area today where Jew St. was located, now part of Bellevue

Why They Came

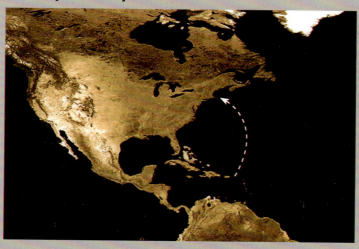

What prompted the migration of Jews from Barbados to Rhode Island? The tale of these Sephardic Jews truly symbolizes the eternal story of the diaspora, with all of the various elements rolled into one.

Everyone knows of the Inquisition, requested by the Spanish monarchs Ferdinand and Isabella and implemented by the Catholic

Church to "cleanse the soil" of Spain from Jews and Muslims. What is not generally known is that the Inquisition moved on from there to Portugal (in 1497) and literally stalked the Jews from country to country for more than 340 years.

The Inquisition was not officially after openly practicing Jews. It had been devised two centuries earlier as a mechanism of the Church to eliminate heretics from within the Catholic faith. However, in 1492, Jews in Spain were given the choice to either convert to Christianity or be expelled from the country after all of their property was confiscated; the latter option meant being turned out penniless (in some cases, after their beards had been forcibly torn from their faces and other painful humiliations), with nowhere to go. Given that choice, many converted, determined to retain their faith in secret. It was these New Christians, *conversos* or crypto-Jews, who were actively hunted by the Inquisition, both for their own "heresy" as well as to prevent their "Judaizing" influence on their brethren.

With the spread of the Inquisition to Portugal, many of these Jews fled to Brazil. Despite persecution by the Brazilian Inquisition, they successfully established sugar plantations and mills. By 1624, nearly 50,000 Europeans lived in Brazil, a large percentage of them *conversos*. They thrived there – ostensibly as Christians – as businessmen, teachers, writers, importers, and exporters, even priests. The Dutch took over much of Brazil in that year, and due to their characteristic religious tolerance, many crypto-Jews came out of hiding. Congregation Kahal Zur was established openly in Recife in 1636.

The Jewish community flourished, with refugees of the Inquisition joining their ranks. They excelled in the sugar industry and (unfortunately, from our modern point of view) the slave trade. A well-run community numbering 1,500 souls established a Talmud Torah and a charity fund.

But the haven didn't last long. In 1647, Isaac de Castro was arrested by Portuguese authorities for teaching Jewish practices in Portuguese-controlled Brazil. He was deported to Portugal, where he was found guilty and burned at the stake. Portugal initiated a nine-year war that drove the Dutch out of Brazil in 1654. The anti-Jewish persecution unleashed at that point resulted in mass migrations of Jews from the area.

It was no accident that Jews arrived in New Amsterdam (early New York City) from South America in 1654. They had fought on the side of the Dutch and were fleeing the Portuguese takeover. In that same year, Jews migrated to British-held Barbados and established the Sephardic congregation Nidhei Israel (The Dispersed Ones of Israel) in Bridgetown. *Conversos* already had been living in Barbados for 25 years, encouraged to settle there by the British. It was the first British territory in which Jews obtained full legal rights.

The Jewish community thrived there. Engaged in sugar and coffee cultivation, Jews were also good businessmen and tradesmen. By 1661, Jewish traders had established trade routes with British-held Suriname and had gained considerable wealth.

That's when the curse of the diaspora set in. British merchants grew irritated by the Jews' successes and began accusing them of illegal transactions, and with favoring trade with Dutch enterprises instead of British. By 1668, Jews were officially forbidden to engage in foreign or local retail trade, and were barred from purchasing slaves. They were pushed into a ghetto.

The noose was tightening all around them, so it is no wonder that they began to seek refuge elsewhere. In 1677, some Jews left Barbados, bound for Rhode Island. This time, it was not outright religious persecution that forced their migration. It was the realization that economic opportunity was closed to them and if they wanted a future for their children – outside of a ghetto – they had to find a home that guaranteed religious, economic, and social freedom.

The young colony in Newport, with its high ideals and refreshing perspective, was just the place.

Nine New York merchants settled in Newport in the 1740s, several of them descendants of *conversos*, who had practiced Judaism underground in Spain and Portugal. Some of the most notable Jewish merchant families of this time were named Lopez, Rivera, Elizer, and Seixas. By the 1750s, fundraisers from Palestine began to include Newport in their itinerary, an indication that its Jewish community was gaining recognition.

In 1759, Newport Jews built their first synagogue. It was only the second synagogue built by Jews in the American colonies and, today, the oldest synagogue building still standing in America. Aptly named Yeshuat Israel (Salvation of Israel) by the very Jews whose families had struggled secretly to teach their children Torah under threat of the severest of penalties, this building was designed with the fears of the past in mind.

4. Aaron Lopez (1731–1782), key American merchant and supporter of the rebels in the Revolutionary War, became a leader of Congregation Yeshuat Israel.

While they were proud of their faith and newfound freedom, they were careful not to flaunt it. In building their synagogue, they practiced great discretion. The architect, Peter Harrison, modeled it, in part, after the synagogue in Amsterdam, as described to him by Isaac Touro, Newport's religious leader. It has no Jewish symbols on the outside, nor does it outdo its neighboring churches.

5. Yeshuat Israel (Salvation of Israel), built by crypto-Jews who were accustomed to hiding their Jewish identity, had no Jewish symbols on the exterior. The acute angle to the street positions the ark to face East. It later became known as the Touro Synagogue in honor of a bequest by Judah Touro to save it from ruin.

Inside, however, is a different story: it resembles the Sephardic synagogues of Europe and the West Indies. It has a central, raised *bimah* (platform) facing the Torah Ark, with a women's gallery above. This level is supported by twelve columns with many elaborately engraved Jewish symbols, providing the members with a warm feeling of tradition. A unique aspect of this building, rarely found anywhere else, was that it was built at an acute angle to the street. To the worshippers, the reason for this was abundantly clear: it is traditional to face eastward – toward Jerusalem – when praying, and this position enabled fulfillment of that custom.

6. The interior of the Touro Synagogue provided members with warm feelings and memories of the Sephardic synagogues of Europe and the West Indies.

Reflecting the fear that haunted these Jewish families in the past, they dressed in such a way that one would not be able to distinguish them as Jews on the street. However, in their homes they prominently displayed ritual objects central to their Judaism. Colonial wills mention Torah scrolls, Shabbos candlesticks, Kiddush cups, shofars, and prayer books as part of their inventories.

I spoke with Rabbi Mordechai Eskovitz, the rabbi of the Touro Synagogue (as Yeshuat Israel is known today), who is a historian extraordinaire. He is a wellspring of information about the synagogue's original members and their aspirations.

"This synagogue is the only Jewish shrine in America," he said. He went on to tell me that the people who designed and built it had one eye on the past and one on the future. On one hand, the exterior was built to look like a colonial mansion, rather than a house of worship, still reflecting the fears of the Inquisition days. "There is still a trap door in the *bimah*, opening a way to an escape tunnel,

7. Torah dating to 1492, the year of the Jewish expulsion from Spain

8. Rabbi Mordechai Eskovitz, rabbi of the Touro Synagogue, told me that it is the only recognized "Jewish shrine" in America. He hosts, among others, bar mitzvahs of children with disabilities.

just as they had built into their synagogues in Europe. Fittingly, next to the Ark, in its own sealed enclosure, is a Torah dating from 1492, the year of the expulsion of the Jews from Spain and the same year that Christopher Columbus set sail to the Americas."

More intriguing was their eye to the future. Much of the Touro Synagogue was built based on the number twelve. There are twelve windows, twelve supporting columns, even twelve candlesticks on the chandelier. This was based on the *Shulchan Aruch*, the compilation of Jewish law whose author, Rabbi Joseph Caro, said that the perfect syna-gogue is built with twelve windows representing the twelve tribes of Israel as a reunified na-tion. There was such enthusiasm and hope in their new freedom; they had come to a place where they could transmit the Torah to their children without fear of retribution. They saw this as a center where their study of the Torah would bring the twelve tribes together in a new unity, preceding the com-ing of the *Moshiach*, the Messiah.

They knew that their children were the vital links in the chain of transmission, so they built a one-room schoolhouse at-tached to the synagogue building, leading both to the women's section upstairs and the men's section on the main floor. This type of attachment to a house of worship was almost unheard of in colonial times. At the same time, they built a *mikveh*, demonstrating their commitment to the Jewish laws of family purity, a necessary step to ensure the continuity of the Jewish people in America.

The religious leader at this time was the synagogue's first *chazzan* (a cantor, who in the Sephardic tradition is not just a prayer leader but wears the many hats of a community rabbi), Isaac Touro, who arrived in Newport from Curacao in 1758. When the British captured the city during the American Revolution, he was forced to flee to Jamaica, where he died in 1783. His sons, Abraham and Judah, migrated to New Orleans and made their fortunes there.

The British brought death, destruction, and economic ruin to Newport, and the war sounded the death knoll for the Jewish community. The *mikveh* and schoolhouse were destroyed. The Torah scrolls were sent to New York for safekeeping, and by 1800, the synagogue closed down, seemingly forever. The symbol of newly acquired religious freedom, the "temple" to which all Jews would be drawn as the unified twelve tribes, the hope of the future, seemed doomed to be a home to rats and moles.

The Newport Jewish Community Is Brought Back to Life

Amazingly, after being closed and dark for fifty years, the synagogue was recalled in the will of Abraham Touro, and saved by his and his brother Judah's generosity. (Judah became known as one of the greatest Jewish philanthropists in American history.) Neither of them ever returned to Newport, nor did they retain the traditionalism of their father. Yet they remained concerned about Jewish continuity. Abraham's will mandates that the "synagogue, the street…also the burying grounds, are kept in elegant order…from the proceeds of a legacy…now amounting to fifteen thousand dollars…for the purpose of supporting the Jewish synagogue."

This may have been the first bequest anywhere in America for the preservation of a vacant building, the first act of what we now call "historic preservation." Their generosity, seemingly out of nowhere, reopened this unique synagogue. Now named the Touro Synagogue, it revived a lost community and, perhaps, set the stage for a new Jewish enclave in Rhode Island. For these people, it was all about their legacy to their children.

"We have continued this legacy," Rabbi Eskovitz beamed. "In preparation for their bar or bat mitzvah, I teach the children *Chumash* (Bible), *halachah* (Jewish law), and reading of their Torah or *Haftorah* portions, sometimes even long distance over the phone, five days a week." But these are not ordinary bar mitzvahs! The Touro Synagogue is known worldwide for providing bar mitzvahs for children who are developmentally disabled. "Their sense of pride at having their joyous event at the oldest synagogue in America is an unbelievable sight," said the rabbi. "We have not forgotten the one-room schoolhouse, nor have we given up on the transmission of Torah values in this venerable old building."

9. Just before George Washington's inauguration as the first president of the United States, Moses Mendes Seixas, president of Newport's Congregation Yeshuat Israel (later Touro Synagogue), wrote a congratulatory letter to Washington. In it he spoke of "a government erected by the majesty of the people – a government which to bigotry gives no sanction, to persecution no assistance, but generously affording to all liberty of conscience and immunities of citizenship, deeming every one of whatever nation, tongue or language, equal parts of the great governmental machine." George Washington's famous response, his letter to the Newport Congregation, repeats Seixas's praise: "…the Government of the United States, which gives to bigotry no sanction, to persecution no assistance…." These eloquent words, famously attributed to George Washington, in fact originated in the pen of the oldest son of Isaac Mendes Seixas.

Dorothy Lippman, one of the energizing forces in the founding of the Newport Jewish Home for the Aged, and now one of its active residents, was born in 1915. "Back then," she reminisced, "we were all members of the Touro Synagogue. We had kosher butchers, bakers, a deli, and a *shochet* [kosher

the Government of the United States, which gives to bigotry no sanction, to persecution no assistance requires only that they who live under its protection should demean themselves as good citizens, in giving it on all occasions their effectual support.

It would be inconsistent with the frankness of my character not to avow that I am pleased with your favorable opinion of my administration, and fervent wishes for my felicity. May the children of the Stock of Abraham, who dwell in this land, continue to merit and enjoy the good will of the other inhabitants, while every one shall sit in safety under his own vine and figtree, and there shall be none to make him afraid. May the father of all mercies scatter light and not darkness in our paths, and make us all in our several vocations here, and in his own due time and way everlastingly happy

G. Washington

butcher]. The chief of surgery at the Newport Hospital, a traditional Jew, became the community's *mohel*.

"In those early days, Jewish education was hard to come by, but it was our only chance as children to strengthen our ties. Reverend Friedman [in the early American Sephardic community, the title Reverend was given to rabbinic leaders] would come to our house to teach me Yiddish and Hebrew. I went to Talmud Torah at the Jewish Community Center. My brother's bar mitzvah at Touro was in the European style: the boy would be called up to the Torah, usually during the week, said the blessing and then, afterward, schnapps and kichel were served. This was the whole thing! The important thing was the understanding of the responsibilities the young man had in the continuity of his people, not the size of the party."

10. Dorothy Lippman was member of b Newport ar Providenc synagogu She hel found th Home f the Age

11. Newport Jewish Home for the Aged

At the same time that the Touro Synagogue and Newport underwent a revival, a new Jewish enclave was growing in nearby Providence. Land was acquired for a burial ground in 1849, followed by the founding of its first synagogue, the Sephardic Bnai Israel, in 1854.

12. Old Sons of Abraham building (now a church), with cornerstone still in place

Providence Takes Root

Rhode Island was the first state to industrialize in early America, and the booming economy attracted a large number of eastern Europeans in the 1870s. Orthodox *shul*s appeared all over Providence's north end and Willard Avenue: Ahavath Shalom, Sons of Jacob, Sons of Abraham, Shaare Tzedek, and Anshe Kovne, to name just a few.

One of the elders of Providence, Rabbi Mordechai Weiner, remembered his 1930s childhood: "I had my bar mitzvah in Ahavath Shalom. It had 1,500 men's seats and a balcony for women, with chandeliers all along the ceiling. In those days, we just read the *Haftorah* and had an open house for Kiddush. Everyone spoke Yiddish, a beautiful language. Today, nobody does; it's a shame.

"I grew up being told that everyone in Anshe Kovne synagogue lived to their nineties. Do you know why?" he asked with a smile. "Because every morning, after *davening*, we had schnapps and herring! Our only Jewish education as children came from the Talmud Torah and it wasn't much of an education. We lost a generation of Jews who wanted to become American. The day school came in 1947 and changed everything."

13. Rabbi Mordechai Weiner and son cherishing the memories of Providence in the '30s

A Jewish Day School as Early as 1731!

Jewish education in Providence, as everywhere, was the key link for a Jewish child between his past and his future. The concept of a Jewish all-day school in the US, teaching both Hebrew and secular subjects, is not a new one. As a matter of fact, the fist such school was Yeshivat Minha Areb, established in New York by the Spanish-Portuguese congregation, Shearith Israel, in 1731. The importance these early settlers put on their children's education was shown in the fact that there were seven such schools in New York City by 1854! With the establishment of the free public school system and the immigration of impoverished eastern Europeans, however, the day school system declined.

By the turn of the century, the Talmud Torah system was failing in Providence. In an article written in 1911 under the pseudonym "Aeriel" in a Providence publication,

Ezra: A Journal of Opinion, the author deplored the lack of Hebrew education for the children of Jewish immigrants. He commented that these immigrants were so immersed in their American freedoms that they ignored their obligation to provide for their children's Jewish education, and he called for the establishment of a Jewish day school.

No one answered his call, until a surprising turn of events occurred.

Over thirty-five years later, the only Reform rabbi in the state, Rabbi William (Gershon Zev) Braude, brought this article to the attention of the community, and fought, along with the Orthodox community and Rabbi Bohnen, the Conservative rabbi, to organize the Providence Hebrew Day School. In 1947, an old mansion on Waterman Street became the school that would blend the values of Jewish heritage with the nobility of American democracy. There was a storm of protests: "It might promote more anti-Semitism." "There would be noise on the streets." "What are you trying to do, revive old European customs?"

Lacking funds, the school couldn't pay its teachers. The bus company threatened that it would not pick up the children. As much as sixteen weeks' salary was owed to the teachers, and revolt was in the air! Even the National Society of Hebrew Day Schools, the newly formed Torah Umesorah, was floundering. Who could save this fledgling Torah institution?

Picture this. Rabbi Braude of Temple Beth El steps up to the pulpit and gives a fiery sermon supporting the day school. "It was a chilly night," he said years later, "but no matter what the chill outside, the chill inside the temple as I delivered the sermon was so perceptible you could cut the ice." Undaunted, he said that the results achieved by a weekend Talmud Torah were very meager. The world of Torah is a very great world and it cannot be squeezed into the tiny confines of a Sunday school. Rabbi Braude berated his bewildered congregants: "I do not wish to see Torah shunted off to an hour or so on a Sunday morning! By means of [day] schools, a generation will ride psychologically secure in their American heritage, spiritually rich in knowledge and understanding of Torah and immovably strong in piety and fear of G-d."

14. Lunchroom in the basement of the original
Providence Hebrew Day School on Waterman St.

When this sermon came to the attention of the troubled Torah Umesorah, headed by Dr. Joseph Kaminetsky, it was a tremendous morale booster for the organization. Eighteen years later, the Reform rabbi was honored by the Providence Hebrew Day School. Its president, Dr. Fishbein, commented, "If Rabbis Braude and Bohnen had not backed the school, it would have never gotten off the ground."

In 1962, the day school moved to its new facility. One of the students, Herschel Smith, who had put up a *mezuzah* on the front entrance of the original building in 1947, again conducted the ceremony at the front entrance to the new building. Everyone knew it had been a long, hard road to reach that moment.

15. Providence Hebrew Day School, in its present location since 1962

This is how this small community in New England, through dogged perseverance, enabled its most important asset, its children, to bind themselves to the past and strengthen their bond to the future. The chain of continuity is unbroken.

16. Rabbi Peretz Scheinerman, principal: "The Jewish people of Providence are very into their kids…their families."

And the Beat Goes On…

Today I am accompanying Beatrice Hohenemser, who has lived in Providence all her life, to the *upsherin* of her great-grandson, three-year-old Moshe Shimshon. There was not much written on this custom in Jewish literature until the sixteenth century, when the disciples of the renowned kabbalistic teacher Rabbi Isaac Luria (the "Ari") of Safed reported that their teacher would go to the tomb of Rabbi Shimon Bar Yochai, in nearby Meron, to cut the hair of his young son. Today, on the Jewish holiday of Lag B'Omer, hundreds of thousands of Jews in Israel converge on the tomb to continue this custom.

17. Filled to capacity: the tomb of Rabbi Shimon Bar Yochai in Meron, Israel, on Lag B'Omer

There are many reasons given for this custom at the age of three, all giving beautiful insights into the importance we Jews give to the transmission of the Torah from elder to child. For example, according to the laws of *orlah*, one is not permitted to eat the fruit of a tree in its first three years. A tree has to go through a certain maturation process until it can provide enjoyment to others. At three, a boy reaches a certain state of development – one of understanding and the ability to communicate – making him ready to start his Torah education and give pleasure to others.

The day starts at the yeshivah. "Older" yeshivah boys – kindergarten and first grade – wait with their *rebbe* in great anticipation of the arrival of Moshe with his entourage of parents, grandparents, and great-grandparent. Instructions are given to the children not to make the boy nervous. He enters the room, wearing his *tzitzis* and *yarmulke* for the first time. The *rebbe* approaches, and he and the boy read the *aleph-beis* (Hebrew alphabet) together. The child says the blessing on his *tzitzis* and kisses them. Next, honey is placed over the Hebrew letters and the boy joyfully licks it off the letters. This creates an association in the mind of the child: the study of Torah is sweet! As the children sing the traditional

תּוֹרָה צִוָּה לָנוּ מֹשֶׁה מוֹרָשָׁה קְהִלַּת יַעֲקֹב

"Torah tzivah lanu Moshe, morashah kehillas Yaakov" (Moses commanded us to keep the Torah, an inheritance for the Congregation of Jacob), little Moshe joins in. Maimonides wrote, seven hundred years ago, that this was the first verse to be taught to a child, even prior to *Shema Yisrael*.

The seriousness, joy, and pride on the faces of the family reflect the importance they place on their children carrying this "inheritance" from generation to generation. Moshe is placed on the shoulders of his grandfather, Zvi Herskovits, as the children dance in frenzy around them. The child loves being the center of attention.

I speak to Zvi and his wife, Brina, as they catch their breath during a momentary break. Zvi tells me, with absolute delight, that they noticed a difference in Moshe the minute he first put on his *yarmulke* and *tzitzis* and joined the other boys in dancing. "It's almost as if he crossed over an imaginary line and joined a club that changed his personality forever." Brina says that this is the beginning of acting, feeling, learning, *being* a Jew.

Beatrice, the glowing great-grandmother, watches all of the proceedings as if she has never seen it before. But, of course, she has seen it all – including many an *upsherin* – during her eighty-five years. "Do you ever tire of watching these life-cycle events?" I query. She looks at me as though I were crazy!

"I'm watching his education take flight" she responds, her eyes tearing. "This is the part of *Yiddishkeit* that makes it all worthwhile." Watching the circle of students, teachers, and parents forming around her great-grandson, she comments, "I feel privileged to be observing this moment in his life. *It's a piece of my heart!*" It is clear that for all those gathered here, the Torah is a gift to treasure.

The festivities now move to Moshe's home, where the barber's scissors and a festive meal await. Everyone at the meal gets to cut a lock of hair, while Moshe sits patiently and takes it all in. One custom is weighing the cut hair, and giving charity according to its weight, linking the *mitzvah* of *tzedakah* to the onset of Jewish education. So begins Moshe's formal introduction to Torah education and *mitzvos*.

The sheer joy and smiling faces at this event match what I have seen at bar mitzvahs and weddings, and the reason is simple. At every milestone in our lives, symbols of the continuity of our people abound. There is great satisfaction in witnessing yet another link being forged in our eternal Jewish chain.

18. Moshe Shimshon, with his own *tzitzis* and *yarmulke* for the first time, says the *berachah* on the *tzitzis* at the yeshivah.

At every milestone in our lives, symbols of the continuity of our people abound.

19. Saying the *aleph-beis* with pride

20. How sweet it is! Pouring the honey on the *aleph-beis*.

21. Center of attention

22. Man-time together: the ties that bind. Zeide Zvi Herskovits and grandson looking toward the future.

When Pharaoh was considering letting the Jewish people go from Egypt, he asked Moses who would go with him to serve G-d in the desert. The answer starts off with a firm and telling announcement: "With our elders and with our children shall we journey!" (Exodus 10:9). No commitment to G-d can leave out the children.

This lesson is borne out in our lives and literature. In his introduction to one of the greatest compilations of Jewish law, Maimonides meticulously details the transmission of the Torah from teacher to student all the way back to the giving of the Torah at Sinai. He is telling us that the perseverance and continuity of a scattered people has been dependent on the transmission of the Torah from elder to child for thousands of years.

Faithful teaching of the Torah is the common bond that ties all Jews to each other from generation to generation. For 350 years, the Jews of Newport and Providence clearly have understood that. It's a piece of their hearts.

Synagogues and their members

23. Sons of Jacob, built in 1906

24. With a stunning interior, it is no wonder that Sons of Jacob is entered in the Historic Registry.

25. Beth Shalom

26. Interior of the Orthodox Beth Shalom

27. Rabbi Asher Oser: "We are unpretentious but highly motivated

28. Choir of Congregation Ahavath Shalom, c. 1910. This *shul* preceded Beth Shalom, which went from Orthodox to Conservative to Orthodox.

29. Orchestra of the Orthodox synagogue Congregation Bais Israel Anshay Hestreich, or the Robinson Street Shul, c.1928

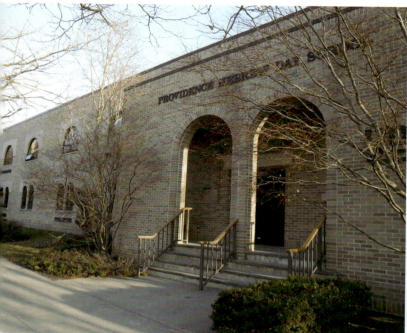

30. Providence Hebrew Day School (PHDS) today

31. Original building of Providence Hebrew Day School on Waterman St., founded 1947

32. Looking to the future: students going to PHDS in 1959, temporarily based in Temple Beth-El

33. Free again! Flag football at PHDS.

34. Time out to pose at PHDS

35. Cornerstone brought from Jerusalem for the new Providence Hebrew Day School

Life

36. Willard Avenue in South Providence, c. 1945. Note the kosher bakery, delicatessen, and meat market.

37. Read all about it! Two paperboys in 1910. It was very common for Jewish youngsters to help augment a family's meager income before World War II.

38. Bar mitzvah boy, c. 1910, Providence

39. Banice and Saul Feinberg becoming bar mitzvah in 1914, Providence

40. Benny Strachman practicing his bar mitzvah *parshah* (Torah reading) with teacher Dr. Lenny Moise looking on. His mother, Amy, says: "We see this not as a chance for a big party…but rather an opportunity to be an *eved Hashem*, a servant of G-d. Instead of focusing on the day itself, it is the beginning of a process of learning."

41. The unforgettable experience of being bar mitzvah in the Touro Synagogue, in front of the Torah dating to the Spanish Inquisition

42. Julius Brier's bar mitzvah, c. 1920s

Bar Mitzv

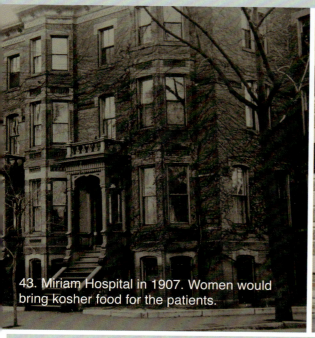

43. Miriam Hospital in 1907. Women would bring kosher food for the patients.

44. Today's Miriam Hospital provides its own kosher food.

45. Tzedakah (charity) box for Miriam Hospital, c. 1907. Inscription in Yiddish: "Help the poor sick."

46. Tzedakah box on the pillar of the Touro Synagogue, given as a gift by the Bevis Marks Synagogue in London in 1763

THE JEWISH CEMETERY AT NEWPORT (1852)
Henry Wadsworth Longfellow (1807–1882)

How strange it seems! These Hebrews in their graves,
Close by the street of this fair seaport town,
Silent beside the never-silent waves,
At rest in all this moving up and down!

The trees are white with dust, that o'er their sleep
Wave their broad curtains in the south-wind's breath,
While underneath these leafy tents they keep
The long, mysterious Exodus of Death.

And these sepulchral stones, so old and brown,
That pave with level flags their burial-place,
Seem like the tablets of the Law, thrown down
And broken by Moses at the mountain's base.

The very names recorded here are strange,
Of foreign accent, and of different climes;
Alvares and Rivera interchange
With Abraham and Jacob of old times.

"Blessed be God! for he created Death!"
The mourners said, "and Death is rest and peace;"
Then added, in the certainty of faith,
"And giveth Life that nevermore shall cease."

Closed are the portals of their Synagogue,
No Psalms of David now the silence break,
No Rabbi reads the ancient Decalogue
In the grand dialect the Prophets spake.

Gone are the living, but the dead remain,
And not neglected; for a hand unseen,
Scattering its bounty, like a summer rain,
Still keeps their graves and their remembrance green.

How came they here? What burst of Christian hate,
What persecution, merciless and blind,
Drove o'er the sea – that desert desolate –
These Ishmaels and Hagars of mankind?

They lived in narrow streets and lanes obscure,
Ghetto and Judenstrass, in mirk and mire;
Taught in the school of patience to endure
The life of anguish and the death of fire.

All their lives long, with the unleavened bread
And bitter herbs of exile and its fears,
The wasting famine of the heart they fed,
And slaked its thirst with marah of their tears.

Anathema maranatha! was the cry
That rang from town to town, from street to street;
At every gate the accursed Mordecai
Was mocked and jeered, and spurned by Christian feet.

Pride and humiliation hand in hand
Walked with them through the world where'er they went;
Trampled and beaten were they as the sand,
And yet unshaken as the continent.

For in the background figures vague and vast
Of patriarchs and of prophets rose sublime,
And all the great traditions of the Past
They saw reflected in the coming time.

And thus forever with reverted look
The mystic volume of the world they read,
Spelling it backward, like a Hebrew book,
Till life became a Legend of the Dead.

But ah! what once has been shall be no more!
The groaning earth in travail and in pain
Brings forth its races, but does not restore,
And the dead nations never rise again.

Longfellow predicts that the Jewish people, like so many others who have come and gone throughout history, is near its end. He's contemplating Newport in 1852, with no *shul*, and only a Jewish cemetery to bear witness to those whose flight from the Inquisition eventually brought them here. In 1854, two years after this poem was written, Bnai Israel opened in Providence. And 96 years after Longfellow set pen to paper, the Jewish State of Israel was declared. A dead nation, never to rise again? Longfellow may have been mistaken this once, though the rest of his lines here seem pretty accurate.

The Upsherin

47. A star is born! Moshe Shimshon draped in a *tallis* and escorted by his proud father, Chaim Lesser, at the yeshivah.

48. Moshe wears his *tzitzis* and *yarmulke* for the first time with his teacher and father looking on.

49. Grandfather Zvi Herskovits dancing with Moshe before going home for the *upsherin*, the ceremonial first cutting of a three-year-old's hair

50. Grandfather Zvi, at three, waiting for his own *upsherin*

51. Rabbi Yehoshua Laufer (back, center) and wife Michla (next to him), on the occasion of their son's *upsherin*, 1989. Rabbi Laufer and his son, Rabbi Yossi Laufer, are prominent Chabad leaders in Providence and Warwick.

52. Take a lot off the top! Great-grandmother Beatrice Hohenemser is beaming as she cuts Moshe's hair with daughter (grandmother) Brina Herskovits looking on. Brina: "This is the beginning…of being a Jew." Beatrice: "I feel privileged to observe this moment."

53. Pièce de résistance!

54. Is that me?

55. We're all in this together. Three boys awaiting their turn in Meron, Israel, Lag B'Omer.

56–58. Over 200,000 Jews come to Meron and the grave of Rabbi Shimon Bar Yochai to celebrate Lag B'Omer and perform *upsherin* on their sons.

59. The proud kiss

**My thanks to
Rabbi Mordechai Eskovitz,
Rabbi Asher Oser,
Rabbi Peretz Scheinerman,
Mordechai Weiner,
Anne Sherman and Jerry Foster
of the Rhode Island Jewish
Historical Association,
Brina and Zvi Herskovits,
Lenny Moise,
Amy Strachman,
and Dorothy Lippman.**

Bibliography

Encyclopedia Judaica. Jerusalem: Keter Publishing House, 1972.

Foster, Geraldine S., Eleanor F. Horvitz, and Judith Weiss Cohen. *Jews of Rhode Island, 1658–1958*. Images of America. Charleston, SC: Arcadia Publishing, 1998.

Friedman, Lee M. *Jewish Pioneers and Patriots*. Philadelphia: Jewish Publication Society of America, 1942.

Goodwin, George M., and Ellen Smith. *The Jews of Rhode Island*. Hanover, NH: Brandeis University Press, 2004.

Libo, Kenneth, and Irving Howe. *We Lived There Too: In Their Own Words and Pictures; Pioneer Jews and the Westward Movement of America, 1630–1930*. New York: St. Martin's/Marek, 1984.

Pessin, Deborah. *History of the Jews in America*. New York: United Synagogue Commission on Jewish Education, 1957.

Rhode Island Jewish Historical Association. *Rhode Island Jewish Historical Notes* 8, no. 4 (Nov. 1982).

Attributions

All numbered photos from the author's collection except as follows. Photos 14, 28, 29, 31, 32, 36–39, 42, 43, 51: Rhode Island Jewish Historical Association; 41: Touro Synagogue collection; 50: Herskovits family collection; p. 57 Lag B'Omer at Meron watermark: Yair Koenig.

"הַעִירוֹתִי מִצָּפוֹן וַיַּאת, מִמִּזְרַח־שֶׁמֶשׁ יִקְרָא בִשְׁמִי..."

ישעיהו מא:כה

"I have raised up one from the north and he has come;
and from the rising of the sun in the east,
he shall call in My name..."

Isaiah 41:25

Bangor, Maine

Beth Abraham
Beth Israel
Old Orchard Beach
Shore Path Cottage, Bar Harbor

Bangor, Maine

Purim and Survival in the Land of the Moose

I t is the week of Purim, and I look down from my airplane window on the frozen expanse that is Maine. All is still. There are few houses and little sign of human activity. I ask myself, how did a Jewish community manage to take root and continue to exist in this remote corner of the world for nearly 160 years?

This state is so far northeast, jutting into Canada and the Atlantic Ocean, that it seems geographically separate from the rest of the United States. You would not think that such an isolated area, with its vast tracts of towering spruce and fir, hidden lakes and snow-covered mountains, would attract Jewish settlers. Nor would you imagine that those few who might venture there would be welcomed by the tight-knit indigenous population. But as Judith Goldstein writes in her book *Crossing Lines* (New York: Morrow, 1992, p. 13), although these conditions would seem to "exclude…ethnic infusions into the native culture," and one would expect to find "few immigrants [a]nd fewer Jews. The reality, however, was much different."

On my visit to this remarkable Jewish enclave, I discovered just how different that reality turned out to be! Bangor is a stirring example of Jewish pride and perseverance. Ironically, its smallness seems to be the chief factor in its survival.

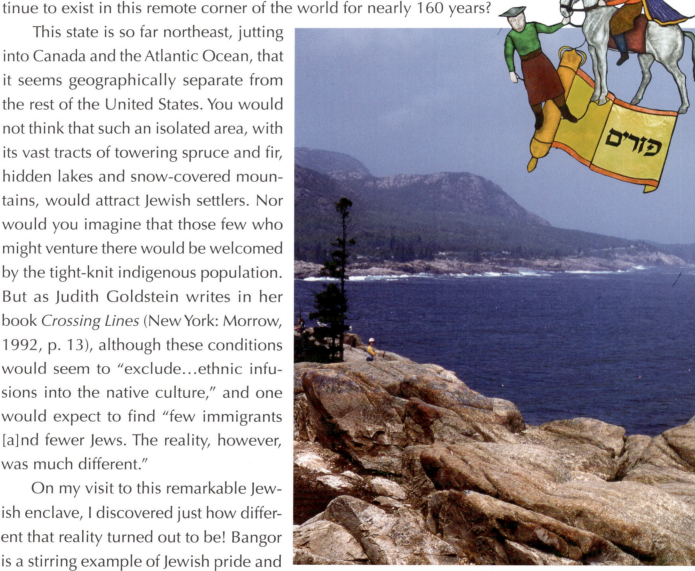

1. At the top of Cadillac Mountain is the easternmost part of the US. One can put on *tefillin* earlier than anyone else in the countr[y]

There had been Jewish residents in Maine prior to the establishment of an actual community. The first was Susman Abrams from Hamburg, Germany, a peddler of old clothing who settled in Waldoboro (about seventy miles southeast of Bangor) during the American Revolutionary War. And there was Joseph Israel, one of the first Jews serving in the fledgling US Navy, who lost his life in 1804 in an expedition against pirates in Tripoli harbor.

A Place of Refuge Hosts a *Minyan*

But our story begins in 1849, when thirteen German-Jewish immigrants settled in Bangor and voted to purchase land for a cemetery and establish a synagogue, both named Ahavath (Ahavas) Achim. Like many other Jews of the mid-nineteenth century, they had fled Germany rather than suffer the wrath of those seeking a scapegoat for their defeat at the hands of Napoleon. When Bangor's economy suffered, the synagogue closed and the Torah was sent to Congregation Ohabei Sholom in Boston for safekeeping. That Torah would resurface fifty years later, seemingly taking on a life of its own.

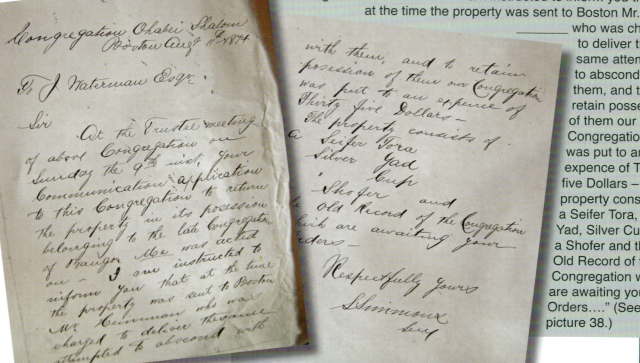

2. Earliest Jewish cemetery in Bangor, with tombstones well over 100 years old. The weather and elements have caused many to fracture. Some are being held together with brackets.

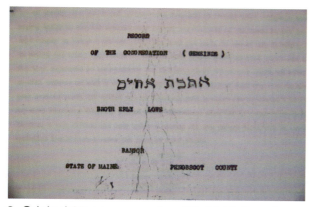

3. Original 60-page record – all in Yiddish – of Congregation Ahavath Achim (Brotherly Love), c. 1849. The *shul* closed in 1856. The Torah was sent to Congregation Ohabei Sholom in Boston for safekeeping, along with this complete record of the congregation, a silver *yad* (pointer used in the reading of a Torah), and a silver cup. (See next two photographs.)

Escaping the pogroms of 1881, Jews from Poland, Russia, and Rumania came en masse to American shores, and Maine got its share. By 1884, observant Jews were numerous enough for the state legislature to liberalize Sunday closing laws to permit Sabbath observers to open businesses on Sunday.

4–5. This is a copy of the original letter sent by Ohabei Sholom in answer to a request sent in 1874 by what seems to be the remnant of Ahavath Achim, asking for their religious articles to be returned, probably to be used in a new congregation to be formed, Beth Israel: "Sir…. Your Communication/application to this Congregation to return the property in its possession belonging to the late Congregation of Bangor Me was acted on – I am instructed to inform you that at the time the property was sent to Boston Mr. _____ who was charged to deliver the same attempted to abscond with them, and to retain possession of them our Congregation was put to an expence of Thirty five Dollars – The property consists of a Seifer Tora, Silver Yad, Silver Cup, a Shofer and the Old Record of the Congregation which are awaiting your Orders…." (See also picture 38.)

6. Joseph Bernstein and other religious immigrants held services in their homes, using the Torah received from Ohabei Sholom. The early *minyan* had no name, no rules, and no constitution. Nor did they have a *chazzan* or *shochet*. This changed in 1888 with their first building.

The founding fathers of Beth Israel, the first synagogue building in Maine, arrived in Bangor in 1888. Ezriel Lemke, Joe Bernstein, and a *minyan* of others, peddlers by trade, held precious the traditions, rituals, and ceremonies of their home cities in Lithuania: Kovno, Grodno, and Vilna, and their surrounding *shtetlach* (villages). All synagogue records were kept in Yiddish.

The Torah that had been sent to Boston for safekeeping almost fifty years earlier was now brought back to Beth Israel. That Torah may very well still be in existence. I found an article written in 1945 about a "flying Torah" lent by Beth Israel to a World

7. April 1945 article describing the Torah that seems to have taken on a life of its own. We will follow it more in photographic images.

War II army chaplain from Bangor. He took it with him as he traveled from base to base all over the world (over seventy-thousand miles, up to that time). The Torah, the article said, was over a hundred years old, so it is very likely the one handed down from the original Bangor congregation. A community dies, but the Torah survives!

At the new Beth Israel, the "entrance fee" (dues) was three dollars per year, payable in quarterly installments of 75 cents. The first Talmud Torah in Bangor was established in 1897, followed by the Hebrew Free School, which, as its name would indicate, offered free education to those who couldn't afford to pay. Its principal was Reb Yehuda Dov Wasserman. In 1898, the Ezras Orchim Society for Destitute Strangers was formed, the first Jewish charitable organization in Maine.

The Jewish community of New York at that time was relatively large and influential. It was led by Rabbi Jacob Joseph, a renowned Talmudic scholar and the only one ever to serve as chief rabbi of New York. He arrived from Vilna in 1895. A typical problem facing the Jews in far-flung communities is demonstrated by

8. The original Beth Israel was dedicated in 1897 and was destroyed in the 1911 Bangor city fire.

9. Reb Yehuda Dov Wasserman was the principal and teacher of the new Talmud Torah held in the basement of the *shul*, c. 1897.

an emergency letter sent to New York from Bangor in 1912: "…Have no meat. Send *shochet* [ritual slaughterer] at once," signed S.E. Rudman.

The story continues: the *shochet* was brought from New York for $20, but it seemed the reverend liked to relax his spirit with spirits (which was not good for the precision needed for this work) and was put on probation! I later found out, through many interviews and research at the Bangor Historical Society, that S.E. Rudman was Shmuel Rudman, the uncle of the first Jewish Supreme Court Justice of Maine, Abraham M. Rudman.

10. Abraham Rudman, who later became the first Jewish Supreme Court Justice of Maine

The Striar Legacy

In every Jewish community throughout history, there is always a notable family that puts the struggling community on its shoulders and carries it. In Bangor, the Striar family did just that. James Gimple Striar, who made his fortune in Maine's woolen mills, was generous to a fault, funding the synagogue, schools, and many charities. His children continued his legacy by helping to build the day school under the leadership of Rabbi Henry Isaacs, and by funding the Yeshiva University division named for their father, the James Striar School of General Jewish Studies. As a fitting memorial, the school teaches the fundamentals of Jewish scholarship and heritage through its unique curriculum.

11. David Pinchas Striar, active member of the early Beth Israel, wanted to institute the *Nusach Sfard* custom for the prayers. When refused, he and a *minyan* of others formed Congregation Beth Abraham Anshe Sfard, which is active to this day.

As Beth Israel was an Ashkenazic synagogue (following the rituals and customs used in Germany and some other European countries), David Pinchas Striar led a group of like-minded congregants to form a new synagogue that would pray using the *Nusach Sfard* (Chassidic) customs more familiar to them. Congregation Beth Abraham Anshe

12. Memorial plaque given in memory of David Pinchas Striar hangs prominently on the wall of today's Beth Abraham. Chief Judge Louis Ko of the US courts in Bangor, an active membe Abraham, told me, "The Striar family is surely 'First Family' in significance to Beth Abraham our existence to them."

13. Beth Israel as it looked in 1913 after the Bangor fire destroyed the original building

Sfard, established in 1902, remains Bangor's only Orthodox synagogue, and still holds to the same *Sfard* tradition. Most of the founding members were either peddlers or cattle dealers.

The official history of Beth Abraham states: "Little is known about the spiritual leaders of Beth Abraham. Most were not ordained rabbis, but *chazzan*s, *shochet*s, *mohel*s or a combination there-of." It was rare to see an ordained rabbi in America until po-groms in eastern Europe forced large-scale emigration in the 1880s.

14. Beth Abraham, shown here in 1933, existed side by s with another large Orthodox *shul*, Beth Israel. It was buil after a fire destroyed the nearby Carr Street *shul* in 1932

A Voice from the Past

I spoke to a couple whose families had been ac-tive in the Bangor Orthodox community for four generations, going back to the early twentieth century. With a gleam in their eyes, Barbara and Sandy Podolsky read me excerpts of a letter written by Barbara's grandfather. He describes escaping the czar's draft in 1908 by running out the back door of his house as recruiters came knocking at the front door, promising his wife and children that he would send for them as soon as possible. As he thought that using his real name at Ellis Island would get him sent back to Russia, he took the name Rolnick, as it was the only "American name" he had ever heard.

He was a peddler six days a week, as were most immigrants, and they all adhered to one rule: no one travels the route of another. In halachic (Jewish legal) terms, taking over another's territory is called in Hebrew *hasagas g'vul* and is strictly prohibited. Though pressed to earn a living, these Jews staunchly abided by that law.

In this letter, he tells that he once knocked on the door of a blind non-Jewish customer, who asked him to move closer so she could feel his head; she was looking for the horns she thought were on every Jew! (This misconception began as a mistransla-tion of the Bible which used the word "horns" to mean the rays of holy light emanating from Moses' face at Mt. Sinai. Michelangelo's famous sculpture of Moses portrays him with these horns on his head, and the myth of "Jewish horns" has survived to this day.)

15. Barbara Podolsky, whose grandparents were pioneers in early Bangor. She and her husband, Sandy, have been an inspiration for years in Beth Abraham. Here she comes "appropriately" dressed for the Purim Megillah reading and celebration.

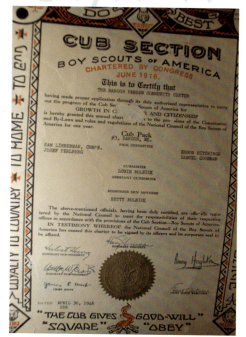

16. Certificate given by the Boy Scouts of America to the Bangor Hebrew Community Center, c. 1946, to allow the meeting of a Cub pack under the leadership of Cubmaster Louis Rolnick, whose father escaped the Russian pogroms in 1908 and came to Bangor

Sandy's grandfather, on the other hand, wound up in Bangor quite by mistake. When he came to Ellis Island, he asked to go to Bangor, Pennsylvania, as he probably knew someone there, and was obligingly routed to Bangor, Maine!

A Lesson in Pride

Zionism was a powerful force in Bangor from early in the twentieth century. All of Bangor's Jews are familiar with the story of the Jewish Legion's visit. During World War I, a British army battalion known as the Jewish Legion, or Zion Mule Corps, fought against the Ottoman Empire in an effort to conquer Palestine. In Bangor, word got out that the Jewish Legion (including David Ben-Gurion) would pass through Bangor on its way to Halifax, to raise money for arms. The Jews of Bangor could not let the opportunity pass without providing a rousing welcome. One soldier wrote about the episode: "…But the town we will remember to the end of our days, the town that will be present before our eyes even in the smoke and thunder of battle, is the little town of Bangor. It was 4:00 AM. We were trying to sleep…suddenly, comes the strains of 'Hatikvah.' Then came a resounding cheer and men, women and children invaded our quarters…with food and gifts. What a wonderful few moments they were!"

By 1920, there were 1,800 Jews in Maine, compared to 690,000 in New York. One can see the continual struggle to maintain a continuity of religious observance with comparatively few people and a harsh environment. But they held on, steadfast in their beliefs, united by their common goals.

Sons and Daughters of Zion, Bangor, Me. June-9th-1920.

17. On Purim day, in 1912, Henrietta Szold and 38 women gathered for what turned out to be a historic meeting in New York, to create a new national organization called "Daughters of Zion" and its "Hadassah" chapter in New York. It was to be devoted to the promotion of Jewish institutions and ideals in Palestine. Szold was elected its first president. Above, a meeting of the "Sons and Daughters of Zion" chapter in Bangor, Maine, c. 1920.

The "Catskills" of the North

Where did Bangor's Jews vacation at the turn of the twentieth century? Very often, it was fifty miles south on the Atlantic shore at Old Orchard Beach, where the Lafayette Hotel, the first strictly kosher hotel north of Boston, was established in 1909. I had the privilege of talking to Harold Goodkowski – 101 years young – whose parents and grandparents had started that hotel. His house is all that's left of this grand place, and I came there to talk with him. The doors to many rooms still have numbers on them!

Sitting here with Harold and listening to his amazingly coherent memories of a life so long ago, I could sense his satisfaction in keeping Orthodoxy alive through two World Wars, the Great Depression, and constant changes in the neighborhood. The hotel lasted only until the 1960s, but the *shul* he supported, the connection to Judaism, still remains. The synagogue is still down the block and in use!

"I remember," he said, as his eyes took on a far-away look, "at the hotel, we had weddings almost every Sunday, bar mitzvahs on Shabbos.

18. Harold "Babe" Goodkowski, whose parents and grandparents started the Lafayette Hotel in Old Orchard Beach, the only kosher hotel north of Boston

We were listed in all the travelogues of the 1920s. People would come from Germany, France, Calgary, Montreal, and all over the US, calling up to make sure we were kosher. Can you beat that? Our guests included well-known rabbis from Denver, New York, and Pennsylvania; New England political families like the Kennedys; entertainers like Benny Goodman; businessmen like the Bronfman family, and so many others. We were like the Catskills!"

After he mentioned all those glorious names, I asked him to think of his fondest memory of Old Orchard Beach in his 101 years. I was sure it would be connected to some illustrious individual – but no! Without hesitation, he replied, "About 60 years ago, on the first day of Shavuos, at the Old Orchard Beach Shul up the block from the hotel, I was asked to *daven Musaf* for the *amud* [to lead the prayer services]. I had never done it before and was so very nervous in front of all those people. I was shaking! I must have been OK, though, because word got around the neighborhood. And they asked me to *daven* again on the second day, too! I consider it, by far, the highlight of my life."

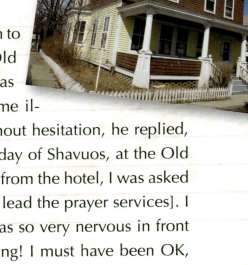

19–20. Postcard showing the Lafayette Hotel and all its annexes, c. 1916. The Rebeka – on the lower left corner of the card – is the only section still in existence. Harold still lives there, and in many ways, it still looks like the hotel it was. The doors to the rooms still have the numbers on them!

21. Just like old times! Congregation Beth Israel in Old Orchard Beach, in the same spot for 100 years, around the corner from the location of Harold's Lafayette Hotel.

The next 40 years saw three thriving Orthodox synagogues, virtually side by side – amazing for such a small community! In 1961, Rabbi Isaacs (mentioned above), chaplain at Loring Air Force Base in northern Maine, became only the second yeshivah-trained rabbi of Beth Abraham. (He was ordained by Rabbi Soloveitchik of Yeshiva University.) He oversaw changes that would reverberate throughout this small community for half a century. From a synagogue where chickens were heard squawking during prayers, where there was a spittoon next to every *shtender* (a lectern or stand used to hold books while praying or studying), and where all speeches were given in Yiddish, Beth Abraham became Americanized and attractive to young members. For the first time, sermons were in English – to the consternation of old-timers – and slowly, the synagogue took on a new spirit. For 39 years he provided the impetus and leadership that made Beth Abraham the center of Maine Orthodoxy, and Bangor a place that took pride in its own yeshivah day school.

Rabbi Fred Nebel, also ordained by the RIETS program of Yeshiva University, has continued this leadership role at Beth Abraham for nearly a decade, conducting adult and children's classes on a daily basis, providing kosher supervision for the only kosher restaurant north of Boston, reading the Torah, leading the services, giving sermons – truly a rabbinic jack-of-all-trades. During my visit on Purim, he told me, "Here is a community seemingly off the map. It is a small community, always struggling, but oh, so proud! To me, Purim is a lesson in pride, pride in being able to overcome annihilation. We provide that same lesson every day!"

22. Rabbi Henry Isaacs, the prime mover in all of Jewish Maine, was the rabbi of Beth Abraham from 1961 to 2000. He helped found a day school and made Bangor the center of Maine Orthodoxy.

> Here is a community seemingly off the map. It is a small community, always struggling, but oh, so proud!

Like those determined early peddlers, Bangor's Jews kept Torah Judaism alive for 160 years. Jo-Ann Kirstein, granddaughter of James G. Striar, told me that life in

23. Rabbi Fred Nebel, of Beth Abraham, as he prepares to read the Megillah. A jack-of-all-trades, he reads the Torah and Megillah, gives kosher supervision, and conducts many classes. "Purim is a lesson in pride in being able to overcome annihilation. We [in Bangor] provide that lesson every day."

Bangor is hard. By its very nature, it forces you to work harder and with more intensity. "And yet," she said, "I feel very blessed to have grown up in that environment." Rabbi Isaacs would say that in Bangor, there was no question you were in *galus* (the diaspora)! Joann's husband, Jerry, confirmed that strongly, saying that here you *know* your presence counts. You have to get involved. Jewish Federation, *minyan*, *chevra kadisha* (burial society), Torah study groups, *mikveh* (ritual bath) – all the institutions of Jewish life depend on you.

Barbara Podolsky added, "There is a saying, 'Remember the past, live the present, and trust the future.' These people have wonderful *emunah* [faith in G-d]. Because of the constant challenges, they built a unique community based on family, hard work, love of learning, and religious commitment. They've held the community together just as their ancestors did 160 years ago. But most of all, they are committed to each other. This community has produced rabbis and teachers who spread their wealth of knowledge throughout the world."

This commitment and pride in Bangor's tight-knit Jewish community is demonstrated in the following story, which says it all. The Podolskys' son, Lee, made *aliyah* (moved to Israel) and became a beloved *rebbe* (teacher) in Yeshivat Hakotel. He had a large student following and was well respected by all.[*] Tragically, he was not blessed with long years. When he was dying of cancer at age 40, he wrote down what he wanted engraved on his tombstone. Now, here was a rabbi with a large following, a *talmid chacham* (scholar), buried in the most religious, prestigious cemetery in all of Israel – and on his tombstone is inscribed this simple expression of his gratitude:

LEE PODOLSKY
FROM BANGOR, MAINE

I admit that I'm spoiled. I was brought up in the New York metropolitan area, where holding on to your traditions comes so easily. Here, in the northeastern tip of our country, where one must strive to make Jewish life endure, I watched and participated in the break-the-fast meal after the Fast of Esther, in the Purim celebrations the next day, enjoying the costumes, the *minyanim*, and all the traditions of Purim, and I realized how deep was the joy and *hakoras hatov* (thanksgiving) that these people feel. It seemed like

---

[*]   We Jews live in a small world. I found out later on that my son-in-law, Rabbi Yudi England, learned with Lee Podolsky many times at Yeshivat Hakotel and, like everyone else, admired and loved him.

they were celebrating not only the survival of the Jews of Persia, but their own survival as a viable community as well. How close they feel to each other, how warm their gratification in making it yet again through another year! I couldn't have asked for a more inspiring experience.

24. One of many stained-glass windows found at Beth Abraham depicting the Jewish holidays

25. Dressed to the nines: costumes abound as siblings get ready for the reading of the Megillah in Bangor, Maine.

פורים

In loving memory of
Ethel and Sam Rosenberg

Synagogues

26. Congregation Beth Abraham Anshe Sfard. The present building was dedicated in 1985 after a fire destroyed the previous building just up the block.

27. Interior of Beth Abraham shows individual *shtender*s (stands) that were handmade years ago and used in the previous *shul* building. That was a time when chickens were heard during davening and every *shtender* had a spittoon next to it. In the *shul*'s 50th anniversary commemorative journal, Rabbi Henry Isaacs said that in those days the *shul* was known by many different names: the "small *shul*," because they were across the street from the Orthodox Beth Israel (the "big *shul*"), the Russisheh *shul* (because the congregants were from Russia), the "cattle dealer's *shul*," and, of course, Beth Abraham. Eli Striar, born in Russia in 1827, came to Bangor and was a cattle dealer. His son, Pinchas Striar, left Beth Israel t[o] found Beth Abraham to have a *Nusach Sfard minyan*, prayer customs of his Russian ancestry.

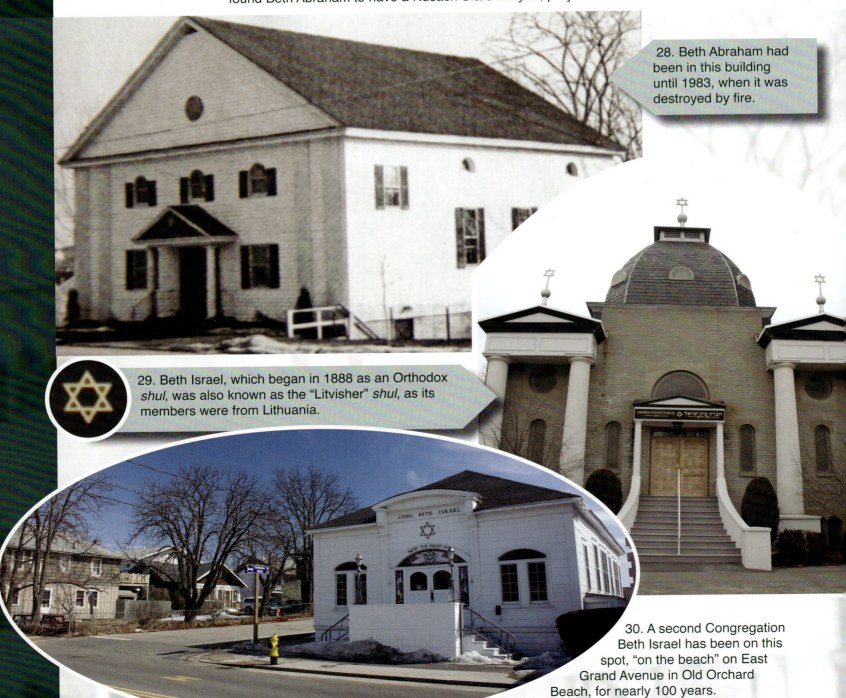

28. Beth Abraham had been in this building until 1983, when it was destroyed by fire.

29. Beth Israel, which began in 1888 as an Orthodox *shul*, was also known as the "Litvisher" *shul*, as its members were from Lithuania.

30. A second Congregation Beth Israel has been on this spot, "on the beach" on East Grand Avenue in Old Orchard Beach, for nearly 100 years.

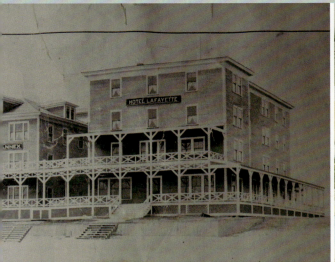

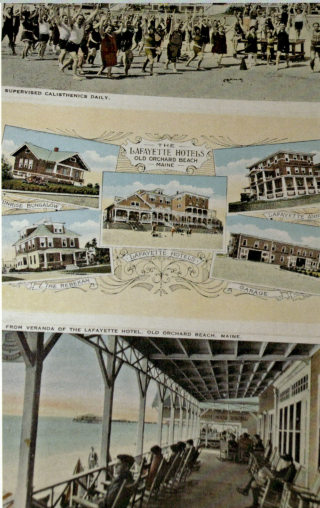

SUPERVISED CALISTHENICS DAILY.

THE LAFAYETTE HOTELS OLD ORCHARD BEACH MAINE

SUNRISE BUNGALOW

LAFAYETTE ANNEX

THE REBEKAH

LAFAYETTE HOTELS

GARAGE

FROM VERANDA OF THE LAFAYETTE HOTEL. OLD ORCHARD BEACH, MAINE.

The Lafayette Hotel

the Sea Wall   I. H. Goodkowsky, Prop.

Old Orchard Beach, Maine

Hebrew Dietary Laws strictly observed.
Fine, Cosy, Airy Rooms with Ocean View.
Spacious Veranda overlooking beach
Beautiful Dance Hall and Card Room.
Excellent Bathing Facilities.
Garage in connection.
Successfully managed since 1909.

——— to ——— September

31–32. Ad for the Lafayette Hotel in Old Orchard Beach. This kosher hotel opened its doors in 1909 and stayed open until the 1960s. Postcard boasting its beaches and calisthenics programs, c. 1916. At this time, there was no running hot water. Maids brought in buckets of hot water as needed.

33. The Lafayette Hotel may be gone but Shore Path Cottage Bed and Breakfast offers the same ocean and kosher food, 170 miles north of it, in Bar Harbor, near the entrance of Acadia National Park. Roberta Chester, an Orthodox woman, originally from New Jersey, owns the B&B and wrote an article for the newspaper *Hamodia*: "I can hardly believe my eyes. There in the early morning sunlight, 15 men are davening here…on Mount Desert Island in Maine. I am quite sure that this house (built in 1880) has never had a *minyan*. Now the sounds of the morning prayers that Jews have recited for countless generations will have penetrated these walls and added a spark of holiness to all the sounds embedded there since 1880."

34. Bangor Hebrew School, 1920–1938

35. W. Lipsky, Jewish peddler from Bangor, Maine. Many men earned their living by peddling in their early years.

BAGEL CENTRAL
HAND-MADE
כשר
947-1654
NO PRESERVATIVES

36–37. Bagel Central, the only kosher restaurant north of Boston. Hot from the oven! The annual specialty: *hamantaschen*, what else?

The Torah

38. Listing of religious articles by "Ohabei Sholom" in a letter dated 1874, asking a congregation in Bangor whether they wanted them returned, including the *sefer Torah* (Torah scroll). This congregation was Beth Israel.

39. Seventy-one years later (April 1945), the war department released the following article (found in the *Bangor Community News*) and accompanying photograph about Chaplain (Captain) Harold Gordon, the custodian of the "Flying Torah," which had flown for a total of over 75,000 miles all over the world.

"The Torah, presented to the chaplain by the Beth Israel Synagogue, Bangor, is more than 100 years old…. Since a Torah may be produced only by tedious hand copying, they are rare…. Chaplain Gordon…providing men of Jewish faith…such home delicacies as salami, pickled herring, dill pickles and spiced beef." Could this be the same Torah originally acquired by the short-lived *shul*, Ahavas Achim, in 1849? It would seem likely.

42–43. Sandy Podolsky, whose family goes back generations in Bangor and Beth Abraham, shows the 200-year-old silver crown saved by Rabbi Isaacs 25 years earlier; it may possibly be the same one saved in 1932. It is now safely inside the ark in the present Beth Abraham.

40. Participation in the rededicati[on of] Beth Abraham in 1933, on York S[t.] after the original structure burned [a] year earlier. The man with the wh[ite hat] holding the Torah is Barney Coo[per who] came from Poland to Bangor in [18__] and opened the first kosher mea[t shop] in Bangor. The silver crown, whic[h was] rescued a year earlier from the fi[re, is on] the Torah on the right.

41. Fifty years later, in 1983, flames gutted the building on York Street yet again. The *Bangor Daily News* wrote, "Tears fell on York St. Wednesday morning as grief-stricken congregation members watched a fire gut Beth Abraham Synagogue.… Donning a fireman's hat and coat, Rabbi Henry Isaacs entered the burning [building] to save a silver crown which adorned the top of a Torah scroll. Moments after the report, he rushed in to rescue the holy Torah scrolls. The original synagogue on Carr St. was destroyed by fire in March of 1932 [two weeks before Purim!]. During that fire, the silver crown adorning one of the Torah scrolls was saved by David Striar. It is believed to be nearly 200 years old."

44. Procession of young men from Beth Israel as they escort a new Torah to the synagogue (not shown), c. 1938

The joy of Purim

45–46. The excitement builds at the Purim Seudah as "Haman" is about to be crushed, freeing the candy inside.

47. Purim poster, date unknown

48–49. Holding half dollars in commemoration of the half shekel that used to be given in Adar for the expense of the sacrifices offered on behalf of the community. In the tractate of *Shekalim* in the Jerusalem Talmud, we are told that there were 13 chests in the Temple for money donated, two of which were set aside for shekel donations. Since the destruction of the Temple, the custom of giving the half shekel before the Megillah reading has remained. Since the Torah, when talking of the shekel, mentions the word *trumah* (donation) three times, one takes three of these half dollars (or half of any of the normal standard of currency), holds them up, and donates the equivalent to *tzedakah*.

50. Purim costumes dominate at Beth Abraham, c. 1950s–'60s

51. Ready for takeoff! Superman and friends enjoying the *seudah* in Bangor.

52. Big Bird reading the Megillah? You bet! C. 1970s.

53. Practicing in preparation to noisily "erase" Haman's name

55. Fulfilling a very important *mitzvah* on Purim: *mishloach manos*, or sending portions made up of at least two foods to one another. Its importance is illustrated by the fact that the rabbis said that even a poor person must give two portions and two gifts (*matanos la'evyonim*, gifts for the poor, or *tzedakah*, charity) each Purim.

54. Taking the more familiar approach to making noise

56. Rabbi Nebel preparing to read the Megillah by folding it so it will read like a letter, as it is written in the Megillah. Beth Abraham's *gabbai*: Uncle Sam!

My thanks to
the people at the Bangor
Museum and History Center,
Rabbi Fred Nebel, Samara Gopan,
Norman Minsky, Judge Louis Kornreich,
Barbara and Sandy Podolsky,
Harold Goodkowski,
Bangor Public Library archives,
Roberta Chester,
and the Old Orchard Beach and
Bangor Historic Societies.

Bibliography

Alpert, Jordan S. *The Alperts and Cohens of Bangor, Maine*. San Francisco: privately printed, 1990.

Cohen, Michael R. "Jerusalem of the North: An Analysis of Religious Modernization in Portland, Maine's Jewish Community." Thesis, Brown University, 2000.

Emple, James Adam, ed. *Congregation Beth Israel's Centennial History, 1888–1988*. Bangor, ME: printed by Bacon Printing and Paper Company for the Congregation Beth Israel, 1988.

Friedman, Lee M. *Jewish Pioneers and Patriots*. Philadelphia: Jewish Publication Society of America, 1942.

Goldstein, Judith. *Crossing Lines: Histories of Jews and Gentiles in Three Communities*. New York: William Morrow, 1992.

Leffler, William II. *A Study of Congregation Ahawas Achim, Bangor, Maine, for 1849 to 1856 from the Minutes of the Congregation*. Cincinnati, OH: American Jewish Archives, 1957.

Peck, Abraham, and Jean Peck. *Maine's Jewish Heritage*. Images of America. Charleston, SC: Arcadia Publishing, 2007.

Risen, Celia. *Some Jewels of Maine: Jewish Maine Pioneers*. Pittsburgh: Dorrance Publishing, 1997.

Scherman, Rabbi Nosson, and Rabbi Meir Zlotowitz, eds. *The Book of Esther*. New York: ArtScroll/Mesorah, 1976.

Photo Attributions

All numbered photos from the author's collection except as follows. Photos 3, 4, 5, 6, 7, 9, 34: Beth Israel archives and Norman Minsky; 8, 13, 35, 40: Bangor Public Library; 10, 17, 39: Bangor Museum and History Center; 14, 22, 28, 47, 50, 52: Beth Abraham archives, Samara Gopan, Barbara and Sandy Podolsky; 18, 19, 31, 32: Harold "Babe" Goodkowsky; 33: Roberta Chester; 41, 44: *Bangor Daily News*.

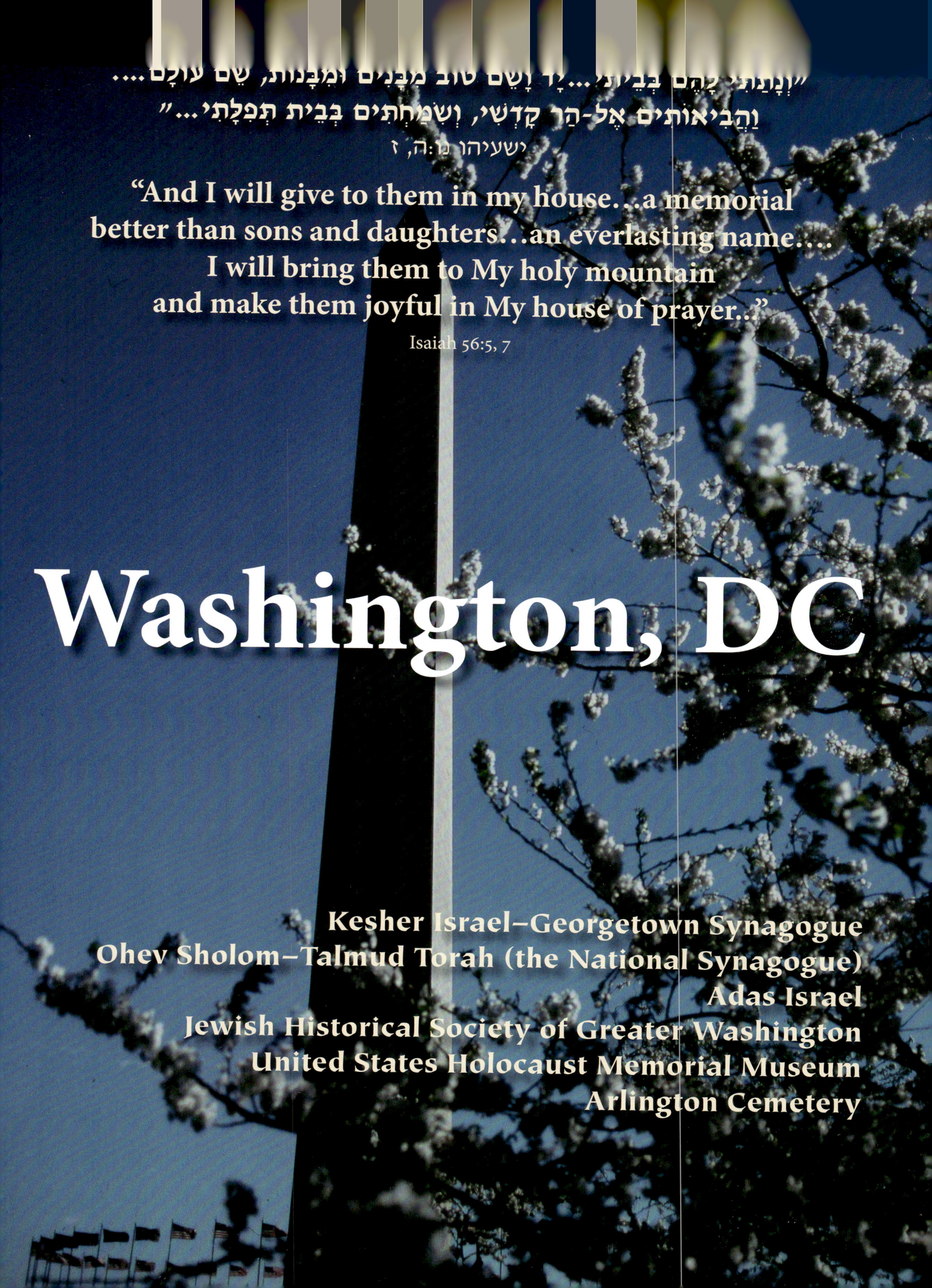

"וּנְתַתִּי לָהֶם בְּבֵיתִי...יָד וָשֵׁם טוֹב מִבָּנִים וּמִבָּנוֹת, שֵׁם עוֹלָם....
וַהֲבִיאוֹתִים אֶל־הַר קָדְשִׁי, וְשִׂמַּחְתִּים בְּבֵית תְּפִלָּתִי..."

ישעיהו נ"ו:ה, ז

"And I will give to them in my house…a memorial
better than sons and daughters…an everlasting name….
I will bring them to My holy mountain
and make them joyful in My house of prayer.."

Isaiah 56:5, 7

Washington, DC

**Kesher Israel–Georgetown Synagogue
Ohev Sholom–Talmud Torah (the National Synagogue)
Adas Israel
Jewish Historical Society of Greater Washington
United States Holocaust Memorial Museum
Arlington Cemetery**

Washington, DC

Holocaust and Rebirth in the Nation's Capital

I am in Washington, DC, the nation's capital, just after Passover (in 2008). The Passover Seder expresses the dichotomy between the devastation of the Jewish people in slavery on one side and the birth of the Jewish nation on the other. So it is appropriate that now, after Passover, is the time of year when we commemorate both the horror and devastation of the Holocaust through Yom Hashoah, Holocaust Remembrance Day, as well as the boundless joy and thanksgiving characterized by the birth of the State of Israel on Yom Ha'atzmaut.

How could I write about the life cycle events of the Jewish people across this country without covering the range of emotions in the two seminal events in our modern history: the Holocaust and the birth of the State of Israel. What was their reaction here, in the political center of this country? How do they remember these events today and what stories do they have for us? The answers are fascinating.

Unlike other cities, Washington, DC's major industry is the federal government, with a generous number of university employers, as well. As a result, its synagogues are packed with an unusually high proportion of lawyers, professors, scientists, and other professionals connected with numerous agencies. These people hold advanced college degrees, and many of them have experienced intense learning in yeshivas as well. In this highly intellectual environment, they have not only retained their Orthodox traditions, they have strengthened them and attracted others to Torah study. Biophysicist Dr. Lee Spetner wrote of this powerful blend of disciplines in the public lectures given in his DC *shul* fifty years ago: "It was certainly an inspiration to hear the nineteenth chapter of Tehillim [Psalms] that begins '*Hashamayim misaprim k'vod Kel* – the heavens declare the glory of G-d, and the firmament tells of His handiwork' profoundly interpreted by an outstanding nuclear physicist; or to have the ethical code [elaborated on in the Torah reading] of *Kedoshim* applied to modern lives by a senior staff member of the Johns Hopkins University applied physics laboratory."

These outstanding individuals were drawn to the nation's capital from all over the country. In fact, it seems like everyone who lives in DC came from somewhere else. There are no ports of call to accommodate large ships bringing immigrants. Yet, over the past 100 years, thousands of Jews have called Washington their home. Where did they come from, and when?

Cornfields and Hunting Grounds

There was little to attract Jews to the area in colonial times. While Jewish communities such as New York, Philadelphia, and Charleston were developing in the eighteenth century, Washington, DC, was nothing but cornfields and Indian hunting grounds. The earliest resident identified as Jewish was Isaac Polock (1795), who came from Savannah as a real estate speculator. He was the grandson of a founder of the Touro Synagogue in Newport, Rhode Island. The first Jewish immigrants to other communities generally were of Sephardic or Spanish/Portuguese origin.

But the first small groups to venture into Washington, DC, in 1840 were German Jews. They came predominantly from the South – Savannah and New Orleans – with a smaller number from New York and Baltimore. At the time of the Civil War, there were no more than 200 Jews living there.

The city's first synagogue was built in 1876 by the Orthodox Adas Israel Congregation, and the prestigious dedication ceremony was held in the presence of President Ulysses S. Grant. This building still exists and houses the Jewish Historical Society. Its chapel is used for weddings.

1. Rendering of the Washington Hebrew Congregation, founded in 1856 as an Orthodox synagogue. President Franklin Pierce signed a bill making it legal to build the first synagogue in Washington, DC.

By the late nineteenth century, an influx of eastern European Jews, fleeing the pogroms and anti-Semitic policies of Czar Alexander III, brought the Jewish population to 3,500. Most of these new immigrants went into the wholesale and retail trades along 7th and 4½ Streets. In 1886, during the administration of Grover Cleveland, a group of these eastern Europeans founded Congregation Ohev Sholom over Myer Fisher's clothing store on 7th NW, while another group founded the Talmud Torah Synagogue in Isaac Levy's clothing store on 4½ Street.

2. This building, now the Jewish Historical Society of Greater Washington, once housed Adas Israel Congregation, dedicated in 1876 with President Ulysses S. Grant present at the ceremony.

3. In 1969, 100 years after its founding, the Adas Israel building was moved to a new location to prevent it from being demolished. It is the only synagogue preserved by actually moving it.

Philanthropy was deep in the mindset of the eastern European Jews and was a ubiquitous feature of their lifestyle. No matter how poor you might be, there was always someone worse off who needed your help! It is not surprising that soon after their migration to Washington began, a number of philanthropic organizations were established, including the United Hebrew Relief Society (1882), the Jewish Foster Home (1911), and the Home for the Aged (1914).

"We All Shared the Joys and Sorrows"

4. Rabbi Moses Yo (second ro second fro left), c. 19 Rabbi Yoe served the Talmud To synagogu as *chazza shochet*, a *mohel*. He also the fa of theater movie sta Jolson.

One of the best-known personalities in DC was Rabbi Moses Yoelson, who served the Talmud Torah *shul* in many capacities from 1892 through the 1920s; he was *chazzan, mohel*, and *shochet* (cantor, circumciser, slaughterer). Moreover, he answered halachic (Jewish legal) questions and performed marriages. He was also the father of one of the great entertainers of the early twentieth century, Al Jolson. When describing the Jewish neighborhood of those times, Al's brother Emil said, "Southwest [Washington] was a little town…like European towns. Everyone knew each other. Whether there were good times or bad, we all shared the joys and the sorrows."

5. Al Jolson grew up as a young Jewish boy in Washington, DC. His legendary role in the play and movie *The Jazz Singer* mirrors these early years. His father, Rabbi Yoelson, never saw his son perform on stage, but, later, did see the movie and was impressed.

giants! Rabbi Joshua Klavan, left, influential leader of ...mud Torah (1936–1953), with Rabbi Jacob Ruderman, ...eshivah (dean) and founder of Ner Israel Rabbinical ...e in Baltimore. Rabbi Klavan provided the leadership ...'s first all-day Hebrew Academy.

Another dynamic leader who played a strong role in establishing and strengthening key institutions was Rabbi Joshua Klavin. Born in Lithuania in 1884, he was a disciple of Rabbi Chaim Telzer at the famous Slobodka Yeshivah. When he came to the United States, he settled in Burlington, Vermont. Legend has it that divine intervention brought this scholar to DC. While visiting his son who lived in Washington, he became ill and had to stay on to recuperate. One evening, as he studied Torah in the Talmud Torah synagogue, congregants urged him to accept the position of rabbi. He was to become one of the most remarkable assets the community ever had.

Rabbi Klavin organized the Rabbinical Council of Washington, improved *kashrus* supervision, and was one of the inspired few who pioneered the founding of the Hebrew Academy in 1943. During World War II, he devoted his energies to the Vaad Hatzoloh, a national organization that sent aid and rescued thousands of Jews from the Nazis. He was an ardent Zionist and worked for the establishment of the State of Israel through the Zionist organization then known as Mizrachi.

So, what was it like living in Washington, DC, over the past century? I had the wonderful opportunity to talk with Paul and Helen Sperling, whose families lived in DC since 1914.

Paul's father was a peddler from the Lower East Side in New York, and he moved to DC to open a clothing store. He took two empty properties and started one of the first department stores in the US. "I can still remember," Paul says, "that we used horse-drawn fire engines. There were troughs on every corner." His father joined the Talmud Torah congregation in 1914. Paul recalls an incident that happened on Yom Kippur in the early 1920s: "We had a guest *chazzan*, a baritone with a powerful voice. My father had a seat by a window and I sat next to him. The *chazzan* hit a high note and the window next to us shattered!"

"It was hard to be *shomer Shabbos* [Sabbath observant] back then," added Helen. "We were government employees and we worked five and a half days a week. Jews here assimilated because of that requirement. Then [President] Truman came along and changed it to a five-day workweek. Some say he was influenced by his friend and ex-business partner who was Jewish. Whether he meant to or not, he saved many Jews from desecrating Shabbos."

The Tumultuous 1940s

The Washington Jewish community reacted in much the same way others did during the two seminal events of Jewish history in the 1940s: the Holocaust and the birth of the State of Israel. Paul spoke of their helplessness and frustration regarding the Jews in Europe: "In 1943, we knew the Jews were being put in boxcars. We heard about the concentration camps. The rabbis expressed their outrage, but their organizations weren't as powerful as they are now. I remember going over to my rabbi and saying, 'Why don't they bomb the tracks? What's the matter with Roosevelt?'"

On the day that a Jewish state was declared for the first time in 2,000 years, "there was a tumult in Washington – dancing, singing, all kinds of celebrations. People were up in the sky with joy! Then, suddenly, there were prayer sessions everywhere; we said *Tehillim* [Psalms] – because we knew it would be really rough. The state was attacked right away and a war was starting. We were unsure of what would happen."

During this era, the Jews of Washington joined in welcoming refugees and survivors of the Holocaust, extending aid in every way they could. By 1945, the Jewish population of DC had hit twenty thousand. Despite the fact that many survivors emerged from their experiences religiously disillusioned, there were others whose steadfastness was an inspiration to all. The Sperlings told me the following story, which not only recounts survivors' determination to do a *mitzvah*, but their pluck and resourcefulness, as well.

7. Paul and Helen Sperling's families have lived in DC since 1914. Their families were members of the Talmud Torah Congregation.

Helen's sister-in-law and her mother had survived the death camps and were looking forward to a truly blessed event. When the time came, the sister-in law gave birth to a son. It was just days before Yom Kippur and she told her mother that she yearned to *"shlug kapores"* with a live chicken, as was their tradition before the war. In this annual ritual of atonement, a chicken is waved over each person's head and scriptural verses are recited, making for a vivid reminder of the fragility of life and the need to examine one's deeds.

So Mama goes to the chicken market, buys a chicken, wraps it tightly in a shawl, and enters the hospital, praying that it will keep quiet. She passes the main desk and the chicken is well behaved – not even a cluck! Now she gets up to the nurses' station and, all of a sudden, the chicken in the shawl begins squawking! Heads turn and someone shouts. Before the nurses can catch her, Mama tightens her grip and runs to her daughter's room. In a flash, she encircles the heads of her daughter and her new grandson three times with the chicken and runs out, passing an open-mouthed nurse on the way!

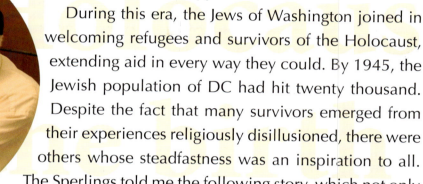

And she never looked back. It didn't matter if the nurse was bewildered, angry, or indignant. To this survivor, it was her chance to return to cherished, age-old traditions, to live as a free Jew, and no force on earth would ever again stop her!

Rabbi Shmuel Herzfeld of the National Synagogue reflected on these qualities of courage and fortitude when he had the honor of bringing to his *shul* a Torah scroll that had been smuggled out of Auschwitz, in pieces, with the help of many who eventually perished in the death camp. It was found just recently and painstakingly restored.

The story was told by survivors that two days before the Nazis came into Oswiecim, Poland, the Torah was buried in a metal box in the Jewish cemetery. Sixty years later, upon hearing the story, Rabbi Menachim Youlis, a *sofer* (scribe), of the "Save a Torah Foundation," went to the cemetery in Poland with a metal detector and found the Torah in the metal box – but it was missing four panels. In response to an ad in the local newspaper, a priest came forward with the four panels! These four panels, he said, were removed before burial and carried by four synagogue members to the concentration camp. As each Jew was about to die, he would hand his panel to his friend. Eventually, they made their way to this priest, who was Jewish and also in the camp. He guarded them, as a priest, for over sixty years. The four panels restored by Rabbi Youlis were all emotionally significant: the first Ten Commandments, with the word *Remember*; the section on the curses; the section on the sacrifices; and the second Ten Commandments, with the word *Shema* in the same panel.

Rabbi Herzfeld summed up what we all feel: "I first learned about the opportunity to host this Torah for the Yizkor service of Passover just before the holiday. As I prayed that evening, I was overcome with emotion and began to weep. I couldn't help thinking about how the Nazis tried to kill us all, but our Torah can never be destroyed. Our Torah lives eternally."

8. Tree of life: on the mantle is written "This Torah was rescued from Auschwitz."

9. Rabbi Youlis carefully watching the completion of the last letters of the Torah that miraculously survived Nazi destruction

A Heartwarming Regeneration

I am walking on the Mall surrounded by the Smithsonian museum complex. Behind me is the domed Capitol building; in front of me, the Washington Monument. When you walk the Mall on any given day, you see hundreds of buses carrying schoolchildren of every age, tour groups, families, memorials, and magnificent buildings. All of that towering Greek architecture was designed to awe visitors, whether foreign dignitaries or American farm boys, and it surely does.

I am on my way to Kesher Israel, better known as the "George-town Synagogue," which has been in the heart of DC for over 100 years. It is fourteen blocks from the White House and less than two miles from the Capitol. In its own way, this synagogue is a symbol of the regeneration of Jewish life in Washington, for in the 1980s the majority of the Jewish community expanded to Maryland and Virginia, leaving only 15 percent of the population in DC. The two original synagogues, Ohev Sholom and Talmud Torah, had already merged in 1958 (and the present synagogue on 16th Street was dedicated in 1960) with Rabbi Klavin's son, Hillel, as its rabbi. In 2006, it was reorganized as the National Synagogue.

Over the last twenty years, the Jews of Washington have witnessed an extraordinary revival. This has been due largely to the leadership of Rabbi Barry Freundel of Kesher Israel for two decades and recently, the exuberance of Rabbi Herzfeld of the National Synagogue.

Rabbi Barry Freundel greeted me cordially. He has been the guiding force in the construction project for an *eruv* (an enclosure that enables the carrying of objects on the Sabbath) around virtually all of Washington, and he is proud of the diverse crowd the synagogue draws. "We have a unique Orthodox synagogue," he said, "whose members and visitors range from those with traditional yearnings to those who are fully observant. On any given Shabbat, our *minyan* can consist of both Chassidic rabbis and Jews just starting out.

10. Kesher Israel, known as the "Georgetown Synagogue," with the foundation stone's inscription: "Organized 1910"

THE WHITE HOUSE
WASHINGTON

Eruv Sabbath, 1990

I am pleased to send greetings to Congregation Kesher Israel and to the Orthodox Jewish community in Washington as you celebrate the inauguration of the first eruv in the District of Columbia.

The construction of this eruv is particularly significant not only because it marks the growth of the Orthodox Jewish community in Washington but also because this city is our Nation's Capital. Indeed, there is a long tradition linking the establishment of eruvim with the secular authorities in the great political centers where Jewish communities have lived. In the words of a responsa of Rabbi Moses Sofer: "Bless the Lord, God of Israel, who has inclined the hearts of kings, rulers, and officers -- under whose sovereign jurisdiction we, the Jewish people find protection -- to grant permission to us to keep our faith in general, and specifically to establish eruvim in their thoroughfares, even on streets where the most important members of the government themselves live . . . in this city, there are places where we need to install a number of objects in order to create an eruv and we have not hidden our work, rather, it is publicized and open to all without doubt and permission has been granted."

Now, you have built this eruv in Washington, and the territory it covers includes the Capitol, the White House, the Supreme Court, and many other Federal buildings. By permitting Jewish families to spend more time together on the Sabbath, it will enable them to enjoy the Sabbath more and promote traditional family values, and it will lead to a fuller and better life for the entire Jewish community in Washington. I look upon this work as a favorable endeavor. God bless you.

Geo Bush

11. A letter of congratulations sent by President George H.W. Bush to Kesher Israel in 1990, on the completion of the first *eruv* in Washington, DC. The date on the letter: Eruv Sabbath, 1990 (misspelled intentionally?). In it he quotes a blessing given by Rabbi Moses Sofer (the Chatam Sofer), the rabbinic leader of European Jewry in the eighteenth century: "Bless the Lord, G-d of Israel…who has inclined the hearts of kings…to grant permission to us…to establish eruvim."

THE RABBI PHILLIP RABINOWITZ MEMORIAL ERUV
IN WASHINGTON, D.C.

12. *Eruv* booklet showing extent of the *eruv*, with maps covering the Capitol building, the White House, and the Supreme Court in a very large area

Our visitors have included the chief rabbi of Israel, Moshe Dayan, and Ezer Weizman. Our membership has included senators, congressmen, many ambassadors, a secretary of agriculture, and several authors. Most of all, we pride ourselves on our warmth and hospitality and an atmosphere of learning combined with intellectual investigation."

During my visit, I was to learn just how true these statements were. I came to Kesher Israel the day of a *yom iyun*, a day dedicated to Torah study, celebrating the sixtieth anniversary of the State of Israel. Located in the center of the political universe, the Washington *shul* had unsurprisingly invited a prominent political figure, Rabbi Michael Melchior (member of the Israeli Knesset and former chief rabbi of Oslo, Norway), as the guest speaker. Addressing the packed audience, he spoke passionately about the need for stronger Jewish education in Israel in order to retain its Jewish character, saying, "We can't cut off Judaism from the state. It would be creating a body without a soul!"

I have to admit I was emotionally unprepared for the moving event in Rabbi Herzfeld's National Synagogue on Yom Hashoah. With shoes removed, everyone – including three Holocaust survivors – sat in a circle, some on the floor, others on chairs. Six large candles, representing the six million Jews slaughtered by the Nazis, were lit in the center of the darkened room, while we read in hushed voices a "Haggadah" for Yom Hashoah, edited by Rabbi Avi Weiss. It begins, "Just as the Haggadah [for Passover] provides an external framework for each of us to experience the Exodus from Egypt, so, too, a ritual for remembering the Holocaust – one of the greatest catastrophes that ever befell our people – is needed to transform Yom Hashoah from a day in which we are spectators to one in which we feel like participants. Soon, the only ones left to tell the story will be those who did not live through the events themselves… it will fall on succeeding generations…to repeat the narrative and re-experience it as if they themselves were there."

The thought and care that went into this program was characteristic of Rabbi Herzfeld. He has led a revival of Orthodoxy in northern Washington through his weekly Sunday radio show, "Shmoozin' with Shmuel – Torah, Prayers, and Yiddishkeit on the Air," and other creative ideas such as building a *sukkah* in Lafayette Park, near the White House.

I thought about the faces of the participants at the National Synagogue event as I made my way to the US Holocaust Memorial Museum. For me, as for many Jews, Yom Hashoah is a time for memories. I was in a somber mood as I walked slowly into the large receiving area of the museum.

13. Rabbi Barry Freundel of Kesher Israel, a diverse congregation whose membership has included senators, congressmen, ambassadors, and several authors. Here he is seen leading a discussion celebrating Yom Ha'atzmaut, Israeli Independence Day.

14. Rabbi Michael Melchior, member of the Israeli Knesset and chief rabbi of Norway, celebrating the 60th anniversary of the State of Israel at Kesher

15. Rabbi Shmuel Herzfeld, rabbi of Ohev Sholom–Talmud Torah (the National Synagogue), lighting six candles (representing the six million) at the Yom Hashoah seder ceremony

My first reaction was disappointment, almost anger, for the place was noisy, with children, teens, even seniors, joking, laughing, and speaking freely of mundane affairs. "Do you think the weather will hold? Where should we go for lunch? Will this take long?" I had the same sinking feeling I get when I go to a *shivah* ready to console the mourners, and find everyone chatting amiably, as though they were at a party.

Nevertheless, I followed a group up a large staircase to an enormous rotunda. It was almost empty, with nothing but candles waiting to be lit by anyone who felt the need, and a small podium with a flame behind it, reflected numerous times in glass. All day long, anyone who wanted to could step up to the podium and read names of Holocaust victims aloud. In this cavernous room for the "Reading of the Names of the Six Million," the quiet, somber sound of the readings is all you hear. So I went with the noisy groups into the rotunda and, as if a switch had been turned off, without any prodding or admonishment, there was silence.

In the stillness, only the echoes of names break the air. Each name pounds on you – like an endless succession of ocean waves. Each name calls to you, until you feel a sense of guilt – or is it shame?

The visitors who lit candles and recited names each had his or her own reasons. I spoke to a woman from Romania who carried with her a book of photographs of people murdered in the Holocaust, including members of her own family. "Look," she said, pointing, "there's my grandmother, and there's my aunt and uncle, and their little boy…" Her eyes dart back and forth to the photos and she lights her candles in the silent room. "I had to come here," she sighs. "I didn't want to, but I had to come."

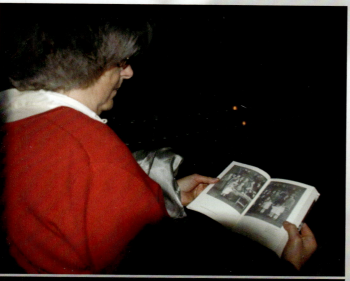

16. After lighting the candles, a woman sees her lost loved ones in a book describing the Holocaust

People of all ages step up to light candles and recite the names, and I am no exception. I feel the need to do something. You can't just stand there.

When I emerged from the museum, I was shaken and profoundly aware of myself as a Jew. I thought of how many lives had been cut short, how this dark doom had overtaken my people. But then, I looked around at the sunshine bouncing off the marble buildings, the folks rushing past me in their ordinary daily pursuits.

And I thought of the incredible, busy revival of the Jewish nation and Judaism all over the world, and especially in this city. Right here in Washington, where the Torah is cherished by so many, there is vibrant outreach and continuous teaching. Like the Torah that survived Auschwitz, the attempt to reach every Jew with the wisdom and beauty of our heritage is alive here, and everlasting.

17. "Lest you forget." Lighting candles of remembrance. There are hundreds of these candles in the vast rotunda, waiting to be lit by the solemn procession on Yom Hashoah.

18. Ohev Sholom, founded in 1886 to serve Russian Jews fleeing the czar's pogroms. The first services were held above Myer Fisher's clothing store on 7th St.; the building dates to 1869.

19. Talmud Torah Congregation, formed nearly parallel to Ohev Sholom, was in the Southwest neighborhood of DC, on 4½ St. SW. The original minyan was in the home of Isaac Levy. The building dates to 1903. Rabbi Moses Yoelson acted as spiritual guide until 1912. His son was the famous actor of early "talkie" films like *The Jazz Singer*, Al Jolson.

20. In 1958, the two congregations merged to become Ohev Sholom–Talmud Torah, later known as the National Synagogue, under its new charismatic leader, Rabbi Shmuel Herzfeld.

21. A new sales pitch for the National Synagogue.

Your Happiest New Year Ever...
CELEBRATE ROSH HASHANAH
...at the National Synagogue
WWW.THENATIONALSYNAGOGUE.ORG

THE NATIONAL SYNAGOGUE
OHEV SHOLOM
202-882-7225
WWW.OSTNS.ORG

...her Israel, or the Georgetown Synagogue, founded in 1910, ...4 blocks from the White House. The membership, which ...politicians, ambassadors, and scientists, also includes many ...chachamim (Torah scholars) as well. Its rabbi, Barry Freundel, ...eaded the *eruv* encircling most of Washington, DC.

23. Kesher Israel as it was in 1930.

24. Jewish Community Center, built in 1925, and blending in with the architecture of the capital city. It was the meeting place for B'nai B'rith, Hadassah, and the American Jewish Committee, among other organizations. It was sold in the 1960s and repurchased in the 1990s to accommodate the rebirth of the growing Jewish community.

DISTRICT OF COLUMBIA
JEWISH COMMUNITY CENTER
IRWIN P. EDLAVITCH BUILDING

KLIVITZKY'S
בשר כשר
MEATS & GROCERIES

25. Klivitsky's, with the familiar sign, "Basar Kosher" (or is it the other way around?), "kosher meat," sold fresh bread and groceries as well. C. 1918.

26. Eli's Kosher Deli may not have the familiar window sign, but continues the tradition of Klivitsky's service to the Jewish community.

27. The *Chevra Kadisha*, or Holy Group, was responsible for the proper ritual cleansing of a Jewish body in preparation for the burial. They met once a year to make a *siyum* (a celebration marking the completion of the learning of a tractate of Talmud or Mishnah), usually on the anniversary of Moses' death, the 7th of the Hebrew month of Adar, because the Torah tells us that G-d buried Moses. The annual meeting shown here took place in 1928.

28. President Ronald Reagan speaks to an audience in the East Room of the White House in the first Days of Remembrance ceremony, c. 1981. Since then, the United States Holocaust Memorial Museum has organized and led national Days of Remembrance in the US Capitol Rotunda with Holocaust survivors, liberators, members of Congress, and community leaders in attendance.

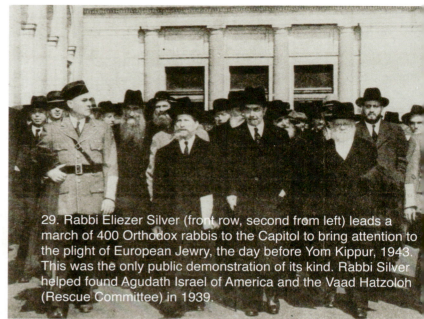

29. Rabbi Eliezer Silver (front row, second from left) leads a march of 400 Orthodox rabbis to the Capitol to bring attention to the plight of European Jewry, the day before Yom Kippur, 1943. This was the only public demonstration of its kind. Rabbi Silver helped found Agudath Israel of America and the Vaad Hatzoloh (Rescue Committee) in 1939.

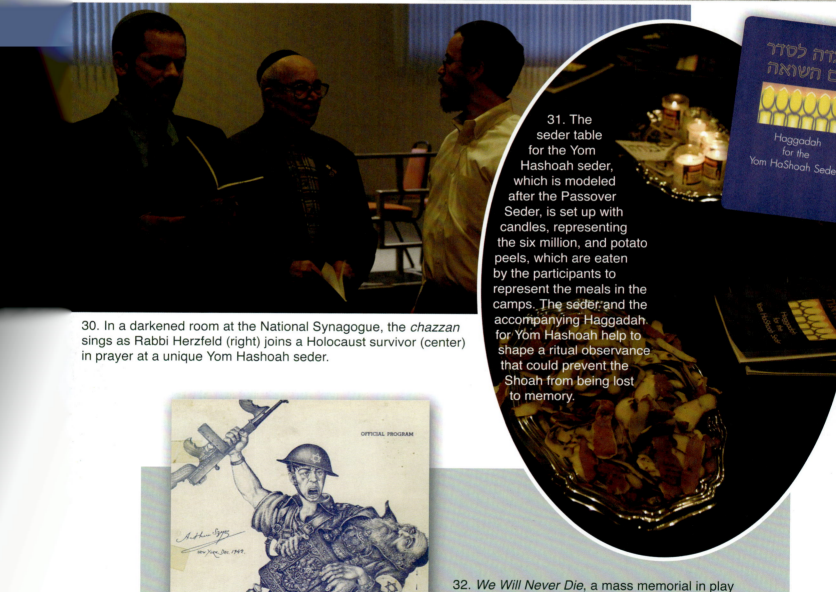

30. In a darkened room at the National Synagogue, the *chazzan* sings as Rabbi Herzfeld (right) joins a Holocaust survivor (center) in prayer at a unique Yom Hashoah seder.

31. The seder table for the Yom Hashoah seder, which is modeled after the Passover Seder, is set up with candles, representing the six million, and potato peels, which are eaten by the participants to represent the meals in the camps. The seder and the accompanying Haggadah for Yom Hashoah help to shape a ritual observance that could prevent the Shoah from being lost to memory.

32. *We Will Never Die*, a mass memorial in play form, dedicated to the then two million Jewish dead of Europe in April of 1943. Among the actors were Edward G. Robinson, Paul Muni, and Luther Adler. This was sponsored by the "Committee for a Jewish Army of Stateless and Palestinian Jews," for the purpose (as Sen. Edwin Johnson of Colorado stated) of "permit[ting] the formation of an all-Jewish army to fight as Jews against those who are exterminating them because they are Jews."

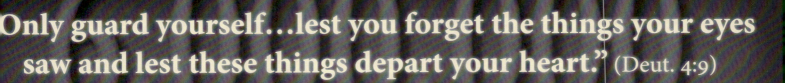

"Only guard yourself…lest you forget the things your eyes saw and lest these things depart your heart." (Deut. 4:9)

33–35. From morning to night, anyone who cares to can step to the podium and publicly read the names of the six million.

36. As the names are read in this massive rotunda, with candles lit all around, the solemnity of the moment is palpable.

גבעת וושינגטון
GIV'AT WASHINGTON

Funded mainly by Washingtonians, Giv'at Washington established a school and home for ...aned Holocaust survivors in Palestine. C. 1944.

38. Many Jews who gave their lives fighting the Nazis are buried at Arlington National Cemetery. Headstones have the Magen David inscribed on top.

39. Jewish sailor participating with Rabbi Herzfeld in the ser... for Yom Hashoah

40. A crowd of American Jews assembled outside the offices of the Jewish Agency in Washington, DC, to celebrate the proclamation of the State of Israel, May 19, 1948. In the center the group dances the hora.

41. "Children should grow up, not blow up." Many children have participated in rallies in support of Israel, for more than 60 years.

42. Banner in front of Ohev Sholom–Talmud Torah (the National Synagogue) says it all.

43. Jewish New Year's card depicts a Daughter of Zion carrying the Zionist banner, c. 1910. This group later became Hadassah, the women's Zionist organization.

44. The Jewish National Fund and the Keren Kayemet L'Yisrael presented these certificates to those who funded the growing of new trees and forests in Israel, c. 1940.

TREE FUND תרומת עצים

JNF קקל

THE OBJECT OF THE TREE FUND IS THE REFORESTATION OF ERETZ ISRAEL

יער הרב מאיר ברלין

תעודת התרומה היא לטעת בארץ ישראל יערות עצים

JEWISH NATIONAL FUND

RABBI MEYER BERLIN FOREST

קרן קימת לישראל

PLANTED IN HONOR OF OHEV SHOLOM CONGREGATION

עצים ONE TREES

WASHINGTON, D.C.

APRIL, 1940

AND LET THEM MAKE ME A SANCTUARY: THAT MAY DWELL AMONG THEM

rt Security & Peace for

RAEL

My thanks to
Rabbi Barry Freundel,
Rabbi Shmuel Herzfeld,
Caroline Waddell at the
United States Holocaust
Memorial Museum,
Claire Uziel at the
Jewish Historical Society of
Greater Washington,
Paul and Helen Sperling,
and Leonard Goodman.

Bibliography

Eban, Abba. *My Country: The Story of Modern Israel*. New York: Random House, 1972.

Ganz, Yaffa, and Rabbi Berel Wein. *Sand and Stars: The Jewish Journey through Time*. New York: Shaar Press, 1994.

Garfinkle, Dr. Martin. *The Jewish Community of Washington, D.C.* Images of America. Charleston, SC: Arcadia Publishing, 2005.

Gilbert, Martin. *The Holocaust: A History of the Jews of Europe during the Second World War*. New York: Henry Holt, 1985.

Rosen, Dov. *Shema Yisrael: A Guide to a Deeper Appreciation of the Jewish Heritage, Past and Present*. Translated by Leonard Oschry. Tel Aviv: Shema Yisrael, 1972.

Wein, Berel. Travels through Jewish History. TES CD-ROM.

——. Triumph of Survival: The story of the Jews in the Modern Era, 1650-1995. New York: Shaar Press, 1999.

Weiss, Avraham. *Haggadah for the Yom HaShoah Seder*. Hackensack, NJ: Coalition for Jewish Concerns – Amcha/Jonas, 2000.

Photo Attributions

All numbered photos from the author's collection except as follows. Photos 3, 4, 32, 37, 41, 43, 44: Jewish Historical Society of Greater Washington; 6, 18, 19, 25, 27: Ohev Sholom–Talmud Torah; 11, 12, 23: Kesher Israel archives; 28, 29, 40: United States Holocaust Memorial Museum; p. 86 images and watermark: Gabi Eden.

"...כִּי אֲנִי ה׳ עֹשֶׂה חֶסֶד, מִשְׁפָּט, וּצְדָקָה בָּאָרֶץ,
כִּי-בְאֵלֶּה חָפַצְתִּי..."
ירמיהו ט:כג

"...For I am G-d Who exercises righteousness,
justice, and charity in the earth,
for these things I desire..."
Jeremiah 9:23

Baltimore, Maryland

Lloyd Street Synagogue
B'nai Israel
Shearith Israel
Ner Israel
Lombard Street
The Associated

Fort McHenry

Baltimore, Maryland

Sukkos, the Four Species, and the Ties that Bind Us

As a boy in yeshivah, I was taught a good deal about the "four species" of plants comprising one of the central *mitzvos* of the Sukkos festival. Three of these, the *lulav* (date palm branch), *hadassim* (myrtle leaves), and *aravos* (willow branches), are physically bound together, and the *esrog* (citron) must be held together with the others when the blessing over them is said.

I learned from a *midrash* (*Vayikra Rabbah* 30) that the four species and their individual characteristics represent all Jews, from all walks of life; from those with few or *no* good deeds or Torah learning to those who possess both good deeds and much learning. What does G-d tell us about these diverse species? He commands, "Let them all be held together, and they will atone for one another."

It was my first lesson in the power of Jewish unity, spelled out right there in Jewish law. And what a magnificent concept it is!

And that was one of the reasons I naturally migrated to Baltimore for the holiday of Sukkos: it has been known by many as the "city of *chesed*" – a metropolis renowned for its benevolence and charity, a city bound together by unity and caring – precisely as represented by the *mitzvah* of *lulav*.

1. Nariman House in Mumbai, India, site of terrorist attacks on Chabad family

I had tasted a bit of this remarkable communal quality just a week after the tragic massacres in Mumbai, India, in November of 2008. You may recall that there were more than ten coordinated shooting and bombing attacks by terrorists across Mumbai (formerly known as Bombay), India's financial capital and largest city. Among the chosen sites for the attacks was the Nariman House, also known as the Mumbai Chabad House, where a Jewish family, including Rabbi Gavriel Holtzberg and his pregnant wife, Rivkah, were among six Jews murdered in cold blood.

Mumbai may seem like a long way from Baltimore, but not to the Jews of that caring community. I heard that a large rally was planned in the Jewish Community Center to honor the fallen of Mumbai. I had to be there.

After a long drive from my home in New Jersey, I found myself in a large room filled to capacity, with the overflow

2. An evening of unity: rabbis and lay leaders of Baltimore in attendance at Mumbai memorial

crowd sitting in another room watching the proceedings on a video screen. The governor of Maryland, the mayor of Baltimore, rabbis representing the diversity of Baltimore's synagogues, and Jews from all walks of life were in attendance in what was truly an evening of unity.

This was not meant to be only a commemorative service; the Jews in that room wanted to take that tragic experience and turn it into a stimulus for benevolence. I listened as the president of the Associated (Baltimore's Jewish Federation), Marc Terrill, spoke about the need to respond to this tragedy by making an extra effort in some positive area – reaching out, together, as one, to the downtrodden, the needy…

I reflected that just as the *sukkah* – the temporary abode that we live in during this holiday – represents the protection that G-d provided His people in the wilderness, so, too, Baltimore and its charitable organizations have protected its people for nearly 200 years. Why Baltimore, you ask? Why did this extreme form of compassion take root in that particular place?

The story is fascinating, and more than a tad ironic.

3. The four species according to some commentaries represent different Jewish characteristics, and according to others they represent different key organs of the body uniting in the service of G-d.

Jews Break in to the Colony of Maryland

You see, initially, Jews were forbidden to tread on Maryland's soil. Established in 1634, Maryland was named after Henrietta Maria, the wife of King Charles I. Jews did not venture there for 100 years because of what was ironically known as the "Toleration Act," enacted in 1649: the "Act Concerning Religion" clearly stated, "Whatsoever person or persons within this Province [...who shall] deny our Saviour…shall be punished with death…."

The first Jew in Maryland was the "Jew Doctor," Jacob Lumbrozo, who came in 1656 and had the distinction of being the first Jewish physician in the country. He was also a farmer, innkeeper, businessman, and Indian trader. He was also in flagrant violation of the "Toleration Act," but was pardoned when Richard Cromwell was named the new Lord Protector in England.

In 1729, Baltimore Town was chartered, and by the 1750s this tiny port town became a leading commercial center. At about this time, the merchant Jacob Hart signed his name to a petition and became the first known Jew to live in Baltimore.

But Jewish families are not known to have settled there for another quarter of a century. Benjamin Levy and his wife, Rachel,

opened a shop on Market Street in 1773, selling "Spices, tea, coffee, chocolate, pickled salmon, hats, and umbrellas," announced the largest ad in the local newspaper. Around the same time, Isaac Abrams, an Orthodox Jew, came to Baltimore and closely minded the religious observances of others. (He once saw a Philadelphia Jew shaving on the Sabbath and promptly reported it to his Philadelphia synagogue, Mikveh Israel!)

Jewish Baltimore was growing. By 1790, Baltimore was attracting Jews from Philadelphia and beyond. The two most prominent families at this time were the Ettings and the Cohens. In 1782, Solomon Etting became the first Jew born in America to become a *shochet* (ritual slaughterer). Jacob Cohen started one of the first public lotteries to help raise public funds. Both the Cohen and Etting families were among the American forces at the Battle of Fort McHenry in 1812 (during which "The Star-Spangled Banner," the American national anthem, was written).

4. Solomon Etting (1764–1847), first native-born American to become a *shochet*. He was an early fighter for Jewish equality in Maryland. His family also fought in the War of 1812.

Solomon Etting was the first Jew to work for civil equality and against bias. Perhaps giving us a glimpse of the future, in one of the first partnerships with a non-Jew, he and Thomas Kennedy pressed the legislature to pass a bill in 1826 heralding Jewish equality in Maryland, called, appropriately enough, the "Jew Bill." It was no surprise that the Jewish population in Baltimore was on the increase by 1830.

Put a few Jews together and what do you have? An organization. In 1830, the legislature approved the formation of the first Jewish organization, Nidchei Israel (Dispersed of Israel), which evolved into Baltimore's first synagogue. Did the membership know that the *gematria* (totaled numerical value of each Hebrew letter in its name) came to 613, the number of *mitzvos* in the Torah?

Within five years, there were 55 members, and a source of income for the fledgling synagogue was the auctioning of *aliyos* (being called to the Torah), a common custom. But the main sources of income were the fines

5. As the British bombarded Ft. McHenry for two days, Francis Scott Key watched from his boat, in amazement "that our flag was still there," and composed a poem which became the lyrics of "The Star-Spangled Banner." It did not become the national anthem until 1931. Painting held by the Maryland Historical Society.

6. One of the oldest Jewish cemeteries in America, the Etting Cemetery was purchased by Solomon Etting in 1801. It contains the burial plots of the Etting and Cohen families, the two most prominent and patriotic Jewish families in Baltimore in the eighteenth and nineteenth centuries. Members of both these families fought in the War of 1812, when the British planned to take over the city of Baltimore.

levied for decorum, or rather the lack of it. There were fines for talking, for putting away one's *tallis* before the end of the service, and for singing louder than the *chazzan*! These fines became quite a livelihood for the synagogue. In 1852, two policemen were called in to prevent congregants from leaving during the Torah reading and congregating on the sidewalk. (Imagine if these fees were enacted today throughout American Jewish communities! Many *shul*s wouldn't need a building fund.)

In 1841, an appeal was sent out to out-of-town synagogues to help in the building of the first real synagogue in Baltimore. A synagogue from as far away as Jamaica, West Indies, sent $170.

The building housing this new synagogue, Baltimore Hebrew Congregation on Lloyd Street (also called the Lloyd Street Synagogue, 1845), was a magnificent structure in the Greek

7. Baltimore Hebrew (the Lloyd St. Synagogue, 1845) was the first synagogue built in Maryland. Its Greek Revival style was a popular mid-nineteenth-century American style of architecture, as we see in Washington, DC. The Central European members first called themselves "Nidchei Yisrael" (the dispersed or scattered of Israel). The synagogue boasts a matzo oven and a *mikveh*.

classical style with a women's balcony and a stained glass window over the ark forming a Jewish star. It was the first time this star was used in the United States.

"The religious life in this land is on the lowest level…. I wonder whether it is even permissible for a Jew to live in this land…."

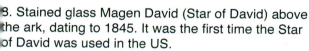

8. Stained glass Magen David (Star of David) above the ark, dating to 1845. It was the first time the Star of David was used in the US.

While the first Jew arrived on American shores in 1654, it would be 186 years before this country had its first ordained rabbi. Abraham Rice, from Bavaria, was retained by Baltimore Hebrew Congregation in 1840, and was a pioneer of Orthodox Judaism in America. The first American Hebrew school was founded in 1845 in the Lloyd Street building with Rabbi Rice as the prime teacher and the tuition set at 62.5 cents per month!

But in less than a decade, the rabbi was so discouraged by the number of congregants who desecrated the Sabbath, violated dietary laws, and intermarried, that he wrote a letter to his mentor in Germany: "The religious life in this land is on the lowest level…. I wonder whether it is even permissible for a Jew to

9. Rabbi Abraham Rice, 1800–1862, first rabbi in Baltimore, c. 1840s–50s

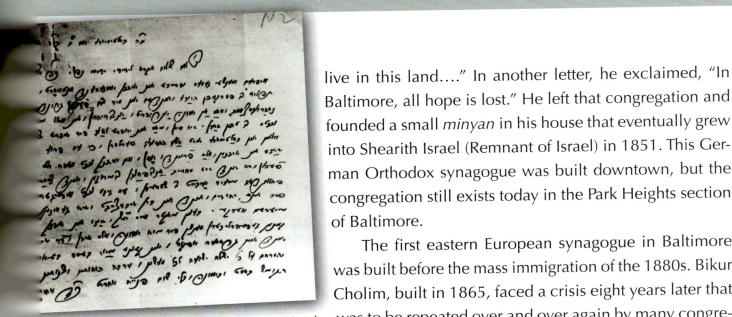

10. Letter written by Rabbi Rice to his friend Isaac Leeser stating that "in Baltimore all hope is lost," c. 1831

live in this land…." In another letter, he exclaimed, "In Baltimore, all hope is lost." He left that congregation and founded a small *minyan* in his house that eventually grew into Shearith Israel (Remnant of Israel) in 1851. This German Orthodox synagogue was built downtown, but the congregation still exists today in the Park Heights section of Baltimore.

The first eastern European synagogue in Baltimore was built before the mass immigration of the 1880s. Bikur Cholim, built in 1865, faced a crisis eight years later that was to be repeated over and over again by many congregations. As immigrants from a given *shtetl* increased, they created one split after another, forming many small *shul*s that gave each group its little touch of the familiar Old Country. B'nai Israel – called the Russishe Shul – broke off from Bikur Cholim in 1873. Over 40,000 Jews came to Baltimore from 1880 to 1915 and, by the turn of the century, there were more than 20 Orthodox synagogues.

In the 1860s, Jews lived primarily in the blocks around Lloyd Street, but over the past 100 years the Jewish neighborhoods have migrated from downtown and Fells Point to East Baltimore and finally to the northwest. In 1917, a small group of Orthodox Jews moved into the outlying area around Park Heights, which became the home of the largest Orthodox congregation, Beth Tefillah, in 1921.

11. Shearith Israel, founded by Abraham Rice in 1851 when he broke from the Baltimore Hebrew Congregation. It is today the oldest continuously operating Orthodox congregation in Baltimore and one of the oldest in the US. Structure was built in 1926.

In the first decade after the arrival of the eastern European immigrants, Hebrew education was completely in the hands of the old-fashioned *melamed* (Hebrew teacher). Baltimore's first large Hebrew school was a Talmud Torah established in 1889. In 1917 the Yeshiva Torah Ve-Emuna Hebrew Parochial School of Baltimore City (today called Yeshiva Chofetz Chaim Talmudical Academy), was incorporated, founded by Rabbi Abraham Schwartz. This school for boys is still going strong today, as is the all-girls' school, Bais Yaakov.

12. B'nai Israel today. The "Russishe Shul," 1873, was one of the many synagogues that split from its original congregation as immigrants from the same eastern European village came in numbers to Baltimore. It is the oldest Orthodox synagogue building in continuous use in Baltimore and still houses an active congregation. Its Moorish Revival style is reflected in the graceful arches that adorn the building's exterior.

In 1933, Rabbi Yaakov Ruderman of the Slobodka Yeshiva established the Ner Israel Rabbinical College. It currently hosts 600 students from all over the world, including South America, Europe, and Russia. Ner Israel was named for Rabbi Yisrael Lipkin Salanter, the founder of the Mussar movement, an educational program emphasizing ethics and morality. Apart from its world-renowned Talmudic studies program, it is also recognized as an accredited college by the state of Maryland. It has agreements with Johns Hopkins University, as well as the University of Maryland and other colleges, to obtain degrees from these schools with academic credits for religious studies. While many other yeshivos have tried to duplicate this concept, Ner Israel was and is still a groundbreaker in expanding its students' horizons.

13. Rabbi Yaakov Ruderman had a dream to bring his Slobodka Yeshiva to America. Ner Israel was the result.

14. Inscription on the cornerstone of the Hebrew Benevolent Society building, c. 1866

Baltimore Earns Praise – from the Poor and Destitute!

So far, Baltimore seems to have followed a familiar pattern, similar to the growth of other Jewish communities across the USA. But what about that remarkable reputation for *chesed*? When and how did that evolve?

As far back as 1813, Baltimore Jewry had acquired a reputation as a charitable community among whom a poor Jew was never lost. In those days, believe it or not, the reputation of a community depended on the opinion of professional beggars! Through their own grapevine, they knew which communities would favor them with kindness. In one instance, when a certain *shnorrer* became dissatisfied with the assistance given to him by the Shearith Israel Congregation of New York, he knew it was time to move to the very giving Baltimore community.

At first, from 1830 on, Baltimore Hebrew Congregation, as the only Jewish organization in the city, took care of all Jews' needs from cradle to grave. In 1834, Baltimore's first charitable organization was formed – the United Hebrew Benevolent Society of Baltimore (known simply as "the United"). Many such organizations followed, which led the *Baltimore American* newspaper to comment in 1856, "The Jews take care of their own poor and contribute to the poor of all religions."

15. Ladies' apartment in the Hebrew Friendly Inn and Aged Home, c. 1890s

The United was not only the first secular Jewish organization in Baltimore; it was also the first German-Jewish society in which Sephardic Jews, who never joined Ashkenazic synagogues, participated. This was the key to all future activities of various charity organizations in that rapidly evolving city. Charity in its widest forms was to be the unifying force of a community divided in many other respects.

Isaac Leeser, the prominent Orthodox voice in the US in the first half of the nineteenth century, wrote in his newspaper, the *Occident*, in 1851 that he foresees a time when "Every effort will be made… to unite for a common good, though they worship in different synagogues." Little did he know how long it would take to accomplish this goal. There was a deep rift between the Reform and Orthodox Jews; and the Civil War further divided the politically passionate residents of this city, which borders both North and South. In the book *Memoirs of American Jews, 1775–1865*, edited by Jacob Rader Marcus (New York: Ktav, 1975), the merchant Haiman Philip Spitz is quoted: "The war broke out. One partner was a rebel; the other a Union man. They broke up business."

"There is a degree of suffering such as no pen can describe. Emigrants arrive every day…and expect gold to be found in the streets. Instead of gold they find distress of every kind meeting them at every step." This sounds like a description of the Russian immigrants. It is not. It is a report in the *Occident* of 1855, describing the arrival of German-Jewish immigrants.

Perhaps remembering what they had gone through 50 years earlier, the German Jews, with their gift of organization, threw themselves into helping the eastern European immigrants in every way possible by giving charity, restoring health, or finding work opportunities. There was no end to the fairs, picnics, collections at social gatherings, banquets, and balls. The balls given by the Purim Association proved to be a great source of income for charitable causes and were attended not only by Jews, but by the "elite" of Baltimore. The Purim Association was organized by Joseph Friedenwald (of the prominent Friedenwald family) in 1868 and became one of the models for such balls all over the country.

Just two years earlier, Dr. Jonas Friedenwald, an Orthodox German immigrant of great influence, joined with the ultra-reformer William Raynor to create the Hebrew Benevolent Society. It was a breakthrough in cooperation and mutual respect. Their historic charter recognized their common bond: "Sixteen free white persons [accepted language in those days] above the age of 21 years…Israelites desirous to associate togeth-

16. Invitation celebrating the 90th birthday of Jonas Friedenwald, 1801–1893, early strong Orthodox voice and founder of the leading Baltimore family of community workers and physicians, c. 1891

er for the purpose of providing for the relief of the destitute of their religion…." Here, in the cause of charity, natives were united with immigrants. The walls separating religious ideologies and between natives and immigrants had fallen.

Dr. Aaron Friedenwald was president of the Orthodox synagogue Chizuk Emunah (founded 1871), a seceded branch of the "Greene Street Synagogue," when it broke with Orthodox traditions. The synagogue was a supporter of the Jewish Theological Seminary and the Jewish Publication Society, both Orthodox at their inceptions. Dr. Friedenwald was director and vice president, respectively, of these two organizations. Though Dr. Friedenwald remained Orthodox his entire life, the JTS and the JPS affiliated with the Conservative movement, and Chizuk Emunah (today, Chizuk Amuno) affiliated with the United Synagogue (USCJ).

The German Jews also formed the "Milk and Ice" fund in 1894, providing milk for the poor and ice for the summer months. They also formed the Federation of Jewish Women in 1915, among other organizations.

The immigrants formed their own charitable associations as soon as they were able to muster some funds, adding considerably to the number of caring organizations in the community. Chesed Shel Emes began to provide free burials in 1899. The Friendly Inn and Aged Home (established in 1890) eventually evolved into today's Levindale, Baltimore Jewry's primary facility for the care of the elderly and disabled. Immigrants also formed the most important of the mutual assistance societies, known as the Hebrew Free Loan Association or the Gemilut Hassadim, in 1898.

> Here, in the cause of charity, natives were united with immigrants. The walls separating religious ideologies and between natives and immigrants had fallen.

Henrietta Szold: Baltimore Girl Makes Good

17. Henrietta Szold (top row, second from right), founder of Hadassah and later Hadassah Hospital in Israel, standing with nurses at a hospital, c. 1905–1920

Rabbi Benjamin Szold, a key figure in Baltimore in the second half of the nineteenth century, had no interest in the land of Israel or its people. He asserted, as did the German Jews, that "we are Russians in Russia and Americans in America." His daughter, Henrietta, on the other hand, felt differently. She joined Chovevei Zion (Lovers of Zion) in the 1890s. In the same year in which Herzl wrote his now famous brochure, *Der Judenstaat*, presenting his plan for a Jewish state, Henrietta Szold read a paper on the same topic before the Council of Jewish Women. Appalled by the poor health conditions she observed on a visit to Palestine in 1912, she founded Hadassah, the women's Zionist organization, with its mission to improve health services for Palestinian Jews and Arabs. Her group ultimately led to the creation of Jerusalem's Hadassah Hospital.

The situation of the various charitable activities during this period was one of chaos, but a chaos that clearly produced results! At first, there were two umbrella organizations: the Federated Jewish Charities (1906) and United Hebrew Charities (1907). Order was imposed at last in 1921, when all Jewish charity and social service organizations in the city merged to become the Associated Jewish Charities. It was obvious that such unity would lead to greater accomplishments.

As you can see, much of the uniqueness of the Baltimore Jewish community lies in the historic efforts of its early pioneers to lay the foundation of charitable institutions, binding the Jewish people as one. However, I came to this city to see whether this foundation of *chesed* was strong enough to continue as a legacy 175 years later. I was amazed at what I found.

Ner Israel Plays a Dynamic Role in Shaping Community Leaders

I visited Ner Israel Rabbinical College, founded in 1933 by its *rosh yeshivah* (dean) Rabbi Yaakov Ruderman. Rabbi Herman Neuberger came five years later and subsequently became its president. I spoke with Rabbi Sheftel Neuberger, his son and now the president of Ner Israel, about the many roles this rabbinical college serves in charity-minded Baltimore.

"Through the years we have always taught [the concept of] *achrayus* – responsibility – that no matter where you are in the world, you must be involved [in your community]. For this reason, students from Ner go on to leadership not only in Torah, but are intrinsically involved in *tzedakah* and *chesed*." There is no doubt that the yeshivah produces both rabbis and professionals: physicians, dentists, lawyers, and many of today's leaders of charitable organizations.

I asked Rabbi Neuberger about the uniqueness of a rabbinical college allowing students to matriculate to a university. Isn't there a danger, I asked, of a student losing his love of Torah? "No," he answered, "Rabbi Ruderman felt strongly that any student who is well grounded in Torah could handle any kind of outside influences. He felt that one had to confront the challenges of life, not run away from them. Boys here are always questioning themselves. It's part of the nature of this institution. Those who choose not to go to college ask, 'Am I preparing myself sufficiently for the future?' Those who go to college ask, 'Am I short-changing my Torah study?' That question must always remain alive. It's part of the fabric of this institution. That's what is unique about Ner Israel."

I spoke to Eli Schlossberg, a graduate of Ner Israel, now a prime mover in an all-volunteer organization called Ahavas Yisrael (Love of Israel) Charity Fund. It provides food and clothing, and pays the

18. Rabbi Herman Neuberger and the *rosh yeshivah* (dean) and founder Rabbi Ruderman at the signing of the contract for the original Ner Israel building on Garrison Boulevard, c. 1941.

19–20. Rav Sheftel Neuberger, son of Rabbi Herman Neuberger (inset) and president of Ner Israel

rent, utility, and medical bills for 500 needy families, distributing over two million dollars annually.

"Baltimore has always been a town of *chesed*," he tells me proudly. "It evolved that way based on the infrastructure that had been laid in the 1880s. Our reputation is so strong that religious leaders of other communities have told their constituents to go to Baltimore for help. We have become an *ir miklat* – a city of refuge."

He noted that each Jewish section in Baltimore organizes its own *chesed* group, but always with a connection to the Associated.

"Sixty years ago, we had fewer than 200 Orthodox families in this city. Jews of all backgrounds needed each other. And even though we have 100 Orthodox families moving here every year now, we are unique in that it has always stayed that way. Rav Ruderman and Rabbi Herman Neuberger, the founders and builders of Ner Israel, always kept close to the Associated, working together."

Eli explained that the parents and students at Ner Israel are always volunteering; the desire to do *chesed* is transmitted from parent to child. When people move to Baltimore and see the number of charitable organizations, they are inspired and feel impelled to join.

"In 1939," he continued, "my father was earning $9 a day and desperately wanted to bring his parents from Germany to the US. But how? A Mrs. Ney donated $3,000 (a fortune, in those days) without even knowing for whom she was putting up the money. When my grandmother arrived in Baltimore, she developed a reputation as a tremendous *baalas chesed* – a charitable woman. She had been brought here through *chesed*, and she imbued that characteristic in her children and grandchildren. This is how it works at Ner Israel. This is Baltimore."

Eli told me of his 13 wonderful years at the Talmudical Academy, graduating high school in 1968, and then eventually going to Ner Israel after a brief stint at Yeshiva University.

"You have to understand," he said, "I was not your typical *yeshivah bochur*. I was introduced to my new *rebbe* (instructor) in Ner Israel and informed him that I would miss two days in the next week…*informed him* without asking permission! He suggested that I speak with the *mashgiach* about my plans. [*Mashgiach* has two meanings: it can be a person who monitors the food in the kitchen to make sure it is kosher, or, in a yeshivah setting, he is the spiritual mentor. Eli was unaware of the second meaning.]

21. Eli Schlossberg, Ner Israel graduate and administrative trustee for the all-volunteer Ahavas Yisrael Charity Fund.

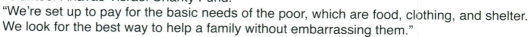

"We're set up to pay for the basic needs of the poor, which are food, clothing, and shelter. We look for the best way to help a family without embarrassing them."

Dovid Kronglas,
ach, Ner Israel

"Why, I thought, would the kitchen staff need to know my weekend plans? When I did go to the *mashgiach*, Rabbi Dovid Kronglas, I found myself arguing my case in front of everyone studying in the *beis midrash* – with the revered *mashgiach*! A few months later, Rav Dovid wanted me to explain the Super Bowl experience. 'Schlossberg,' came the question, '*vos ist der* Super Bowl?' [What is this Super Bowl?] Do you realize what it is to explain a football game to a *gadol baTorah* [a giant in Torah knowledge]? This *gadol* who escaped the horrible tragedy of Europe, a person who fled to Shanghai with the Mir Yeshiva and then put his whole existence into teaching Torah – how *do* you explain the Super Bowl to such a person?

"Look," Eli said with a knowing smile, "even if I wasn't a diligent student, and even if I was a bit of a rebel, I really learned to appreciate who my rabbis were – and the tremendous contribution each made to Torah and the Baltimore community."

Eli told me how the calls for assistance and advice would pour in to Rabbi Herman Neuberger's office from Vienna, London, Jerusalem, Sidney, Paris, and cities across the USA. Some people were looking for the best doctor, or wanted help preventing an autopsy, comforting mourners, dealing with political crises, or finding employment.

"He called me into his office," Eli recalled, "to discuss how to run the Ahavas Yisrael Charity Fund. He began with our important commitment to the broader Jewish community and the roles we needed to assume by being active in the Associated Jewish Charities. He made me promise that we would never, ever pay a salary. He wanted Ahavas Yisrael to be pure *chesed*. So it remains today a completely volunteer group."

I spoke with Marc Terrill, longtime president of the Associated, celebrating its 90th anniversary as the groundbreaking Federation of greater Baltimore. "My philosophy is that to the Associated, community means community. People in the *kehillah* are responsible for one another, no matter what 'flavor' of Jew. Everyone has a role in the community. The role of the Associated is to provide a large tent under which everyone has the ability to participate. No matter the problems of the day, lines of communication always remain open. There is a mutual respect and realization that we are stronger as a *kehillah* than as disparate parts competing with one another."

He told me that 70 percent of Orthodox Jews participate in this Federation. When considering employment options, he decided to work for the Associated because, "no matter what your background, your work is welcome here.

23. Marc Terrill, president of the Associated, speaking at "An Evening of Jewish Unity: A Tribute to the Mumbai Victims." "Defeat the violence by helping each other," he implored.

"The rally for the victims of Mumbai," he remembered, "was organized by the Orthodox community, but I was there along with Jews and non-Jews alike. You can grieve for Mumbai and leave it at that, or you can defeat [the violence] by volunteering and helping each other. The tent is vast."

Baltimore is home to the Orioles, the Ravens, and the Social Security Administration; birthplace of Henrietta Szold, Babe Ruth, Edgar Allen Poe, and "The Star-Spangled Banner." It is home to a dozen Jewish day schools, yeshivos, and seminaries. It has 70 synagogues, kosher butchers, Judaic stores, bakeries and eateries galore. But most of all, Baltimore is the home of *chesed*, benevolence, and charity. Ahavas Yisrael delivers food packages to the poor, Bikur Cholim arranges meals and visitation to the sick, the Jewish Caring Network provides help to the terminally ill, Hachnosas Orchim arranges housing for visitors throughout the world, Chaveirim help with flat tires, Hatzalah gets to emergencies before 911, and Shomrim help the police avert crime.

Yes, being here for Sukkos was a natural choice. As I take the four species and hold them tightly together, I remember the lesson that I had learned so long ago about the unity of our people. Baltimore has proven true to its exalted reputation, reinforcing this idea of community, of *kehillah*, beyond my expectations. Since my visit to Baltimore, holding the *lulav*, the *hadassim*, the *aravos*, and the *esrog* tightly together will never be the same. For G-d said, "Let them all be tied together in one band, and they will atone for one another." The tent is, indeed, quite vast.

24. *Descendant of the High Priest* by Isador Kaufmann, c. 1903. The young Chassidic boy holds a *lulav* and *esrog*.

25. Generation to generation: "Let them all be held together and they will atone for one another."

Synagogues and the old neighborhood

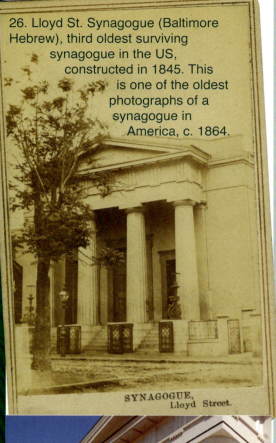

26. Lloyd St. Synagogue (Baltimore Hebrew), third oldest surviving synagogue in the US, constructed in 1845. This is one of the oldest photographs of a synagogue in America, c. 1864.

SYNAGOGUE, Lloyd Street.

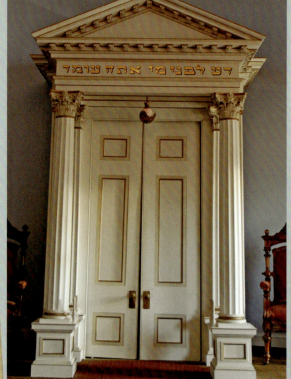

28–29. Replica of actual ark found in Baltimore Hebrew, which was lost in the 1920s. The Greek Revival look: the four Doric columns, peaked pediment, recessed portico, and steps from the ground all look eerily similar to the ark shown in the front page of most books of the Talmud.

27. Baltimore Hebrew today, 150 plus years later.

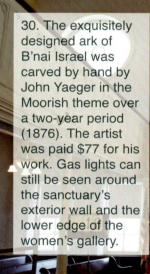

30. The exquisitely designed ark of B'nai Israel was carved by hand by John Yaeger in the Moorish theme over a two-year period (1876). The artist was paid $77 for his work. Gas lights can still be seen around the sanctuary's exterior wall and the lower edge of the women's gallery.

31. The place to be at the turn of the century, c. 1890s. Produce and chicken market on Lombard St.; the chickens were taken up the street to be ritually slaughtered.

32. The intersection of Lombard St. and Horseradish Way. Harry Tulkoff, who was the largest supplier of horseradish in the country in the 1930s, was directly across from the famous Attman's Deli, which still exists today.

33. Silverman's Dairy Restaurant on Baltimore St. in the old neighborhood, c. 1921

34. Dairy restaurant on the Lombard St. of today: Reisterstown Rd.

35. Fell's Point, along with Locust Point, was the main port for 10,000 Central European Jews from 1820 until the Civil War. It was built in 1730 as a shipbuilding and trade center by William Fell.

36. Pride of Baltimore: Henrietta Szold, Zionist, philanthropist, c. 1930s

37. Szold founded a night school for Russian immigrants, and was the director of the Jewish Agency's Youth Aliyah to help refugees come to Israel. Here, she greets one of 800 Polish children who succeeded in crossing the Russian border, reaching Persia and finally six months later, through Suez to Palestine, c. 1943.

Education

BALTIMORE, MARCH 28, 1842.

SIR,

You are respectfully invited to attend the Consecration of the *New School-house*, erected by the *Hebrew and English Benevolent Academical Association* of Baltimore, in BOND STREET, between Pratt and Gough Streets, on Wednesday morning, the 30th inst., at 9 o'clock.

R. Goldsmith   Secretary.

38. Invitation to attend the consecration of a Hebrew school, c. 1842

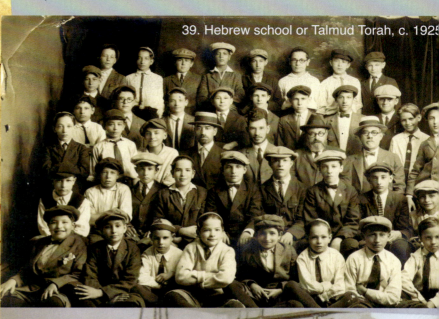

39. Hebrew school or Talmud Torah, c. 1925

40. Classroom in the original Ner Israel Yeshiva building, c. 1940

41. Ner Yisrael *beis midrash* (major study hall) today. There is usually a full house with hundreds of students; however, they have the week off during the holiday of Sukkos.

42. Ner Israel today: while the original school was founded in 1933, this campus was built in 1968 on 50 acres.

43. Rav Shepsel Neuberger told me that this stone, now embedded in the wall at Ner Israel, was originally taken from Har Zion in Israel and presented to the yeshivah to be used in the original building on Garrison Ave. in the 1930s or '40s. It was eventually moved to its present site.

44. Baltimore's Iranian Synagogue owes much to Ner Israel. In the mid-1970s, when the religious revolution in Iran was inevitable and the Shah, who was friendly to the many Jews in Iran, was to be deposed, Rav Herman Neuberger and Rav Ruderman smuggled 50–60,000 Jews through Pakistan and Turkey to the US. The Iranian community has maintained a strong, active voice in the Baltimore community

46. Sinai Hospital today

47. "I am my brother's keeper." An ad in the Baltimore Sun of 1928 announcing all the donors to the seven-year-old Associated. This Federation has set a fine example for Federations around the country for 90 years.

45. Hebrew Hospital and Asylum. The initial ten-room building opened in 1868. The first patient said he hoped he would get a diet more suited to his disease. This was his way of saying he wanted kosher food.

48. "We are Associated." The tent is vast with most Jewish organizations of every background participating, announcing their participation for all to see. Here is the popular sign outside the Suburban Orthodox Congregation.

49. Ahavas Yisrael Charity Fund was established over 30 years ago and now has a $2 million budget. It distributes food, helps with funding and even provides a choice of wedding gowns!

50. *Gemach* – the word is a short version of *gemilas chesed*, providing for charity and benevolence. This is only a partial list of items available for free and donated by people all over Baltimore: air conditioners, air mattresses, flower centerpieces, baby formula, cradles, medical equipment, fax machines, cell phones, even large tents for celebrations. The list is in the multiple hundreds and the organization controlling all these items does it with understanding and compassion. This is a community that has acted with benevolence for over 200 years.

Sukkos

51–52. The custom of Tashlich – "throwing" our sins into the river – has no origin in the Talmud. Yet it is a custom performed every year from Rosh Hashanah until Hoshanah Rabbah during Sukkos, by both Ashkenazim and Sephardim. The midrash tells us that Satan tried to interfere with Abraham taking Isaac for a sacrifice, by placing a deep river in front of him to provide an excuse to give it up. Our forefathers overcame the temptation. This custom is another attempt for us to improve ourselves as individuals and as a nation.

53. *Shlugging kapores* or providing charity to the poor before Yom Kippur is another custom to try to improve ourselves at this solemn time of year. In the old neighborhood a live chicken was used to circle around the head three times and then donated to the poor. Today some use money – a neater option. For some, like Yael Englard of Baltimore, the chicken is scary!

55. Cutting and placing the *s'chach* requires teamwork and a knowledge of Jewish law. *S'chach* can only come from something that grew from the ground and is no longer connected to it.

54. Putting the *sukkah* up is hard work and the *s'chach* or covering is the most important facet. *S'chach* and *sukkah* come from the same word, meaning "cover."

56. Choosing a beautiful *esrog* is a science and a joy in the glorification of the *mitzvah*. Here Rabbi Zvi Teichman carefully inspects an *esrog* with his son.

57. A soldier performing the *mitzvah* of *lulav* and *esrog* during World War II, possibly at Fort Meade, Maryland.

58. Rabbi Silber making the *brachah* (blessing) on the *lulav* and *esrog* in the *shul*'s *sukkah*.

59. Far right: on "Yeshiva Lane," where all the families of Ner Yisrael live (on campus), *sukkah*s are built on balconies, on the ground, and everywhere in between!

SUKKOS

60. Image of the Lutsky family taken in their *sukkah* full of decorations, including what seems to be a picture of Theodore Herzl hanging on the left, c. 1904

61. There is no joy such as there was when the *kohanim* brought to the Altar the water offering in the time of the Temple. It says in the Talmud: "He who has not seen the rejoicing of the water-drawing has never in his life seen rejoicing." Here, this occasion of the *simchas beis hashoeivah* is taking place in the *sukkah* of Rav Shmuel Silber of Suburban Orthodox, as hundreds of people come in and out for hours on end to enjoy singing and a *l'chaim*!

62. Multitasking *morah* (teacher) at Rambam Yeshiva helps her students with their *sukkah* decorations while making sure that her baby gets a soothing "piggy-back" ride.

63–64. Commemorating the circling of the Temple Altar seven times on Hoshanah Rabbah, the men circle the *bimah* with their *lulavim*. At the end of the ceremony, the lowliest of the four species, the *aravos*, are beaten on the ground, symbolizing our humility and our prayer for rain.

65. A joyous completion and an inspiring beginning: Simchas Torah

My thanks to
Rabbi Sheftel Neuberger,
Rabbi Shmuel Silber
Eli Schlossberg, Marc Terrill,
all the devoted workers at the
Jewish Museum of Maryland,
Rabbi Tzvi Teichman,
and to my daughter Jennifer
and her husband, Yudi,
for housing and feeding me.

Bibliography

Besdin, Abraham, ed. *Man of Faith in the Modern World. Reflections of the Rav*, vol. 2. Adapted from the lectures of Rabbi Joseph B. Soloveitchik. Hoboken, NJ: Ktav, 1989.

Fein, Isaac M. *The Making of an American Jewish Community: The History of Baltimore Jewry from 1773 to 1920.* Philadelphia: Jewish Publication Society of America, 1971.

Feuer, Avrohom Chaim, and Nosson Scherman. *Tashlich*. New York: ArtScroll/Mesorah, 1980.

Silberman, Lauren R. *The Jewish Community of Baltimore*. Images of America. Charleston, SC: Arcadia Publishing, 2008.

Zevin, Rabbi Shlomo Yosef. *The Festivals in Halachah: An Analysis of the Development of the Festival Laws*. New York: ArtScroll/Mesorah, 1991.

Photo Attributions

All numbered photos from the author's collection except as follows. Photos 10, 26, 31, 33, 36, 37, 38, 39, 45, 57, 60: Jewish Museum of Maryland; 13, 18, 20, 22, 40: Ner Israel archives; 14, 15, 16, 45, 47: the Associated archives; 51:

THE
South

MEMPHIS

It's hard to measure the love, commitment, and passion that the Belz family has had for Jewish life in Memphis, as well as in Israel. The family's leadership, beginning with

Sarah and Philip Belz, a"h,

and Ruthie and I. E. Hanover, a"h,

has led the way for generations to come to continue that legacy.

Jan and Andy Groveman and the Belz family

DALLAS

In loving memory of my parents and grandparents,

Esther Rochel and Meyer Getzel Moore, a"h,

and Max and Florence Moore, a"h,

who came to this country with little more than the clothes on their backs.

Their lives were dedicated to building a home for their children, where they could not only survive as Jews – but thrive. When they came to Houston in 1922, it was difficult to maintain the rituals of Jewish life. Their dedication and unwavering commitment to tradition instilled in their children the conviction necessary to build a Jewish community, which continues to thrive today.

Evelyn (Moore) Reichenthal

„עשה תורתך קבע... והוי מקבל את כל האדם בסבר פנים יפות.‟

מסכת אבות א:טו

"Make the study of Torah a fixed habit…
and receive all men with a cheerful countenance."

Pirkei Avos 1:15

Charleston,
South Carolina

**Brith Sholom-Beth Israel Synagogue
Coming Street Jewish Cemetery
Charleston Hebrew Institute
Addlestone Hebrew Academy
Minyan House
College of Charleston Library-Special Collections**

Charleston, South Carolina

Shavuos and the Family

1. One hundred fifty years of history

It was the first Shabbos in June of 2008, and I was asked to lead the services. Normally, this request would not faze me. But I was in Charleston, standing on the *bimah* in the oldest Ashkenazic Orthodox *shul* that had been in continuous existence in North America: Brith Sholom Beth Israel Synagogue. I was filled with a sense of awe and respect for the history and beauty around me: the ark with its elegant Corinthian columns, the marbled Ten Commandments, the columns supporting the women's gallery encircling the sanctuary. They had been there for more than 150 years. It seemed to me that I did not deserve the privilege.

The ancestors of many of the synagogue's current members had prayed here. My research revealed that the Jewish presence in this major southern city goes back over 300 years, and it was easy to believe. I had toured the area and marveled at the antebellum homes, unchanged – with their piazzas facing east and west to catch the cool breezes. I had learned of the Jewish involvement in the Revolutionary War and the Civil War, resulting in unimaginable division and devastation. Yet, through it all, there had been perseverance and continuity from generation to generation. My mission on this visit was to learn how they had done it.

Traditional Judaism is still vibrant in the heart of the Bible Belt of the Deep South. The youthful spiritual leader of the synagogue, long known by its initials (BSBI), is Rabbi Ari Sytner. On this Shabbos, he speaks about the weekly Torah portion, *Bamidbar* – the counting of the Jewish people specifically by its families – and emotionally emphasizes how the family unit is the key focus of Jewish life. How appropriate, I thought, this concept of family in a synagogue where many members can trace their lineage in Charleston back three, four, even five generations!

It has not always been easy. The history of Charleston Jewry is sometimes dramatic, sometimes terrifying, and the community was nearly lost more than once. Let's go back to the beginning.

2. Piazzas on these old southern mansions that sit on the Atlantic, built to catch the breezes

A Historic Act of Tolerance

The first known Jew to set foot on southern soil was Joachim Gans, a metallurgist who accompanied Sir Walter Raleigh on a voyage to the New World in 1585, and set up the first smelting furnace in North America. The Fundamental Constitutions of the Carolinas (1669), attributed to John Locke, specifically stipulated that "heathens, Jues, and other dissenters" were entitled to the same civil and political rights as Anglicans.

This unusual toleration (for even in the colonial states, "tolerance" too often only applied to the differing forms of Christianity) attracted Jews almost as soon as Charleston was established on its present site in 1680 as Charles Towne. Governor John Archdale, in writing about the province of Carolina in 1695, tells how he employed a Spanish-speaking Jew as an interpreter between himself and the Florida Indians. The first Jew known to have settled in Charleston was Simon Valentine, a family name associated with Jewish patriots who gave their lives in the War of 1812 and the Civil War.

Historically, we find that when Jews are in a friendly, tolerant non-Jewish environment, they have a tendency to assimilate and lose their identity. In Charleston, however, there has been a strong element of generational continuity in Jewish tradition for over two centuries.

3. Beth Elohim Synagogue as it stood in 1794, drawn by Solomon Carvalho

In the eighteenth century, Jewish settlement steadily increased. Hailing from London, France, and Holland, as well as Jamaica, Barbados, and other West Indies islands, they helped build the city's colonial prosperity largely as shopkeepers, traders, and merchants. The first formal congregation, established in 1749, was called Kahal Kadosh Beth Elohim (KKBE); it followed Sephardic customs. The cemetery this community established on Coming Street in 1764 is the South's oldest Jewish burial ground.

5. Plaque found at main gate

4. The Coming St. Cemetery, the South's oldest Jewish burial ground. Beth Elohim bought this cemetery in 1764 from the Jew Isaac da Costa, who had bought it for his family. Trustees included members of congregations from the Caribbean island of Jamaica; New York; Newport, Rhode Island; and Savannah, Georgia.

Early in its history, the model for KKBE was the renowned London synagogue Bevis Marks. The congregation took a no-nonsense approach, stipulating, for example, "Whoever openly desecrates the Sabbath loses his rights as a member." Some of its rules, which were the norm in that era, would be considered outrageous in our generation. Fines were imposed for "offending the president of the congregation… for refusing to accept office…[and] for refusing to read the Torah portion aloud when called upon." Excommunication was the penalty "for attending or failing to report an unauthorized *minyan*"!

Charleston grew to become home to one of the largest and wealthiest Jewish communities in North America, at times outranking those of New York and Philadelphia. Until 1830, Charleston was the "capital" of American Jewry. Just as Carolina was good for the Jews, the Jews were good for Carolina.

Jewish Charleston embodied the principles of duty and patriotism from its beginnings. Francis Salvador, a distinguished congregant of KKBE, became the first Jew in America to serve in a legislative assembly and, in 1774, was elected to the first provincial congress in Charleston. He was also the first Jew – and likely one of the first Americans – to die for the cause of American liberty. In the summer of 1776, while serving in the Revolutionary War, he was killed and scalped by Cherokee loyalists. So many Jews in the South rallied to join Washington's army, a Charleston company was formed and named the "Jews' Company." The period between the Revolution and the Civil War was the golden age in the history of the Jews in Charleston.

Famous Charleston Jewish names associated with this era are Seixas, Cardozo, Moise, and Harby. In July 1826, Isaac Harby, a prominent Jew, wrote that "America truly is the land of promise spoken of in our Scriptures." This sounds like an early version of the *Goldeneh Medinah* lauded by the eastern European immigrants sixty years later. In fact, it was the forerunner of the Reform movement's sentiment that one's homeland – be it Germany or America – was the new Promised Land, as opposed to Palestine. Harby led a major Reform insurrection at Beth Elohim Synagogue. It eventually ended in a bitter split with the Orthodox, who formed Shearith Israel.

Charleston Jews were pioneers in forming organizations to care for their own.

Charleston Jews were pioneers in forming organizations to care for their own. Indeed, they could boast some of the oldest charitable organizations in America: Hevrah Gamulut Hasadim (1750), Hebrew Benevolent Society (1781), and Society for the Relief of Orphans and Indigent Children (1801). The first Hebrew school was established in Charleston in 1838.

Interestingly enough, and diverging from the pattern seen in other Jewish communities in the United States, eastern European Jews from Poland and Russia came to Charleston to join the German and Sephardic Jews over a half century before the mass migration of the 1880s. It was this group that formed the Ashkenazic congregation Berith Shalome in 1854 – a direct antecedent of the present Brith Sholom Beth Israel Synagogue. Influenced by the spread of Reform in Europe, KKBE became a pioneer in the American Reform movement.

6. Berith Shalome on Philip St., c. 1900

A number of descendants of Berith Shalome's founding officers are members of BSBI today. Synagogue historian Jeffrey Kaplan proudly told me that he himself is fifth-generation Charlestonian, and he can indirectly trace his family back to the original formation of Berith Shalome! As in most relatively isolated Jewish enclaves, Charleston's early Jews married among themselves. "We are so interrelated that you must watch when you speak about someone – a relative is probably listening nearby!"

Loyal Confederates

In the decades before the Civil War, the heyday of the South was coming to an end and the country was fiercely divided on the slavery issue. By 1830, 83 percent of Charleston's Jews owned slaves. To be fair, most of the free blacks of the South owned slaves as well. While there were some rabbis who were abolitionists, most held that Jews must uphold the law of the land, and slavery was the law of the land. It was the way of life in the South. Some rabbis wrote that our forefathers had slaves and that the Torah gave instructions for "the government of slaves – not their abolishment!"

At the outbreak of the American Civil War – or as they call it in Charleston, the War of Northern Aggression – the Jewish communities, for the most part, rallied around the Confederacy. Jews were soldiers in the battery that fired on Fort Sumter, in the Charleston Bay battle that began the war, and many served in the Confederate army. Among notable Jewish names in the Confederacy were Isaac, Edwin, and David Moise, who were all officers of the Confederacy; Dr. Marx Cohen; and Charleston's own Judah P. Benjamin, secretary of state and war in the Confederate government. His likeness appeared on the Confederate two-dollar bill. With Lee's surrender to Federal forces, Benjamin lost no time in escaping to the Bahamas and then to England under a false name.

7. Tombstone of Marx Cohen, 26, one of many Jews killed in the Civil War. The self-sacrifice of this voluntary soldier made him a prominent name in the Confederacy.

One of the most dramatic events of the war had a profound effect on the Jews of Charleston. Toward the end of 1864, it was clear that Union General William Tecumseh Sherman would soon march on South Carolina, not only as part of a general campaign to subdue this southern stronghold, but to exact vengeance upon the state that had dared to be the first to secede from the Union. All of the misery and carnage of four years of war had brought the Union troops to a frenzy of hatred for this state that had begun the war, and Sherman himself said, "When I go through South Carolina it will be one of the most horrible things in the history of the world. The devil himself couldn't restrain my men in that state."

Southerners presumed that Charleston would be one of the main targets, and the capital city of Columbia was thought to be the safest place in the state. Residents of Columbia were confident that they would remain well protected; in fact, they graciously hosted refugees from ravaged areas. Treasures of all kinds were sent there from all over South Carolina for safekeeping – including the Torah scrolls and silver ornaments of the Kahal Kadosh Beth Elohim in Charleston. Surely, Columbia would be the best place for them should the Yankees actually take Charleston.

But no one realized the antipathy General Sherman and his men had for this "haughty" capital of the state that had soaked America in blood. The elitist citizens of Columbia never thought of fleeing their city of magnificent homes and gardens, beautiful buildings, and broad promenades – until the Union forces were just a scant few miles away. By then, it was too late, and a large population of women, children, and old men were at the mercy of the invaders.

On Friday night, February 17, 1865, thousands of Union soldiers went on a drunken rampage through Columbia, plundering everything in sight and torching buildings all over the city. A gusty wind spread the fire until most of the city was utterly destroyed. Though it is claimed that Sherman never gave an order for revenge, it is recorded that

he emerged from his headquarters and, seeing the sky red with flames, he breathed, "They have brought it on themselves."

Caught in the conflagration and pillaging was the synagogue housing the refugee Charleston Torahs. Rabbi Jacobs rushed to the synagogue and found only a few burnt sheets of parchment and a single Torah bell. Mournfully, he had to inform the Jewish leaders of Charleston that all had been lost.

Not only was the Jewish community of Columbia decimated and its wealth destroyed, the Jews all over the South suffered greatly from the war. In Charleston, the devastation was so complete that the city would not fully recover until after World War II.

United by Tradition

Though they fought each other to the death, the Jews of the North and South were still bound together by ancient religious ties. Myer Levy, a Union soldier in an occupied southern town, saw a little boy eating matzoh during Passover and asked him for a piece. The child ran inside, shouting, "Mother, there's a 'damnyankee' Jew outside!" The mother emerged and, to Levy's relief, invited him to the family Seder.

In a letter written in 1864, Confederate soldier Isaac Levy (no relation to Myer) describes his brother's attempt to observe Passover during the Civil War in Charleston. "Zeke was astonished to find on arriving in Charleston that the first Seder was to be held that day! He purchased matzot sufficient…at two dollars a pound. [At the time, matzoh cost six cents a pound in New York City!] We are observing the festival in true orthodox style." Isaac Levy was killed in battle four months later.

8. Depiction of a Civil War Seder using anything they could get their hands on, including a brick to stand in as the *charoses* (usually wine and nuts to represent the mortar used to make bricks) and bitter grass for the *maror*

The war left the Jews decimated and impoverished and began a long decline of Jewish Charleston soon thereafter. Though KKBE and the newly formed Conservative synagogue temporarily had to close their doors, the Orthodox community persevered and grew strong despite the devastation. The strength of Brith Sholom can be traced to the arrival in the early 1850s of Rabbi Hirsch Zvi Margolis Levine from a distinguished rabbinical family

in Lithuania. His animated rhetoric fit the fiery southern style. "We are all in danger…of wrath and anger and even death," he thundered, "if we fail to mend our ways!" As he resisted becoming their official rabbi, the synagogue looked for a *chazzan-shochet-mohel*, offering a salary of $200 per year. The synagogue grew, despite the excesses of the Union army occupation of Charleston. In 1874, construction began on its first permanent building of brick and wood.

In the spirit of communal harmony found among Jews in this war-ravaged town, and continued even to today, KKBE donated the ark with its Corinthian columns to this Orthodox group, still found in the synagogue. Beginning in the 1880s, Brith Sholom joined the *chazzan* craze (hiring the best-known *chazzan* available for a concert or holiday) that had started on New York's Lower East Side – a sign of status for an immigrant congregation.

9. Rabbi Hirsch Zvi Margolis Levine arrived in 1850 to become spiritual leader of the Orthodox community of Brith Sholom. While he never wanted to be their official rabbi, when he was not peddling his wares with his horse and buggy, he was apparently their *mohel*, *shochet*, and *chazzan*. This oil painting by an unknown artist hangs in today's Brith Sholom Beth Israel as a reminder of a man who was responsible, from the earliest days, for their growth.

10. Brith Sholom, the brick building, c. 1949

11. Brith Sholom began forming a choir in 1894. With the East European mass immigration in the 1880s, many synagogues "Americanized" by boasting that they had in residence a professionally trained cantor, who would entertain the members who paid top dollar to be present at his performance. During this "*chazzan* craze," there were bidding wars to secure star talent, as it was a sure sign of American Jewish status for the synagogue. Many of these famous cantors, from Romania, Austria, and France, performed at "out of town" engagements, such as Charleston.

12. "The little *shul*," as Beth Israel was known, was formed in 1911 just three blocks from the established Brith Sholom, as a protest against the lack of strict practice of religious customs by some of the members of Brith Sholom. These new immigrants were poor and couldn't afford a rabbi, so they relied on the services of their competitor's rabbi, Benjamin Axelman.

A Daring Rabbi Speaks Up!

By the turn of the century, tension was building between the eastern European immigrants and the Americanized "older members." In response, a new Orthodox synagogue, Beth Israel – called "the little *shul*"– was established in 1911, three blocks from Brith Sholom, "the big *shul*." This rift was not fully resolved for forty years.

Shirley and Arnold Prystowsky discussed this era of deep disagreements between the two *shul*s. Shirley recalled, "The rift was external, political, superficial, but it was there. The young people didn't care about it. I remember that on the *yomim tovim*, especially Rosh Hashanah, we walked back and forth, from *shul* to *shul*, visiting friends. Oh, we had the best times! To us, it didn't matter."

Arnold, an elder statesman of BSBI, can trace his genealogy back to the end of the Civil War. "My grandparents first came here in the 1860s because Charleston had the reputation of being one of the most observant cities in the nation. My grandfather's name was Ezra. He and my parents owned a clothing store in 1911 on King Street, called E. Prystowsky's. They once told me that they had to go to the city council to have a special law passed permitting them to have a cow and chickens behind the store: this was unheard of on fashionable King Street! We were always closed on Shabbos, from 1911 till we closed permanently in 1990. Many of our valued customers were black. Why, you ask? Because black customers figured that anyone who would close on the busiest business day of the week had to be honest!"

I asked them what they remember from the two most memorable

13. E. Prystowsky's was a clothing store named for Arnold's grandfather, Ezra. It was on King St., the fashionable center of town.

Jewish events in Charleston's more recent history: the formation of a major citywide Hebrew school and the merger of the two synagogues who were always at odds with each other. Shirley told me that 1927 was a turning point for the community's growth. They hired

14. Shirley and Arnold Prystowsky. Arnold traces his genealogy back to the end of the Civil War. Shirley told me that when the two *shul*s were close to merging and then drew apart yet again, it was like (to the southern way of thinking) "Merger, secession, merger, secession!"

Rabbi Benjamin Axelman to the pulpit of Brith Sholom. He was the first American-born, English-speaking rabbi they ever had, and he had been ordained by the Rabbi Isaac Elchanan Theological Seminary on the Lower East Side (the predecessor to today's Yeshiva University). To bring back the synagogue's youth, he focused his full attention on successfully creating a united Hebrew school. The Charleston Hebrew Institute was established in 1938 along with the Charleston Junior Congregation.

15. The Charleston Hebrew Institute was founded in 1938. Shown is the dedication of the new building by all the students in 1956.

Arnold went on and said, "One of the miracles of this community happened when Brith Sholom and Beth Israel merged; and the man most responsible for the peaceful accord was Rabbi Nachum Rabinovitch, a true *talmid chacham* [scholar] from the Ner Israel Yeshiva in Baltimore." Shirley continued the story in her wonderful southern drawl, mixed in with some Yiddish.

"Rabbi Rabinovitch was a '*shah shtill*' type of rabbi – quiet and unassuming. Except once. He was there when the boards of the two *shul*s were, as usual, heatedly discussing the merger. Suddenly the rabbi got very dramatic – he rushed up to the *aron*, opened it in anger, grabbed a Torah and held it up high, shouting, 'Y'all quit fighting! THIS is what's important!'"

16. Rabbi Nachum Rabinovitch as he enters the new Charleston Hebrew Institute in 1956. He was responsible for getting the two *shul*s to resolve their differences and merge in 1954.

And, so, they merged in 1954, becoming BSBI, dancing the *sifrei Torah* under the *chuppah* from one *shul* to the other. Rabbi Rabinovitch was also responsible for the founding of the community-wide day school that later became Addlestone Hebrew Academy.

In 1970, Rabbi David Radinsky came to BSBI and, for thirty years, was successful in strengthening the community's commitment to Jewish tradition. During his term, Charleston became a center for youth organizations all over the East and has had *kollel* learning groups coming down virtually every Shabbos.

17. Bringing the Torahs, as is traditional, under the *chuppah* from Brith Sholom to Beth Israel on Rutledge Ave., c. 1956. After 40 years the new Brith Sholom Beth Israel (BSBI) was founded.

Shavuos and the Family: Coming Home

My visit to Charleston falls the week before the holiday of Shavuos – when we commemorate not only the giving of the Torah at Mount Sinai, but also the first time that the people of Israel gathered together, family by family, to become a nation by their united acceptance of the Torah. It is easy to see the dedication to Torah that has kept this community vibrant.

Rabbi Ari Sytner has been BSBI's spiritual leader for the past four years and has clearly put his own stamp on this historic community. He teaches numerous classes, each appealing to a different segment of the population: "Blessings and Bagels" on Wednesday mornings; "Lunch and Learn" in the afternoons; Women's Siddur Class on Thursdays; and, of course, his seventh-grade class on Talmud at Addlestone Hebrew Academy. As I accompanied him on the way to his many commitments, we spoke of

"Who is honored? He who honors mankind."

the source of his dynamic drive. "My rabbi and mentor is Rabbi Berel Wein, who wants to attract people who 'get it,'" he told me.

"What does that mean?"

"Well, if you look at history, you must zoom out to see the destiny of the Jewish people – not just your own. There is an opportunity here to balance the growth of the total community, of people from all backgrounds. I always believed in the wisdom of the Mishnah that says, 'Who is honored? He who honors mankind.' When you respect everyone, they respect you. They will listen to what you have to say."

18. It is no wonder that Rabbi Ari Sytner has a great sense of history, as he received his *smichah* (rabbinic ordination) from Rabbi Berel Wein, a prominent Jewish historian and author of many Jewish history books. Rabbi Sytner is very active in Charleston in many capacities, especially as a teacher of numerous classes to adults and children alike.

19. Rabbi Sytner proudly showing his computer-generated *kashrus* symbol, "the Palmetto-K," on the door of the kosher bakery Sweetsmith, one of the many places he supervises

One of his innovations is a new kashrus symbol for the Charleston area, the "Palmetto K," a symbol he generated on his own computer. He supervises the kashrus at a bakery, a restaurant, and other food places, as well as the famous Bed and Breakfast Guest House.

In terms of education and community growth, Rabbi Sytner assured me, "We are definitely on the upswing. I can even see a high school coming in the near future. People come here because there is a feeling that's hard to describe – a feeling of coming home."

That feeling is quite real to Mr. Charlie Markowitz, the *gabbai* who called me up to the Torah. I had the honor of interviewing him the next day, and it was an emotional experience for both of us. You see, Charlie is a Holocaust survivor. I had never spoken to a survivor in depth, one on one. I shuddered when I asked him if I could take photographs of him putting on his *tefillin* over the numbers tattooed on his arm. He agreed, and then he started to talk. It was a chilling story.

"I was in twenty-one camps – Buchenwald, Auschwitz, Bergen-Belsen, among others. In 1941, my brother was shot on the fence trying to escape from the Warsaw Ghetto. My father had a heart attack. In Warsaw, the Nazis came looking for my brother, not knowing that he had already been shot, so they took me instead. I was eleven years old. I could not keep up my Jewish tradition, constantly working, changing camps.

"In 1943, I tried to escape with a friend, Yaakov Borenstein. He was twenty-five years old. We were caught, and they built a gallows to hang us. I dragged the coals in our little room to form a mound to the small window covered by bars. I climbed up to the bars and called for Yaakov to help. Maybe we could still escape somehow! But he just wanted to die, to get it over with. There were many times that I know that Hashem [God] was watching over me. I know it. I bent those bars to escape the gallows – impossible!! Yaakov was hanged. I was caught a second time, but delayed getting on a 'death line.' The boy in front of me was shot and the shooting stopped. Who knows?

"I was liberated in '45, April 30th at 4:00 PM. Hitler died at 3:00 PM. I wandered around at age sixteen, doing odd jobs in Germany. In 1948, a British officer gave me a pair of *tefillin*. I've been wearing them ever since.

"In 1949, I came to Charleston through New Orleans. Why Charleston? I don't know. As soon as I got here, it felt like home to me. In 1950, I was drafted into the US Army to fight in the Korean War. Can you believe it? I wasn't a citizen, didn't speak much English, but there I was! I volunteered to join the paratroopers. I had twenty plus one jumps – twenty day jumps and one night jump. My friend Schulman asked me, 'What kind of job is that for a nice Jewish boy? You're just out of the camps!' I told him that I volunteered because it was fifty dollars more pay.

20. Mr. Charlie Markowitz, *gabbai*, hero. "Charleston feels like home to me."

"Buchenwald, Auschwitz,
Bergen-Belsen...
the Warsaw Ghetto...
I was liberated...
I came to Charleston...
it felt like home...
so I stayed."

"When I got out of the service, I went back to Charleston. It still felt like home, so I stayed."

Home: the magic word to survivors in every generation. For centuries, the Jew has longed for home, for refuge, for safety in a violent world. That Shabbos, as I led the services in this hallowed *shul*, I felt honored beyond words.

I thought of what the rabbi said about the counting of the Jewish people, how important families are for strengthening the ties that bind us from generation to generation. "You can't look ahead," he said, "without looking back."

Many of today's Charlestonian Jews, some of whom I had the pleasure to meet, are proud descendants of old and distinguished families. They feel at home because their ancestors walked these narrow streets for two centuries or more, sat on the city councils, and fought for their country in every war. There is a certain reverence for the past that surpasses most communities. Perhaps being steeped in its history and strengthened by their families has brought Charleston's Jews to an even deeper, unbreakable respect for the traditions of their fathers.

For me, this concept of extended family unity reverberates well in Charleston, especially on this week before Shavuos. The Torah describes the encampment of nearly three million Jews at Mount Sinai as *vayichan* (encamped), written in the singular form of the word, instead of the plural. The commentators tell us that the usage of the singular connotes one nation, "like one person," as a family with one heart, united by the Torah and their experiences.

The Jews of Charleston implicitly understand that Jews are held together in a vertical line throughout the generations, and in a horizontal line, from one contemporary Jew to another. And from the security of their rich history and traditions, they can warmly welcome "home" even newcomers like Charlie, and travelers like me.

21. Is there a better time to have a *Chumash* party than the week of Shavuos, commemorating the giving of the Torah to a united Israel? The children at the Addlestone Hebrew Academy are acting out the moment of prayer and thankfulness in front of their friends and relatives.

Food and prayer

22. Exterior of BSBI (Brith Sholom Beth Israel)

23. Interior of BSBI with the original ark and its Corinthian columns the marbled Ten Commandments, and the columns supporting the *ezras nashim* (women's balcony) dating back well over 100 years

24. Minyan House is another *shul* founded on the other side of town. Here, the members are saying the Havdalah ceremony that concludes Shabbos, c. 1983.

Making a living with food

25–26. The Broad St. Guest House is a kosher bed and breakfast in this historical Charleston mansion. It is owned by Hadassah Rothenberg, who told me that people have lived in these homes for over 150 years; they would come off their ships and live here.

27. Shirley Prystowsky's father, William Feldman, ran this grocery 80 years ago in Charleston.

28. One man who played no favorites: Joshua Kamenitzki was president of Brith Sholom in 1910 and of Beth Israel in 1912.

29. Rev. Jacob Cohen served as *chazzan* and *shochet* for Beth Israel, c. 1913–1919.

In Judaism, digging the earth can evoke very different emotions:

tudents planting a tree next to Brith Sholom, Rabbi Rabinovitch helping out. The occasion was Shevat, Jewish Arbor Day, c. 1956.

31. Young adults prepare to participate in the burying of holy books at the cemetery after they were destroyed in Hurricane Hugo. Jewish tradition requires disposal by burial for any books or documents that have the four-letter name of G-d in them. They must be buried exactly as a person would be. These worn holy items are called *sheimos*, Hebrew for "names," because they contain the Holy name. In the Temple in Jerusalem they were kept set aside in a place called the "Genizah," and Jewish communities around the globe still maintain such storage areas. When too much is accumulated, the items are buried.

2–33. There is a big challah bake appening at Addlestone Hebrew cademy, and Rabbi Sytner is there to ulfill a *mitzvah* he doesn't get a chance o do very often: *hafrashas challah*, or eparating the dough. This *mitzvah* is abbinic in nature but similar to the tithe that was given to the *kohen*. A small piece of dough the size of an egg is set aside to remind us that it is His land that we are taking from. Although both men and women can do this *mitzvah*, this is one that is usually entrusted to the women. We do not give the piece to the *kohen* as it was in the past because we cannot verify his lineage beyond any doubt. So we destroy the challah (the small piece) beyond the point where it is edible. Very often, you will see a small burnt piece in a pizza store on top of the oven.

Shavuot preparation in Charleston

34. Lena Berkman studying *Chumash* (Torah), c. 1945

35. The Torah learning continues from generation to generation. Student at Addlestone today.

36. Hebrew school at Beth Israel, c. 1949

37. Rabbi Benjamin Axelman leading a women's study group on King St., c. 1935

38. Rabbi Sytner, today, leading a popular women's study group on the meaning of *tefillah* (prayer)

39. Rapt attention! Rabbi Sytner's favorite time: teaching his classes.

Shavuot preparation in Charleston

„טוב לי תורת פיך מאלפי זהב וכסף"

תהילים קי"ט, ע"ב

"The Torah of your mouth is better to me than thousands of gold and silver." –*Tehillim 119:72*

40. Preparing for the big moment: the presentation in front of family and friends at the graduation *Chumash* party

41. Saying it with feeling! They are ready for Shavuos.

42. A sight that must provide *chizuk* (strength) to all whom Charlie Markowitz inspires

My thanks to Rabbi Ari Sytner, to all the people at the Jewish Historical Society of South Carolina, the Special Collections Department of the College of Charleston Library, Hadassah Rothenberg, Arnold and Shirley Prystowsky, Charlie Markowitz, Jeffrey Kaplan, and Addlestone Hebrew Academy.

Bibliography

Besdin, Abraham. *Reflections of the Rav: Lessons in Jewish Thought Adapted from the Lectures of Rabbi Joseph B. Soloveitchik*. Hoboken: Ktav, 1979.

Breibart, Solomon. *Explorations in Charleston's Jewish History*. Charleston, SC: The History Press, 2005.

Gottesman, Milton M. *Hoopskirts and Huppas: A Chronicle of the Early Years of the Garfunkel-Trager Family in America, 1856–1920*. New York: American Jewish Historical Society, 1999.

Gurock, Jeffrey. *Orthodoxy in Charleston: Brith Sholom Beth Israel and American Jewish History*. Charleston, SC: College of Charleston Library, 2004.

Pearlstine, Jean. *Bicentennial Celebration: Charleston Jewish Community, 1750–1950*. Charleston, SC : Bicentennial Committee, 1951.

Pessin, Deborah. *History of the Jews in America*. Illustrated by Ruth Gikow. New York: United Synagogue Commission on Jewish Education, 1957.

Reznikoff, Charles, with Uriah Z. Engelman. *The Jews of Charleston: A History of an American Jewish Community*. Philadelphia: Jewish Publication Society, 1950.

Scherman, Rabbi Nosson, and Rabbi Meir Zlotowitz, eds. *Shavuos Handbook: A Treasury of Prayers and Readings Recited on Shavuos with an Overview and a Commentary Anthologized from Talmudic, Midrashic and Rabbinic Sources*. New York: ArtScroll/Mesorah, 1990.

Williams, Arthur V. *Tales of Charleston 1930s*. Charleston, SC: College of Charleston Library in association with the Jewish Historical Society of South Carolina, 1999.

Zevin, Rabbi Shlomo Yosef. *The Festivals in Halachah: An Analysis of the Development of the Festival Laws*. New York: ArtScroll/Mesorah, 1991.

Photo Attributions

All numbered photos from the author's collection except as follows. Photos 6, 9, 10, 11, 12, 15, 16, 28, 29, 36, 37: BSBI archives; 8: American Jewish Archives; 13, 27: Shirley and Arnold Prystowsky; 17, 24, 30, 31, 34: Special collections, College of Charleston Library.

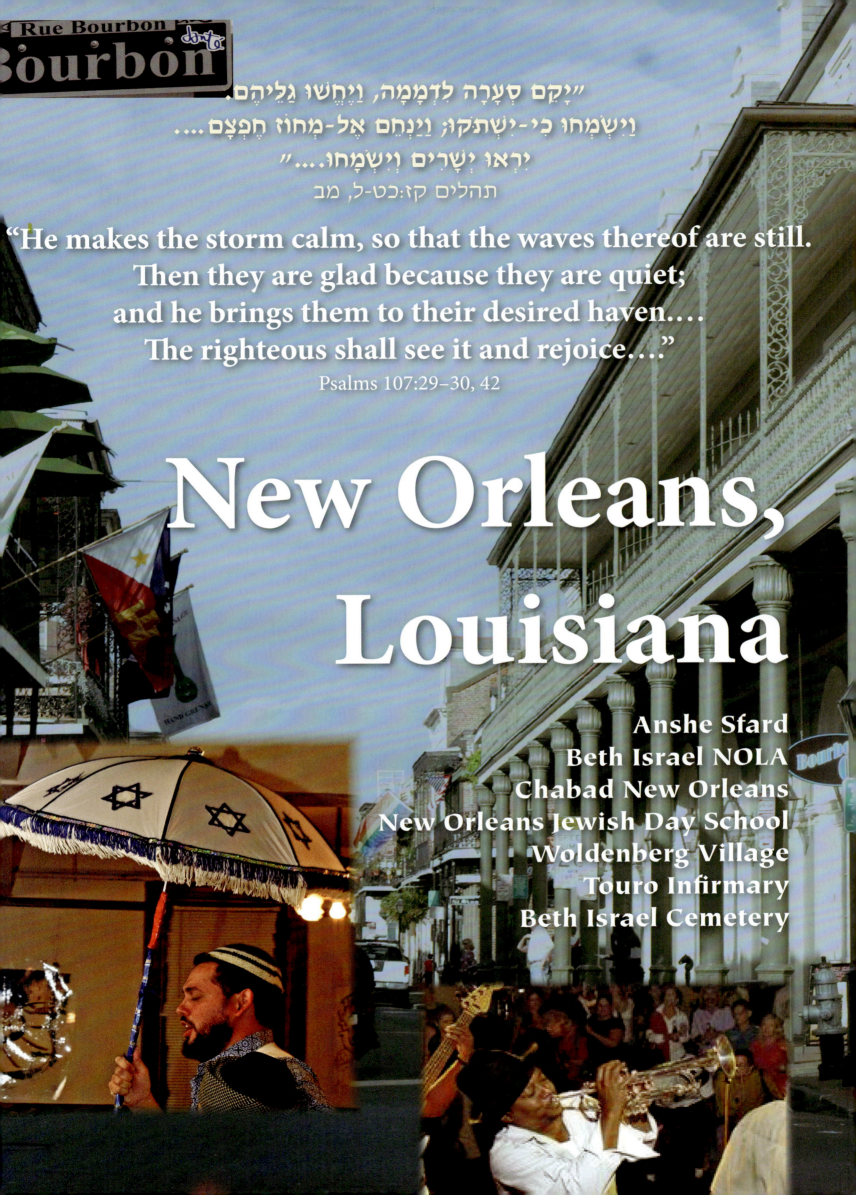

"יָקֵם סְעָרָה לִדְמָמָה, וַיֶּחֱשׁוּ גַּלֵּיהֶם.
וַיִּשְׂמְחוּ כִי-יִשְׁתֹּקוּ; וַיַּנְחֵם אֶל-מְחוֹז חֶפְצָם....
יִרְאוּ יְשָׁרִים וְיִשְׂמָחוּ...."
תהלים קז:כט-ל, מב

"He makes the storm calm, so that the waves thereof are still.
Then they are glad because they are quiet;
and he brings them to their desired haven....
The righteous shall see it and rejoice...."
Psalms 107:29–30, 42

New Orleans, Louisiana

Anshe Sfard
Beth Israel NOLA
Chabad New Orleans
New Orleans Jewish Day School
Woldenberg Village
Touro Infirmary
Beth Israel Cemetery

New Orleans, Louisiana

The Joy of Purim in the Land of Katrina

1. Volunteer from the organization ZAKA, which often handles bodies after a bombing, pulling out seven Torahs from ten feet of water, by boat. The Torahs were all lost and had to be buried.

I'm standing in the ruins of what was once the main sanctuary of Congregation Beth Israel, now just a shell after Hurricane Katrina tore through it on August 29, 2005. I feel my eyes tearing. When the rain-swollen waters of enormous Lake Pontchartrain broke through nearly all of the levees, 80 percent of the city flooded, and almost 2,000 people lost their lives. Rescue workers were dodging floating bodies to save people who had been on rooftops for days, begging to be saved.

Here in Beth Israel, seven Torah scrolls were submerged in ten feet of water for nearly three weeks before being rescued. Three thousand holy books tossed atop the water until they became too waterlogged to float and sank down to the bottom. The scenes are so vivid and powerful you want to ask, as Moses did of G-d, to know why people must suffer. At the time he was answered, "I will show you My Back," meaning that humans cannot understand tragedy as it is happening. But we do have the ability to experience G-d's "Back" – the eventual retrospective comprehension of what happened. Hopefully, we will also grasp the ultimate good in what transpired.

When we enter the Hebrew month of Adar, we are told that we should have an abundance of joy. I arrived in New Orleans a day before the start of Purim to examine how a Jewish community – so devastated less than three years earlier and still suffering physically and emotionally from the effects of Hurricane Katrina – can lift themselves up and reach for the joy of Purim. Frankly, I didn't know what to expect.

The story of Purim is described in the Megillah in one phrase: *v'nahafoch hu*, i.e., everything was turned "upside down." Our commentators use yet another phrase to describe the story: *hester panim*, the concealment of the face of G-d. Is the story of the Jewish community of New Orleans a microcosm of the Purim saga? When everything is topsy-turvy, are there blessings in disguise?

An Unlikely Haven

New Orleans is often called the Crescent City because its original area, the French Quarter, lay along a giant curve of the Mississippi River. It is renowned as the birthplace of jazz and, of course, Mardi Gras parades and celebrations. How does a city known for sin, seafood, and carnivals become a Jewish enclave?

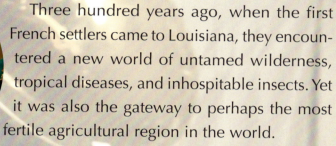

2. Jazz band in New Orleans' Beth Israel.

Three hundred years ago, when the first French settlers came to Louisiana, they encountered a new world of untamed wilderness, tropical diseases, and inhospitable insects. Yet it was also the gateway to perhaps the most fertile agricultural region in the world.

In 1718, Governor Bienville named the capitol of the Louisiana colony New Orleans in honor of the Duke of Orleans, Philip II. Perhaps more than any other American city, New Orleans experienced a unique mingling of the old world and new: the Creoles of today are descendants of the original French, Spanish, and African settlers. There is a culture of independence and individualism in this city of seemingly endless potential.

If French colonial laws had been strictly enforced, there would be no early history of Jews in New Orleans. According to the Code Noire (the Black Code) of 1724, all Jews were to be expelled from this French colony. Yet when the first known Jewish settler, a Sephardic Jew named Isaac Rodrigues Monsanto, arrived in New Orleans from Curaçao in 1757, he faced few obstacles. The restrictive law of expulsion was never enforced, owing to general recognition of valuable Jewish experience and connections in shipping and commerce. The early Jewish pioneers did nothing to build a Jewish community in New Orleans, however. As one historian put it, there were Jews in the city – but no Judaism.

3. History trying to repeat itself: "The Black Code" of 1724

When the United States purchased Louisiana from France in 1803, Jewish pioneering in the area began in earnest. The most influential person in the early nineteenth-century Jewish community was Judah Touro. While he had no desire to be directly connected to this community, his legendary philanthropy has left a mark on Jewish life in New Orleans (as well as other parts of the country) to this day. Raised in Rhode Island, where his father was the *chazzan* (spiritual leader) of the Newport congregation, he arrived in New Orleans in 1801 and built a successful trading and real estate business. Touro was seriously injured as he fought against the British in the Battle of New Orleans during the war of 1812. In 1852, he established the Touro

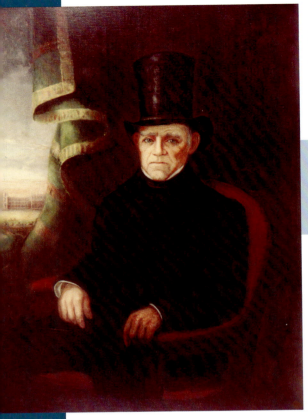

infirmary, a charity hospital supported by the local Hebrew Benevolent Association, which has developed into one of the leading medical centers of the South.

4. Judah Touro, who had little contact with the organized Jewish community during his lifetime, became the first great Jewish philanthropist. Oil painting by Solomon Carvalho.

5. Famous Touro will leaving money to almost every Jewish charity in the US, including the Hebrew Benevolent Association and the "Orphan's Home and Asylum."

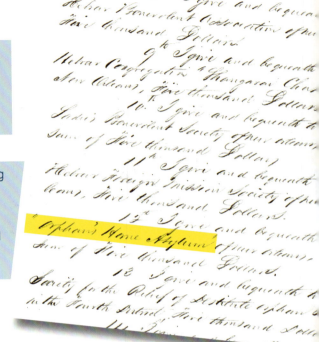

The Legend of a Buccaneer Boychik

It can be said that a Jewish pirate saved Louisiana from the British in the War of 1812. It can also be said that he wasn't Jewish. It depends who you believe. If you take Lafitte's diary seriously (for it is deemed a forgery by some historians), he was born in Saint Dominque in 1782 (others say 1776), and was raised by his grandmother, the Sephardic Jewess Zora Nadrimal. He recounts that the family – originally named Lefitto – fled the Spanish Inquisition, scaled the Pyrenees, and made it into France, where they changed their name to Lafitte. His first marriage was to a Danish Jewess, Cristiana Levine.

Infamous as a daring "privateer," a term he preferred to "pirate," Lafitte roamed the Louisiana area for decades. When the British offered him a small fortune for his expertise navigating the waterways of Louisiana in their attempt to capture New Orleans, he warned the Americans and fought valiantly alongside them. He's a revered local hero.

Ghost seekers say Lafitte still hovers in the area, keeping watch over his beloved New Orleans, and appearing (most often to fishermen) on the prow of his phantom ship whenever an ill wind bodes harm. The last "sighting" of Jean Lafitte, by those in the know, was just before Hurricane Katrina.

6. Artist's conception of Jean Lafitte (1776–1823). Born in the same year as this country's birth, he helped it survive the War of 1812.

7. Shaarei Chessed (Shangarai Chasset was the original spelling) was the first permanent house of worship in Louisiana.

8. Gershom Kursheedt (1817–1863). Religious activist, grandson of Revolutionary War patriot Rabbi Gershom Mendes Seixas, and close friend of Isaac Leeser, publisher of the *Occident*. Kursheedt helped found the Hebrew Benevolent Association and convinced Judah Touro to provide the funds for the new congregation Nefutzot Yehudah (cleverly named after Touro), or Dispersed of Judah.

The first congregation in New Orleans, Shangarai Chasset (later Shaarei Chesed or "Gates of Mercy") was founded in 1827, when Jacob Solis, a Sephardic merchant from New York, was unable to find Passover matzoh. So he had to bake his own. Anger turned to inspiration and he decided to organize a congregation following the Sephardic ritual, the first congregation in America outside the original thirteen states.

In 1845, under the leadership of the first religious Jew to live in the city, Gershom Kursheedt, a new Sephardic congregation, Nefutzot Yehudah (Dispersed of Judah) was named in honor of Judah Touro, in the hope that Touro would assist them. He did. Kursheedt was the grandson of the renowned Revolutionary War patriot and rabbi in Philadelphia and New York, Gershom Mendes Seixas.

Yellow Fever

was a constant threat in New Orleans. The city was particularly hard hit for three years in a row (1853–1855), when nearly thirteen thousand residents lost their lives. Due to these ravages, the Jewish Widows and Orphans home was founded in 1856 – only the second of its kind in the US.

9. Dispersed of Judah Cemetery

10. The Jewish Widows and Orphans Home, opened in 1856 by members of the Hebrew Benevolent Association to help victims of Yellow Fever and other deadly diseases

By 1860, two thousand Jews lived in New Orleans and there were 245 different Jewish-owned businesses there. Much of the development of Jewish institutions in New Orleans was due to the effects of the Civil War, which brought many Jews from the surrounding areas to the safety of the city. Most Jews were loyal supporters of the Confederacy and many took up arms for the cause. This was not surprising; many were accepted leaders in the community and held prominent political positions in the state. The most notable of these was Judah P. Benjamin, the first Jewish senator in the US. Known as the "brains of the Confederacy," he came to New Orleans in 1827 and served as the Confederacy's secretary of state. After the war, he was forced to flee the country, eventually building a successful career as a lawyer in England. He burned all of his papers related to the Confederacy and never spoke of the ill-fated secession. He died in Paris in 1884.

11. Judah P. Benjamin (1811–1884) held three different cabinet positions for the Confederacy.

Backtalk!

In the annals of famous Jewish comebacks to anti-Semitic remarks, Judah P. Benjamin ranks high. High-profile Jews of that era were regarded with open suspicion, and Benjamin was never allowed to forget his ancestry when in the public forum. In the Senate, he was often attacked because he was a Jew, but he rarely responded, preferring to display a "perpetual smile."

Once, however, during a debate on slavery, Senator Ben Wade of Ohio chided that Benjamin was "an Israelite with Egyptian principles." It is reported that Benjamin answered, "It is true that I am a Jew, and when my ancestors were receiving their Ten Commandments from the immediate Deity, amidst the thunderings and lightnings of Mount Sinai, the ancestors of my opponent were herding swine in the forests of Great Britain."

This story bears a remarkable similarity to one about his contemporary, British Prime Minister Benjamin Disraeli. Born of Jewish parentage, Disraeli was baptized at the age of thirteen and remained an observant Anglican for the rest of his life. Nonetheless, his political opponents and the press often depicted him as a "Shylock." He never denied his heritage. In fact, after a British politician made a particularly snide remark about him, Disraeli reputedly retorted, "Yes, I am a Jew, and when the ancestors of the right honorable gentlemen were brutal savages on an unknown island, mine were priests in the Temple of Solomon."

Benjamin made his remark in the 1850s, while Disraeli pontificated in 1835. Did Benjamin usurp his well-said barb from Disraeli? It's quite possible but we'll never know.

In 1860, Rabbi Yissachar Dov (Bernard) Illowy, who had received *smichah* (rabbinic ordination) from the Chasam Sofer of the Pressberg Yeshiva, arrived as the new rabbi of Shaarei Chesed. He proudly declared that after his first sermon, forty important merchants began closing their businesses on Shabbos, and ten other congregants fully kashered their houses. When he discovered that one congregant was raising strange-looking birds called Muscovy ducks for food, he caused a controversy when he declared the bird non-kosher. He based his opinion on a common rabbinic guideline that a bird species cannot be eaten if one cannot trace a valid *mesorah* (tradition) that permits it. He sent a letter to Rabbi Samson Raphael Hirsch of Germany and Chief Rabbi Dr. Nathan Adler of London for adjudication, both of whom concurred with his opinion.

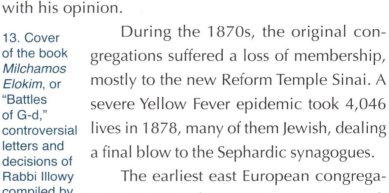

12. Rabbi Bernard Illowy (1814–1871), only the second ordained rabbi to be employed in a *shul* in the US. He served congregations in New York, Philadelphia, St. Louis, Syracuse, and Baltimore before coming to New Orleans.

ספר
מלחמות אלהים

BEING

THE CONTROVERSIAL LETTERS AND THE CASUISTIC DECISIONS

OF THE LATE

RABBI BERNARD ILLOWY PH. D.

WITH

A SHORT HISTORY OF HIS LIFE AND ACTIVITIES

BY HIS SON

HENRY ILLOWAY M. D.

Formerly Professor of the Diseases of Children in the Cincinnati College of Medicine and Surgery; Formerly Visiting Physician to the Jewish Hospital in Cincinnati, Ohio. One of the collaborators on the American text-book of the diseases of children. Author of "Constipation in Adults and Children", of "The Summer-Diarrhoeas of Infants" (German edition "Die Sommerdiarrhoeen der Kinder" — Karger, Berlin) etc. etc. Fellow of the Academy of Medicine, New York City, etc. etc.

M. POPPELAUER, BERLIN
1914

13. Cover of the book *Milchamos Elokim*, or "Battles of G-d," controversial letters and decisions of Rabbi Illowy compiled by his son, a physician, in 1914.

4.

A letter addressed to Chief-Rabbi Dr. N. Adler, London, and Rabbi S. R. Hirsch of Frankfurt a/M. as to Muscovy Ducks.

ב"ה פה נואָרלעאָנס יום ד' עש"ק פ' בחקותי הרכ"ב לפ"ק.

אלנא יחר בעיני אדני מכ"ת ר' הרפה כי טלאתי [עוו] לבוא עמו במגלת ספר והעמסתי עליו בדברי, ולכן לפני הסכל מלכא בדרכותי בבקשתי לחת את שאלתי, הנכרת לא יונה, כי בע"ה יד העת גרשתני מנחלה אבותי על ארץ טמאה, ארץ אכלה יושביה ואנשיה כמהים נחשבו כי עורים הם כלטו, כי עם עיניהם מראות נוגה החמנה והמדע, ושמש החכמה עליהם לא יורח, ורבים הם עמי הארץ וכן כולם חכמים כולם נבונים כולם בעיניהם אף כי אינם יודעים את התורה, ונעם ככהן, כי מאשרי העם הזה הם אנשים אשר מעולם לא למדו ולא שמשו ואינם יודעים בן דין לדין בין טמא לטהור, חונים הם ומכבירים את ד' בגרונם ולא כלבבם, חוויס הם ועיניס אין להם לראות נגע הצרעת הממארת הקרוי בית ישראל, הכמים הם מצוינים בבגדיהם כחכני בבל, הם הסוררים הם הסורים ומסרדים גיטין וקדושין ופוטרים יבמות מיבום מהירים ענונות ומערבין זרע קודש עם זרע העמים רק כי יתן הכבד את ערלתו אשר חרפה היא לנו בעד אהבתו לבתולת בת יהודה אף כי אינם יודעים להתיר בזעא ככוחחא כי כל כוחם רק כפה, לענן היטיב והלל ולשבח את עצמם וכל המרכה לספר בשבחו הרי זה משובח, כי יודעים כל גנון וגנון כמשפטו וכהלכתו ורובם כולם אינם יודעים לקרא בלשון הקודש בלי נקורוה, בכל זאת ירהבו בנפשם עוו להורוח ולהתיר את אמורים, כי איך ישפילו את עצמם להשיב לשואל (שמחזק) כל חון לצורבא מרבנן) שאינם יודעים תשובה, וחתוק עצומה היא כחא

14. Letter to Chief Rabbi Adler of London and Rabbi Samson Raphael Hirsch as to the *kashrus* of Muscovy duck

During the 1870s, the original congregations suffered a loss of membership, mostly to the new Reform Temple Sinai. A severe Yellow Fever epidemic took 4,046 lives in 1878, many of them Jewish, dealing a final blow to the Sephardic synagogues.

The earliest east European congregation in New Orleans was Tememe Derech (the "Right Way"). It was founded in 1858, a full 22 years before the mass immigration from Russia following the assassination of Czar Alexander. Along with other smaller *shul*s, it was located in what was to become *the* Orthodox neighborhood for over half a century, best known as the Dryades Street neighborhood. The Chassidic Anshe Sfard, the prominent *shul* in this "old neighborhood," was founded in 1896 and still functions today.

Jews in New Orleans were fortunate that they faced little anti-Semitism in the nineteenth century. In fact, even the first king of Mardi Gras, in 1872, was Lewis Solomon, a Jew. On the other hand, he was also the last Jewish

15. Congregation Agudas Achim Anshe Sfard, organized in 1896. This building went up in 1925 and is open today despite the deterioration of the neighborhood. Anshe Sfard hosted the Megillah reading and Purim seudah for Beth Israel after Hurricane Katrina destroyed the Beth Israel building.

king of Mardi Gras, a position that has since become very restrictive. One New Orleans urban legend, recounted in many interviews, tells the story of a Jewish merchant who was so accepted in the larger community that he was asked to join the notoriously anti-Semitic Ku Klux Klan. Politely declining the invitation, he must have taken secret joy in the fact that the Jew-hating Klansmen unknowingly were buying the white sheets they used as a disguise from this Jew's dry goods store!

The financial prosperity of the 1920s allowed Orthodox congregations to build larger *shul*s. Anshe Sfard built a large synagogue in 1925 that still stands today, and Beth Israel built a structure with a seating capacity of 1,200; in both, the women's sections overlook the men's. At 350 members, Anshe Sfard considered itself the largest Orthodox *shul* in the Deep South.

I chatted with two re-markable people who gave me of their time (and spared little emotion) in showing me the devastation of Hurri-cane Katrina: Jackie Gothard is a president of Beth Israel and she's one of its real movers and shakers. Her cousin Irwin Lachoff is the preemi-nent Jewish archivist and historian of the New Orleans Jewish community. Their fami-lies have been in New Orleans

16. Congregation Beth Israel bought the home of former city mayor Joseph Shakespeare in 1905 for their first building.

for generations. They gave me such a vivid picture of the old neighborhood and Katrina, I could not have written this without them.

"My grandfather," Irwin told me, "was a baker in Odessa. Following a bakers' strike in 1905, a pogrom ensued, because most of the bakers were Jewish. He'd had enough! So he came to New Orleans, where some of his relatives lived." Jackie chimed in. "He came to Ellis Island with the Russian name Conchas, and left with the name of Kansas, owing to the clerk's incorrect spelling."

"Yup, 'Fisher Kansas' opened a bakery on Dryades Street," continued Irwin, "and by World War II, he was selling chickens too. As a matter of fact, he sold more chickens than was allowed by the rationing laws, got arrested, and was put in jail!"

Jackie told me of the thirty-two aunts and uncles they had, all of whom lived in the Dryades area. "The *shochet* would come on Fridays. He worked out of my uncle's garage, with two inches of sawdust on the floor. My cousins and I would chase the chickens; we loved to see the sawdust fly!

"My father started Pressner's Kosher Deli on Dryades Street in 1941, and when my dates came to pick me up, they would have to walk through the deli to get to our apartment above the store. To me, it was embarrassing, but the boys loved it because my mother always offered to let them reach into the pickle barrel, or she'd make them a salami sandwich!"

17. Anshe Sfard's interior as it appeared for the wedding of Sarah Carp in the '40s

Fond Memories of Another Era

I learned further about how dear the memories of the Dryades Street neighborhood are from Sarah Carp, a young lady of 86. Her father came to the neighborhood as a peddler from Kiev, escaping from the vicious Russian military in the early twentieth century. When the community asked him to be their butcher, he changed occupations, not knowing anything about the meat business. This is how occupations were established in the 1920s! "My fondest memories are of walking down Dryades Street after Shabbos in the '30s and '40s – I still remember all the stores: there was Glinsky's dress shop, Handelman's department store, Levine's hardware store, Perlman's bakery, and Pressner's deli. Wonderful places, wonderful memories!"

18. Interior of Anshe Sfard today with original menorah, chandelier, columns, and *ezras nashim* (women's balcony)

Jackie told me that the first Beth Israel structure was the former residence of Mayor Shakespeare, which the congregation purchased. Of course, they were proud of their grand new building, erected in 1904. "That building is now a Baptist church," sighed Jackie. "Those of us who remembered growing up there wanted to go back, so we chartered a bus and made arrangements with the minister. When we arrived, we saw the minister and his congregants waiting to welcome us. We went in and, you know, it still felt like our *shul*, 38 years later! Our parents and grandparents all had specific seats where they regularly prayed, and with tears flowing, we all instinctively ran to them, women upstairs, men downstairs.

"Our *shul* had the only *mikveh* in the Deep South, from Houston to Florida! When our visit was done, one of the church lead-

19. Sarah Carp remembering the old days on Dryades St.

ers came over to me and said, 'You know, I have always had a question that I wanted to ask. This building was constructed with such care and beauty. Can you tell me, please – why did you make the swimming pool so small?'"

It was time to talk about Katrina. Jackie took me to the shell of what had been the recent magnificent structure of Beth Israel. We stood in pained silence in the *beis midrash*, known as "the little *shul*" – with its empty *aron kodesh*, save for a few Torah *gartels* (cloth ties used to bind the Torah scrolls) – and the *bimah* of beautifully carved wood, now in pieces. "Our *shul* is actually situated in a bowl below sea level. When the levees a few blocks away failed, the waters from Lake Pontchartrain crashed through our

We stood in pained silence

20. The remnant of "the little *shul*," as the *beis midrash* with its hand-carved *bimah* was known. Note the high water mold markings on the walls reaching up to ten feet high!

front entrance glass windows and inundated the *shul* with ten feet of water. The water didn't subside for three weeks! During that entire time, our members – who evacuated to Baton Rouge, Houston, Dallas, San Diego, and Memphis – couldn't get back here at all. Our seven Torahs, under water for all this time, were rescued by ZAKA, the organization that also does the gruesome cleanup in Israel after a suicide bombing. They rowed into the *shul* on navy rafts.

21. Jackie Gothard, president of Beth Israel, showing me the damage wrought by Hurricane Katrina

"Becky, our non-Jewish secretary, took these Torahs from ZAKA – with the parchment just falling apart – and buried them temporarily in her back yard, because the cemeteries were still under water. She was our 'righteous Gentile'!"

Once they were allowed to return to the area after Katrina, Jackie and her volunteers worked day and night to see what could be salvaged. "I had a good cry when I first stepped into the *shul*," she said. "We began collecting the *siddurim* [prayer books]. I was tempted, out of curiosity and nostalgia, to open them up and read the dedications. Would you believe it, the very first one I opened said, 'Dedicated to my mom, the first female president of Congregation Beth Israel.' That was me!

"We buried 3,000 holy books. The men formed long lines at the cemetery, handing one or two at a time down the line until they were placed in a large mass grave.

"Meyer Lachoff, Irwin's father, died in a nursing home two days after Katrina hit. He had been our *gabbai* at Beth Israel for forty years. When he was finally put to rest at the Beth Israel Cemetery [he had to be temporarily buried elsewhere until the water subsided], we found that there happened to be one burial plot right next to his, in an otherwise crowded area. We took all seven Torahs and buried them next to Meyer. How appropriate it was: the *gabbai* who watched over our beloved Torahs for forty years would now continue to watch over them in perpetuity!

"We had our first services on Yom Kippur in a Comfort Inn. How we cried! We needed our Beth Israel back. We needed *machzorim* [holiday prayer books] too," Jackie recalled. "Someone called from a nursing home in Monsey, New York, to tell me a story. He said they were once in desperate need of *machzorim* a long time ago, because they were just starting out, and an old *shul* in New Orleans, Chevra Thilim (long since gone), generously donated many *machzorim* to help them out. Now, many years later, their *gabbai* had passed away, and new *machzorim* were donated in his memory. Would we like to have the old

22. "The parchment is consumed." The final burial place for over 3,000 *seforim* (holy books).

הנבלין נשרפין והאותיות פורחות למעלה

"THE PARCHMENT IS CONSUMED, BUT THE LETTERS FLOAT UP ON HIGH"

HERE REST MORE THAN 3,000 HOLY BOOKS REMOVED FROM CONGREGATION BETH ISRAEL IN THE AFTERMATH OF HURRICANE KATRINA. WE BURY THESE PAGES, BUT THEIR LETTERS ENDURE

DEDICATED AUGUST 31, 2008

HURRICANE KATRINA
AUGUST 29, 2005

BOOK BURIAL
DECEMBER 21, 2005

23. "Let all bear witness to the tears of our community." Inscription carved into the headstone at the burial site of seven Torah scrolls lost in the waters of Katrina. Meyer Lachoff, *gabbai* of Beth Israel for forty years, buried next to his beloved Torahs.

machzorim back? We were overjoyed! We told him of the loss of our longtime *gabbai*. They overnighted all the *machzorim*, originally from New Orleans, and put the following inscription in each one: 'In memory of Beth Israel lost to Katrina, and in memory of our *gabbai*, and Meyer Lachoff, *gabbai* of Beth Israel.' It was such a touching gesture."

Jackie told me that the winter before Katrina, a retirement community in New Jersey asked them, through an old friend, if they had a spare Torah to sell them. Since they had eight Torahs, they were able to spare one. Before sending it, they made a new cover for the Torah with the inscription that it was from the Beth Israel congregation. After they lost all of their Torahs, the New Jersey *shul* contacted Jackie and asked if Beth Israel would like their Torah back. "I said no. This was Hashem's [G-d's] way of saving a *sefer Torah* from being lost with the others – it was *bashert* [predestined]!"

After the hurricane, the rabbi of the *shul* left New Orleans with his family. The situation seemed bleak. "So we're interviewing for a new rabbi," Irwin tells me, "and after a few candidates, Rabbi Uri Topolosky calls me and asks about the position. 'Well, I said, we have no *shul*, we have no Torahs, we have nothing, and we're probably not going to make it, but if you want to come down, okay. He did, and he took it! This rabbi was our gift – our survival.'"

When I met Rabbi Topolsky, I could see why. Effervescent and energetic, the rabbi had gone from Phoenix to Silver Spring to Riverdale, and had found his calling in July 2007 in New Orleans, filling the void left by Katrina.

As I was visiting at Purim time, I asked the rabbi if he sees any Purim relevance in the Katrina experience. "We have learned," he answered wisely, "that when one door closes, another opens. Often, after a tragedy, the general public tends to forget. But in Judaism, part of our responsibility is to remember and learn. When we read the Megillah on Purim, we acknowledge that each experience we face as Jews, whether good or bad, offers something to learn, something on which to build. Look, nobody wanted Haman and nobody wanted Katrina! We were losing in numbers, before Katrina. But out of disaster comes an opportunity for resurgence – to make a difference, to participate, to lead, and shape Jewish life in New Orleans."

24. Rabbi Uri Topolosky, wife Dahlia, and son Itai entertaining the seniors at Woldenberg Village

Out of disaster comes an opportunity

And that is why he took the position. "For our family," Rabbi Topolsky continued, "the most attractive offer is the opportunity to make a difference. Unlike many other communities around the country, New Orleans offers the gift of necessity. Each person has the opportunity to have a great impact."

Just before Rosh Hashanah in his first year in New Orleans, Rabbi Topolosky came striding up to the *shul*, dragging a bunch of colorful, festive balloons! Responding to the questioning looks of his congregants – who were still despondent from the effects of the disaster not two years earlier – he said that this wasn't an anniversary, but a birthday, a time for renewal. Soon after, he redid the synagogue's website, using the biblical symbol of a dove with an olive branch. When the dove returned with the branch to Noah, who was waiting for a sign of hope, Noah rejoiced because he realized that this was a sign that the worst was over. The rabbi succeeded in lifting everyone's spirits; they began to view the future with new optimism.

I have this story in mind as I sit in the hundred-year-old *shul*, Congregation Anshe Sfard, waiting to hear the Megillah read on Purim night. The members of Beth Israel and Anshe Sfard are here together to celebrate as one. The acting rabbi of Anshe Sfard gets up to read the Megillah in his distinctive Yemenite accent in front of 200 people. A six-piece jazz band sits nearby to drown out Haman's name, New Orleans style. (What do you expect in the jazz capital of the world?) And then there's the vibrant Rabbi Uri, getting up and booing, egging everyone on, protesting vocally (in jest), when the reader tries unsuccessfully to run through Haman's name without the congregants noticing. Watching him run up and down the aisles, getting the children and adults involved, I wonder if, for a minute, he forgot what happened to this community just a few short years ago.

25. Acting Rabbi Nachum Amosi, named after two prophets, reads the Megillah as if he were reading a letter (as we are supposed to). Originally from Yemen, he was sent from Israel to help out after Katrina.

26. BOOO! Reaction from Rabbi Uri Topolosky as he ensures that Rabbi Amosi doesn't run too fast through Haman's name.

No, he never forgets it any more than his congregants do, he tells me later. "Our building sits there," he says, "sort of a relic, a shell of what it once was, and it's incredibly intense to walk through there." Yet, the memory cannot obliterate the festive Purim atmosphere; even tragedy cannot obstruct our annual Jewish buoyancy. Despite everything, mirth bubbles to the surface.

Rabbi Mendel Rivkin, a Chabad rabbi in uptown New Orleans, offered a new and very meaningful insight. "As a people," he said, "we learn to see miracles in everything. The commentators say that when we read the story of the Megillah, we are obligated to read it as if it were happening now. How ironic! We Jews wrote the textbook on how to handle a crisis. We stayed for Katrina, until the breach in the levees forced our evacuation. And the Jewish community's response, both locally and nationally, was far ahead of everyone else. The idea of viewing the Megillah as if it is happening now means that sometimes, like the Jews of Shushan, we need a wakeup call and a fresh start. Do you know that after Katrina there has been a slow, yet steady influx of new Jewish residents in New Orleans? There's a new energy here!"

There is a "for sale" sign in front of the Beth Israel complex near Lake Pontchartrain. The congregation must look for a new site for their sanctuary. To date, three Torahs have been donated from Jews in other parts of the country. I watch Rabbi Topolosky, with his equally energetic wife, Dahlia, and their two boys, constantly on the move in a flurry of activity – like a spinning *gragger*, if you will – at the Purim carnival at the Jewish Community Center, then at the retirement home for the aged. His guitar never leaves his arms, and he wears a constant joyous smile. "I'm a Purim Jew!" he laughs.

When Rabbi Topolosky contemplates the phrase *v'nahafoch hu* in the Megillah, he sees not a world turned upside down, but an opportunity to turn ourselves upside down – to redefine ourselves.

27. *L'chaim*! Rabbi Mendel Rivkin proposing a toast at the Chabad Purim *seudah*. *L'chaim* is always welcome in the land of Katrina!

We learn to see miracles in everything

"We have an opportunity here to spin a wonderful story out of absolute destruction," he explains. He has made that opportunity his challenge, his mission.

Yes, we can view this Jewish community as a microcosm of the Purim story, I conclude. The original event was followed by a happy ending, the building of the Second Holy Temple in Jerusalem. Perhaps, with the renewed enthusiasm of a revived community and the generosity of Jews everywhere, a new *shul* will rise on high ground, and we will catch a glimpse of that dove returning to New Orleans.

28–29. "When one door closes, another opens." So says Rabbi Uri, as he, Dahlia, and sons Itai and Elyon bring joy and hope to everyone they meet. Here, they entertain the seniors at Woldenberg Village. Rabbi Topolosky goes everywhere with his guitar. I'm told he visited Sderot in the south of Israel, near Gaza, as the rockets were raining down daily. He ran with everyone, Israelis and Arabs alike, to the shelters, leaving everything behind…except his guitar. He started playing in the shelter and kept on playing until the place was rocking with the music!

30. Congregation Shaare Tefillah, or "Gates of Prayer." Its small wood structure was purchased in 1855.

31. Later Gates of Prayer building, now abandoned

32. Some of the oldest headstones in the city were found at the Gates of Prayer Cemetery, 1850.

33. The second Beth Israel building (1924) is now a Baptist church, which has retained the menorah, tablets, and the Stars of David.

34. Anshe Sfard was not only built in 1924, the same year as Beth Israel, but was designed by the same architect.

35. This photo was taken inside the original Beth Israel, in 1917, during the announcement of the Balfour Declaration, a statement of support for forming the State of Israel. The man in the lower left corner with hands to his eyes is the Reform Rabbi Heller, an ardent Zionist, unlike most of his Reform colleagues of that time.

36. Opened by Theodore Danziger in 1848, Danziger's was one of the leading dry goods houses in the South.

. Kosher Cajun New York Deli and Grocery: ur source for everything kosher in New Orleans

38. Touro Infirmary, serving the public for over 150 years

39. Ad for Touro Infirmary, 1850s. Terms: $1–5 per day, slaves $1 per day.

40. First issue of the *Jewish Ledger*, 1895, one of the most influential Jewish journals in the country

41. Moise Steeg, Jr., continued the work of his grandfather, until he left to serve in World War II. Publication officially stopped in 1963.

Katrina

42. Rescuing a Torah submerged in ten feet of water for three weeks.

43. Irwin Lachoff, author and historian, being married in the main sanctuary of beautiful Beth Israel just months before Hurricane Katrina

44. Jackie standing in the midst of the ruins of the main sanctuary, reminiscing about the once stately *shul*

45. Gloved volunteer removing one of the seven lost Torahs for eventual burial, under the watchful eye of a National Guardsman

IN MEMORY OF
ABRAHAM J. & ALICE W. GOLDBERG
אברהם יעקב ועלקא גולדברג
BY GRANDCHILDREN
JONAH D. GOLDBERG   BRENDA S. HECKLIN
AARON R. GOLDBERG   LARRY E. HECKLIN

46–48. Seven Torahs, countless *talleisim* (prayer shawls), 3,000 holy books, shofars (rams' horns), and hundreds of pieces of Judaica lost in the devastation.

49. Sadly, Beth Israel for sale

AVAILABLE
504-831-2363

The hope of Purim

50. Did you ever see an alligator do *hagbah* (lift the open Torah)?

51. "Their laughter and their loveliness can clear a cloudy day" – John Denver

52–53. How apropos for the community: "Who is rich? One who is happy with his lot."

54. Playing the *gragger* (noisemaker used when the evil Haman's name is spoken) with the jazz band

55. The jazz band, Haman, and the Megillah

איזהו עשיר השמח בחלקו

56. Audiovisual bonus! Reading the Megillah while the story is shown on screen.

57. Is this heaven? Purim *seudah* and a New Orleans jazz band.

The New Orleans Community-Wide PURIM PARADE

58. Boxes for the *machatzis hashekel* (the half coin used traditionally on Purim) and *matanot la'evyonim* (gifts for the needy)

59. Rabbi Uri escorting Rabbi Amosi under the ever present (but with a twist) New Orleans umbrella

60. Rabbi Uri entertains the seniors and kids alike on Purim.

61. Rabbi Uri and family giving hope through music and *tefillah* at the Purim Carnival

My thanks to
Rabbi Uri Topolosky,
Dahlia Topolosky,
Sandra Carp,
Jackie Gothard,
Irwin Lachoff,
Rabbi Mendel Rivkin,
Moise Steeg,
Touro Infirmary Archives,
and Linda Epstein.

Bibliography

Friedman, Lee Max. *Jewish Pioneers and Patriots*. Philadelphia: Jewish Publication Society of America, 1943.

Lachoff, Irwin, and Catherine C. Kahn. *The Jewish Community of New Orleans*. Charleston, SC: Arcadia Publishing, 2005.

Simons, Andrew, Irwin Lachoff, et al. *Jews of New Orleans: An Archival Guide*. New Orleans: Greater New Orleans Archivists, 1998.

Zevin, Rabbi Shlomo Yosef. *The Festivals in Halachah: An Analysis of the Development of the Festival Laws*. New York: ArtScroll/Mesorah, 1991.

Photo Attributions

All numbered photos from the author's collection except as follows. Photos 1, 42, 45: Beth Israel archives; 4, 5, 38: Touro Infirmary archives; 7, 8, 10, 11, 12, 16, 29, 36: Lachoff and Kahn, *The Jewish Community of New Orleans* (Charleston, SC: Arcadia Publishing, 2005); 17: Sarah Carp; 40: Moise Steeg Jr.; 43: Irwin Lachoff.

"...כִּי אוֹת הִוא בֵּינִי וּבֵינֵיכֶם לְדֹרֹתֵיכֶם, לָדַעַת כִּי אֲנִי ה' מְקַדִּשְׁכֶם."

שמות לא:יג

"...For it is a sign between Me and you
throughout your generations,
that you may know that I am the Lord
Who makes you holy."

Exodus 31:13

Dallas, Texas

Shaare Tefilla
Tiferet Israel
Akiba Academy
Yavneh Academy
Dallas Jewish Historical Society

Dallas, Texas

Symbols of Continuity in the Lone Star State

Abe and Rosa, a young immigrant couple from eastern Europe, get off the boat in New York in 1900 and Abe is diagnosed with "lung problems." He is told to go out West for a cure. Promising Rosa to send for her soon, he boards a train for Arizona, but it stops in Dallas late Friday afternoon. He gets off the train so he won't have to ride on Shabbos. A policeman directs him to the Orthodox synagogue, Tiferet Israel. By Sunday, Abe's lungs are feeling better, he's had a great Shabbos, and he sees no reason to continue on to Arizona. Before long, he brings Rosa to Dallas and it becomes their home. What one Shabbos can do for a family!*

In the Torah, Shabbos is called in Hebrew *os*, a sign or symbol. There are many times in the Torah that this word is used in reference to a *mitzvah* or an event. Three of those times are quintessential events of continuity for the Jewish people: *bris milah*, circumcision (Genesis 17:11); putting on *tefillin*, phylacteries, first done when a boy reaches bar mitzvah (Deuteronomy 6:8); and our weekly spiritual recharge, called Shabbos (Exodus 31:17).

1. Postcard depicting the lighting of the Shabbos candles. Made in Germany, c. 1914.

The stereotypical Texan stands tall, hands on hips, proclaiming that everything is bigger in Texas. Among the myriad precepts in Judaism, there is no concept that has a bigger impact on our people than Shabbos.

The Talmud (*Beitzah* 16a) recounts a Midrash about Shabbos. Early in the history of the Jews as a nation, G-d says, "I have a good gift in My treasure house whose name is Shabbos. I seek to grant this gift to the Jewish people." The great author of *Sfas Emes*, Rabbi Yehudah Aryeh Alter of Gur – whose profound discourses have been an inspiration for generations – says that He gave us this gift not because of our merit, but because of our potential. Our potential for what? The Gerrer Rebbe tells us that Shabbos is such a wonderful gift because its holiness brings the potential for *achdus*, unity, into the hearts of all Jews. It is the greatest unifying force. Rearranging the last five letters of "continuity," we see that in order to have continuity in a people, you must first have unity.

---

*   This story was told by Irwin Waldman about his parents in a film called *A Dallas Jewish Journey*, sponsored by the Dallas Jewish Historical Society.

Shabbos is the best time to appreciate the wonders of creation, when families are together, without mundane worries of the week. This unity is recreated every week.

And our story in Dallas is one of family unity and national continuity, all that Shabbos represents. It is the story of three symbols: Shabbos, *bris milah*, and bar mitzvah. I am very fortunate. I am in Dallas for only four days, but I will have the honor of witnessing all three.

2–4. Three *osos* (signs)

Throughout my travels to the Jewish communities in the United States, I have found that their histories are invariably written from their "East Coast" origins. Fleeing persecution in Europe, Jews board a crowded ship for America, stare with moist eyes as they pass the Statue of Liberty on their way into the *goldene medinah*, and join the massive crowds of immigrants at the embarkation point at Ellis Island.

But the story of many Texas Jews begins at a port far from Ellis Island and its quintessential statue, and far indeed from the colorful ambience of the Lower East Side.

In fact, the earliest Jews to arrive in this area came with the conquistador explorers, coming from the Sephardic (Spanish-Portuguese) communities. The untamed Southwest, teeming with hundreds of Indian tribes and Spanish Catholics, must not have seemed very inviting, with the fires of Inquisitions still fresh in their minds.

A wave of Jewish immigration began with Jews from Central Europe – Alsace-Lorraine and Germany – in the 1820s. Before 1821, Jews who openly practiced their religion could not legally live in the Spanish colony of Texas, where only Catholics could take up residence. After the Louisiana Purchase of 1803, boundaries bordering Texas were vague and there was considerable push and pull between Mexico and the United States.

5. Map showing borders of the Louisiana Purchase and Texas. There was a constant struggle for possession between the US and Mexico.

Rabbi Henry Cohen, the first researcher to document Texas Jewish history in the early 1900s, writes of Henri Castro, a surveyor and explorer who came to the area in 1820. He was descended from the old Portuguese family of de Castro, and was probably a *converso* himself. During his surveying tours, Cohen tells us, Castro would leave his companions to retire to the forest for the purpose of "binding his phylacteries" (*tefillin*). How important was this *os* (sign) to this "secret Jew"?

While not actively establishing communities, Jews had their share of heroes in the early days. A. Wolf, called "the Jewish Davy Crockett," brandished a sword at the Battle of the Alamo in 1836, where he lost his life. But shortly after, when the Mexican general Santa Anna lost the decisive battle of San Jacinto to General Sam Houston, the Republic of Texas was born, opening the way for increased Jewish settlement. By 1838, Jews were living in the Texas towns of Bolivar, Nacogdoches, San Antonio, and Galveston.

Many of the early Jewish settlers at the time of Texas statehood (1846) began – as was the wont of Jews all over the young country – as backpacking peddlers. The settlement pattern of Texas Jews reflected that of Jews all over the country: first, the formation of a benevolent society to acquire land for a cemetery, followed by a synagogue. The first cemeteries were established in Galveston (1852), Houston (1854), and San Antonio (1856). The first Jewish congregation in Texas was the Orthodox Congregation Beth Israel in Houston, founded in 1859 (it turned Reform fifteen years later). An Orthodox congregation, Tiferet Israel, was founded in Dallas (1890) and still flourishes today with a more traditional service. Other *shul*s founded at the turn of the century in Dallas include Agudas Achim and Anshe Sphard.

6. Shearith Israel, or "the Jackson St. Shul," c. 1892. In 1884, twelve men gathered in the back of Wasserman's store on Elm St. to form a *minyan*.

DEDICATION OF CONGREGATION OF ANSHE SPHARD SYNAGOGUE
SEPT 6, 1936

7. Dedication of Congregation Anshe Sphard Synagogue, an original turn-of-the-century synagogue, c. 1936

A unique feature of the early pioneer years in Texas was that new Jewish arrivals scattered all over the state. By the mid-1800s, Jewish communities emerged in such towns as Texarcana, Palestine, Amarillo, Crockett, and Lubbock. This can be attributed to the fact that new Jewish settlements popped up, with their cemeteries and synagogues, wherever there were newly established railroad lines. An interesting example of that phenomenon can be found today in the small town of Corsicana. In 1871, a new railroad line came into the area, and in that very same year, Jewish merchants came in and established their cemetery. Predictably, their first synagogue, Temple Beth-El, was built soon after. Both still exist today. Isaac Leeser, the publisher of the Philadelphia-based *Occident*, the preeminent Jewish newspaper of the nineteenth century, commented on his Texas readership: "The *Occident* goes out to fully one hundred small places where we have a single subscriber in each!"

Frontier Jews not only survived, but many retained their Judaism, often in astonishing ways. In 1852, in the absence of a *mohel*, a member of the Galveston community performed his infant's *bris* himself. Another couple in Houston resolved to postpone the *bris* for their son until a *mohel* was available. The ceremony was performed eight years later! These were the sacrifices that one made for this *os* of continuity.

Corsicana Hebrew Cemetery, established 1875. This Jewish community was typical among many scattered across Texas. Metal staircase inscription: "Made by the Oil City Ironworks, Corsicana, 1918."

Frontier Jews not only survived, but many retained their Judaism, often in astonishing ways.

9. Temple Beth-El, Corsicana. Jewish settlers arrived in 1871, the year the railroad lines were built to the area. Built in 1900, the building features octagonal towers, a Star of David in the center, and windows depicting the two tablets of the law, just below. It is interesting that these Russian immigrants chose to use the onion-shaped domes found commonly on the Russian Orthodox churches of the eighteenth and nineteenth centuries. They were used to symbolize burning candles.

Sometimes, all one needed was a little Texas imagination to perform *mitzvos*. Helena Landa (no relation to this author) spent weeks preparing matzoh for family and friends for the Passover Seder. The dough was rolled out on the table in thin long sheets and a large tin form was used to cut them to the proper size. But how would she punch the all-important air holes in the dough? Scanning the room, she came up with spiked cowboy spurs, and quickly ran them over the dough! How Texan can you get?

Jonas Weil, an early Jewish pioneer after statehood, was an actual "rainmaker." He would explode a hot-air balloon filled with sulfuric acid and iron shavings, which was often followed by a downpour! Another Jew who integrated well into turn-of-the-century Texas culture was Hungarian-born Maurice Faber, a Reform rabbi. He served as chaplain of St. John's Masonic Lodge, until the Ku Klux Klan infiltrated that organization in 1915. Appointed by the governor as the first clergyman to sit on the Board of Regents of the University of Texas, he was amused to find that he was referred to officially as "Father Faber"!

Rainmaking Nothing New to Texas Ranchers

By GRADY STILES

RAINMAKING is nothing particularly new to Texas ranchers; they were flirting with the clouds 60

Editor's Note.—Jonas Weil, member of a pioneer South Texas ranching family, in the accompanying

10. Let it rain! Jonas Weil, rainmaker, from *The Cattleman*, 1940.

Egg Eaters and Merchant Princes

Alex. Simon,
North East Corner of the Pa Square,
DALLAS, TEXAS,
Wholesale and Retail Dealer in
DRY GOODS, GROCERIES,
READY MADE CLOTHING,
Crockery, Wood and Glass Wardrobe Paints, Oils,
&c &c
NOW OPENING, a large and complete assortment
of SPRING AND SUMMER GOODS,
Cheaper than the Cheapest!
Dallas, Texas May 8, 1858–45:tf

11. "Cheaper than the Cheapest!" Ad for Alex Simon, the first Jewish settler of Dallas, found in the *Dallas Herald*. He served in the Confederate army.

The Dallas Jewish community is one of the oldest in the state, as the frontier town welcomed newcomers to help guarantee safety against hostile Indians, outlaws, and the challenges of nature. The first Jewish settler in Dallas was a merchant, Alex Simon, in 1858. His advertisement read, "My merchandise is cheaper than the cheapest!"

The impact of early Jewish merchants on fledgling Dallas is evident in a comment of a visitor upon seeing shops closed all along Main Street for the Jewish New Year in 1865. He remarked in the French periodical *Archives Israélites*, "If Jews ever left the city, nothing would reward the interest of an observer."

GTT (Gone to Texas!) was printed on the doorposts of many southern residences after the Civil War. During this time, Dallas grew because it was not touched by the war and economic opportunity was there. When the railroad came through in 1868, a new wave of pioneer entrepreneurs, known as the "merchant princes," arrived in Dallas. These men started off as peddlers and were known as "egg eaters," signifying their diets on the road, which consisted mainly of eggs, the only kosher food they could find. Numerous retail stores – later to become chain stores – were started by these newcomers, including Kahn's, Zales, and Neiman Marcus.

Jewish Dallas experienced a watershed year in 1872, heralded by the arrival of fifteen Jewish families led by the Sanger brothers. These enterprising young men opened the first Jewish-run dry goods store, which became the largest Texas dry goods chain. Their inventory included Bowie knives, harnesses, saddles, pistols, and musical instruments. (How's that for a well-rounded inventory?) Not forgetting their roots, the Sangers helped found the first Jewish organization – the Hebrew Benevolent Association, in 1872.

12. Sangor Bros. dry goods store, c. 1890. The original store opened in 1859.

With the mass immigration of the eastern European Jews, the centers of Orthodoxy became concentrated in Houston and Dallas, with Jewish newspapers established in both – the *Jewish Herald Voice* in Houston (1906) and the *Texas Jewish Post* of Dallas (1946).

The Galveston Movement

Credit for the most definitive presentation of the history of Texas Jewry goes to the aforementioned Rabbi Henry Cohen (1863–1952), who served Congregation B'nai Israel in Galveston from 1888 until his death in 1952. Along with Rabbi David Lefkowitz of Dallas, he interviewed as many early settlers and their families as possible, producing a historical account of Texas Jewry in 1936 for the Texas Centennial. However, his most definitive contribution was his integral role in the "Galveston Movement."

Between 1865 and 1924, two hundred thousand of the immigrants who came to America did not sail through the shadow of the Statue of Liberty. Their journey took them south through the Gulf of Mexico to the port of Galveston, Texas, one of the largest immigrant ports of nineteenth- and twentieth-century America. It has been known as the "Forgotten Gateway" and the "Ellis Island of the West."

When there was talk of closing New York's gates of immigration in the early 1900s, Rabbi Cohen and others devised a method to divert the Jews (fleeing the pogroms of Russia) away from the congested communities of the East Coast. Two possible ports were

Charleston and New Orleans. But Charleston wanted only Anglo-Saxon immigrants and New Orleans was in constant threat of yellow fever. Thus was born the "Galveston Movement." Between 1907 and 1914, thousands of immigrants disembarked on the Texas shore, with Rabbi Cohen meeting virtually every ship and directing them everywhere from Texas to Fargo, North Dakota.

In a film titled *West of Hester Street*, a "greenhorn" confessed, "I told them I was a blacksmith. So who knew from a blacksmith? I had to say something…. So, I became a peddler. Peddler schmeddler…if it earned me an honest living, I'd do it!"

A typical immigrant story is told of Abraham Rosenthal, who came to Dallas in 1904. He was a *shochet* and the *chazzan* at Shearith Israel. When he sent his fifteen-year-old son, Harry, to buy cattle, the boy herded the cattle through the Dallas streets. Even in 1906, Dallas was trying to establish city gentility. The lad was given a ticket for "driving too large a herd" through downtown! What a strange place America is, the perplexed father must have thought – *nu*, what size herd would have been acceptable?

Rabbi Cohen's deep emotional involvement in this movement comes to life in the story told of an immigrant stowaway, Deninchick, who was threatened with deportation and inevitable execution in Russia. Unable to persuade local authorities, Cohen met with President Howard Taft, who denied his request as well. Yet Taft remarked, "How wonderful how you Jews do so much for each other."

"He is not Jewish," the rabbi exclaimed, "but rather Greek Catholic!" Stunned, the president released Deninchick to the rabbi's custody.

An ardent supporter of a Jewish state in Palestine, Rabbi Cohen's enthusiasm certainly inspired early Zionist feelings at the turn of the century. At a 1909 convention in Waco, the Texas Zionist Association adopted plans to purchase land in Palestine for a colony called "Texas." In 1934, they created "Nachalot Texas" for Jewish colonies in Palestine. Because of this constant, strong support for Zionism, Texas was often a stepping-off point for such notables as Chaim Weizmann and David Ben-Gurion.

13. Historic visit: Chaim Weizmann (second from left), president of the World Zionist Organization, on a visit to Dallas in 1924. On the steps of the YMHA center.

During the height of the Galveston Movement, the pioneer Jews in Dallas lived in an area called "Deep Elm," near Elm Street. The ultimate combination of Harlem and Delancey Street, it was a place of Yiddish conversation and calls to "get a bargain," along with the sounds of "Black Blues."

14. Elm St., 1884

"Oyvey un dulles"

I was very interested in finding someone who remembered the old Jewish neighborhood, someone who could give me a tour of the streets the Jews called home. To my rescue came Ginger Jacobs, born and raised in Dallas, who is a Jewish historian extraordinaire, an author, and a founder of the Dallas Jewish Historical Society. Her husband, Mike Jacobs, is an author and Holocaust survivor of five years in ghettos and concentration camps, where he lost his mother, father, and five siblings. Mike is the founder of the Dallas Holocaust Memorial Center. They both have committed themselves to teaching students of all ages about the destruction that hatred causes, and the power of faith.

15. Ginger Jacobs, author, historian, founder of the Dallas Jewish Historical Society, and my wonderful guide, shows me the South Dallas block where she was raised.

"My father came through Galveston in 1914 and picked up sacks to fill with peddling goods. When the bags became worn and unusable, he would repair them, having no money to buy new ones. One day, a merchant approached him to buy his repaired bags and that became his business for decades!"

"I grew up in South Dallas in the 1930s and '40s, and I remember Goldin's, the kosher butcher shop – with that wonderful barrel of pickles in the front of the store! Ninety percent of the Dallas Jewish population lived in that area, home of the original Dallas Jews." She remembered that there was one rule in the house that stood out among all the others: "Whether in *shul* or at home, you never interrupt Daddy when he's *davening*!"

16. Blatt's Bakery on Forest Ave., c. 1923

Ginger went on to tell me that she went to Talmud Torah five days a week from the age of five until she was eighteen. It was *Ivrit b'Ivrit* – the Hebrew language taught in Hebrew. This was very unusual for those days – speaking and writing Hebrew was not yet accepted in most Jewish schools. The curriculum was also groundbreaking for the era: prayers, *Chumash* (Bible), *Nevi'im* (Prophets), *historia* (Jewish history). She described it as "an intense program of being totally immersed in the Hebrew language." Way ahead of its time, the Talmud Torah became known as one of the top Hebrew schools in the country. "It served as a model for the first Dallas day school of 1961 and it was crucial to the continuity of our Jewish community."

Reverend Abraham Frand was the *chazzan*, as well as the community's *shochet* and *mohel*, and his "Tin Lizzie" (Model T Ford) was something of a local spectacle. He would slaughter chickens in the yard behind the kosher meat shop, or bring them to a customer's house and *shecht* them there for 25 cents. "I was told," Ginger said, "that in the 1930s, when business was bad, there was a butcher who would throw nickels on the street and people would come running to his store." I guess you could call it the first stimulus package.

Eventually, one pawnshop after another emerged in the "Deep Elm" area, as immigrant peddlers prospered and "graduated" to running pawnshops. Elm Street was alive with Jews intent on earning a living in this land of promise. "In the afternoon, they would get together to form a *minyan* – the pawnbrokers, tailors, shoe repairmen, and liquor store owners."

17. Uncle Sam's Pawnshop on Elm St. was one of many in the 1930s.

Ginger took me to the block she grew up on, and pointed down the street. "See down the block," she said, smiling, "that highway wasn't there. Railroad tracks were there, and cows would graze alongside the tracks. We would wave to the conductor as the train went by."

She was an active Zionist from the age of eight. "In anticipation of the United Nations vote on the Jewish state, we all gathered at the home of Rabbi Levine, the principal of our Hebrew school and founder of the Zionist Camp Habonim [1939]. What a celebration we had!"

On our tour, Ginger and I passed Ervay Street and it reminded her of a famous local story. A Jewish immigrant writes home to his mother in Poland wanting to tell her that he moved to Ervay Street in Dallas. He writes in the only language he knows, Yiddish, saying he moved to "*Oyvey un dulles*," which, loosely translated, means, "Woe is me, in misery and sickness!" (Fortunately for the distressed mom, it was all cleared up in the next letter.)

What about anti-Semitism? Oh, it was there, Ginger assured me. The Ku Klux Klan thrived in Texas in the 1920s, but Jews weren't their main target. Moreover, people like Rabbi Henry Cohen formed a potent opposition to the Klan's activities. The story is told of the Jewish shoe salesman who was able to recognize the masked Klansmen by the shoes they wore – because they all shopped in his store. Another legendary story is about an important Klansman who tried to convince a friend to join the Klan. "I can't! I'm Jewish!" the man answered in surprise. "That's too bad," the disappointed recruiter replied, "you would have made a good Klansman!"

18. Ku Klux Klan at the height of their power in the 1920s

Four Generations Come Together

For me, there is no greater evidence of the continuity of our people then observing a family of four generations preparing and celebrating a Shabbos together. I'm at the home of Rabbi Jeffrey and Naomi Schrager, along with their three children, Naomi's parents, and her grandmother. I watch as they set up multiple sets of Shabbos candlesticks representing untold histories going back over a hundred years.

To the matriarch of these four generations, great-grandmother Evelyn Moore, family is "everything." Each family is a microcosm of the nation and it's the key to *achdus*, the unity of our people.

Evelyn was born in Houston in 1924, to parents who had come through Ellis Island and then New Orleans. Like so many other young men, her father came first, and then had to earn enough money to bring over his wife and relatives.

"Father used to tell us stories about Jews who would purchase a horse and buggy, then go to 'Produce Row' to pick up bananas and oranges to sell. They didn't know much English, so when an English-speaking merchant in his horse and buggy would yell out, 'Bananas! Twenty-five cents a bunch!' the new peddler would quickly align his horse and buggy behind him and yell out, 'Same thing!'

"When I was eight, my father borrowed money from a bank to buy a truck for his new scrap metal business. Every few months, my mother would give me $300 and I would hop on a streetcar and bring the money to the bank. Seeing this, a friend said to my mother, '*Du bist meshugah?* Are you crazy giving so much money to such a little child? It could be stolen!' But my mother knew just what she was doing. There was no safer place than the pocket of an eight-year-old. Who would suspect that a child would be carrying so much money?

19. Shabbos tradition through the generations

"I went for a brief period of time to *cheder* and learned to read Hebrew. It almost got me in a lot of trouble! One day, I took my *siddur* home, turned it to the back, and started practicing my Hebrew reading. Suddenly, my father jumps up and yells to my mother, '*Vey iz mir, Evelyn zogt Kaddish!*' (Evelyn is saying *Kaddish*!)

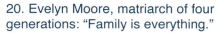

20. Evelyn Moore, matriarch of four generations: "Family is everything."

"In the days of the Great Depression, there was tremendous unity in our neighborhood. My father would barter scrap metal for two chickens. If a neighbor couldn't afford food, he would give them a chicken.

"When I was twenty-five, Israel began selling bonds. Oh, all the Jews in Houston were scrambling to buy $1000 bonds. But they never expected to be paid back – they thought it was just giving *tzedakah* [charity]!"

Remembering a Passover with all the generations together, Jeffrey and Naomi recounted that whenever the children would make too much noise, Great-Grandma Evelyn would say in her best Houston Yiddish, "My mother would have said that you're giving us '*agasinfish*.'" Naomi laughed as she remembered everyone trying to figure out what kind of "fish" she was talking about. Of course, she was really saying *agmas nefesh*, a "troubled soul," in a language spoken only in Texas!

Evelyn stands there with her family, representing four generations of continuity in Texas, lighting the Shabbos candles, singing "*Shalom Aleichem*," and blessing the children. All I could think of while watching this scene of unity and peace were the words of the *Sfas Emes* telling us about this gift of Shabbos, given to us because of our potential to use this unity to return to our roots, to appreciate where we have been and to prepare for where we are going. This is a scene not to be forgotten.

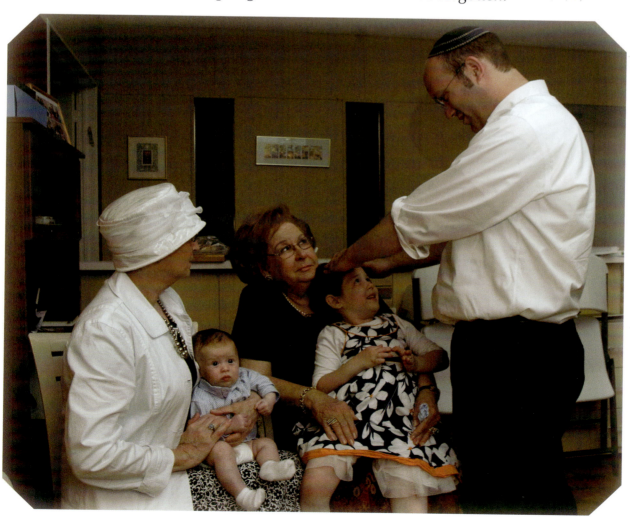

21. Evelyn looks on as her great-granddaughter is blessed by her father, Rabbi Jeffery Schrager, before making Kiddush. See also photo 49.

ישימך ... כשרה, רבקה, רחל ולאה

The next day it was Rosh Chodesh, and I sat with Rabbi Zev Silver, principal of Judaic studies at Akiba Academy, who was proudly watching a student putting on his *tefillin* for the first time as a bar mitzvah. I asked the educator how he felt about his former students. He corrected me gently.

"What's nice about going to these life-cycle events is that these are never 'former students.' They stay your students forever. I have been here long enough that I am now invited to the weddings of students that I taught. Just last year, I was invited to a wedding, in Atlanta, of a student I taught in the fourth grade. Of course, I went, and the whole class was there. Suddenly they all came over and danced in a circle around me! It's an unbelievable feeling."

> "...these are never 'former students.' They stay your students forever."

One day later, I attended a *bris*, the third symbol of our unbreakable national bond with our Creator. I thought of the early pioneers sacrificing so much to do what many of us find easy today. And those immigrants of the Galveston Movement, who maintained such unity of purpose to retain their traditions – how did they persevere?

As I am contemplating this question, the father of the bar mitzvah boy gets up to speak, and he provides me with an answer. He quotes the Netziv, Rabbi Naftali Zvi Yehuda Berlin. "A *tzaddik*, a good person," he says, "falls seven times and gets up seven times. A *rasha*, an evil person, falls once and doesn't get up ever. One has total *emunah*, faith in G-d, and the other has none."

I reflect that this unshakeable *emunah* is at the core of this community. Bolstered by that *emunah*, the parents, grandparents, and great-grandparents of Jewish Dallas turned every dif-

22. Rabbi Zev Silver, principal of Judaic studies at Akiba Academy

ficulty they encountered trying to maintain Jewish life here into a source of unity and strength. They fought hard for every *os*, every sign of Jewish life, and today the Dallas community has boys' and girls' yeshivas, kosher restaurants, a *kollel*, and flourishing *shul*s.

אות היא
לעולם

Os – a word with just three simple Hebrew letters, but how powerful a concept it is. I have been privileged to witness here the three events on which the Torah has conferred the title *os*. As we say of Shabbos, "*os hi l'olam*," it is an eternal symbol of the bond between G-d and His people. And here, under the Texas sun, those signs of our Covenant are more precious and more enduring than ever.

23. Reading the Torah while wearing *tefillin*, a symbol of continuity.

Prayer and education

25. Akiba Academy and Yavneh Academy

24. Hebrew school on Park Row, c. 1935

27. Tiferet Israel on Highland St. was founded in 1890. Photo c. 1916.

28. Tiferet Israel today offers a traditional service and is the home of the "Kosher chili cookoff," a Texas-wide event benefiting many local charities.

29. Interior of Congregation Shaare Tefilla, founded 1986

26. High school students studying on the extraordinary campus of Akiba and Yavneh, which has a deep bond with Israel. A river runs through the campus, representing the Torah flowing from one side of the world to the other. Plants on the campus are indigenous to either Israel or Texas, and the seven species of Israel enumerated in the Torah are grown on campus.

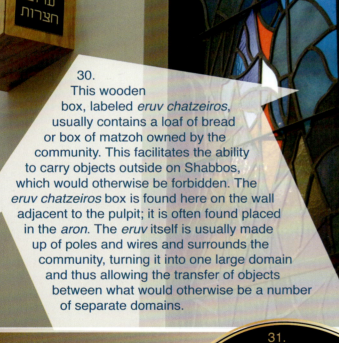

30.
This wooden box, labeled *eruv chatzeiros*, usually contains a loaf of bread or box of matzoh owned by the community. This facilitates the ability to carry objects outside on Shabbos, which would otherwise be forbidden. The *eruv chatzeiros* box is found here on the wall adjacent to the pulpit; it is often found placed in the *aron*. The *eruv* itself is usually made up of poles and wires and surrounds the community, turning it into one large domain and thus allowing the transfer of objects between what would otherwise be a number of separate domains.

31.
This unique *aron* (ark) in Shaare Tefilla has a fascinating origin. The *shul*'s founder, Rabbi Howard Wolk, told me this story: *Chevra* Bikur Cholim, an old *shul* in Bardejov, Czechoslovakia, had a beautiful *aron* which by some miracle survived the Nazi destruction. When a family in Dallas wanted to bring the *aron* to Shaare Tefilla after the Bikur Cholim *shul* had to close, the Polish authorities stripped it and virtually destroyed it. It survived the Holocaust but couldn't survive the Polish authorities. A replica was constructed from memory and placed here in Shaare Tefilla.

Life

32. The Pioneer Cemetery in Dallas, dating from the 1850s, is composed of remnants of four early graveyards. Some of the land was once used by the earliest of Jewish settlers as part of the Hebrew Benevolent Association in 1852.

33. Rev. Abraham Frand, *chazzan*, *shochet* (ritual slaughtere 25 cents per chicken), and *mohel*. He drove a Model T Ford

34. Frand's butcher shop today is the Emerald Grill (with the blue awning).

35. The old Jewish neighborhood: Willow Grove Salon, c. 1903. Baby Jennie Wolfe with grandpa Mattathias Garonzik and uncle Harry.

36. Café Carmel in the new Jewish Dalla

37. *Mishnayot* learning group at Shearith Israel, 1940s

Tefillin as a sign

38. Rendition by unknown artist of father teaching his son to put on *tefillin*, an everlasting sign, helping to secure the bond between Hashem and his people

39—40. Thumbs up for a job well done

41. Covering the Torah and their heads, waiting for the candy to fly towards the bar mitzvah boy from the men and women

42. Collecting his just rewards. There is no source found in the literature for this custom. It started with throwing candy at the *chassan* (groom), wishing him a sweet life. It was later extended to the bar mitzvah, hoping for a sweet life of doing *mitzvos*!

The *bris* as a sign

43. "*Baruch haba*" – the *mohel* and the entire assembly welcome the infant.

44. The *mohel* says the first prayer: "This is the throne of Elijah." Elijah the prophet is invited to sit on the throne because he championed the *mitzvah* of the *bris milah* when no one else would.

45. The *sandak*, or "companion of the child," sits in the designated chair next to the throne of Elijah. The *mohel* quickly (we hope!) performs the *milah* as the father looks on.

46. As grandpa holds the baby, a blessing on the wine is recited and the father gives the name. The custom of naming the boy at the *bris* is connected to the fact that it was in conjunction with the *bris* of Abraham that Hashem changed his name – it symbolizes a whole new identity.

47. "The Child Enters the Covenant," by Moritz Daniel Oppenheim, 1837

זכור את יום השבת לקדשו

Shabbos as a sign

48. No peeking! The blessing is made over at least two Shabbos candles: one corresponding to "Remember the Sabbath day" (Ex. 20:8) and the other for "Observe the Sabbath day" (Deut. 5:12). Four generations welcome the Sabbath as Tamar Schrager, on the left, can't resist a little peek.

49. The family brought in Shabbos early, allowing the author to take these photos before accepting Shabbos himself. Before Kiddush is recited, the father, Rabbi Schrager, blesses the children.

50. Tamar grabs a Shabbos kiss from great-grandma Evelyn Moore, as Kiddush, or sanctification of the Sabbath, is about to begin. Two challahs, representing the double portion of manna that fell on Friday, are covered.

51. When Shabbos is over, Havdalah (separation) is recited, including a blessing over spices to restore the soul saddened by the departure of the Sabbath.

52. Shabbos blessing on the child, c. 1900

53, 54. "L'hadlik ner" (to light the candles); young students at Akiba Academy welcoming the Sabbath (archival photos)

My thanks to
Rabbi Zev Silver,
all the wonderful people
at the Akiba Academy,
Rabbi Jeffrey and Naomi Schrager,
the Dallas Jewish Historical Society,
Rabbi Ari Perl,
Ginger and Mike Jacobs,
and Evelyn Moore.

Bibliography

Grunfeld, Dayan Dr. Isadore. *The Sabbath*. Jerusalem: Feldheim, 1972.

Jacobs, Mike. *Holocaust Survivor: Mike Jacobs' Triumph over Tragedy*. Edited by Ginger Jacobs. Austin, TX: Eakin Press, 2001.

Mondell, Allen, and Cynthia Salzman Mondell. *A Dallas Jewish Journey* (film). Dallas Jewish Historical Society, 2009.

Ornish, Natalie. *Pioneer Jewish Texans: Their Impact on Texas and American History for Four Hundred Years, 1590–1990*. Dallas: Texas Heritage Press, 1989.

Stern, Yosef. *The Gift of Shabbos: Ideas and Insights of the Sfas Emes on the Tefillos, Seudos and Hashkafah of Shabbos*. New York: ArtScroll/Mesorah, 2005.

Weiner, Hollace Ava, and Kenneth D. Roseman. *Lone Stars of David: The Jews of Texas*. Brandeis Series in American Jewish History, Culture, and Life. Waltham, MA: Brandeis University Press, in association with the Texas Jewish Historical Society, 2007.

Photo Attributions

All numbered photos from the author's collection except as follows. Photo 1: American Jewish Archives; 6, 7, 11–14, 16–18, 24, 27, 35, 37: Dallas Jewish Historical Society; 47: Jewish Museum of New York; 52: courtesy of the Jewish Museum of Maryland (accession number 87.137.103); 53, 54: Akiba Academy archives; shoes p. 175: S. Kim Glassman.

„בשר רומז לגשמיות ועל ידי שהצדיק אוכל
הגשמיות ביחודים הוא שואב השפעות מעולמות העליונים."
נועם אלימלך, שמות, פרשת משפטים

"Meat alludes to the commonplace,
but when a *tzaddik* eats of the commonplace,
he draws influence from Heaven above."

Noam Elimelech, Exodus, *Parashat Mishpatim*

Memphis, Tennessee

B'nai Israel
Baron Hirsch Synagogue
Anshei Sphard–Beth El Emeth
Center for Southern Folklore
Peabody Hotel
Graceland
Beale Street

Memphis, Tennessee

Elul and the Que in the Bible Belt

1. Pre-contest grill gridlock in Memphis

Memphis is the largest city in Tennessee and a major commercial force in the South. Just thinking about it conjures images of B.B. King and the blues, Elvis and rock 'n' roll, with strong overtones of working-class culture accompanied by Bible Belt fundamentalism. And barbeques. In fact, food is the clearest symbol of southern distinctiveness. The passwords in Memphis are southern hospitality and the Que.

It's the Hebrew month of Elul in the South, and that means it's time for the Anshei Sphard–Beth El Emeth/Kroger twentieth annual Kosher BBQ Cooking Contest and Festival, quite possibly the year's most anticipated event in Jewish Memphis. In the words of syndicated columnist Ted Roberts, this event has "perfumed the skies over Memphis for nineteen years – the first and only kosher barbeque contest in America, maybe in the whole Diaspora, maybe in the whole solar system." Trust me, we will come back to this mouthwatering topic.

But first, I must ask the question that is no doubt haunting you: how can Jews be comfortable in a place where catfish is easier to find than kreplach? To find the answers, let's start at the beginning.

Located on the bluffs overlooking the Mississippi River, Memphis is in the heart of one of the largest cotton-growing areas in the country. Early on, it was an ideal place for riverboat trade. Because it was founded in 1819, long before the Civil War, it had the uniquely southern characteristics of cotton and slavery.

1b. A booth at the barbecue contest – part of the contest is coming up with witty name for the teams and decorating booths

The First *Shul* – and the First Breakaway!

The established theory concerning Jewish settlement is that Ashkenazic Jews from Germany and a handful of Jews from eastern Europe came to Memphis in the 1830s looking for the economic opportunity and adventure offered by the American thrust for territorial expansion.

However, there is evidence from skeletons found in 1889 in Tennessee that there might have been Jews here as early as 32–769 CE! Engravings on a stone, at first thought to be a Cherokee message, were turned upside down by an expert in Middle Eastern languages who believed the scratchings were Hebrew, and translated them to mean "for Judea." The script was eerily similar to that found on Hebrew coins from around 100 CE.

2. B'nai Israel historic marker. The first permanent Jewish house of worship in Tennessee, it affirmed the American principle of freedom of religion.

Okay, you don't have to believe that one. The first *reliably* documented Jewish presence was of a gentleman named David Hart, a Memphis resident who emigrated from Germany in 1838 to open Hart's Inn and Saloon. The second name attached to Memphis Jewry is Joseph Andrews, who arrived with his wife, Sally, the daughter of Haym Salomon, noted patriot and financial supporter of the American Revolutionary War. Andrews is considered the founder of the Memphis Jewish community, for he donated the land for the first Jewish cemetery when his brother died in 1847. The necessity to care for the cemetery prompted the 1850 formation of the first charitable institution, the Hebrew Benevolent Society. Soon after, the first Yom Kippur service was held by the first congregation, B'nai Israel, followed by the inevitable building fund. The first synagogue was erected using $2,000 given by Judah Touro of New Orleans. This would be the first of

3. Baron Hirsch Cemetery, the earliest Jewish cemetery in Memphis. Note the Israeli flag flying with the American flag, indicating the passion for Israel.

many times that Memphis and New Orleans would help each other in times of need.

With the help of Philadelphia's Isaac Leeser, the Orthodox leader of his time, B'nai Israel hired Rabbi Jacob Peres, who founded the first Hebrew school. While the circumstances are not clear, it seems he was dismissed when it was discovered that his grocery store was open on Shabbos – probably to subsidize his monthly $50 salary. This caused a split in the synagogue: Reform-leaning members stayed at B'nai Israel; in 1862 Orthodox members founded Beth El Emeth ("the true house of G-d"), seemingly sending a message through its name.

It was the forerunner to one of the largest Orthodox congregations in the South, Anshei Sphard–Beth El Emeth. The ironic aspect of this affair is that Jacob Peres was hired as the rabbi of the breakaway Orthodox synagogue Beth El Emeth, and the Peres family became a force for Orthodoxy in the South for decades to come.

Jewish peddlers did very well and eventually opened small stores, which led to larger stores such as Goldsmith's (the first department store in the South) and Lowenstein's. The story is told of one such peddler named Abraham Boshwitz, who arrived in 1850 and went from town to town by horse and wagon. His travels took him all the way to Illinois where, one day, his horse died. After buying a new horse and continuing his journey in the morning, he realized that his horse was blind. When he was refused a refund, he ended up in Springfield, where he consulted with a young, little-known attorney who sued the seller and won. The lawyer's name: Abraham Lincoln.

4. Rabbi Jacob Peres (c. 1852), lecturer, leader, and choir leader. An early force for Orthodoxy in the Deep South.

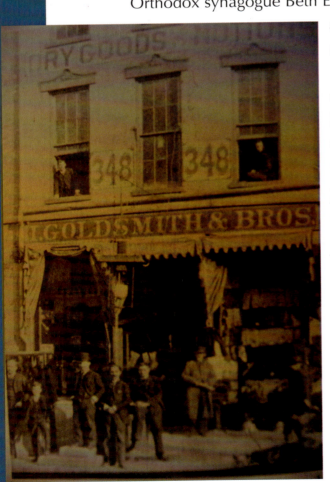

5. Goldsmith & Bros. store, c. 1870. First department store of the South. Their first customer was a little girl named Loretta. The brothers were so delighted that they sent her a gift every holiday season until she died in 1921. Her last gift? A fur coat!

1862

"Old Country" Discrimination and Yellow Fever

Generally acculturated to southern mores by the early 1860s, most Jews in Memphis favored secession from the Union. Although there was little overt anti-Semitism in the history of Jewish Memphis, it was a great shock when General Ulysses S. Grant issued the infamous General Order No. 11, the only anti-Semitic order in American history, in December of 1862. Singling out Jews on suspicion of running contraband during the Civil War, Grant ordered the immediate expulsion of the Jewish population from Tennessee, Mississippi, and Kentucky. Jewish leaders appealed to "father Abraham" Lincoln and he rescinded the order within a few days. A few years later, when the Jews of Memphis campaigned nationally for the defeat of Grant in the presidential election, it marked the only time in recorded American history that the Jewish community took such a totally united action in a presidential election.

> GENERAL ORDERS No. 11.
> HDQRS. 13TH A. C., DEPT. OF THE TENN.,
> Holly Springs, December 17, 1862.
>
> The Jews, as a class violating every regulation of trade established by the Treasury Department and also department orders, are hereby expelled from the department within twenty-four hours from the receipt of this order.
> Post commanders will see that all of this class of people be furnished passes and required to leave, and any one returning after such notification will be arrested and held in confinement until an opportunity occurs of sending them out as prisoners, unless furnished with permit from headquarters.
> No passes will be given these people to visit headquarters for the purpose of making personal application for trade permits.
>
> By order of Maj. Gen. U.S. Grant:
> JNO. A. RAWLINS,
> Assistant Adjutant-General.

6. "The Jews, as a class violating every regulation of trade established by the treasury department and also department orders, are hereby expelled from the department within twenty-four hours from the receipt of this order"

Memphis, as a whole, suffered very little damage due to the Civil War. However, two events in the next two decades would help to define the ability of the Jewish community to survive. From 1873 to 1879, poor sanitary conditions in the city led to the outbreak of a devastating yellow fever epidemic. Half of its population of 40,000 either died from the disease or fled. The Jewish population went from 2,100 to just 300. Tens of thousands of dollars came in from national Jewish organizations such as B'nai B'rith and local ones such as the Hebrew Hospital and Relief Association. Jewish homes around Memphis in the South opened their doors to their brethren, demonstrating the well-known attribute of Jewish (and southern!) hospitality. This attribute would play a large role yet again, when Memphis Jews opened their doors to victims of Hurricane Katrina 150 years later.

I walked through the old Baron Hirsch Cemetery, originally started by Beth El Emeth, and saw many tombstones with fading inscriptions

From 1873 to 1879... half of its population... either died from the disease or fled.... Jewish homes around Memphis in the South opened their doors to their brethren, demonstrating the well-known attribute of Jewish (and southern!) hospitality.

in Hebrew memorializing the staggering number of Jews lost in the yellow fever epidemic, including Rabbi Jacob Peres.

Rabbi Joel Finkelstein, spiritual leader of the present Anshei Sphard–Beth El Emeth congregation, notes that the recorded history of the *shul* "died" in 1877 and reappeared out of nowhere in 1880. Perhaps, he conjectures, some members who had fled the city returned to their homes to rebuild their lives and their community.

7–8. A testament to devastation: Peres tombstone and cemetery registry. Many of the Peres family were lost to the plague. The translation of the tombstone's Hebrew inscription reads, "Moses the son of Peretz fell in the yellow plague in 1873."

CEME[TERY]

Number.	Year.	Month.	[ ].	Day.	Hebrew Date.	NAME.			
38	1873	Oct.	1	Wednesday	תרל"ד יתשרי	Alexander Ma[			
39	1873	Oct.	1	Wednesday	יתשרי	Dora Hertzfelder	20 yrs.	Memphis.	103 Main
40	1873	Oct.	1	Wednesday	יתשרי	Henry Hellman	11 yrs.	Memphis.	104 Cour[
41	1873	Oct.	1	Wednesday	י'תשרי	Moses Klein.	20 yrs.	Germany.	Infirm[
42	1873	Oct.	5	Sunday.	יר'ד'תשרי	Albert Herzfelder.	26 yrs.	Germany.	103 Main
43	1873	Oct.	7	Tuesday	טו'ד'תשרי	H. L. Oppenheim.	31 yrs.	Germany.	51 Mark[
44	1873	Oct.	8	Wednesday	יזתשרי	Isaac Freiberg	65 yrs.	Germany.	41 Popla[
45	1873	Oct.	8	Wednesday	יזתשרי	Infant child of L. Wexler.	2 mos.	Memphis	Exchan[
46	1873	Oct.	8	Wednesday	יזתשרי	Lewis Wexler.	28 yrs.	Germany	Exchan[
47	1873	Oct.	8	Wednesday	יזתשרי	Mrs. H. Beatus.	48 yrs.	Germany.	Second
48	1873	Oct.	9	Thursday.	יח תשרי	Mrs. Charlotte Gaus.	36 yrs.	Russia	Main + Pont[
49	1873	Oct.	9	Thursday	יח תשרי	Mrs. S. B. Warzawski	25 yrs.	Germany	131 Second
50	1873	Oct.	12	Sunday.	כאתשרי	Ludwig Goldstein	38 yrs.	Hungary.	59 Fourth
51	1873	Oct.	12	Sunday	כא תשרי	Nicolai Phillipsen	22 yrs.	Denmark.	Exchange +
52	1873	Oct.	14	Tuesday	כג'ת'שרי	Louis Rosenthal.	46 yrs.	Germany	183 Main
53	1873	Oct.	14	Tuesday	כג'ת'שרי	Theresa Friedlander.	36 yrs.	Germany	Popla[

Life in "the Pinch"

At the turn of the twentieth century, the anti-Semitic tract *The Protocols of the Elders of Zion* was distributed in Russia. A pure hoax based on earlier anti-Semitic writings, it was rumored to have been written by an official of the Russian secret police, exposing the "international conspiracy of the Jews" to dominate the world from generation to generation. Hundreds of thousands of Jews fled the pogroms that ensued. Many of these refugees wound up in a twelve-block area near the Mississippi River known as "the Pinch," the Memphis version of the Lower East Side. It had been nicknamed for the pinched stomachs and faces of the Irish immigrants who first came there, fleeing the Great Potato Famine of the 1840s.

In its heyday of the early 1900s, the Pinch encompassed four Jewish groceries, three delicatessens, several butcher shops, and a kosher fish market. Life there remains vivid to its former residents. They recall women tapping the backs of live chickens to see whether they were fat, then *hondeling* (bargaining) the price to 40 cents a chicken. They paid an extra five cents for "flecking" the chicken (removing its feathers). To buy a schmaltz herring, they would reach into a big barrel, pull out a herring, and wrap it in the newspaper they had brought with them.

The central institution for the Orthodox population was the synagogue. As early as 1884, Baron Hirsch Synagogue, now one of the largest Orthodox congregations in the US, was formed. It was named after a wealthy Belgian Jew, Baron Maurice de Hirsch, who devoted much of his fortune to help Jews flee the pogroms and resettle in America. In 1898, Anshei Sphard was founded with Israel Peres, son of Rabbi Jacob Peres, drawing up

9. The Pinch: the Lower East Side meets the Deep South. Home of the Jews until the 1930s.

DISEASE. | PHYSICIAN.

Yellow Fever. | Dr. W. E. Rogers
Yellow Fever. | Dr. Szenniya
Accidental discharge Pistol. | Dr. F. M. Primer
Yellow Fever. | Dr. Szenny
Yellow Fever. | Dr. Szenniya & J. W. [...]
Yellow Fever. | Drs. Szenniya & N. W. [...]
Yellow Fever | Drs. Szenniya & Mitchell
Yellow Fever. | Drs. Szenniya & William
Yellow Fever. | Drs. Szenniya & William
Yellow Fever. | Dr. F. W. Lacey
Yellow Fever. | Dr. A. H. Taylor
Yellow Fever. | Dr. A. H. Taylor & Armstrong
Yellow Fever. | Dr. Szenniya
Yellow Fever. | Dr. Lacey & Rogers
Yellow Fever. | Dr. Szenniya

4E 82

THE PINCH

In the mid-1800s this twelve-block area became a stepping stone for European immigrants, and is known as Memphis' first commercial district. The name "Pinch" is traced to Irish settlers who fled the great potato famine. Their "pinch-gut" appearance prompted this slang description which became synonymous with the area. In the 1890s Jewish immigrants settled here, transforming the area to a merchant community. Pinch was home and business center to most of Memphis' Jews until the 1930s.

the charter. (It later merged with the old Beth El Emeth, evolving into the present congregation.) With the influx of Jews shortly thereafter, numerous *shuls* emerged – each representing a different group from eastern Europe – such as Anshei Mischne (1900) and Anshei Galicia (1912), whose members were known as the "G Men."

I was sitting with Harold (Hosh) Katz and his wife Dorothy (Dottie), age 83, whose family in Memphis goes back five generations! With her feathery, colorful, wide-brimmed hat and cane, Dottie is as elegant and gracious a southern belle as you will find. With her charm and manner, she transports you back to the antebellum days of *Gone with the Wind*. Her grandfather, David Goldberger, was one of the founders of the forerunner to the Baron Hirsch synagogue in 1864. His son Leo founded *Hebrew Watchman*, the Memphis Jewish newspaper, in 1925, and it continues to be run by his grandson Herman.

Harold's father came here during the mass eastern European migration, and Harold has warm recollections of life in the Pinch. "My father was one of the first in the 1920s to own an auto parts store. Back in 1929, there was a family that kept a cow in their backyard so they could have *cholov Yisrael* (kosher milk supervised by a Jew).

"No one put on airs, there was no one-upmanship between people," he sighed, "and we visited each other, ate together, cooked together; there was true *hachnasas orchim*, Jewish hospitality." [As an outsider, I observed that to this day, Memphis hospitality is automatic: no stranger goes uninvited, no greeting is missed on the street.] "We had five *shuls* within a mile of each other, and Anshei Mischne was a one-man show, run by a man named Blockman. He owned a junk yard down the block from the *shul*. He also had the only *mikveh* [ritual bath]. In the waning days of the Pinch in the 1940s, he would stand on the corner and pull people in to form a *minyan*, telling them they were the ninth or tenth man. He did this for years. After he would get you in there, he would stand for the Amidah [prayer]

10. Dotty's grandfather, one of the founders of the forerunner of Baron Hirsch Synagogue in 1864

11. Leo Goldberger, founder of the *Hebrew Watchman* in 1925

12. The 1928 issue of the *Watchman* reporting the dedication of the new Yeshiva College in New York: "the blending of religious and secular education." It was a new concept in college education.

Memphis hospitality is automatic: no stranger goes uninvited, no greeting is missed on the street.

for an hour or so: we'd want to close the *shul* for the night, but he was still *davening*!"

"Do you know how I met Harold?" Dottie drawled. "I was at the Reform temple and I felt something was missing in my life. Without knowing why, I hopped on a trolley, stepped off at Baron Hirsch [synagogue], and the first and only person I met was Harold. You have to understand, Reform and Orthodox never mingled in those days! This was pretty radical!"

Israel, Elvis'll, and Moonshine

The invisible wall between Orthodox and Reform congregations was quite real back then. But with the creation of the State of Israel, Memphis Jews of all stripes were brought together for the first time in a hundred years. This unity has enabled the community to build the Jewish Community Center and to form the Jewish Welfare Fund, which fund-raised to build the Jewish old folks home as well as many other charities.

13. Southern comfort: Dorothy (Dotty) and Harold (Hosh) Katz reviewing their photographs. Both their families go back five generations in Memphis, to the Civil War.

Rabbis Nathan and Ephraim Greenblatt are the foremost *poskim* (authorities on Jewish law) in the South and long-time Memphians. I spoke to Rabbi Ephraim about the strong Memphis ties to Israel. He told me he was born in Jerusalem in the late 1920s and fought in the 1948 War of Independence. As a sergeant in the Israeli army, he took his 500 troops to the Egyptian border and wanted to cross into Egypt. This move was against the wishes of David Ben-Gurion, who was so angry that he flew down to the battle site and asked for the "guy in the *yarmulke*" defying his orders. He came face to face with Ephraim Greenblatt, who continued to argue his point. Suddenly, Ben-Gurion slapped him in the face and gave him a *pinkus*, the Israeli equivalent of our pink slip, and he was out of the army. Nevertheless, the Greenblatts are staunch backers of Israel and encourage the Jews of Memphis to participate in its support. Zionism is strong in all Memphis synagogues: year in and year out, Memphis is a leader in Israel Bond campaigns.

Another Memphis rabbi can claim an odd distinction. The story goes that in the 1950s, when Rabbi Alfred Fruchter needed a "*Shabbos goy*," his wife would call on a shy young neighbor, whom she called "Elvis'll," to come help them. Of course, he would later become the best-known entertainer to come out of Memphis: Elvis Presley. The term *Shabbos goy* is one of honor – a person kind enough to help out a Jew with tasks forbidden to him on Shabbos. We can add Elvis to our national register of prominent men who served as a *Shabbos goy* in their respective home communities or as a friend to a religious Jew: the list includes novelist Pete Hamill, Mario Cuomo, Colin Powell, and Barack Obama.

I had the honor of chatting with Jack Belz, whose grandfather, Moses, came here in 1904. Son of the town *shochet* (slaughterer) in Lancut, Galicia, Moses started as a peddler until he saved enough for a small grocery store. During the Prohibition of "intoxicating liquors" (1920–1933), everyone had to find ingenious ways to acquire and hide wine and liquor. A hollowed-out place beneath the windowsill was big enough to stash the bottles in their home. Seven-year-old Philip – Jack's father – acted as courier, taking the bottles, hidden in his belt, to customers.

14. The Belz family, respected community builders and philanthropists and ardent Zionists, entertaining Natan Sharansky (left) at their home

For nearly a hundred years, this family has been among the most respected community builders and philanthropists in the South. They have literally changed the face of Memphis. Philip Belz was instrumental in building one of the largest Orthodox synagogues in the South, as well as the Jewish Community Center, and the Belz School of Jewish Music at Yeshiva University in New York.

Jack and his son-in-law, Andrew Groveman, are proud of the accomplishments of the community in Memphis: 30 percent of the Jewish population is affiliated with Orthodox synagogues, as compared to 7 percent nationally.

How to Grow a Jewish Community

The keys to this growth are hospitality and education. Jack spoke of the attribute of hospitality that is unique in this community. "Every year, on the [eight-day] holiday of Sukkos, my mother and Aunt Bertha would have 50 people over every day, two meals a day. They had a family recipe for strudel that's as secret as Coca Cola!"

While there were Hebrew schools to provide a basic Jewish education, the future of Orthodoxy was shaky. Realizing that the only way to ensure continuity was through quality Jewish education, Memphis residents made the first Jewish day school in the South become a reality in 1949. Today, thanks to the dedicated efforts of many philanthropic families over the years, there is now an Orthodox elementary school and two yeshivah high schools.

"We had 650 kids in the Talmud Torah [Hebrew school]," Jack recalled, "before the yeshivah came along."

Andrew added an ironic note: "Three years ago we started the Memphis Jewish High School, which utilizes the progressive Harkness method of learning: all of the students meet around a large oval table, no desks." We both laughed as we thought of the eastern European *cheder*, which used the same method hundreds of years earlier.

"Forty years ago," Jack said, "my cousin Cheryl Loskove, who lived in Chattanooga [one of the first Jewish enclaves in Tennessee], was driving by a junkyard when she saw something flash out of the corner of her eye. Upon closer inspection, she found an *aron kodesh* [Torah ark] with two stained-glass windows that open vertically via a pulley system. It stayed in her basement until it was handed down to me and finally found its way to the *beis midrash* of our new Jewish high school."

I visited Memphis in the Hebrew month of Elul, the month preceding the High Holy Days. Sitting at the Shabbos table with me were Lynne and Lenny Mirvis, whose daughter, Tova, wrote the novel *The Ladies' Auxiliary*, about Orthodox Memphis. Also at the table are Herman and Barbara (Bobbie) Goldberger, editors of *Hebrew Watchman*, and Dottie and Hosh Katz. There were so many generations of southern Jewish history around this table and yet, to me, they still felt like family.

15–16. Standing the test of time. The Harkness method of learning around the table at the new Memphis Jewish High School.

17. The ark found in a junkyard in Chatanooga, Tennessee, now in the Jewish High School

The Peabody Duck Walk

Lynne Mirvis told me that her daughter was married at Jack Belz's Peabody Hotel. The roof of the hotel is known as the legendary Peabody Duck Palace. In the lobby, at precisely 11:00 AM, spectators come to witness the daily march of the Peabody Ducks – a line of mallards who parade to the music of John Philip Sousa down a 50-foot red carpet to spend the day in the hotel fountain. At precisely 5:00 PM, the music strikes up again and the ducks march back into the hotel's elevator, which takes them home to their rooftop palace.

18. Ducks marching to Sousa

When Tova Mirvis got married, the wedding band was given a strict warning: Don't start playing "Od Yishama" to bring the groom to the bride for the bedeken (placing of the veil over her face before the ceremony) until the ducks' Sousa serenade is finished. Two pieces played at the same time will confuse our feathered friends! No one dared disobey.

When we started talking about customs of the upcoming Rosh Hashanah, they told me about the time the police showed up at Tashlich, a prayer customarily said near a body of water. More than 50 people had gone down to the bayou – a marshy area overlooking the river – to say Tashlich. They stood on the cliff and began saying the appropriate prayers while gazing at the river, 15 feet below them. This went on for about a half hour when, all of a sudden, a police car came racing in from nowhere, lights flashing, sirens blaring. Coming to a screeching stop ten feet from the shocked group, two state troopers bounced out of their vehicle, hands on holsters. Running toward the group, they shouted, "Ok, where's the body? Where's the body?" Evidently, a passerby had seen them looking down at the river and called the police: such a large group must have been staring at a floating body!

At the time, no one was laughing, but with the distance of time, we all enjoyed the story. We started to dig in to the fabulous meal that had been placed before us. Our Shabbos menu was a perfect bicultural blend: gefilte fish, chicken soup, southern fried chicken, black-eyed peas, string beans accompanied by a fine scotch, and for dessert, pecan pie. Kosher traditional meets southern comfort! Dottie, of course, is not the least bit surprised. She has written food columns in the local papers and published a kosher cookbook of recipes she's gleaned over the years. You want southern cooking? How about her Aunt Esther's Gedempte Chicken or Carrot Kishke with Vegetable Fritters?

The Famous Kosher Que!

We reflected on the fact that food is the clearest symbol of southern culture, but that it is also an integral part of Judaism. We celebrate daily life, holidays, and life-cycle events with meals, and every bite must be kosher.

Kashrus is not just a set of rules; it's a way of life. Wherever the Torah speaks of the kosher food laws, the word *kodesh* – holiness – is used. The Talmud says that, in this regard, every home is a temple, every table an altar, every meal a temple offering, and every Jew is like a *kohen* (priest). Yes, we use food as a way to improve ourselves spiritually, to bring us closer to G-d, and to each other. I would soon have a taste of this mixture.

19. Dotty Katz's cookbook contains recipes and "a little chit chat."

20. Ribs and beans – let the grillin' begin!

When Shabbos ended, it was time to turn my attention to the preeminent event in Jewish Memphis: the Anshei Sphard–Beth El Emeth/Kroger twentieth annual Kosher BBQ Cooking Contest and Festival. The passion for the Que in Memphis is indescribable. Memphis Jews are bonded by southern culture and have adjusted their eating habits to those of their neighbors, despite the fact that the typical Memphis Que is as *treif* as could be. An old Memphis joke reflects this dual identity: An elderly Memphis Jew is going through customs and the agent discover five sets of teeth. The agent asks him, why five? "Well," he explains, "one set is for dairy and one for meat."

"And the other three?"

"One is for meat and one is for dairy for Passover."

"And the last set?"

"Barbeque."

There is nothing like the Memphis Kosher Que! This year, fifty teams came from New York, Louisiana, Florida, Mississippi, as well as representing every Jewish organization in this community. They converge on Memphis, the barbeque capital of the world, to compete for prizes for best brisket, ribs, and beans, as well as best booth design and name.

The teams are given their portions of meat, and a large table is laden with spices and ingredients provided for common use, all under the supervision of Rabbi Joel Finkelstein of Anshei Sphard. In the classic barbeque contests (of which Memphis has the largest in the world), contestants bring their own grills, meats, secret sauces, and spices. In this ko-

21. Rabbi Joel Finkelstein of Anshei Sphard

sher contest, the teams come with nothing but the shirts on their backs. The *shul* even provides the grills – two for each team and a two-page set of rules about *kashrus*. In this contest, the teams are answerable to a higher authority: Rabbi Finkelstein.

There is frenzy on Saturday night, in the social hall and meat kitchen, as participants frenetically prepare their slabs of meat with rubs, spices, and marinades. This goes on until two o'clock in the morning!

The following day, services conclude at 8:30 AM, and the heavenly aroma of barbeque wafts into the synagogue. I walk out into the parking lot – almost the size of a football field – and smoke is everywhere! The Que has been going on since 6:00 AM. The ten-piece jazz band is slowly assembling and the judges, representing television, radio, the press, and local politicians, arrive and take their seats. The emcee, George Klein, a member of Anshei Sphard, has his own claim to fame: he was best man at Elvis Presley's wedding and Elvis at his.

The booths are going up, each with its own theme, vying for top prize: among them, "The Alta Cookers," "Indiana Jonestein and the Temple of Israelites," "Fleish Gordon," "Jews Can Q, Can You?" "Blue Suede Jews," "Grillin' & Tefillin" (Chabad, of course!). The five-car train ride for adults and children goes from booth to booth for an up-close and personal look at the grilling. Despite the sense of competition, camaraderie is evident among all the participants; they're swapping cooking stories and recipes. There's a congenial mingling of *yarmulkes* and *tzitzis* from Flatbush, *baalei teshuvah* from Mississippi, Israel Bond ladies from Florida. A Memphis police officer tells me that despite the enormous crowd, this will probably be the easiest assignment he will have all year. By the end of the day, it doesn't matter who won!

What a place. Jews have lived in the South for hundreds of years and each generation had to find a balance between its Jewish and southern identities. Judy Peiser, executive director of the Center for Southern Folklore in Memphis, remembers her eastern European roots and growing up in a southern home with a black housekeeper who prepared kosher versions of southern dishes like fried chicken greens, hot-water cornbread, and cobblers, a scenario repeated all over the South throughout the years. In an interview she gave for the book *Matzo Ball Gumbo** – a must-read to appreciate the true flavor of the Jewish South – she said, "We always have the 'pack' on our backs. We walk in two worlds."

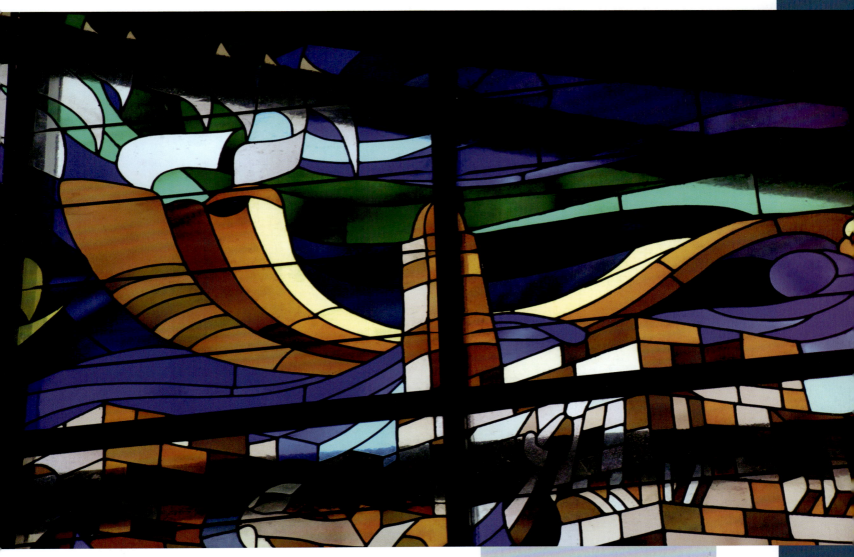

22. Stained glass shofar (ram's horn) representing Rosh Hashanah, the Jewish New Year. This is one of many windows depicting the Jewish holidays at the Baron Hirsch Synagogue, one of the oldest and largest in the country.

---

*   Marcie Cohen Ferris, *Matzoh Ball Gumbo: Culinary Tales of the Jewish South* (Chapel Hill, NC: University of North Carolina Press, 2005).

Evolution of the synagogues

23. Present-day Baron Hirsch, dedicated in 1988

24. Rabbi Shai Finkelstein of Baron Hirsch: "There is a thirst for learning in Memphis…. The southern accent affects both Hebrew and especially Yiddish."

25. Baron Hirsch Synagogue, built in 1957 with seating for 3,000 – one of the largest Orthodox *shul*s in the country

CONGREGATIONS MERGED
(Moving Further East)
MEMBERSHIP CAMPAIGN BEGINS JULY 31
≡Both Properties For Sale Now≡

Anshel Sphard
PROPERTY
N. PARKWAY and BELLEVUE
.Modern Sanctuary and Educational Bldgs.
.Beautifully Furnished
.Prestige Mid-town Location

Beth El Emeth
PROPERTY
3771 POPLAR AVE.
.Prime Location
.4 Bldgs. on 86,000 Sq. Ft. Land
.Paved Parking Area
.Main Bldg. 7 Yrs. Old

For Details Call:
MESSINGER REALTY COMPANY
685-5548 1079 N. Hollywood 458-3411
Member American Real Estate Assn.

28. Congregation B'nai Israel, built in 1883 as a Reform temple and sold to the Orthodox Beth El Emeth in 1917, was the predecessor to the present-day Anshei Sphard–Beth El Emeth.

26–27. Anshei Sphard and Beth El Emeth merged in 1970 as their properties were put up for sale.

29. In the first year of the historic Memphis Hebrew Academy day school (1949), today called Margolin Hebrew Academy, students celebrated the first anniversary of the creation of the State of Israel.

30. The students of the Margolin Hebrew Academy proudly show off their artwork demonstrating the key concepts of the High Holy Days: repentance, prayer, and charity.

31. Students at the Hebrew Academy studying Talmud in the *beit midrash* (study hall)

32. The Pinch's Baron Hirsch boy scout troop, c. 1920

The game is on! The Jew and the Que

33. Proudly wearing the BBQ contest logo

36–37. MC George Klein is a DJ, TV and movie actor, radio host, and member of Anshei Sphard–Beth El Emeth. He was the best man at Elvis Presley's wedding and Elvis reciprocated at his.

40. Relaxed grilling with an eye on the competition

The game is on! The Jew and the Que

34–35. Smokin'! This serious griller has won awards for best ribs and best brisket three years running!

38. All eyes on the two remaining contestants, who, deep in concentration, stuff their faces in the pickle-eating contest.

39. Out of this world! The "Fleisch Gordon" team of (L to R) Mitch Kaplan and Steven Weinberger from Flatbush, NY, holding a brisket for the judges.

41. Are these beans ready for the ultimate test of the judges?

The game is on! The Jew and the Que

INDIANA JONESTEIN and the Temple of Israelites

Memphis Jewish Home & Rehabilitation Center

42. Does this win the Best Booth trophy? "Indiana Jonestein and the Temple of Israelites."

44. Chabad – who else?

CHABAD LUBAVITCH of Tennessee

GRILLIN & TEFILLIN

NECK CHUCK RIB SHOULDER BRISKET

47. Poster advertising the "Annual Barbeque and Dance" in the Memphis Zionist District to benefit the American Zionist Fund in the 1940s

Make Your Plans Now
TO ATTEND
THE OUTSTANDING EVENT
OF THE SUMMER SEASON
15TH ANNUAL
BARBECUE and DANCE

Chairman   President

AL BALLIN   LOUIE KOTLER

Sponsored By
THE MEMPHIS ZIONIST DISTRICT
HONORING
THESE TWO
OUTSTANDING
ZIONISTS

SUNDAY, AUG. 27
RAINBOW LAKE
Private Picnic Grounds
PROCEEDS FOR
AMERICAN ZIONIST FUND

JOE SHANEMAN   WILL EPSTEIN

DINNERS $2.50 Plate including soup; Children Under 12—75c DANCING Starts 8
An All Day Event That You W

46. These Klezmer musicians serenade the serious rib eater.

MAJYC'S X-WING FIGHTER

STEAK WARS
RETURN OF THE RIB-EYE

43. May the schmaltz be with you!

Abraham
Skywalker & the
Bar-B-Q
Eating
Empire

BLUE SUEDE JEWS

45. Gotta do at least one Elvis!

PRIME RIB-EYE COOK

48. Too tired to grill? Take a tour of all the cooking on the "Chatanooga Choo Choo."

Business and food

W WAT

EWS AND JEWISH NEWS"

ENN. OCTOBER 8th, 1926

RIST
3TH

HARVARD OPENS KOSHER CAFE

Boston, Mass., Oct. 5 — A Kosher cafeteria and students' house with eating accommodations for more than 100 and lodging for about 25 Jewish students was opened last week at the beginning of classes at Harvard University. This is the first time, according to those in charge of the house, that proper provisions have been made for the spiritual as well as physical being of the Jewish students.

The house in Cambridge, is operated of Orthodox Jewish Con- America. Any Jewish provided he prom the Jewish tradition ating.

rnment; proceed- hality of en hour aw, the Oregon 907-1914 munici- ing the m 1900 Savings

49. Newspaper article in the *Watchman*, 1926, covering the groundbreaking opening of a kosher café at Harvard

50. Kosher butcher in the Pinch in the 1920s

52. Memphis kosher bakery brings back memories of the popular Ridblatt's Bakery in the Pinch in the 1920s. It was famous for Ridblatt's son, a prizefighter who was nicknamed "Rye" in honor of the bakery's bestselling bread.

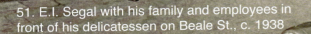

51. E.I. Segal with his family and employees in front of his delicatessen on Beale St., c. 1938

53. Cantor Aryeh Samberg of Anshei Sphard, in his 21st year, is originally from Brooklyn, NY. "When I first came here, all barbeque meant [to me] was throwing a hamburger on the grill. Here it is an art form, a science."

54. New Year's card depicting Rachel's tomb, c. 1947, one year before the creation of the State of Israel

L'shanah tovah tikaseivu

55–56. Jewish New Year postcards, c. 1912, printed in Germany

Blowing the shofar

59. Rabbi Isadore Goodman
of Baron Hirsch Synagogue
with unidentified shofar
blower, c. 1945

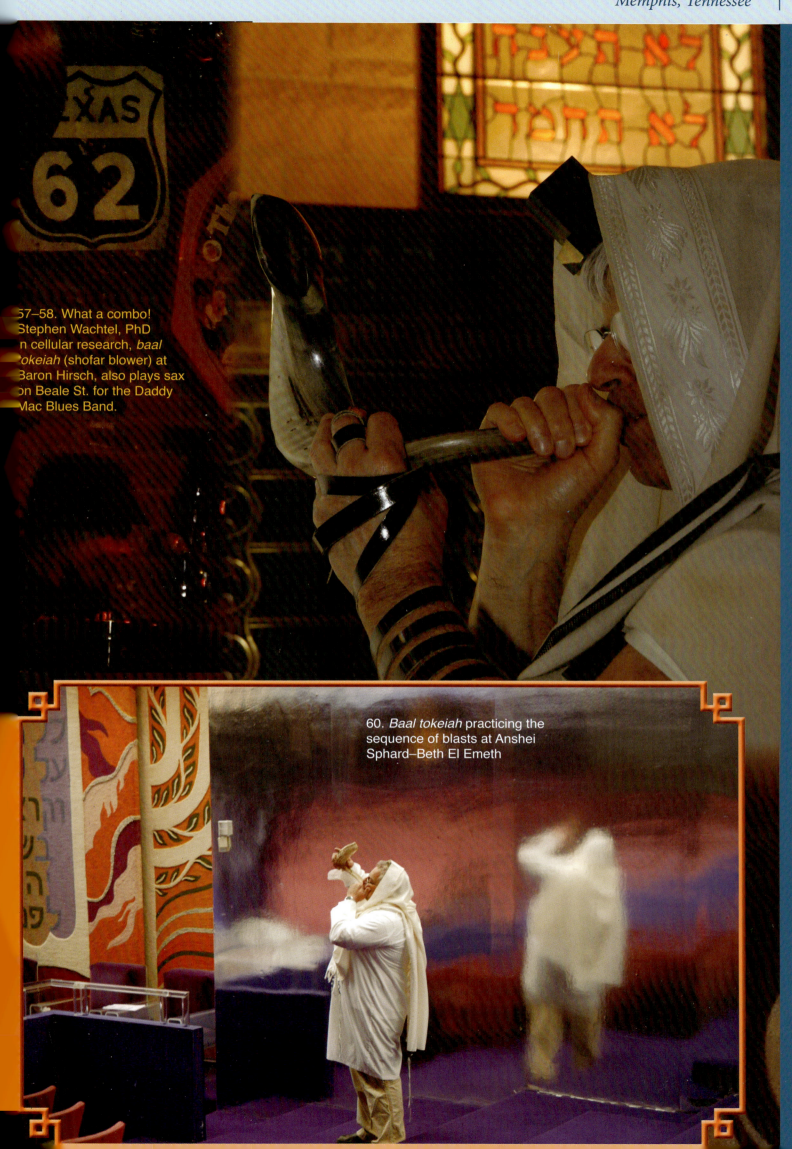

57–58. What a combo! Stephen Wachtel, PhD in cellular research, *baal tokeiah* (shofar blower) at Baron Hirsch, also plays sax on Beale St. for the Daddy Mac Blues Band.

60. *Baal tokeiah* practicing the sequence of blasts at Anshei Sphard–Beth El Emeth

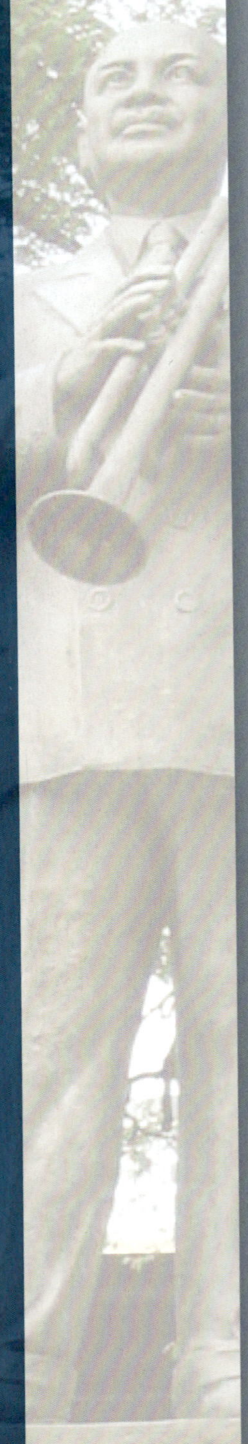

**My thanks to
Jack Belz, Andy Groveman,
Judy Peiser and the
Center for Southern Folklore,
Rabbi Shai Finkelstein,
Rabbi Joel Finkelstein,
Rabbi Gil Perl,
Harold and Dorothy Katz,
Herman Goldberger,
and the devoted people at the
Margolin Hebrew Academy and
the Memphis Jewish High School.**

Bibliography

Katz, Dotty. *The Purr-fect Line to Good Eating*. Memphis, TN: Starr Toof, 1996.

Lewis, Selma. *A Biblical People in the Bible Belt: The Jewish Community of Memphis, Tennessee, 1840s–1960s*. Macon, GA: Mercer University Press, 1998.

Lipschutz, Yacov, and Sheah Brander. *Kashruth: A Comprehensive Background and Reference Guide to the Principles of Kashruth*. New York: ArtScroll/Mesorah, 2000.

Mervis, Tova. *The Ladies Auxiliary*. New York: W.W. Norton, 1999.

Sacks, Margaret. *Life on a High Note: The Philip Belz Story*. Intermark Publishing, 1994.

Scherman, Nosson, Hersh Goldwurm, Avie Gold, eds. *Rosh Hashanah: Its Significance, Laws, and Prayers; A Presentation Anthologized from Talmudic and Traditional Sources*. New York: ArtScroll/Mesorah, 1983.

Photo Attributions

All numbered photos from the author's collection except as follows. Photos 4, 5, 25, 26, 28, 29, 32, 47, 50, 51, 54, 59: Center for Southern Folklore; 10, 19: Dorothy and Harold Katz; 11, 12, 49: the *Watchman* and Herman Goldberger; 14: Jack Belz and Andy Groveman; 37: George Klein; 55, 56: American Jewish Archives; Mississippi River p. 188 and statue of Father of the Blues WC Handy p. 212 watermarks: Yedida Lubin.

THE
Midwest

This chapter is dedicated to
my beloved *"Tante* and Uncle"

Regina and Wolf Diamant, a"h,

and to their children:

Ben and Estelle, a"h,

Irving and Kay, and Henry and Marlene,

who have distinguished themselves
through their acts of *chesed* and *tzedakah*
not only for their families,
but for their communities and *Klal Yisrael* as well.

This chapter is also dedicated
in loving memory of my mother,

Ida Uncyk, a"h

(Regina Diamant's niece),
who bound our families together
despite the obstacles of distance and time,
and taught me how precious family can be.
– Sylvia Berger

Dedicated by:
**Sylvia and Mark Berger
and their children
Allison and Pesach Zaromb
Jocelyn and Shmuel Jonas**

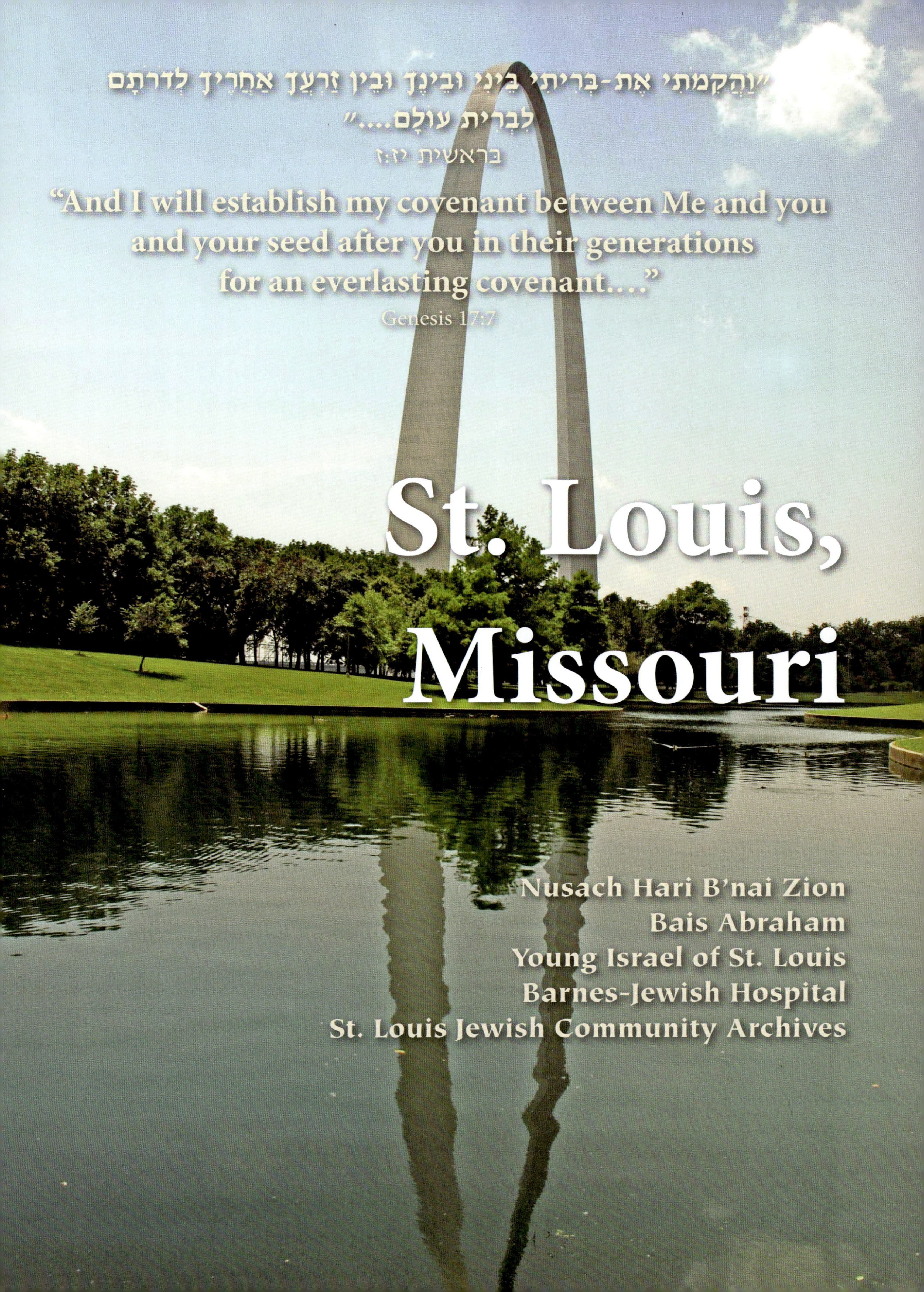

"וַהֲקִמֹתִי אֶת־בְּרִיתִי בֵּינִי וּבֵינֶךָ וּבֵין זַרְעֲךָ אַחֲרֶיךָ לְדֹרֹתָם לִבְרִית עוֹלָם...."

בראשית יז:ז

"And I will establish my covenant between Me and you
and your seed after you in their generations
for an everlasting covenant...."

Genesis 17:7

St. Louis, Missouri

Nusach Hari B'nai Zion
Bais Abraham
Young Israel of St. Louis
Barnes-Jewish Hospital
St. Louis Jewish Community Archives

St. Louis, Missouri

A Covenant of Continuity in the Midwest

The message came suddenly. It usually does. A longtime friend, Allison Zaromb, was expecting a baby very soon and I told her that if it was a boy, I would be happy to come to the *bris* (circumcision). Allison and her husband, Pesach, live in St. Louis, 1,300 miles away from my home. I explained apologetically that, due to my work schedule, the only day of the week I would be able to come on such short notice is on a Wednesday. It had to be a boy and it had to be on Wednesday.

She called. It's a boy. The *bris* is Wednesday. So the next thing I know, I'm on a plane going to this Midwestern city, a little dumbfounded by the Providence that put me there – but thrilled to participate. A *bris* is so special. It's a covenant between man and G-d, a defining moment in the generational continuity of the Jewish people for the past 3,000 years. I consider attending a *bris* a privilege: it's worth going out of my way.

1. A hand-painted wimple, a Torah binder made from the swaddling cloth that wraps the infant during his circumcision, c. 1849. The brass plate and Kiddush cup were used at circumcisions from 1850 to 1894.

I decided that this was an ideal opportunity to delve into the St. Louis community. In researching the 200-year Jewish presence in St. Louis, I noticed many historical similarities with other area communities: first came the German Jews, then the eastern Europeans; first a *minyan*, then a cemetery, synagogue, and social institutions. Does St. Louis Jewry have anything unique about it, something that cries out for recognition? To me, the answer became obvious. You decide.

First, let's put the community in context. Named after the French king Louis IX, St. Louis lies on the west bank of the Mississippi River, making it a natural location for shipping. A raucous frontier town in the 1760s, it was governed by the French, who did not allow non-Catholic settlement. Jews of that era, such as the Philadelphia Gratz family and the Franks

2. The Mississippi River, the longest river in the US, flows from Minnesota to New Orleans.

3. Gateway Arch in Gateway National Park commemorates the great westward expansion of the US. It is the nation's tallest man-made monument.

of Illinois, sent Indian agents to St. Louis to participate in the fur trade. As part of the Louisiana Purchase, St. Louis was transferred from France to the United States in 1804. The first Jew recorded in the city was Joseph Philipson, who opened a store there in 1807, but there was no Jewish community as yet.

Incorporated as a town in 1809, St. Louis became known as the "Gateway to the West," represented today by its famous Gateway Arch, 630 feet high, the nation's tallest monument. It became an important "last stop" for covered wagon trains before they braved the wilderness during the westward expansion.

It wasn't until 1837 that a Jewish community began to take shape. With the arrival of the Block family (23 members) and a Torah scroll from Philadelphia, the first *minyan* was held near the riverfront over "Max's grocery store." Abraham Schwartzkopf was the *shochet* (ritual slaughterer) and Abraham Weigle served as *mohel* (circumcisor), the only one in the mid-Mississippi area. Dedicated to his mission of bringing Jewish children into the Covenant of Abraham, Weigle would travel as far as 200 miles on horseback, without compensation, to perform a circumcision!

4. B'nai Emuna Cemetery, one of the oldest in the area, was founded in the early 1870s.

This first community also bought a plot of land for a cemetery. One of the first *chevrei kadisha* (burial societies) in the Midwest was formed here in the 1840s. In accordance with Jewish tradition, bodies were purified and prepared for burial as soon as possible. A bizarre story was reported in the columns of the *Daily Missouri Republican* of December 7, 1843, concerning the death of Ann Roseta Wolf in St. Louis:

> A young lady belonging to a Jewish family…died of a nervous disease…and her friends started with her remains for interment. The body was taken to…a house to wash it with cold water and anoint it for its final resting place. While performing this ancient custom upon the body of the corpse, a healthful warmth evaporated and evident signs of life became manifest. On arrival of the physicians, the certainty of her being alive was established. Every person who reads this circumstance will exclaim, "How providential that she was a Jewess!" … This fact should caution the public against hasty burials!

5. B'nai El, the first synagogue in the Mississippi Valley (1855), had a unique octagonal architectural design.

While Congregation B'nai El was the first synagogue in the Mississippi Valley, the United Hebrew Congregation – Achduth Israel (1840) was the prime mover for the 100 Jews in the city, mostly German immigrants. The community revolved around the synagogue, whose assumed responsibility was providing a *shochet*, *mohel*, *chazzan* (cantor/teacher), and matzoh for Passover. It was clearly stipulated that all of this must be in conformity with "the customs and laws of German and Polish Jews" guided "only by laws laid down in the *Shulchan Aruch* [a key Jewish law book directly based on the Torah]." In the congregation's minutes of 1852, its expectations of the *shochet* are recorded: "In the warm season, he shall kill three times a week – Sunday, Tuesday, and Thursday, and from December to March, twice a week – Monday and Thursday."

By 1853, the Jewish population was still no larger than 500. Three events led to this stagnancy, all in 1849: the devastating St. Louis fire; a cholera epidemic; and the California Gold Rush, which lured significant numbers to the west.

Nevertheless, United Hebrew Congregation organized a Hebrew day school in 1851 and a *mikveh* (ritual bath) was completed by 1862. It is thought that the *mikvaos* of St. Louis were used by Orthodox pioneer women going west. Fees for the *mikveh* ranged from 25 cents for a man to 50 cents for a married woman, and one dollar for an unmarried woman. (In some communities, it was customary for all Jewish men and women to go to the *mikveh* before Yom Kippur.)

Though all of these Jewish institutions had been established for some time, no one held the position of rabbi until 1854. United Hebrew Congregation hired the first known rabbi in St. Louis – Bernard Illowy from the Chasam Sofer's yeshivah in Pressburg, Hungary. The first synagogues in the Mississippi Valley were the German temples, Emanuel (1847) and B'nai Brith (1849), which held on to their Orthodox customs, but with liberal tendencies. Isaac Leeser, the well-known Orthodox leader from Philadelphia, tried to merge these three congregations, but failed. All three eventually turned to the Reform movement.

By the outbreak of the Civil War, there were 5,000 Jews living in St. Louis. Only one was known to have owned slaves. A Jew from St. Louis, August Bondi, was one of the most outspoken opponents of slavery in the US. He was one of the "freedom fighters" who joined abolitionist John Brown.

In order to "Americanize," the German Jews of the post–Civil War era distanced themselves from what they thought of as antiquated religious practices. These Reform Jews held on to only key life-cycle events such as *bris* and bar mitzvah celebrations. They formed the first of St. Louis Jewry's charitable institutions, at first by themselves, and then, after the 1880s, along with the Orthodox community.

There was a strong ethic among all Jews in St. Louis of *tikkun olam*, the biblical mandate to "repair the world." For example, to serve the mass arrival of refugees from the Great Chicago Fire of 1871, they formed the United Hebrew Relief Association. This organization later evolved into the United Jewish Charities in 1879, and then into what is now the Jewish Federation in 1925.

From 1860 to the mid-1880s, approximately 80 percent of all synagogues in America turned to the Reform movement. Orthodoxy

6. Rabbi Bernard Illowy, United Hebrew Congregation (1854), was the first rabbi in St. Louis. He also served in New York, Philadelphia, Syracuse, Baltimore, New Orleans, and Cincinnati. Illowy fiercely opposed Reform leaders.

There was a strong ethic among all Jews in St. Louis of *tikkun olam,* the biblical mandate to "repair the world." ...[T]hey formed the United Hebrew Relief Association. This organization later evolved into...what is now the Jewish Federation.

persevered in small *shul*s that tenaciously upheld their traditions until bolstered by the arrival of the eastern Europeans in the 1880s. In 1879, Beth Hamedrosh Hagodol was established and it is now the oldest extant Orthodox congregation in St. Louis. In 1891, Rabbi Shalom Elchanan Jaffe became its rabbi. He held a prestigious ordination from Rabbi Yitzchak Elchanan Spektor of Kovno, Lithuania.

7. YMHA, early community organization

In 1881, eastern European mass immigration was under way, just when the earlier German-Jewish settlers had become comfortable with their non-Jewish neighbors. The newcomers, accustomed to their *shtetlach* (small villages), preferred to live in an area called "the Ghetto" on the northeast side of the city's central corridor, near the Mississippi. They practiced their Judaism in the Orthodox way, representing everything the German Jews had tried to escape. The earlier settlers saw these newcomers as a threat to the lifestyle they had worked so hard to establish, and resentment ran high.

Despite these strong differences, when it came to a need for mutual cooperation, Jews of every stripe worked together to found the Home for the Aged and Infirm Israelites (1882) and the Jewish Hospital (1902).

The new immigrants came through Ellis Island in New York. Why come all the way to St. Louis from Ellis Island? For one thing, it was the fourth largest city in America (after New York, Chicago, and Philadelphia), and the economic opportunities were more plentiful than in other cities. Eventually, most found their way to the Ghetto.

8. The "Harris Shul," one of the many "Ghetto" *shul*s near the Mississippi, at the turn of the century

9. The Home for Aged and Infirm Israelites (1882), a fine example of mutual cooperation of Jews of every stripe

Shawn Ferguson Comes to America

An apocryphal story demonstrates the confusion of new immigrants coming through Ellis Island in New York. An Orthodox Jew, Yoel Reuven Ben Avraham, tried to anglicize his name and nervously practiced the new pronunciation. But when asked his name, he couldn't remember it. He answered the clerk in Yiddish, "*Ich hab es shoin fargessen* (I have already forgotten it)!" So the clerk responded, "Shoin Fargessen – that would be Shawn Ferguson." And that's how one European Yoel Reuven Ben Avraham became the American Shawn Ferguson. **(**Only G-d and Shawn Ferguson know if the tale is true!**)**

Though not enclosed like a true ghetto, the area had numerous defining characteristics: one of these was the proliferation of *shul*s, many of which were small rented rooms above a butcher or grocer. Often, they lasted no longer than a few weeks, for they came about for trivial reasons. If an individual was offended because he did not receive a particular honor, or if he wanted to be *shul* president, all he had to do was gather a *minyan* of friends, provide schnapps for a Kiddush, and he was in business! There were, at times, twenty or more synagogues in the small area.

> There were, at times, twenty or more synagogues in the small area.

Two other *shul*s whose origins were in the Ghetto and still exist today are Bais Abraham (1894) and Ohavay Shalom Nusach Hari (1901), which is based on different prayer customs. It's known today as Nusach Hari B'nai Zion. Each synagogue had its own Talmud Torah and butcher. There could be more than a dozen *shochtim* at any given time. Such was the situation in St. Louis at the turn of the twentieth century.

10. Bais Abraham, one of two "Ghetto" *shul*s still active today, was founded in 1894. This building housed the *shul* 60 years ago. "The beauty of St. Louis is how important its past is. It's a big Jewish community yet everyone knows each other." – Rabbi Hyim Shafner, present rabbi of "Bais Abe"

A Unique Development

Perhaps it was the chaos of the times in the Orthodox community that eventually brought about a fascinating development found virtually nowhere else in the United States: the St. Louis Jews decided to create an authority known as the Vaad Hoeir, the United Orthodox Jewish Community, and to create the position of chief rabbi of St. Louis!

In itself, this was not an innovation, for an important vestige of their former way of life that eastern European Jews brought with them was the concept of the *kehillah*, a self-contained communal existence dating back to the Middle Ages. In the *kehillah*, Jews traditionally called upon the chief rabbi to arbitrate all sorts of disputes, social as well as halachic. In the early St. Louis community, they lacked rabbis of stature, so they looked to other leaders. Solomon (Shlomo) Weissman, known as the peacemaker of the Ghetto, was reverentially dubbed "Shlomo Hamelech" (King Solomon). Nathan Harris, who came in 1890 and helped found the Orthodox Jewish Home for the Aged (Beth Moshav Zekeinim) and the Jewish Shelter and Aid Society, was also looked up to for his leadership.

The lay leader who had the biggest impact was Herschel Yawitz, who hoped to unite the Orthodox community by creating a St. Louis *kehillah*, a reincarnation of the centralized Jewish authority that had flourished in the old country. The first step was the formation of a Vaad Hakashruth to supervise the many butchers and their *shochtim* with the joint executive authority given to two eminent Orthodox rabbis, Zechariah Joseph Rosenfeld and Bernard Dov Abramowitz. Rabbi Rosenfeld, who received ordination at the age of fifteen, came to St. Louis in 1893 and made it his first order of business to build an *eruv* (halachic boundary) around the city to prevent Sabbath transgression. It was the first of its kind in 1896, utilizing existing boundaries

ELEVENTH ANNUAL REPORT

OF THE

Jewish Orthodox Old Home

BETH MOSHAV Z'KEINIM SOCIETY

11. Eleventh annual report of Beth Moshav Zekeinim, the Orthodox Jewish Home for the Aged, 1917. This was the original building.

12. Rabbi Bernard Dov Abramowitz, early leader in the Vaad Hakashruth (kosher supervising organization)

including the Mississippi River. He was one of the founding members of the Agudas Harabanan and helped develop a unified system of education in 1922 to replace the disparate system of Talmud Torahs.

In 1924, the natural extension of this centralized authority was the St. Louis Vaad Hoeir. Charged to supervise all aspects of Orthodox Jewish life in the city, it soon engaged Rabbi Chaim Fishel Epstein to be the officially recognized chief rabbi. This was a unique event in this country and the position still exists today, one of the few such institutions in the US. The idea of having a chief rabbi had been tried in New York and was a dismal failure; but in St. Louis, the time was right and the leadership united. (The Vaad sometimes played a role outside the community as well. In 1961, for instance, a bill in the state legislature would have banned some slaughtering methods mandated by Jewish law. Rabbi Menachem Eichenstein, chief rabbi at the time, appeared before the legislature and persuaded its members to drop the clause.)

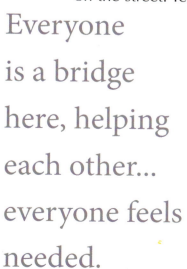

13. Rabbi Chaim Fishel Epstein, the first chief rabbi of St. Louis, who helped unite the religious leadership. Shown here in 1924.

I sought out Don Makovsky, an educator and historian who wrote a thesis on the early Jewish community in St. Louis. His legacy, too, goes back a long way. "My *zeide* came here in 1905 and was a *mohel* and a *shochet* in the heart of the Ghetto. His father gave him five pairs of *tefillin* [phylacteries] and it turned out later that he had five sons!"

He confirmed that the success of the Vaad Hoeir gave St. Louis a unique edge. "We started out with brilliant Talmudists such as Zechariah Rosenfeld, who was not officially the chief rabbi, but served the same purpose of unifying and stabilizing the community. He had the reputation of greeting everyone on the street. Ten thousand people attended his funeral. He set the stage for the Vaad to be formed.

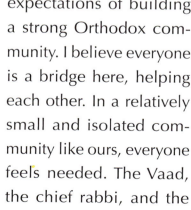

"People came here in the late nineteenth century with great expectations of building a strong Orthodox community. I believe everyone is a bridge here, helping each other. In a relatively small and isolated community like ours, everyone feels needed. The Vaad, the chief rabbi, and the

Everyone is a bridge here, helping each other… everyone feels needed.

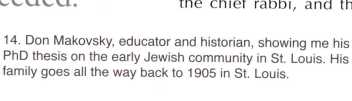

14. Don Makovsky, educator and historian, showing me his PhD thesis on the early Jewish community in St. Louis. His family goes all the way back to 1905 in St. Louis.

Hebrew School Organization – with schools ranging from elementary day schools to *kollel*s for advanced Talmudic study – have helped keep the community together for the last hundred years."

Zionism also played a strong role in solidifying the community. Two important events in 1904 gave singular impetus to St. Louis Zionism. One hundred years after its purchase, St. Louis became the site of the Louisiana Purchase Exposition (also called the St. Louis World's Fair), and the Olympic Games were hosted there. Theodor Herzl had died on July third of that year and in his honor, the organizers of the Jerusalem Exhibit wanted to fly a flag. But what flag? At the Basel congress, Herzl had urged creating an attractive banner to add to the spirit. A friend pointed out that Jews already had one: the stripes of the traditional *tallis* (prayer shawl) and the colors of the *tzitzis* fringes, which in ancient times were blue and white. Add a six-pointed Magen David star, and the Zionist flag is born. At the fair, the flag was unfurled at the All Nations Building and, within a few days, it appeared at seven more exhibits. It was the first time the Magen David flag was displayed in public in the Western Hemisphere, spotlighting St. Louis as a center of influential Zionist activity.

Back in 1897, Herzl had held a successful conference in Basel, Switzerland (where modern political Zionism came into being). In 1902, another conference was held in Poland. This gathering of Orthodox Jews tried to resolve the dilemma of whether encouraging a Jewish homeland at that point in history was consistent with traditional religious belief. A religious party within the World Zionist Organization was formed. It was called Mizrachi – an acronym of the Hebrew words *mercaz ruchani*, meaning "spiritual center." Two early St. Louis Zionist leaders were the aforementioned Rabbi Rabinowitz and Leon Gellman. The latter became the president of the Mizrachi Organization of America in 1949.

15. Zionist flag flies at the St. Louis World's Fair, in 1904. The Magen David (Star of David) was first used by the Jewish communities of Prague and Vienna in the mid-1600s. The flag in its present form was first used in Rishon LeZion in 1885 and was unknown to the First Zionist Congress in Basel in 1897. The white represents the purity of the faith and the blue, the heavens.

15b. Theodor Herzl in Basel 1897 and beneath, his proposed sketch of a symbol for the Zionist movement, in his own handwriting: "Here is my draft of our flag, white field, seven golden stars." Taken from his diary, June 14, 1895: "We have no flag; we need one.... I would suggest a white flag, with seven golden stars. The white field symbolizes our pure new life; the stars are the seven golden hours of our working day. For the Jews are going to the new land under the sign of work.... [W]e are a modern nation and wish to be the most modern in the world."

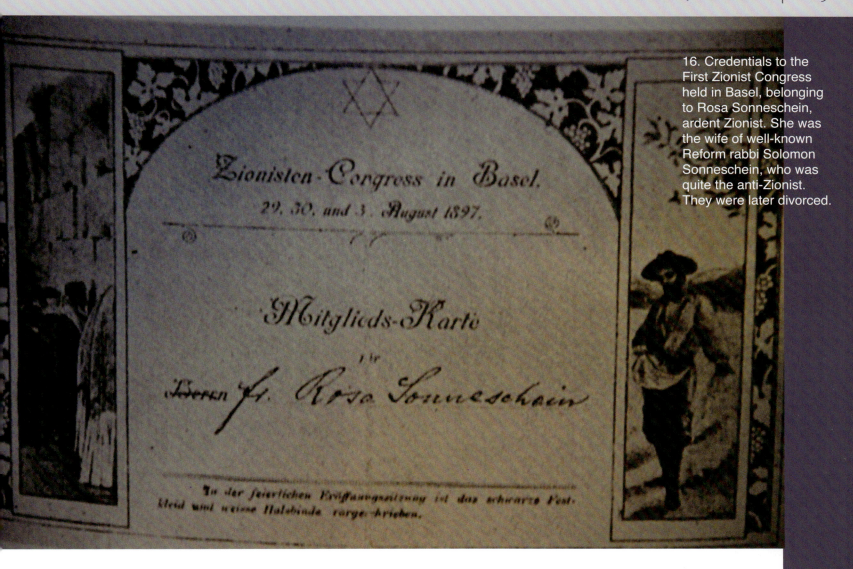

16. Credentials to the First Zionist Congress held in Basel, belonging to Rosa Sonneschein, ardent Zionist. She was the wife of well-known Reform rabbi Solomon Sonneschein, who was quite the anti-Zionist. They were later divorced.

The Case of the Telltale Bullets

In 1945, Bill Cohen owned a drapery store on South Broadway. Many years later, after he sold his store, he asked his son-in-law, Arnold Goodman, to clean out some storage areas there. Imagine Arnold's surprise when he came across several dozen loose bullets! He had heard rumors that his father-in-law had once been involved in some kind of hush-hush activities, and finding these bullets confirmed his fear that he had married into a criminal family!

He confronted Cohen with the evidence, demanding an explanation. The old man laughed! "Well, I might as well tell you. It doesn't matter now," he said. "Back in the 1940s, it was very important to help the Jews of Palestine arm themselves against Arab attacks. I recruited some of my closest friends and we started a clandestine operation in the basement of my store to ship arms to them. It was illegal, of course, so we had to keep it very quiet. We managed to send hundreds of thousands of bullets. I guess you found a few that were left over."

Arnold sheepishly apologized. He knew his father-in-law had been an ardent, lifelong Zionist, but who knew that he had such guts?

Today, the main Jewish population of St. Louis is in the western part of the city. Leaving the Ghetto behind in the 1920s, the population moved, but brought with them the warm atmosphere they had established so well. In the old days, most of the stores were of the "mom-and-pop" variety; groceries, butcher shops, dry goods, clothing. Wives worked long hours, side by side with their husbands. They managed to educate their children, pass on their traditions, and somehow achieve economic self-sufficiency.

17. Irving Diamant, owner of Diamant's Meat and Poultry for 52 years. "This community is my family."

I visited with the 2008 version of two such people, Kaye and Irving Diamant. They have owned Diamant's Meat and Poultry for 52 years, and it hasn't changed in all that time. I stepped into their shop to the sound of the cowbells hanging on the door. I was greeted with smiles, a sandwich, and a soda. The wonderful warmth made me feel like I was stepping back in time, to an era when store owners had time to *shmooze* with their customers.

I quickly discovered that Irving was not a native of St. Louis. "I was born in Poland in 1935," Irving relates with pride, making sure that my tape recorder is working. "I went to *cheder* and my father was a rancher, a cattle driver. Well, actually, he took one cow from one town to the next to eke out a living."

Along with his brother, they soon had to run from the Nazis. "My father was always one town ahead of the Nazi armies, all the way to Russia. He was arrested by the Russians; and I was selling water in a tin cup for a kopek. We grew up fast. We suffered, but the suffering of our people in Germany was far, far worse. We knew. We heard.

"After the war, *shlichim* [representatives] were sent to our detention camps to teach us about farming and cattle, to prepare for a life in Palestine. As fate would have it, my family wound up at Ellis Island instead. Through much traveling, and with the kind help of the Jewish aid societies, we came to St. Louis. We were unsure about living here, but the first language my father heard in this city, to his utter amazement, was Yiddish! St. Louis, instantly, became his kind of town."

Kaye, on the other hand, can trace her southern family back to pre-Civil War times. Her father was one of twelve siblings born in St. Louis to an Orthodox family. Commenting on Irving's dedication to his customers, she mused, "I might work here, but this is his shop, his love. There's no one in this town who doesn't love him. Rarely does anyone take advantage of his good nature. We have always felt that the more you give, the more you get."

Irving greets every customer by his or her first name and writes down all transactions by hand. You don't just get a piece of meat or a sandwich, you get a conversation. "So how's your mother doing?... Did you enjoy Israel?... No, you don't have to pay; your father will take care of it..."

"I know every face here," he remarks. "I sold meat to their parents and grandparents. In other stores, you take a number. Not here."

But his devotion goes further than that. "I never had the experience of the love of a family; we were always running," he explains. "So I adopted this community as my family. We send candy packages to the students in the Torah Prep School across the street, especially on Chanukah. We were honored by the community last year," he adds with satisfaction.

The community's love for this couple goes beyond official honors. Kaye was in a serious auto accident five years ago and was disabled for months. People spontaneously came forward to take her place at the store. They came by to work the meat slicer or the cash register, never missing a day. That wouldn't happen just anywhere.

I came here to participate in the joy of my friends' *bris* ceremony and I came away inspired. Pesach movingly expressed his feelings, pointing out that the *bris* is a unique commandment in that it cannot be performed completely: every *mitzvah* requires full intention and concentration. Since that is beyond the infant's ability, the *mitzvah* is only complete in the next generation, when that boy participates in *his* son's *bris*. This is the intention of the Torah, he said, when it says that the *bris* is a covenant that must be performed throughout the generations. These are truly the ties that bind us from generation to generation.

וּבֶן-שְׁמֹנַת יָמִים,
יִמּוֹל לָכֶם כָּל-זָכָר
לְדֹרֹתֵיכֶם:
בראשית יז:יב

So what is special about the Jewish community of St. Louis? I believe the answer lies in a *mohel* who would travel two hundred miles on horseback to perform a circumcision. It's a chief rabbi who would labor to put up the first *eruv*. It's a community that would fly the Jewish flag at the World's Fair, when a Jewish state was just a dream. It's an organized community of rabbis uniting a divided enclave of Jews with a system never tried before. The first Orthodox synagogue here was called Achduth Israel – literally, United Israel. Perhaps this name also describes the singular ability of this wonderful community to survive and prosper from generation to generation.

18. A mitzvah spanning the generations.

The neighborhood

19. Original Jewish Hospital, 1902–1926

20. Barnes-Jewish Hospital today

21. Mr. Klingler of the Freund Bakery, together with a wagon boy and a horse-drawn delivery van, St. Louis, 1908

22. The man in the doorway with a *tallis* may be the owner, Yaakov Hirsch Fox, who advertises himself on the window as both a "*shochet* and a *mohel*" (ritual slaughterer and circumciser). The photo probably dates from the 1920s.

24. Men around the table studying Jewish law at the Orthodox Jewish Home for the Aged. These study groups were conducted by the rabbi five times weekly. A brochure describes the home as providing "a rich spiritual life."

23. Diamant's Meat and Poultry, a mainstay for 52 years

25. Rabbi Zechariah Joseph Rosenfeld, a key early leader in 1893, shown here in the early 1900s. He built the first *eruv* (halachic boundary) in 1896, using the Mississippi as a boundary. He was one of the founding members of the "Agudas Harabbanim," a national rabbinic committee, and helped develop a unified system of education.

26. A unique event in this country: Rabbi Chaim Fishel Epstein became the first officially recognized chief rabbi, Vaad Hoeir, 1930–1942.

27. Rabbi Menachem Eichenstein, chief rabbi, Vaad Hoeir, 1942–1981.

28. Rabbi Ze'ev Smason, spiritual leader of Nusach Hari B'nai Zion, which has been around for over 100 years, received *smichah* (ordination) after eight years of study in Jerusalem. Under his leadership NHBZ has become a major influence in St. Louis. "We were recently named one of the top ten Jewish cities in America. Our seven-rabbi Vaad Hoeir creates a sense of *achdus* [unity] among our rabbis, with a trickle-down effect to the entire community."

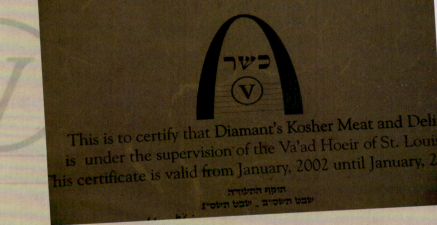

29. *Kashrus* symbol of the Vaad Hoeir of St. Louis

30. Ad inviting everyone in St. Louis to hear "R' Joseph-Isaac Shcneierson [*sic*: it's Schneersohn], the chief rabbi of the Lubawitz Chassidim" speak, May 8, 1930

31. The Lubavitcher Rebbe greeted by Rabbi Sholom Rivkin, left, chief rabbi of St. Louis

A synagogue

32. Interior of today's Nusach Hari B'nai Zion, founded 1901

33. Groundbreaking for NHBZ, 1956. Present, among others, were Rabbi Eichenstein, the then chief rabbi, and Rabbi Rivkin, future chief rabbi.

34. Minyan at NHBZ, 1921

35. Minyan at NHBZ, 2001

Fiddler on the Roof meets Bob Marley

36–42. Born Mathew Paul Miller, but better known by his Hebrew name, Matisyahu is an American Chassidic Jewish reggae musician with some rock and hip hop sounds included. I had the opportunity to sit and talk with him in his dressing room before a St. Louis concert. I walked into a room with many Miller's cheese wrappers decorating the floor and counter and the star resting on the couch wearing his *tzitzis*. I asked him who was his musical inspiration and who does he hope to inspire. He counts Bob Marley (the reggae king) as well as Rabbi Shlomo Carlebach as his inspirations. He also told me that although he did not set out with any agenda, he seems to have inspired his fans with a sense of pride in their Jewish heritage. As I watched and photographed him performing – constantly moving and dancing like a dreidel, arms outstretched, *tzitzis* flying in all directions, with the audience unable to sit still to the beat – I too, was inspired and proud.

The covenant of continuity

Turnus Rufus, the roman ruler who tortured the great sage Rabbi Akiva to death, asked him about the importance of circumcision. Rabbi Akiva told him that it was an eternal mark to remind us of our constant striving for perfection. So then why, Rufus asked, wasn't man created that way? Is man's handiwork greater than G-d's? In answer, Rabbi Akiva showed him raw grain and baked goods. We are on a mission to perfect ourselves, using everything given us by a generous Creator to transform ourselves from human animals to human beings.

43. All in the family: the family of Don Makovsky, my St. Louis expert, who go back generations in St. Louis. His *zeide* (third from left, in white), Avraham Osher, was a *mohel* and a *shochet*. His *kaballah*, or certificate of knowledge as a *shochet*, was signed by the Brisker Rov. His uncle, Yechezkel (second from right), was a *mohel* as well.

45. Continuity through the generations: circumcision implements in St. Louis

44. Eighteenth- and nineteenth-century circumcision implements: silver knife, Near East, 1819; silver foreskin bowl, Germany, eighteenth century; silver protective shield, France, nineteenth century; book of rules and prayers for ceremony, Germany, 1729

46. *Kisei Eliyahu* (Elijah's throne) found in Sephardic Bikur Holim in Seattle, Washington. The custom of using this chair dates to Geonic times (sixth to tenth century). After the reign of King Solomon, the kingdom split and the ten tribes refused to perform the ritual of circumcision. The prophet Eliyahu was angry and restrained the heavens from giving rain. As a reward for his protection of this generational *mitzvah*, G-d gave him the privilege of being present at every *bris milah*.

51. The naming: everyone waits in anticipation to hear the name recited for the first time. After Abraham performed his own circumcision at age 99, G-d changed his name forever. In Judaism, an infant's name takes on a significance beyond its letters – it is a definition of what we aspire for him to be, and even captures his personality.

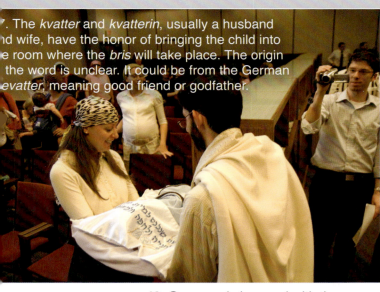

7. The *kvatter* and *kvatterin*, usually a husband and wife, have the honor of bringing the child into the room where the *bris* will take place. The origin of the word is unclear. It could be from the German *gevatter*, meaning good friend or godfather.

48. One man is honored with the role of holding the child during the *bris*: this is the *sandak*, from the Greek word *suntekos*, patron or companion of the child. Here, Dr. Mark Berger, the grandfather, has the honor of taking the child from his father, Pesach Zaromb. He bridges the centuries going back to Abraham. He cradles the infant, engulfs him with his *tallis*, binding him to his great heritage.

49. Keep your eyes on *zeide*! The *mohel* prepares for the *bris*, as the infant looks for support.

50. After the *bris*, the child is mollified with a little wine, as a curious boy looks on with interest (or is it trepidation?).

52. The pride of St. Louis! Three generations of continuity forging another link in the unbroken chain of perseverance that goes back thousands of years.

The covenant of continuity

**My thanks to
Rabbi Ze'ev Smason,
Rabbi Hyim Shafner,
Diane Everman at the
St. Louis Jewish Archives,
Don Makovsky,
Allison and Pesach Zaromb,
Barbara and Marty Aft,
and Irving and Kaye Diamant.**

Bibliography

Ehrlich, Walter. *Zion in the Valley: The Jewish Community of St. Louis*. 2 vols. Columbia, MO: University of Missouri Press, 1997.

Encyclopedia Judaica. Jerusalem: Keter, 1972.

Krohn, Paysach. *Bris Milah: Circumcision – The Covenant of Abraham*. New York: ArtScroll/Mesorah, 1985.

Photo Attributions

All numbered photos from the author's collection except as follows. Photo 1: College of Charleston Special Collections; 5, 43: archives of Donald Makovsky; 7–9, 11–13, 19, 21, 22, 24–27: St. Louis Jewish Archives; 15, 16: Ehrlich, *Zion in the Valley*; 30, 31, 33–35: Nusach Hari B'nai Zion congregation archives.

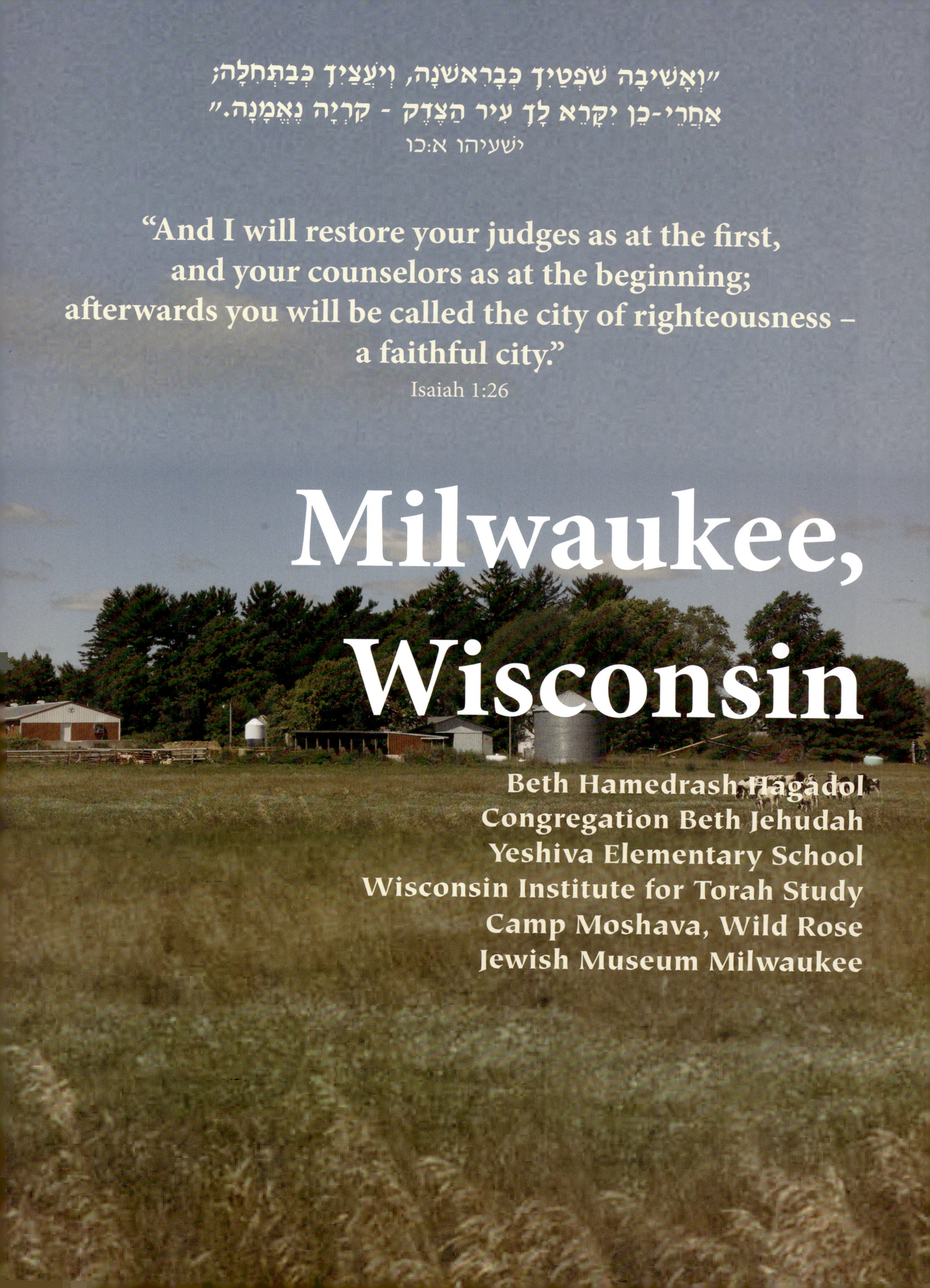

„וְאָשִׁיבָה שֹׁפְטַיִךְ כְּבָרִאשֹׁנָה, וְיֹעֲצַיִךְ כְּבַתְּחִלָּה;
אַחֲרֵי-כֵן יִקָּרֵא לָךְ עִיר הַצֶּדֶק - קִרְיָה נֶאֱמָנָה.“
ישעיהו א:כו

"And I will restore your judges as at the first,
and your counselors as at the beginning;
afterwards you will be called the city of righteousness –
a faithful city."
Isaiah 1:26

Milwaukee, Wisconsin

**Beth Hamedrash Hagadol
Congregation Beth Jehudah
Yeshiva Elementary School
Wisconsin Institute for Torah Study
Camp Moshava, Wild Rose
Jewish Museum Milwaukee**

Milwaukee, Wisconsin

Destruction and Renewal

"There is nothing as whole as a "broken heart." This paradoxical Chassidic saying always had me baffled. A teaching in the Chassidic work *Tanya* (chapter 31) describes two types of sorrow. In Hebrew, the first is called *atzvus* – a destructive grief where all hope is drained to total despair. The second is *merirus* – a constructive grief, in which one agonizes over missed opportunities, but refuses to become indifferent to what is deficient in himself or in the world. It is a grief that becomes a springboard to action.

I am flying to Wisconsin, during the Nine Days leading up to Tisha B'Av. The saddest time of the year, it is a vehicle for reliving the destruction of the successive two Holy Temples that stood on a Jerusalem hilltop for 830 years. But it is more than the burning of an edifice that we mourn: on Tisha B'Av we face the spiritual decline that led to the physical destruction of G-d's Sanctuary, and we bitterly admit the resulting distance from G-d, then and now, manifested by our continuing exile. Deep down, we know that we can rebuild our relationship with G-d and see the Temple rebuilt, but we must first muster the courage to renew ourselves spiritually. It is a time conducive to contemplation, but can we overcome the grief?

So I am traveling to two Wisconsin destinations – Milwaukee and Camp Moshava in Wild Rose – to try to resolve my puzzlement: can deep despair really become a springboard to action? Will I find the answer to this question there?

The plane lands and I am in Milwaukee, the largest city in the state of Wisconsin. Located on the beautiful shores of Lake Michigan, 90 miles north of Chicago, the area attracted individual Jews from Bohemia and Germany early in the nineteenth century. But it wasn't until the 1840s that group migration from New York to Milwaukee was tried.

1–2. On Tisha B'Av, both the First and Second Temples were destroyed. No flame is completely extinguished within a Jew.

High Hopes Are Nearly Extinguished

The first congregation was established by 12 observant Jews. The organization of the Imanu-Al Cemetery Association in 1848 led to the formation of Milwaukee's first Jewish Congregation, Imanu-Al (the spelling was later changed to Emanu-El). It conducted services for the High Holy Days in a room over Nathan Pereles's grocery. In the original minutes to their meetings, it is noted that fines were imposed on any individual who talked during services or even prayed out loud! The *chazzan* functioned as cantor, Torah reader, *shochet* (slaughterer), *mohel*, shofar blower, and gravedigger! In case his salary (which sometimes consisted of bread, turnips, and potatoes) wasn't sufficient, he was permitted to peddle rags and dry goods. It seems that the *chazzan* had occasion for his first turn with a shovel at the burial ground, known since then as Jew's Cemetery, in 1848.

3. Temple Emanu-El (1872) was originally established as Milwaukee's first congregation by 12 observant Jews.

One of the first Jewish residents, Sophia Heller Goldsmith, recalled her pioneering days in 1848: "The first 25 dollars saved built a small frame cabin of two rooms…on 6th Street near Chestnut. In the rear was a high hill on which the Indians still resided in their tents."

The *New York Jewish Chronicle* wrote about a group leaving the city for the wilds of Wisconsin in 1849: "The present party means to establish a congregation [in Milwaukee] at once and they came provided with teachers…and other officers to carry their intentions into effect."

Within a decade, dissension over custom resulted in the formation of two Orthodox synagogues, Anshe Emeth and Ahabath Emuno (1854). A year later, the latter reunited with Emanu-El under the new name B'ne Jeshurun.

The general populace was impressed with the devotion of Milwaukee's Jews to their traditions. The *Sentinel* wrote with respect about the "shut stores of the Jewish inhabitants…on Yom Kippur…and other Jewish festivals."

When Isaac Mayer Wise, the leader of the Reform movement, began to influence members of B'ne Jeshurun synagogue to abandon Orthodox practices, Isaac Leeser, the Orthodox champion from distant Philadelphia, warned the community in 1857 that "an attempt to force a new creed…upon the people will only end in

4. Shaarei Tzedek, the Hopkins Street Cemetery, was also known as the "Jew's Cemetery" (1848). Few plots still remain there, the bodies having been moved to other cemeteries. The last burial was in 1888.

confusion." His prediction proved accurate. By 1865, the choir of B'ne Jeshurun consisted mainly of paid Christian singers, and the second day of Shavuos was "dedicated" to the assassinated Abraham Lincoln.

Two thousand Jews lived in Milwaukee by 1873, but Orthodoxy was almost nonexistent and the outlook was bleak: only Anshe Emeth, reduced to a small synagogue in a series of rented rooms, kept Orthodoxy alive.

The assassination of the Russian czar saved the situation. In 1881, Alexander II was assassinated when a bomb was lobbed at him in St. Petersburg, and rumors quickly spread that the Jews were responsible. (What else is new?) Pogroms and harsh economic sanctions followed, driving 600,000 Jews to seek refuge in the US from 1881 to 1900. Many of these came to Milwaukee, where Jews from Russia and Lithuania had already settled. With the new influx of Jews, new synagogues were established, including Beth Hamedrash Hagadol (1894), which retained the first eastern European rabbi in Milwaukee, Solomon Isaac Scheinfeld. The establishment of Anshe Sfard and Anshe Hungari followed in 1905.

5. Anshe Sfard (1905), later consolidated with Beth Hamedrash Hagadol (1894) in 1920

One day, in June of 1882, 350 Jewish immigrants arrived in Milwaukee without prior warning. And the community was ready. Many charitable organizations, such as the Hebrew Relief Society and the Jewish Alliance, had been created to handle just these emergency situations. Later, from the merger of earlier charitable societies such as the Gemilath Chesed Society of 1862 and the Ladies Relief Sewing Society (among others), the Federated Jewish Charities arose in 1902.

6. Rabbi Solomon Isaac Scheinfeld (1860–1943), the first eastern European rabbi brought to Milwaukee, came to Beth Hamedrash Hagadol in 1892.

The Jewish peddlers prospered and eventually became storekeepers – clothiers, grocers, hardware dealers, pharmacists ("free advice given"), and delicatessen proprietors. Jewish trade associations, paralleling eastern European occupational *hebrot*, were formed, such as the Jewish grocer club, and the junk dealers association.

Zionist organizations appeared as early as 1895 in the form of Hovevei Zion and later Poale Zion (1906). Jewish colonization efforts in Palestine attracted many Milwaukee Jews – rabbinic leaders such as Victor Caro and Solomon Scheinfeld, as well as lay leaders. The most celebrated of these was a young lady named Golda Mabowitz (Myerson). She immigrated to Palestine in 1921 and later became prime minister of Israel as Golda Meir.

7. Goldberg's Pharmacy on Walnut St., c. 1938. "Free advice given" was the slogan.

8. A young Golda Mabowitz, later Golda Meir (at center), in Poale Zion Chasidim Pageant, c. 1919. The photo was taken two years before she immigrated to Palestine.

A Chassidic Rebbe Revitalizes a Dying Community

Though Rabbi Scheinfeld was universally respected as the preeminent Orthodox rabbi, the Orthodox presence was again losing ground, as it had in the 1870s. This desperate situation gave rise to a new force. In 1927, Rabbi Yaakov Yisroel Twerski, a scion of a long line of Chassidic rabbis going all the way back to the Baal Shem Tov (the founder of the Chassidic movement), established himself in the city as rabbi of Congregation Anshe Sfard. A considerable following developed around him and his wife, Leah, the sister of the Bobover Rebbe (another Chassidic dynasty). The community differed from all others in the US at that time in that it revolved around its Chassidic leader. Struggling to adapt to an American way of life that challenged their most precious traditions, the followers had found a leader who reminded them of their boyhood *shtetlach* and who could return them to enthusiastic worship with renewed feeling and energy.

Rabbi and Rebbetzin Twerski had a profound sense of reality and had the rare ability to connect with people of every background. Helping others with total commitment was their way of life. Milwaukee Jews were drawn to their warmth and understanding, and soon Congregation Beth Jehudah, founded in 1939, went from its simple beginnings in the Twerski house to a building that became the center of Milwaukee's Jewish activity.

Harry Rubin, an active member of Beth Jehudah all his life, remembers the influence the Rebbe had on people, whether or not they were observant Jews. "There was only one country club that accepted Jews. Word got around the club that Reb Twerski needed $10,000 for his *shul*. In the early '50s, you know, that was a small fortune! All the golfers pulled out their checkbooks and put together the whole sum in one day!"

When Rabbi Michel Twerski, his son, and his wife, Feige, returned to Milwaukee in 1961 to join his father, they found an aging congregation with fathers and sons separated by their memories and experiences of European and American life. Their rabbinate, which has been ongoing for more than four decades, has been dedicated to rebuilding the fragments of Jewish life into a caring community, as Rabbi Twerski's father did before him.

This is an Orthodox community in a neighborhood that is as culturally diverse as any found in America. There has been no fleeing

…the followers had found a leader who reminded them of their boyhood shtetlach and who could return them to enthusiastic worship with renewed feeling and energy.

Rabbi Yaakov Yisroel Twerski of Congregation Anshe Sfard, c. 1930s. A scion of a long line of Chassidic rabbis going back to the Baal Shem Tov (the founder of the Chassidic movement), Rabbi Twerski revitalized Milwaukee's Orthodox presence.

10. Congregation Beth Jehudah today. Founded in 1939 in the house of Rabbi Twerski, it became the center of Judaism in Milwaukee.

11. Rabbi Michel Twerski breaking the fast after Tisha B'Av. He has been the prime force behind the creation of the elementary school and the *kollel* for adult learning in 1989. He is also a composer, singer, and guitarist.

12. Rebbetzin Feige Twerski has devoted her life to Jewish education and outreach, lecturing worldwide. Rabbi Benzion Twerski represents the third generation of Twerski leadership at Beth Jehudah. He has served as scholar in residence in Denver, Chicago, Baltimore, and Phoenix, among others.

to the suburbs. As a matter of fact, the *shul* and the yeshivos have had a remarkably stabilizing effect on the community. They were the guiding force behind the founding of the Yeshiva Elementary School (YES) in 1989, the *kollel*, and WITS (Wisconsin Institute for Torah Study), the yeshivah high school.

I spoke with Rabbi Twerski – known affectionately as Reb Michel – and his son, Rabbi Benzion. A key member of the synagogue and resident historian, Howard Karsch, joined us. Mr. Karsch worked closely with Rabbi Twerski in the founding of the yeshivah and many other Jewish projects. To understand the impact of this Chassidic family on this community, sit with me as I listen to these perspectives.

"My grandfather was a cattle dealer in Colorado," Karsch began, "and I came to Milwaukee to go to college. I decided to stay here and settle down. When I came into the *shul* for the first time, Rabbi Twerski Sr. came to say hello, took my kids up to the *bimah*, and the rest is history.

"It might be surprising to some people that as children the Twerskis went to public school and were taught Jewish subjects at home by a *melamed* [private tutor]. But, of course, they had no alternative: there was no yeshivah in Milwaukee back then. The Rebbe sent his sons to universities so they could survive in case they didn't pursue the rabbinate. They became, among other things, a famous psychiatrist and author (Rabbi Dr. Abraham Joshua Twerski) and an attorney and dean at Hofstra University School of Law (Dr. Aaron D. Twerski).

"It has always been the Twerskis' goal to break through to each generation and convince them that Orthodoxy is not outdated or antiquated. Reb Michel started a group known as Orthodox Perspectives to reach out to young families, and it had a profound effect. They were pioneers in the *kiruv* [outreach] movement before it was ever popular! Because of their influence, people started taking their children out of public school and putting them in day school. Moreover, Reb Michel has a down-to-earth sense of reality. He started the Torah Foundation to help fund Jewish projects and, through his influence, our yeshivah became the first Orthodox institution in the US to accept vouchers for those in need.

"The Twerskis have the *rebbe ayin* [the "eye" of a Rebbe] – a sort of magnetism. They hold your attention. They don't judge me; they accept me for who I am. Look, I have five children and 47 grandchildren and they all say, 'You can be my Rebbe, Reb Michel!' This community would not have existed for a minute and a half without the Twerskis."

13. Waiting to get in: a student waits at Yeshiva Elementary School or YES, founded in 1989.

The Fervor Takes Hold

At one point in his life, Reb Michel was just a dissertation short of his PhD in psychology. "Did you ever feel pressure," I ventured, "to join your father on the pulpit of Beth Jehudah, since your brothers went into other professions?"

"I remember walking with my father one day when I was 20," he said in reply, "when, out of the blue, he asked me, 'So, *nu*, what would you like to do?' It was then I said out loud what I had always known inside: 'I want to stay with you.'

"It has always been my goal to personally absorb, teach, and influence each of the families who came to this community. I want families to be committed to learning [Torah], to *gemilus chasadim* [kind works], to improving themselves on a daily basis."

His Claim to Fame

To say that the Milwaukee community is focused on the Twerski family is an understatement. Rabbi Pinchas Avruch, executive director of the Milwaukee Kollel, tells a great story. "There was a wedding in Milwaukee and the Bobover Rebbe was invited. Now, you must understand the greatness of this man. He lost his wife, family, and community to the Nazis, came to America with nothing, and despite this enormous loss, rebuilt the Bobover dynasty virtually from scratch. Everyone recognized his greatness. A local fellow is brought over to meet him and the Rebbe notices the lack of recognition in the man's eyes.

"The Rebbe asks gently, 'Do you know who I am?' When the man shakes his head no, he smiles and says, 'I'm the Bobover Rebbe.'

"'Oh!' says the man, aglow with new understanding. 'You're Rebbetzin Twerski's brother!'"

14–15. Milwaukee Kollel adult learning program

Reb Michel's son, Rabbi Benzion Twerski, has decided to join his father in nurturing the community, as his father did for his grandfather. He is a perfect fit. After being schooled at the Yeshiva of Philadelphia and then at Bobov, he returned to Milwaukee in 1989.

Rabbi Benzion's joy, fervor, and pride are apparent as he discusses his family; this is the same fervor, I realize, that must have been a trademark of his ancestor, the Baal Shem Tov. To demonstrate his father's influence, he told me the following story.

"There was a therapist who came to the community and was making a modest living. He came to my father and told him that he wanted to buy a pair of *tefillin*. My father knew him, as he made sure to know everyone.

"'But you already own *tefillin*,' he said.

"'Well, I actually saved up for a top-of-the-line laptop computer – and then I heard you talk so passionately about *hidur mitzvah* [beautifying a *mitzvah*]. I was mesmerized, and I began to think, "What right do I have to purchase a top-of-the-line computer, when I don't even have a top-of-the-line pair of *tefillin*!" So first, I'll get the *tefillin*. The computer can wait.'"

To further characterize the passion of his ancestors, he recounted a moving Passover memory about his late great-uncle, Rabbi Shlomo Halberstam of Bobov, *ztz"l*.

"It was the last year of his life: he was frail and weak, ravaged by disease, when the family wheeled him to the Pesach Seder. The Rebbe was being nourished through a feeding tube, clearly unable to drink the four cups of wine or eat the matzohs. The family knew he would be broken by his inability to fulfill these holy *mitzvos*. They were filled with trepidation as they waited for his reaction.

"The Rebbe looked up from his wheelchair…, looked around at the anxious faces of his children, and said in Yiddish, '*Kinderlach, kinderlach*, listen well. I can no longer drink the four cups and I can no longer eat the holy matzohs. But children, I thank Hashem [G-d] that He allowed me another year to fulfill the wonderful *mitzvah* of *sippur yetzias Mitzrayim* – retelling the story of the exodus!'"

Rabbi Benzion Twerski, heir to this remarkable Chassidic dynasty in Milwaukee, had shown me all I needed to know about the passion of this family. The boundless joy and energy of the Twerskis in living a Torah life, in loving people through three generations, renewed a community on the verge of destruction – an appropriate lesson on the eve of Tisha B'Av.

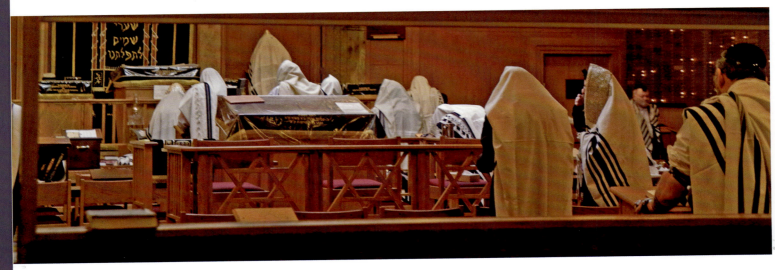

16. Reb Michel Twerski leading davening from the *bimah* at Beth Jehudah on Tisha B'Av

Tisha B'Av Questions and Some Surprising Answers

I traveled two and a half hours north of Milwaukee to Camp Moshava, a Bnei Akiva sleepaway camp. Rabbi Benzion wanted me to stay in Milwaukee for Shabbos ("You can't appreciate our community without experiencing a Shabbos here"). But I had planned to stay at the camp for Shabbos and, at its conclusion, the beginning of Tisha B'Av, for I had more questions that needed answering: How would the religious youth in a Midwestern community handle the roller-coaster emotions of a Shabbos followed by Tisha B'Av?

In the middle of an obscure town called Wild Rose, I drove up to the gate of Camp Moshava. As I noted its fluttering American and Israeli flags, I thought of the history of Bnei Akiva. The Zionist movement of the early twentieth century consisted mainly of secular Jews. It was joined in 1901 by the religious Zionists of Mizrachi, whose motto was "The land of Israel, for the people of Israel, according to the Torah of Israel." Owing to the powerful influence of the secular Zionists, Jewish youth moved away from the religious movement, posing an existential threat to the future of Mizrachi.

In the winter of 1929, Yechiel Eliash of Mizrachi formed a religious youth movement, Bnei Akiva, whose two perspectives were "Torah and Avodah," working for Israel while studying Torah. Today, there are 150,000 members of Bnei Akiva throughout the world and its youth camps throughout the US are called Moshava.

Interestingly enough, at the same time that Yaakov Yisroel Twerski arrived in Milwaukee and began the revitalization of Orthodoxy in that community, Bnei Akiva was founded to revitalize the Orthodox Jewish youth throughout the world. Rabbi Michel went to this camp in his youth.

17. Entrance to Camp Moshava, a Bnei Akiva camp representing religious Zionists

It was the eve of Shabbos. The *shul* was an outdoor structure open on all sides, in a serene atmosphere, surrounded by trees. The services were conducted with uncharacteristically sad tunes, as is the tradition before Tisha B'Av. Even the usually joyful tune of the "*Lecha Dodi*" hymn was sung to a sad melody. Suddenly, spontaneously, as the *chazzan* approached the last two stanzas, there was an explosion of emotion. Fifty teenage boys got up and started to dance and sing around the *bimah*. I moved up from my seat to observe this sight and saw the girls doing the same thing on the other side of the *mechitzah* (separation). They danced and sang for over thirty minutes, building to a crescendo of energy and joy – the same that I've seen in Chassidic enclaves! The stark contrast from the mournful beginning of *Lecha Dodi* to the ecstatic dancing at the end accentuated for me the refusal of Jews in Wisconsin (and everywhere) to submit to the despair of previous times. *Zemiros* (Sabbath songs) were on the lips of the waiters as they served, and the campers sang throughout that night and the next day.

I knew it was just hours away from the saddest time of the year for every Jew, but I couldn't help feeling the joy of the moment that these campers spontaneously exhibited on this Shabbos day.

ימין ושמאל תפרוצי

ואת ה׳ תעריצי

על יד איש בן פרצי

ונשמחה ונגילה

בואי בשלום עטרת בעלה

גם בשמחה ובצהלה

תוך אמוני עם סגלה

בואי כלה בואי כלה

Tisha B'Av started immediately after Shabbos, and the mood became somber and introspective. After the traditional reading of the prophecy of *Eichah* (Lamentations), groups of four to ten teens spread out throughout the camp. In the darkness of night, well past midnight, they discussed the destruction of the ancient Holy Temples of Jerusalem and why it happened. It is an unshakable Jewish belief that G-d allowed the Temples to be destroyed by human hands at these specific junctures in history because the Jewish nation no longer deserved them. Inherent in this tradition is the understanding that when we rectify the sins that caused these destructions, the Temple will be rebuilt and the Kingdom of G-d will once again reign on earth. For these Jewishly sensitive teens, the discussion began to revolve around what they could do to improve themselves.

I walked around, listening in on these conversations, and I was awed. By the time I left the camp the next day, I was thinking to myself, "So this

is how today's Bnei Akiva teens react to the divergent emotions of Shabbos and Tisha B'Av. They feel the joy of our heritage and weighty mission of the Jewish nation with genuine, identical passion!" What a glorious feeling to observe the future of our people.

Back in Milwaukee, I was invited to break the fast at the home of Rabbi Michel Twerski. As we sat around the table with his brothers, their wives, and his son, Benzion, the question was asked by another guest why the Jews let the Holocaust happen – why didn't they take up arms and fight? Everyone

18. Somber atmosphere: reciting *Eichah* on the night of Tisha B'Av

> I walked around, listening in on these conversations, and I was awed.… They feel the joy of our heritage and weighty mission of the Jewish nation…. What a glorious feeling to observe the future of our people.

took part in the debate, but Reb Michel sat there, thinking, singing a soft melody, and observing with his "*rebbe* eyes." As the debate wound down to silence, and everyone's attention turned to him, he said that no matter how much we think we are in control, there is a Higher Authority. We don't always understand, but He has the ultimate plan.

The Rebbe asked to see me privately in his office and elaborated on this point. "When I married off my sons, I was introduced to each prospective bride and considered whether she would be right for my son. I pondered and struggled and debated in my mind until it made me sick thinking about it. Then I realized I could struggle and ponder all I want, but in the end, it's not really up to me. A *shidduch* [marriage match] is up to Him."

In addition to his other talents, Reb Michel is a musician and has written his own compositions, setting Jewish thoughts and prayers to music. Since 1967, he has produced numerous albums that have been played by the Milwaukee Symphony Orchestra. His music is so sensitive and deep with emotion, you can feel the meaning of each holy word. When I was sitting at Reb Michel's *tisch* (rebbe's table) and listening to him softly singing a song, I realized that there is royalty here in Milwaukee. Not the kind of royalty that is separated from the people, but one intertwined with every Jewish soul.

In the Twerski living room is a large, five-foot-long document of the Rebbe's *yichus* – his family tree – all the way back to Adam! The Twerskis' pride in their ancestry is not empty glory, nor an excuse for vanity. On the contrary, it bespeaks a humble acceptance of responsibility toward G-d, toward the nation of Israel, toward all humanity. I share the pride at the table on a more personal level for I, too, am a Twerski (on my father's side) and related to the Baal Shem Tov. Rabbi Michel Twerski and his son Rabbi Benzion are products of their past, but very much in touch with the present. I look forward to seeing how their community will grow in the future.

On the flight home, one day after Tisha B'Av, I close my eyes and hear the songs of Reb Michel, with the depth, the joy, the energy characteristic of him. In my mind's eye, I see the campers singing and dancing around the *bimah*. Reviewing the stories I had heard in these past 48 emotion-laden hours, I am transported back to a time of grief and despair over the nearly lost community of Milwaukee, then uplifted as I recall the Orthodox leaders who refused to become indifferent. I can easily envision these leaders rejecting complacency, eschewing despair, and instead becoming springboards to action. In this place, there had been deep, genuine renewal, the kind of renewal that rebuilds the Holy Temple. And I can feel myself smile – so this is how revival feels. It feels good.

19. Beth Hamedrash Hagadol Cemetery. The *matzeivah* or memorial stone of Rabbi Michel Twerski's father lists the family tree all the way back to the Baal Shem Tov.

20. Reb Michel leading his family in *zemiros* (songs) as they break the fast. Many of the Twerski family gather on this night as it marks the *yahrzeit* (anniversary) of the passing of Rabbi Yaakov Yisroel Twerski, the founder of today's Milwaukee Orthodox community.

Making a living

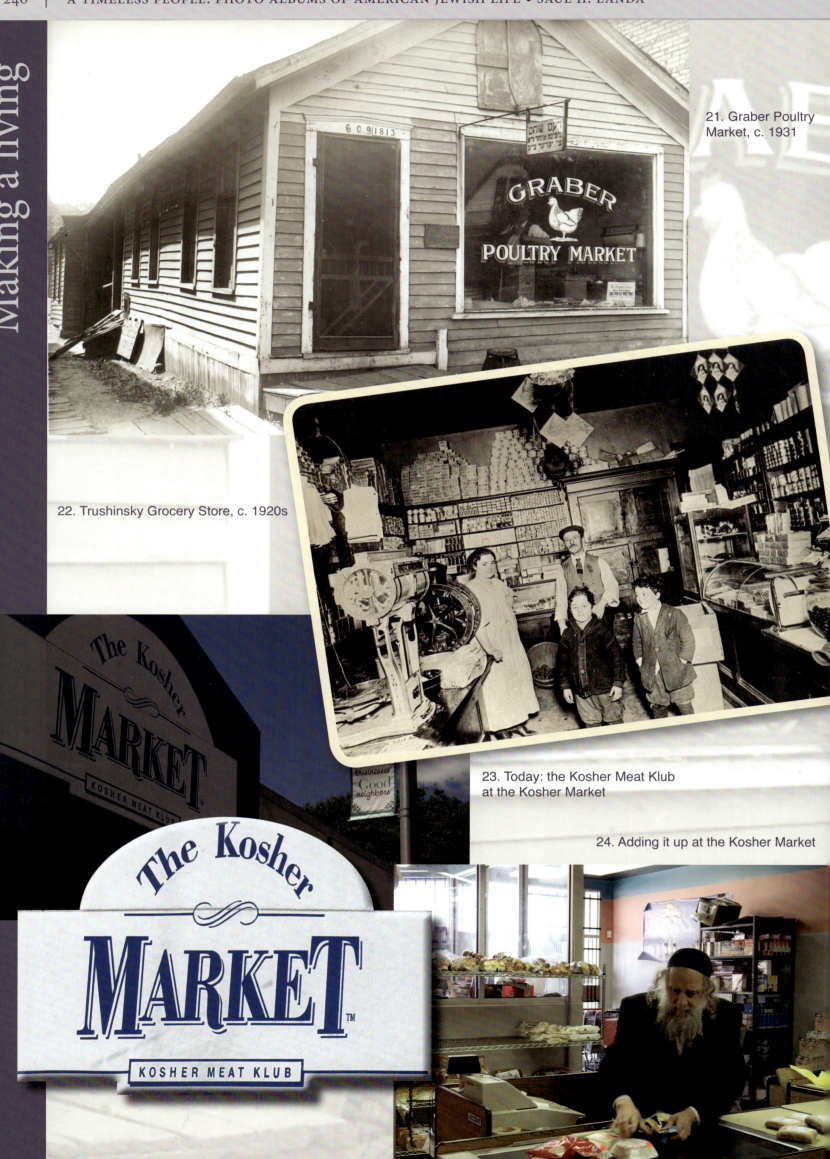

21. Graber Poultry Market, c. 1931

22. Trushinsky Grocery Store, c. 1920s

23. Today: the Kosher Meat Klub at the Kosher Market

24. Adding it up at the Kosher Market

25. Man in doorway next to sign in Yiddish: Congregation Anshe Roumanin, c. 1910

26. Behind the synagogue building, c. 1910

27. At Beth Israel synagogue, holidays were a formal affair with men in top hats in front of the *aron*. L–R: cantor, president, vice president, sexton.

28. "Open to Me the gates of righteousness." Congregation Beth Jehudah, the center of Orthodoxy in Milwaukee.

By the turn of the twentieth century, the area between 3rd and 8th Streets not only held three *shuls*, but this Yiddish-speaking village within the city was well stocked with kosher meat markets, milk stands, and all the necessities to lead a Jewish life.

Emotion, contemplation, prayer: Tisha B'Av at Camp Moshava

"The elders of the daughter of Zion sit on the ground in silence…"
Lamentations 2:10

29. Photo taken in the early days of Camp Moshava near Annapolis, Maryland, c. 1940s

"יֵשְׁבוּ לָאָרֶץ יִדְּמוּ, זִקְנֵי בַת-צִיּוֹן..."
איכה ב:י

30. Havdalah ceremony brings in Tisha B'Av at the end of Shabbos

31–41. Tisha B'Av scenes at Camp Moshava.

Emotion, contemplation, prayer: Tisha B'Av at Camp Moshava

Golda Meir

Golda's mother, having come from
the experience of the pogroms in
Russia, was always terrified of police
on horseback in her new country,
even during the entertaining parades.

42. Golda Meir visits Milwaukee, her hometown, 1969

43. Goldie Myerson later became Prime Minister Golda Meir.

44. With Paul Zuckerman and David Ben-Gurion

In 1948, the first lady of Israel revealed the Israeli secret weapon in holding back five Arab armies. "It's called '*ein bererah*' – no alternative. The Arab armies have an alternative – they can run back. So they run."

(*Wisconsin Jewish Chronicle*, June 11, 1948)

Twerski legend

45. Rabbi Yaakov Yisroel Twerski

46. Twins Michael (Reb Michel) and Aaron Twerski at their bar mitzvah reception

47. Bar mitzvah invitation, 195[...]

48. Reb Michel cutting challah at his wedding

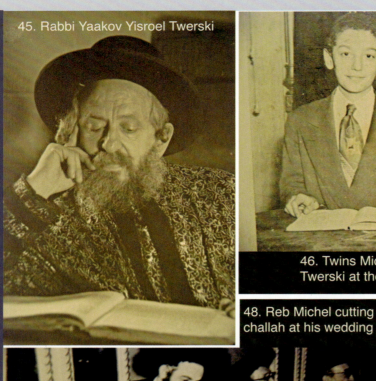

49. Reb Michel and his father at the wedding

50. Reb Michel Twerski on the pulpit at Beth Jehudah

51. Reb Michel writing a letter of a *sefer Torah* as son Benzion looks on

Rabbi and Mrs. J. Twerski
...est the honor of your presence at the
Bar Mitzvah
of their sons
Michael and Aaron
at the
...eth Jehudah Synagogue
2700 North 54th Street
...y morning, May twenty-fourth
...teen hundred and fifty-two
...Milwaukee, Wisconsin
...n at the Synagogue Hall
...day evening, 8:30 p. m.
...inday, 2 to 10 p. m.

52–55.
Dancing
with the
Torah
and
placing
it in the
aron

56. Old rendition in oil of Kiddush Levana, sanctification of the moon. Note the artist's inclusion of exactly ten men to form a *minyan*. Painting from the author's collection; unknown artist.

57. Immediately after breaking the fast, Rabbi Twerski and his followers go outside for Kiddush Levana. It can be recited from the third evening after the appearance of the new moon until the 15th day of the month. It is recited in the open air, only when the moon is clearly visible. It is customary to recite it after Shabbos, when one wears his best clothes. Another custom is rejoicing, dancing, and singing during the recitation.

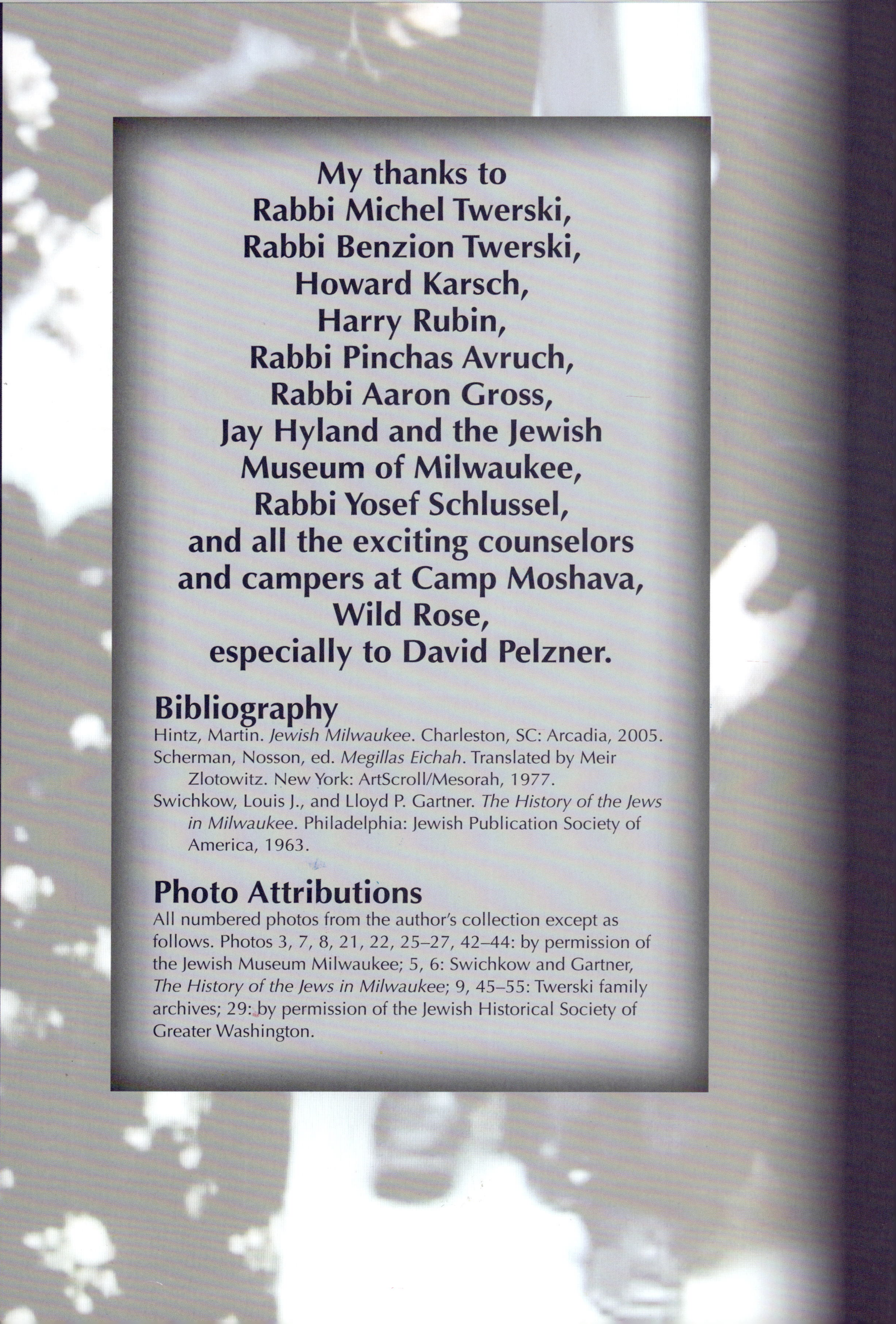

My thanks to
Rabbi Michel Twerski,
Rabbi Benzion Twerski,
Howard Karsch,
Harry Rubin,
Rabbi Pinchas Avruch,
Rabbi Aaron Gross,
Jay Hyland and the Jewish
Museum of Milwaukee,
Rabbi Yosef Schlussel,
and all the exciting counselors
and campers at Camp Moshava,
Wild Rose,
especially to David Pelzner.

Bibliography

Hintz, Martin. *Jewish Milwaukee*. Charleston, SC: Arcadia, 2005.
Scherman, Nosson, ed. *Megillas Eichah*. Translated by Meir Zlotowitz. New York: ArtScroll/Mesorah, 1977.
Swichkow, Louis J., and Lloyd P. Gartner. *The History of the Jews in Milwaukee*. Philadelphia: Jewish Publication Society of America, 1963.

Photo Attributions

All numbered photos from the author's collection except as follows. Photos 3, 7, 8, 21, 22, 25–27, 42–44: by permission of the Jewish Museum Milwaukee; 5, 6: Swichkow and Gartner, *The History of the Jews in Milwaukee*; 9, 45–55: Twerski family archives; 29: by permission of the Jewish Historical Society of Greater Washington.

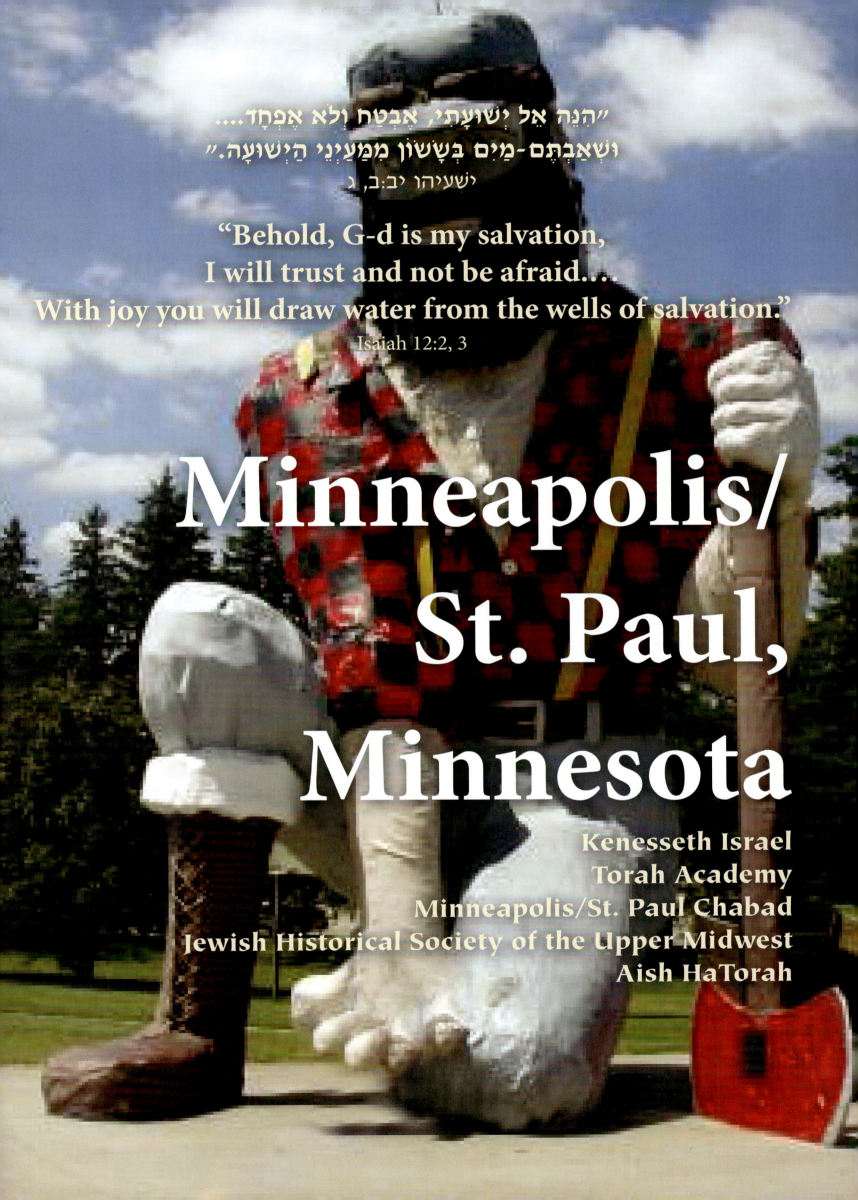

"הִנֵּה אֵל יְשׁוּעָתִי, אֶבְטַח וְלֹא אֶפְחָד....
וּשְׁאַבְתֶּם-מַיִם בְּשָׂשׂוֹן מִמַּעַיְנֵי הַיְשׁוּעָה."
ישעיהו יב:ב, ג

"Behold, G-d is my salvation,
I will trust and not be afraid....
With joy you will draw water from the wells of salvation."
Isaiah 12:2, 3

Minneapolis/ St. Paul, Minnesota

Kenesseth Israel
Torah Academy
Minneapolis/St. Paul Chabad
Jewish Historical Society of the Upper Midwest
Aish HaTorah

Minneapolis/St. Paul, Minnesota

Bonfires, Bar Mitzvahs, and Bitachon at "the End of the World"

1. Lag B'Omer bonfires – a common custom throughout the world

I arrived in the Twin Cities of Minneapolis and St. Paul, situated on either side of the Mississippi River, just in time for Lag B'Omer. Today, these are bustling cities, full of life, but 150 years ago, the area was well beyond civilization. When Amelia Ullman, the first Jewish woman to settle in St. Paul, arrived here from the Rhineland of Germany, she gaped at the wilderness and exclaimed, "I did not think that the time to go to the end of the world had come so soon."

She was not alone in her assessment of this bleak outpost. A Jewish pioneer spent several grueling months traveling up the Mississippi in the mid-1850s. He then crossed the prairie under the most rugged conditions, arriving in a frigid area now known as North Dakota. When he finally met another person, he cried, "Is this the end of the world?"

"It might not be the end of the world," came the reply, "but it's close!"

2. End of the world? Not quite, but close.

3. Lag B'Omer celebration outdoors: a time for celebration and contemplation

Heart-Thumping Pioneer Tales

In a book by Linda Mack Schloff about Jewish women in the Upper Midwest titled *And Prairie Dogs Weren't Kosher*, Henry Fine recounts the events surrounding the birth of his Aunt Sarah in Fargo, North Dakota. "My grandfather was away peddling, the rain had cut a hole in the roof of the sod farmhouse and my grandmother, about to give birth, was in pain and evidently suffering. All of a sudden, two Indians appeared in the house, looked at my grandmother and, without saying a word, walked out. Within ten minutes, two squaws were in the house and they delivered my Aunt Sarah. They never knew where these Indians came from."

Rachel Minenberg Baker told of a tornado that coiled like a snake in the sky and tore the roof off the house. The rain came down in torrents, and even heavy objects were buoyed up, bobbing around the house like toys. Her mother thrust Rachel and her brother in the closet to keep them from drowning.

That summer, a prairie fire traveled very quickly towards the house and her mother, terrified, ran up a hill and screamed for help. Alone and weeping, she began to call on G-d to help her. Just then, men in buggies from nearby farms came and put out the fire.

Why come to the "end of the world" at this time of the year? It seems to me that Lag B'Omer is the perfect time to observe these wonderful Jewish communities of the North Country. The connection is the substantial refinement of a human quality called in Hebrew *bitachon* – trust in the ever-present goodness of G-d, despite difficult circumstances.

The message of Lag B'Omer helps Jews develop this awareness. The Talmud tells us that almost 2,000 years ago, the beloved scholar Rabbi Akiva lost 24,000 of his adult students to a deadly plague within just a few weeks. Imagine the devastation, the incredible despair of a teacher for his students – young men who held the promise of the Jewish nation's future leadership! According to most sources, the plague ceased on Lag B'Omer, the 33rd of the days counted between the festivals of Passover and Shavuos. That fact alone is ample reason for celebration.

But that is not the whole story. Despite the enormity of this tragedy, Rabbi Akiva did not lose hope or his faith in G-d's love. He persevered, gathering together five disciples, including Rabbi Shimon Bar Yochai (later the author of the kabbalistic *Zohar*). These five students became the forceful engine of continuity, outstanding leaders who guided the Jewish nation through terrible times and established the study of Torah forever. Between them, they compiled 80 percent of the Mishnah, the foundation of Talmud and Jewish law. The optimism and rock-solid *bitachon* of Rabbi Akiva literally saved the Jewish nation from spiritual destruction.

Remembering his legacy on this balmy Lag B'Omer in the North Country is perfectly natural – for the story of Jewish perseverance here is remarkable. In a place that seemed destined to destroy continuity, feisty Jewish leaders succeeded in transmitting Torah for 150 years. It is the story of Rabbi Binyamin Papermaster, Reverend Shepsel Roberts, Rabbi Moshe Feller, and, yes, even baseball star Sandy Koufax. In short, it is a story of self-sacrifice and *bitachon* worthy of being linked to Rabbi Akiva.

Putting Down Roots

Among the early Jewish settlers in Minnesota were the Samuels brothers, who ran an Indian trading post at Taylor Falls in 1852. At the same time, the oldest Jewish community of the state, St. Paul, was being settled by a group of German Jews. They were fur traders and peddlers who supplied the dry goods for the lumber industry. The Mount Zion Hebrew Congregation, their first synagogue (traditional until 1870) was founded in 1856. There are no remaining Jewish structures from this early settlement downtown, except for the early cemeteries.

4–5. Mt. Zion Cemetery, the oldest Jewish cemetery in Minnesota (1857)

One of the better-known Jewish settlers who arrived in St. Paul (in 1857) was Isaac Nunez Cardozo, namesake and direct descendant of one of America's most important and distinguished Jewish families. He was married to the granddaughter of Rabbi Gershom Seixas, the officiating *chazzan* (spiritual leader) of the first synagogue in America, the Sephardic congregation of Shearith Israel in New York. Seixas was a Revolutionary War patriot who officiated at George Washington's inauguration. Isaac Nunez Cardozo was also the uncle of Benjamin Cardozo, who served as chief justice of the US Supreme Court in the 1930s.

One of the first Orthodox Jews to arrive in St. Paul was Aaron Mark from Vilna, Poland, in 1873. Clearly a mover and shaker, he held a meeting in his home shortly after his arrival to organize the Orthodox Jewish community. In 1875, the Chevrah B'nai Ya'akov (Sons of Jacob) Congregation was founded with twelve families.

With blizzards, tornadoes, Indians, and extreme isolation, life was so hard here in the nineteenth century. Why would anyone in his right mind choose to live in Minnesota?

It seems that some people arrived by serendipity, because it was the place on the railroad line where their money ran out, or they had seen boxes of flour in Russia labeled "Pillsbury Co., Minneapolis, Minn." Perhaps they had come across brochures telling them of the fine jobs they were sure to find in this rugged place that would make them physically and mentally stronger. Once a Jewish family settled there, it was a sure bet that some of their relatives from the old country would follow.

6. Pillsbury's Yiddish-English cookbook, 1930s

7. Kenesseth Israel's second building, 1948

And sometimes, the reasons for migration were more pressing and powerful. Escaping from the czarist pogroms, eastern Europeans from Russia, Romania, and Lithuania flocked to Minneapolis. At the close of the nineteenth century, eastern European immigration was the main contributing factor in the founding and growth of numerous Orthodox congregations in Minneapolis – B'nai Abraham in 1889, Kenesseth Israel in 1890 (and still going strong today), and Agudath Achim in 1903, among many others.

8. Horse and buggy in Minneapolis selling goods door to door

Some of these Jews were farmers, milking their cows at four o'clock in the morning and selling the milk door-to-door by horse and buggy at five cents a quart. There would be a *melamed* or two, scholars who would come to each house to teach the children Hebrew. Uniting the Jewish communities of the Twin Cities with stories about notable individuals and communal events was the newspaper *American Jewish World*, founded in 1912 and still publishing today.

By 1924, there were 40,000 Jews in Minnesota. In that year, the Minneapolis Talmud Torah was organized, replacing the individual *melamdim*. The school became the national model for Hebrew education and achieved fame as one of the outstanding Jewish institutions in North America.

9. Talmud Torah, 1920

Individuals Who Made a Difference

One of the important names in the history of the early Upper Midwest was Papermaster. I visited Dorothy and Ted Papermaster. He is the grandson of Rabbi Benjamin Papermaster, who received his rabbinic ordination in Lithuania in the 1880s. Ted, who is a spry 93, told me how his scholarly grandfather wound up in Minnesota.

One day, his grandfather was called to the home of the leading rabbinic sage of the era, Rabbi Yitzchak Elchanan Spektor (for whom the rabbinical college of Yeshiva University is named) in Kovno. There he was told that there was a great need for a rabbi in America, in a place called North Dakota. Moreover, young Papermaster was told, he was the ideal candidate for the position, as he was a *shochet* (ritual slaughterer), a *melamed* (teacher), a *mohel* (circumciser), and a *chazzan* (cantor) with an impressive tenor voice. How had the elderly Lithuanian rabbi heard of North Dakota?

We don't know. But suffice it to say that he sent Rabbi Papermaster on a mission he couldn't refuse. He arrived in Fargo, North Dakota, just after Chanukah of 1890. Legend has it that on the first Shabbos, he knocked on the door of the president of the Jewish community there. When the door opened, he beheld the president smoking a cigarette, a brazen desecration of the Sabbath. The community was small – only 15 Jews by generous count – and this was their leader. So the bewildered young rabbi made his way to Grand Forks, where presumably there was a stronger religious community. He remained there as rabbi until his death in 1934.

10. A "jack of all trades Jewish," Rabbi Benjamin Papermaster: *shochet, melamed, mohel, chazzan,* c. 1890

But he did not forsake the few Jews remaining in outlying areas. Dorothy said with a smile, "He was always on the move. He traveled all over, first by horse and wagon, then by train to perform circumcisions, weddings, and funerals, and to slaughter meat for Jews in Montana, Idaho, Minnesota, Texas, the Dakotas, and Canada." Far from the comforts of his native Lithuania, he became the one and only Jewish "man of G-d" in the territory.

This was a grave responsibility, so Rabbi Papermaster "rode the circuit" to Jewish farms and communities all over for more than 40 years, even under the most trying conditions. Traveling at the turn of the twentieth century was, at best, an adventure. One day, to perform a *bris* in the middle of the winter, he had to take a train and walk the last three miles to a farm. A sudden blizzard engulfed him as he walked. It was a blinding storm. He became disoriented and was afraid to move. Just as he was ready to give up, a Jewish farmer trying to find a stray cow came across the figure of the half-frozen rabbi, lying in the snow. Rabbi Papermaster regarded his sudden appearance as a miracle. The farmer brought him to the house of the baby, and the *bris* was performed.

11. *Bris* celebration of Philip Cohen. Family gathers on the front porch, c. 1908.

12. Ted Papermaster (grandson of Rabbi Benjamin Papermaster): raconteur, historian, and writer

On another occasion, he was called to the wilds of North Dakota to perform a *bris*, again in midwinter. Due to the frigid weather, he was forced to stay overnight in the home of a gentile "farmer-lady." In the morning, he came down and saw the woman washing dishes with *tefillin* (phylacteries) wound around her arm! Shocked, Rabbi Papermaster asked her where she had gotten them. She answered that she had bought them from a Jewish peddler after she had seen him wearing them and asked what they were for. Not knowing what to answer, the peddler said he wore them for his arthritis. "Good!" she told him, she too had arthritis and wanted to buy a pair. Needing the money, the peddler sold her his extra pair of *tefillin*. Rabbi Papermaster offered her a good deal of cash for the *tefillin*, but she refused. No matter how much he upped his offer, she rejected it.

"But why," he asked plaintively, "why won't you sell them to me?"

"Because," she answered triumphantly, "they work!"

What was it like growing up in the young Jewish community of Minnesota? Just ask Evelyn Zylberg, who has lived in the St. Paul community for nearly 50 years. She's a child of Ellis Island heritage: her grandfather came to New York around 1918 and eked out a living as an itinerant tailor, with a sewing machine strapped to his back. In St. Paul, "we had four or five kosher slaughterhouses. I remember, as a child, going to the *shochet*'s house – Shepsel Roberts was his name – to bring back chickens. Eventually, the government stepped in and stopped him from doing backyard *shechitah*."

Shepsel Roberts. Everywhere I went, I heard that name. It seems there isn't a Jew in Minneapolis who doesn't know of him. To understand what this remarkable man meant to Jewish Minneapolis and the Midwest, I spoke to his daughter, Debbie Weinberg.

Shepsel was born in Bialystok, Poland, and came to Ellis Island in 1918. From there, he went with his family to northern Minneapolis, where his parents raised chickens. Even in his teen years, he knew what he wanted. He hitchhiked to Chicago to attend yeshivah in the nearby suburb of Skokie, and he was ordained there. He selected his wife, Tiba Steinberg, because she was the only girl in Minneapolis in those days (1935) who would not answer the phone on Shabbos!

Astutely surveying the American scene, he answered the call of the hour. He studied to be a *mohel* and a *shochet*, performing his first *bris* in 1938. He traveled to Winnipeg (Canada), Iowa, even Switzerland to perform a *bris*, sometimes walking ten or twenty miles on a Shabbos! He kept records of every single *bris*, including that of one Robert Zimmerman. We all know him today as Bob Dylan, the renowned folksinger and songwriter. At the time of Shepsel Roberts's passing, he had performed 15,000 *bris milahs*; Shepsel's sons and grandsons have continued his tradition as *mohelim*.

13. Shepsel Roberts, a giant of the Minneapolis community, was the *mohel* to over 12,000 children.

Shepsel was a founder of the Torah Academy, the current day school, in 1945 (in St. Louis Park, Minneapolis, the present location of the Orthodox enclave), despite strong opposition, even from the local Orthodox rabbinate. He was told that creating a Jewish day school that would siphon Jewish children out of the public schools was "un-American and unpatriotic!" Support was minimal, so to raise funds for the fledgling school he would frequent the cemeteries, offering to say the Kel Malei prayer for the dead in exchange for a donation to the school.

Rabbi, *shochet*, *mohel*, founder of the day school – Shepsel Roberts did so much for the children of the Midwest and for their future. "My father believed," Debbie said firmly, "that if you take care of Hashem's children, He will take care of yours." The results of that *bitachon*, faith in G-d's goodness, is manifest in Shepsel and Tiba's four staunchly Orthodox generations of children who still live within blocks of each other.

Rabbi Moshe Feller, the chief Chabad rabbi in Minnesota, has been in St. Paul for over 50 years. Born and raised in Minneapolis, he went to public school and to the Minneapolis Talmud Torah. He went to Bnei Akiva Camp Moshava in 1948. Then he met the Lubavitcher Rebbe in 1955, while in New York studying at Yeshiva Torah Vodaath. He was immediately drawn to the warmth and wisdom of the Rebbe, as well as the Chassidic lifestyle. "I liked the songs, the camaraderie, and the unity. He taught me to see what you are, what you are not, and what you could be," recalls Rabbi Feller. The Rebbe sent him back to Minnesota in 1962 to start one of the first Chabad communities in the country. He's been there ever since. You just need a little trust.

"A very strange thing happened to me in 1965," the rabbi offered, with a sly smile. While handing me an article written by Pamela Huey in the *Twin Cities Star Tribune* as proof of his story, he began the tale.

It was in October, and the Minnesota Twins were hosting the Dodgers in the important first game of the World Series. Sandy Koufax, the best pitcher in baseball (some say the best of all time) was scheduled to pitch. But that day was Yom Kippur and Sandy is Jewish. He refused to play! Putting his religion before the game sent shockwaves throughout professional baseball and made headlines worldwide. What an example he had set! The pride felt in Jewish communities all over the country was palpable. (People in numerous *shul*s in Minneapolis claimed to have sighted the star pitcher sitting in their ranks!) As it happened, Don Drysdale pitched that game instead of Sandy and was pounded for many runs. When the manager came to take him out of the game, Drysdale said to him, "I know…you're wishing I was Jewish."

Now comes the interesting part.

14. Rabbi Moshe Feller, director of Chabad Lubavitch of the Upper Midwest. At age 28, he felt divinely inspired to try to see Sandy Koufax in his hotel room on the day Sandy was scheduled to pitch game two of the 1965 World Series in Minneapolis.

Young Rabbi Feller felt so inspired by Koufax's public respect for Jewish tradition, he felt he just had to go to the pitcher personally and thank him. "I get to the hotel where he's staying," the rabbi continued, "just hours before he is supposed to start pitching in the next World Series game. I had the chutzpah to go to the front desk and ask to see Sandy Koufax. The desk clerk must have thought that I was his rabbi, because he allowed me to go to his room! Koufax was gracious enough to let me in and I presented him with a pair of *tefillin*. I talked to him about what his actions meant to American Jewry. As I was leaving the hotel room, Koufax called out, 'You know, Rabbi Feller, they make a big fuss that I don't pitch on Yom Kippur. Well, I don't pitch on Rosh Hashanah either!'" As Pamela Huey wrote at the end of her article, "The Dodgers lost that day, but Koufax won."

15. Pitching great Sandy Koufax became a source of Jewish pride and a reluctant hero.

The Rewards of Unity

Kenesseth Israel, founded in 1890, is the oldest existing Orthodox synagogue in Minneapolis. Its spiritual leader, Rabbi Chaim Goldberger, talked to me on Lag B'Omer about the character and personality of this historic place of worship.

"We have survived two breakaway *shul*s," he reflected. "Each time our imminent demise was predicted, and both times we confounded the prediction. Most of the synagogues of the 1920s, '30s, and '40s did not remain Orthodox. We are the only surviving Orthodox *shul* from the eastern European Jewish enclave on the north side." Unwavering perseverance kept the *shul* from going the way of all the others. If it weren't for the *bitachon* and tenacity of a core of individuals, the *shul* would not be here today. And who were they? A junk dealer, a rag dealer, and a *shochet*.

16. Rabbi Chaim Goldberger, spiritual leader of Kenesseth Israel, the oldest existing Orthodox synagogue in Minneapolis. Shown here on right singing *zemiros* (songs) for Lag B'Omer.

In addition to their spiritual gains, G-d saw to it that their selflessness was rewarded materially. The *shochet* and his sons became the founders of the largest food distributors in the Midwest, and the junk dealer founded the region's most preeminent recycling firm. Their children and others brought the first mini-*kollel* in America to Minneapolis. The city now has the *kollel*, the Torah Academy, and a Bais Yaakov high school for girls.

The sense of *achdus* (unity) prevalent here defies the usual communal tendency for fragmentation. This quality was beautifully demonstrated recently at a rare event.

בָּרוּךְ אַתָּה ה' אֱלֹוקֵינוּ מֶלֶךְ הָעוֹלָם עוֹשֶׂה מַעֲשֵׂה בְרֵאשִׁית

Every 28 years, the sun begins the spring season on the eve of a Wednesday at the same moment when and where it first appeared at creation. The Jewish event surrounding it is called Birchas Hachamah, literally "the blessing of the sun." Jews gather all over the world to recite the simple blessing thanking the Creator.

Birchas Hachamah in Minneapolis, Rabbi Goldberger told me, was an exercise in community unity. "We all *davened* Shacharis [said morning prayers] at Bais Yisroel, the original breakaway synagogue. Then everyone – 250 men, women, and children – walked to my *shul*, Kenesseth Israel, to say Birchas Hachamah together. The police closed off the street and we both, rabbis of the two *shul*s, climbed on top of a flatbed truck. A keyboard pumped out Jewish tunes and everyone sang and danced. So many Jews dancing in the streets was an unbelievable sight. A middle-aged man came over to me and said that he remembered standing just 20 feet from this exact spot 28 years ago at the last Birchas Hachamah. At that time, a total of only 20 other Jews joined him. But this year, we united and stood proudly together at this wonderful event."

17. Birchas Hachamah, the blessing of the sun, a custom observed every 28 years. These pictures were taken at the Birchas Hachamah celebration of Young Israel of East Brunswick, New Jersey.

18. Singing and dancing at the Birchas Hachamah.

Our sages tell us that in ancient times, Rabbi Akiva's 24,000 students perished from a divinely sent plague because of a lack of unity and respect for each other. But on Lag B'Omer the plague stopped. And today, all mourning practices which were in force for the previous 32 days (commemorating this tragedy) are suspended. It is a day of celebration. Weddings are held, three-year-old boys have their hair cut for the first time. In Israel, hundreds of thousands of Jews show up in the northern city of Meron, the burial site of Rabbi Shimon Bar Yochai (the disciple of Rabbi Akiva who wrote the *Zohar*, as noted above), for wild celebrations.

Perhaps the most enduring symbol of Lag B'Omer is the bonfire. Some say it represents the light of Torah that emanated from Rabbi Shimon Bar Yochai as he taught his students the secrets of the Torah on the day of his death. Tradition states that the light that surrounded him was so intense that no one could approach him except his own students. Miraculously, the light of the sun stayed bright without setting until he completed his teachings.

19. A beaming Shlomo Simpser celebrating his bar mitzvah on Lag B'Omer

I stopped at the Aish HaTorah Center (in Minneapolis) where Shlomo Simpser was celebrating his bar mitzvah. A Lag B'Omer bonfire was blazing, and everyone sang and danced. How appropriate it is, I thought, to have a bar mitzvah celebration on Lag B'Omer, a day that celebrates the transmission of Torah from one generation to the next. I watched with joy and reverence as Shlomo's father spoke publicly to him about the importance of using his time to do *mitzvos*. And how moving it was to hear the young man standing near the bonfire of Rabbi Shimon Bar Yochai say how much he, too, wants to continue his Torah education, like the rabbis who preceded him.

> It is a day of celebration…. A Lag B'Omer bonfire was blazing, and everyone sang and danced. How appropriate it is…. I watched with joy and reverence…. And how moving it was…

Standing at the large bonfire at Kenesseth Israel on Lag B'Omer night – watching the crowd rejoice as they roast marshmallows and down hot dogs – I think of how the impressive growth of the Jewish communities in this challenging environment is founded on *bitachon*. These people point with pride to the *bitachon* of a Rabbi Benjamin Papermaster, carrying the mission of Torah from Lithuania to the unknown reaches of North Dakota; of a Shepsel Roberts, hitchhiking from Minneapolis to Chicago in search of a yeshivah; and of a father encouraging his son to hold fast to Torah Judaism on the day of his bar mitzvah. I am reminded of the message given by Rabbi Goldberger on the occasion of the 118th anniversary of the synagogue's founding. At that time, he said, "Our theme is *bitachon* – total confidence that G-d will provide, as He has provided for 118 years, in making Kenesseth Israel a flagship of Midwest American Orthodoxy."

And the light of the bonfires continues to shine.

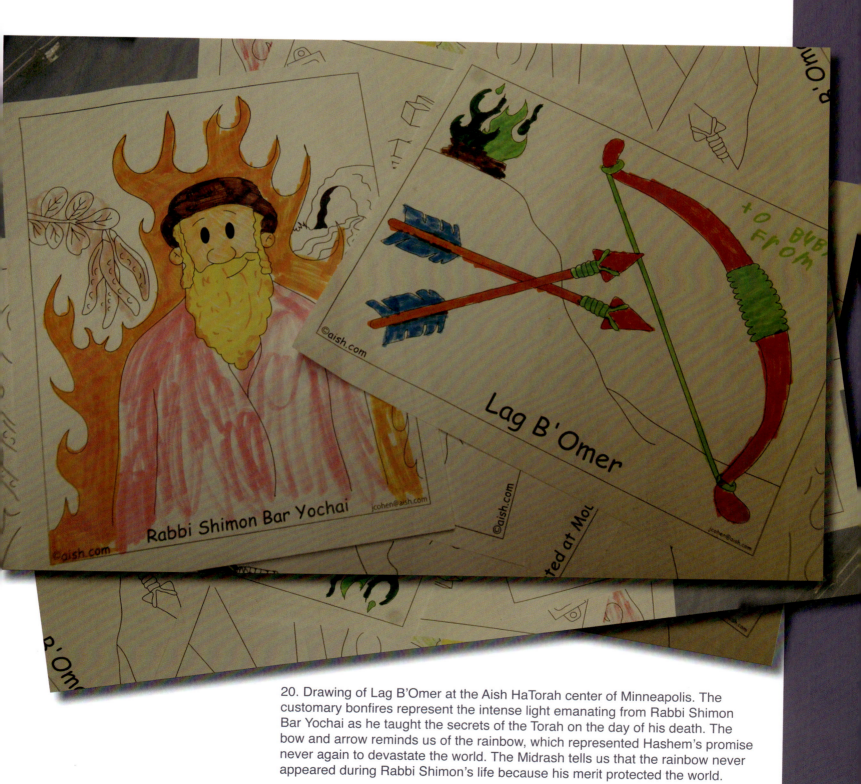

20. Drawing of Lag B'Omer at the Aish HaTorah center of Minneapolis. The customary bonfires represent the intense light emanating from Rabbi Shimon Bar Yochai as he taught the secrets of the Torah on the day of his death. The bow and arrow reminds us of the rainbow, which represented Hashem's promise never again to devastate the world. The Midrash tells us that the rainbow never appeared during Rabbi Shimon's life because his merit protected the world.

Shuls of the Midwest

21. Kenesseth Israel, 4th St. North, c. 1934

"As my fathers planted for me, So do I plant for my children"

TA 'ANIT 23A

22. Kenesseth Israel in St. Louis Park, 2009

23. KI's pews are on permanent loan from a distant Minnesota *shul*; a sign on the wall leading to the main sanctuary reads: "They are the legacy of B'nai Abraham in Virginia, Minn., an Orthodox synagogue that spanned the 20th century seeing to the spiritual needs of the Jewish community of the Iron Range."

24. Sons of Abraham, 14th Ave. South, c. 1913

26. Reb Shepsel Roberts, founder of the Torah Academy, celebrating with several of his grandchildren and great-grandchildren at a Torah Academy *siddur* party

25. Torah Academy of St. Louis Park, Minneapolis, the day school founded in 1945 by men such as Reb Shepsel Roberts

28. Five students learning at the West Side Hebrew Institute in St. Paul, c. 1929

27. Talmud Torah, St. Paul, c. 1915

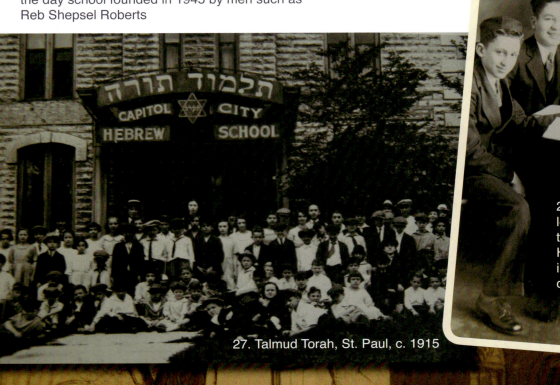

29. Talmud Torah Shelter House, St. Paul, after the flooding of the Mississippi, c. 1920s–30s

Life

31. Fishman's Kosher Deli, for everything kosher today

30. Abe's Delicatessen on Plymouth Ave., where all things Jewish were found, c. 1948

32. Zlota Rivka Svidelsky (second from right) and her family. The photo was taken in the Ukraine, the year this typical Orthodox family moved to the then atypical St. Paul.

33. In 1946, journalist Carey M. Williams labeled Minneapolis "the capital of anti-Semitism." A young mayor, Hubert H. Humphrey, pushed for new laws banning discrimination. Photo of Temple Israel with swastika painted on its column, c. 1929.

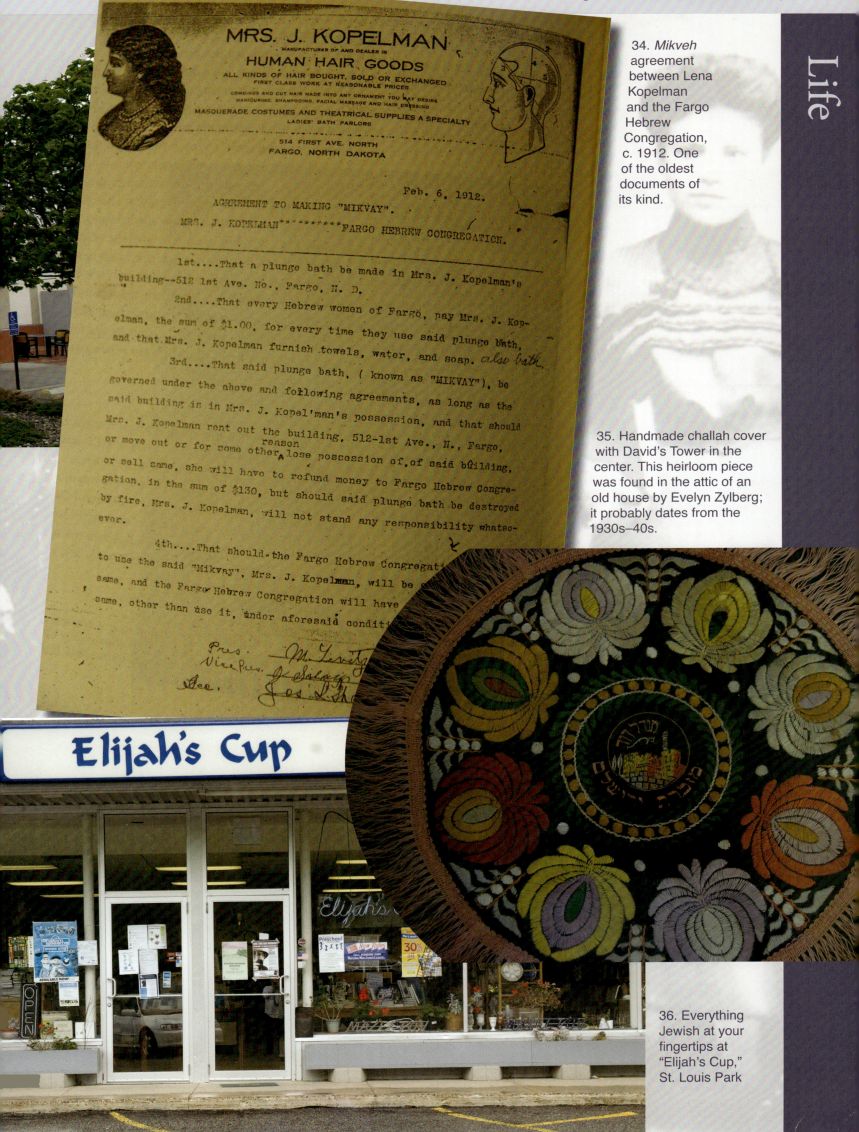

MRS. J. KOPELMAN

MANUFACTURER OF AND DEALER IN

HUMAN HAIR GOODS

ALL KINDS OF HAIR BOUGHT, SOLD OR EXCHANGED
FIRST CLASS WORK AT REASONABLE PRICES

COMBINGS AND CUT HAIR MADE INTO ANY ORNAMENT YOU MAY DESIRE
MANICURING, SHAMPOOING, FACIAL MASSAGE AND HAIR DRESSING

MASQUERADE COSTUMES AND THEATRICAL SUPPLIES A SPECIALTY
LADIES' BATH PARLORS

514 FIRST AVE. NORTH
FARGO, NORTH DAKOTA

Feb. 6. 1912.

AGREEMENT TO MAKING "MIKVAY".

MRS. J. KOPELMAN**********FARGO HEBREW CONGREGATION.

1st....That a plunge bath be made in Mrs. J. Kopelman's building--512 1st Ave. No., Fargo, N. D.

2nd....That every Hebrew women of Fargo, pay Mrs. J. Kopelman, the sum of $1.00, for every time they use said plunge bath, and that Mrs. J. Kopelman furnish towels, water, and soap. *also bath*

3rd....That said plunge bath, (known as "MIKVAY"), be governed under the above and following agreements, as long as the said building is in Mrs. J. Kopel'man's possession, and that should Mrs. J. Kopelman rent out the building, 512-1st Ave., N., Fargo, or move out or for some other reason, lose possession of, of said building, or sell same, she will have to refund money to Fargo Hebrew Congregation, in the sum of $130, but should said plunge bath be destroyed by fire, Mrs. J. Kopelman, will not stand any responsibility whatsoever.

4th....That should the Fargo Hebrew Congregati[on] to use the said "MIKVAY", Mrs. J. Kopelman, will be [ ] same, and the Fargo Hebrew Congregation will have [ ] same, other than use it, under aforesaid condit[ions]

Pres.
Vice Pres.
Sec.

34. *Mikveh* agreement between Lena Kopelman and the Fargo Hebrew Congregation, c. 1912. One of the oldest documents of its kind.

35. Handmade challah cover with David's Tower in the center. This heirloom piece was found in the attic of an old house by Evelyn Zylberg; it probably dates from the 1930s–40s.

Elijah's Cup

36. Everything Jewish at your fingertips at "Elijah's Cup," St. Louis Park

The fires of Lag B'Omer

37. Reb Shepsel Roberts, leader of the Midwest

38. Rabbi Benjamin Papermaster, pioneer

39. Rabbi Moshe Feller, leader for forty years

. Shlomo
mpser at Lag
Omer bar
tzvah celebration
ading the Torah

. Dancing
ound the bonfire

. Marshmallow
asting on Lag
Omer

. A Lag B'Omer
rade in the Twin
ties, a Chabad
dition, 1993

. What's Lag
Omer without
asting hot dogs?

. Rabbi
olberger keeps
e fires lit.

. Pouring oil to
art the bonfire
Lag B'Omer in
eron, Israel

. Lag B'Omer
lebration in
eron, site of the
mb of Rabbi
himon Bar
ochai, the author
the *Zohar*, the
assic work on
bbalah

. Over 250,000
ws make the
grimage each
ar to Meron to
ht the bonfires
Lag B'Omer and
cut their three-
ar-olds' hair.

40

41

42

43

44

45

46

47

48

My thanks to
Rabbi Chaim Goldberger,
Debbie Weinberg,
Rabbi Berel Simpser,
Sara Simpser,
the Jewish Historical Society
of the Upper Midwest,
Dr. Ted Papermaster,
Rabbi Moshe Feller,
and Evelyn Zylberg.

Bibliography

Berman, Hyman, and Linda Mack Schloff. *Jews in Minnesota*.
　　Minnesota: Minnesota Historical Society Press, 2002.

Epstein, Morris. *All about Jewish Holidays and Customs*. New York:
　　Ktav, 1959.

*Upper Midwest Jewish History: The Journal of the Jewish Historical
　　Society of the Upper Midwest*. Vols. 3–4 (2004–2005).

Rosenblum, Gene H. *Jewish Pioneers of St. Paul, 1849–1874*.
　　Charleston, SC: Arcadia Publishing, 2001.

Schloff, Linda Mack. *And Prairie Dogs Weren't Kosher: Jewish
　　Women in the Upper Midwest since 1855*. Minnesota:
　　Minnesota Historical Society Press, 1996.

Bleich, J. David. *Bircas Hachamah*. New York: ArtScroll/Mesorah,
　　1980.

Photo Attributions

All numbered photos from the author's collection except as follows.
Photos 8, 9, 11, 15, 21, 24, 27–30, 33, 34: Jewish Historical Society
of the Upper Midwest; 10, 38: Papermaster family archives; 13, 26,
37: archives of Debbie Weinberg and Shepsel Roberts; 43: archives
of Rabbi Moshe Feller.

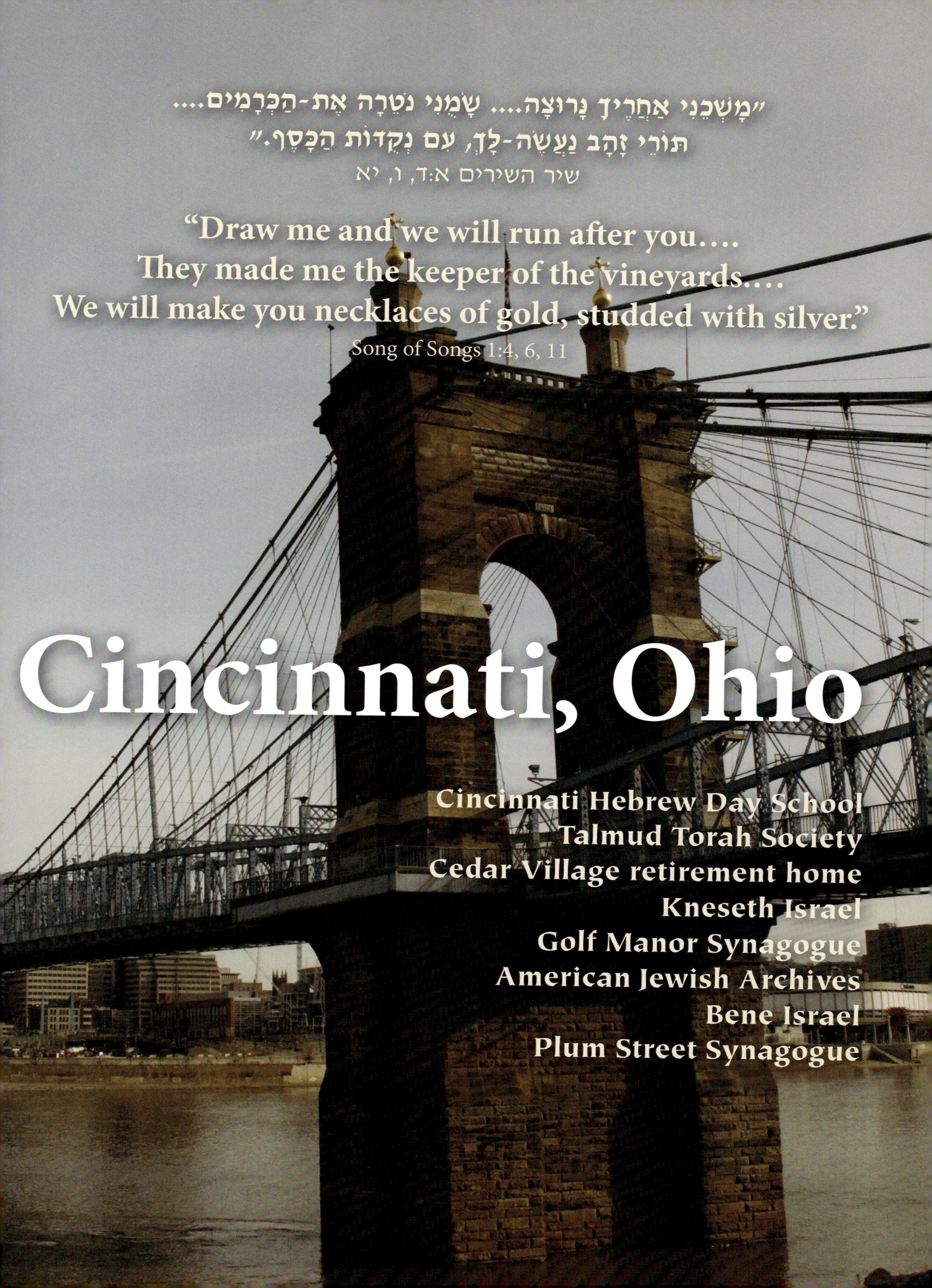
"מָשְׁכֵנִי אַחֲרֶיךָ נָּרוּצָה.... שָׂמֻנִי נֹטֵרָה אֶת-הַכְּרָמִים....
תּוֹרֵי זָהָב נַעֲשֶׂה-לָּךְ, עִם נְקֻדּוֹת הַכָּסֶף."
שיר השירים א:ד, ו, יא
"Draw me and we will run after you….
They made me the keeper of the vineyards….
We will make you necklaces of gold, studded with silver."
Song of Songs 1:4, 6, 11
Cincinnati, Ohio
Cincinnati Hebrew Day School
Talmud Torah Society
Cedar Village retirement home
Kneseth Israel
Golf Manor Synagogue
American Jewish Archives
Bene Israel
Plum Street Synagogue

Cincinnati, Ohio

Passover in the Queen City – with a Touch of Silver

O ften called "the Queen City of the West," Cincinnati was also described by historian Henry Howe as "a sort of Paradise for the Hebrews." I am flying over the Ohio River, which separates Ohio from Kentucky, and I review my research of Jewish history in this area. As it happens to be only ten days before Passover, I wonder, are there parallels to be found here to the Exodus story? In many respects, this too, is a story of a newly independent people crystallizing their religion in the wilderness – and nearly losing it until a leader appears to provide guidance and energy. I found that Cincinnati Jewry's unique history rests very much on the personality of its founder, Joseph Jonas. Let's go back in time.

"You Will Forget Your G-d!"

It is October 1816, and Joseph has just arrived in New York harbor from Plymouth, England. He is young man from a traditional Jewish home. Unlike other immigrants, he is not interested in New York or Philadelphia, the northeastern centers of Judaism at the time. He has read a good deal about America, and he is intrigued by descriptions of the Ohio River, where few explorers have gone. He is determined to settle on its banks, in a place called Cincinnati – a city not twenty years old, but full of beauty and economic opportunity.

He had been warned, somberly and emphatically, by his Jewish acquaintances in Philadelphia: "In the wilds of America, entirely among gentiles, you will forget your religion and your G-d!" Yet he feels that the area's isolation is all the more reason to strike roots there. His response is, "A new resting place for the scattered sons of Israel should be commenced; …a sanctuary should be erected in the Great West dedicated to the L-rd of Hosts." Solemnly promising never to forget his religion or forsake his G-d, he leaves for Cincinnati, hoping to plant there the first Jewish congregation west of the Alleghenies. He arrives there just before Passover.

Writing about his "errand into the Wilderness" in 1845, Joseph implied that he was following the tradition of the Children of Israel going into the wilderness after the Exodus from Egypt. Trekking into a region unknown to them, they will yet become a strong nation.

1. Joseph Jonas (1792–1869), possibly the first Jew to settle in Cincinnati, was a silversmith, watchmaker, and one of the founders of Kahal Kadosh Bene Israel.

2. By the mid-nineteenth century, Cincinnati had become one of the largest cities west of the Allegheny Mountains.

3. Chestnut St. Cemetery, the first permanent Jewish cemetery in Cincinnati, purchased in 1821 for $75

From the first day he entered the town, he was quite a curiosity. One old Quakeress asked, "Art thou a Jew? Will thou let me examine thee?" She made a thorough appraisal and then pronounced, "Well, thou art no different to other people!"

True to his word, Jonas remained Orthodox. One day, a farmer brought him a watch and left it to be repaired. (Jonas had opened shop as a "mechanic" – a watchmaker/silversmith.) He came back a few days later and, to his surprise, found the store closed. Either Jonas went bankrupt, he thought unhappily, or he ran off with my watch! Then he met a neighbor who told him that Jonas was a Jew who kept his store closed on this day, for Saturday was his day of rest. When the customer went home and told his mother, she hurried to Jonas and asked if he was, indeed, Jewish. When he answered yes, she lifted her eyes towards the heavens and cried, "Thank you, O L-rd, that I have lived to see a descendant of Abraham before my death!"

4. Grave in Adath Israel Cemetery of Rev. Bernard Illowy, Orthodox leader of American Jewry in the mid-nineteenth century.

5. KK Bene Israel, 1836, organized by Jonas and nine other Orthodox Jews in 1824

Jonas was later joined by nine more Orthodox Jews from England and they organized the first congregation, Kahal Kadosh Bene Israel, in 1824. Their relationship with neighboring Christians was so favorable that Jonas reported, "Fifty-two gentlemen of the Christian faith donated twenty-five dollars each toward the building of the city's first synagogue." A congregation of Jews from Poland, Adath Israel, formed in 1847. German-Bavarian Jews came next, forming Ahabath Achim in 1848.

The German Jews began with the most typical of all Jewish immigrant occupations, peddling. They would start with five dollars, invest it in a sackful of goods, and travel hundreds of miles, lodging along the way for 25 cents a night (supper, lodging, and breakfast). The five dollars would turn into $150 in a few years. With that, they could start small dry goods stores of their own, and were soon selling supplies to new peddlers.

By 1850, philanthropy had become the hallmark of Cincinnati Jewry. The city boasted "the Jewish Hospital," the first of its kind in America, as well as several mutual aid, benevolent, and ladies' charitable societies. It even had a fund to aid the needy in Palestine. With the onset of eastern European mass immigration of the 1880s, the major Jewish charities federated into the United Jewish Charities – the second Jewish Federation in the country. (The first was in Boston.)

Despite the formation of syna-

7. The Jewish Hospital, established in 1850, was the first of its kind in America.

6. During the first half of the nineteenth century, many central European immigrants started as peddlers, carrying heavy backpacks on foot. Often, they were aided by their more established coreligionists with loans for merchandise. They would later open stores and help the next group of peddlers.

gogues, traditional Judaism found few supporters in Cincinnati. Jonas wrote that "Religious laxity was the rule with little interest in spiritual matters," and ultimately confessed his fear that perhaps Judaism would not be able to survive in this wilderness.

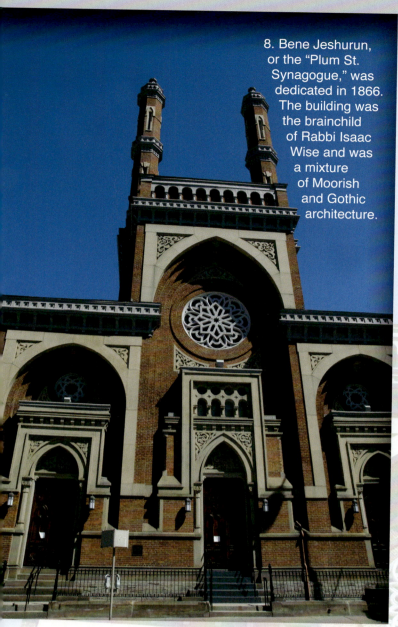

8. Bene Jeshurun, or the "Plum St. Synagogue," was dedicated in 1866. The building was the brainchild of Rabbi Isaac Wise and was a mixture of Moorish and Gothic architecture.

The climate he described later set the scene for the 1854 appointment of Isaac Mayer Wise (a founder of the American Reform movement) as the rabbi of Bene Jeshurun, which had been formed by a group of German immigrants in 1841. His first major pulpit at Beth El Congregation in Albany, New York, had ended quickly in 1846. A series of ritual modifications he instituted stirred a heated controversy that led to a memorable melee on Rosh Hashanah, when the congregation's president lashed out at Wise and knocked off his hat.

In Cincinnati, Wise saw his brand of Judaism replacing the *minhag* (custom) of the Spanish-Portuguese, Polish, and German Jews. He optimistically titled his prayer book *Minhag America*. In 1865, the classic, Moorish-style temple building on Plum Street was erected. Ten years later, Hebrew Union College, the Reform seminary, was founded as the only rabbinical seminary in America, but not without considerable controversy. In 1883, at a banquet celebrating the first rabbinic ordination at the college, a commotion erupted. As the waiters began to serve the food, two rabbis rose from their seats and left, while others refused to eat. Whitened clams had been placed before them, followed by crabs, shrimp, and frogs' legs. It became known as the "*Treifah* Banquet Incident."

Wise later said he had expected the meal to be kosher.

Joseph Jonas once wondered what great things might happen, "If only a few…[Jews] would commence, sincerely, keeping the Sabbath and the festivals." When most of the traditional-leaning synagogues in Cincinnati merged to follow the Reform movement, this seemed like a pipe dream in the wilderness.

This situation, however, was about to change.

Despite the powerful reforming efforts of Isaac Wise, Reform Judaism never gained a monopoly in Cincinnati. Orthodox Jews maintained a continuous presence in the city from Jonas's time onward. In addition to Adath Israel and Ahabath Achim, there was also Shearith Israel (founded 1855), also known as the "Frummer Shul." Its rabbi was Bernard Illowy, one of the most learned and influential Orthodox leaders in the entire country. Staunchly anti-slavery in New Orleans, he fled for his life from the Deep South, hopped on a riverboat disguised as a gambler, and landed in Cincinnati, where he stayed until his death.

Maintaining a Foothold

The roots of the Isaacs family of Cincinnati go back to the pioneering days. In 1853, Schachne Isaacs opened a general store, which stayed firmly closed on Shabbos. His customers learned that it paid to come into town during the week. Known as the "fire-eater" for his zeal, Schachne publicly burned a copy of Wise's prayer book. When his congregation refused to put in a *mikveh* (ritual bath), he

9. Family of Schachne Isaacs, the "fire-eater." He opened a general store and remained closed on Shabbos even though that was the big shopping day for the farmers. They learned that it paid to come on another day during the week.

resigned in protest and began a new congregation, Kahal Kadosh Beth Tefillah, better known as "Reb Schachne's Shul" (1866).

With the assassination of Czar Alexander II in March 1881 – and the vicious pogroms that followed – eastern European Jews came en masse, most in abject poverty. The Society for the Rehabilitation of the Sick and Poor, the Hebrew Free Loan Society, and the Jewish Foster Home galvanized into action.

In 1887, Dov Behr Manischewitz from Salant, Lithuania, arrived in Cincinnati as a *shochet* (ritual slaughterer) and peddler. He and Moses Isaacs started the Cincinnati Talmud Torah Society, the predecessor to today's day schools. The curriculum included Hebrew literacy, *Chumash* (Bible) with Rashi commentary, and *Shulchan Aruch* (Jewish law), all taught in Yiddish.

In 1888, Rabbi Manischewitz, who had studied in the Telz Yeshivah, opened a small bakery to bake matzoh for his friends and family using a coal-fueled oven. By the turn of the century, demand for his matzoh was so great that he switched to gas-fired ovens and matzoh machines to handle the dough. This innovation allowed for more consistent quality

10. Dov Behr and Nesha Manischewitz, founder of America's largest matzoh company, c. 1888

11. The original Manischewitz bakery on 8th St. – the largest matzoh bakery in the world, c. 1920s. Eventually this facility was replaced by the more modern plant opened by Manischewitz in Jersey City in 1932.

and matzoh size and more careful control of the baking speed, a factor especially important for Passover. Though the matzoh machine invented by Isaac Singer twenty years earlier had become the subject of a serious halachic controversy, the scrupulous reputation and piety of Dov Behr Manischewitz helped the company win significant rabbinic allies. He was the first to package matzohs for shipment outside the immediate community, and eventually shipped to England, France, Japan, Hungary, Egypt, and New Zealand. His bakeries would become a model for future kosher bakeries both in America and abroad.

Cincinnati's Orthodox Jews were quite divided between Polish, Romanian, Russian, and Lithuanian factions. Rabbi Abraham Jacob Gershon Lesser of Beth Hamedrash Hagadol (a formidable scholar and founder of Agudath HaRabbonim of America) tried valiantly to bring a measure of unity to the community from 1898 until his death in 1924. Following his demise, however, the community became mired in myriad disputes involving kosher food supervision, Jewish education, and fundraising, among other issues. In an article written in 1928 for the more traditional newspaper, *Every Friday* (as opposed to the Reform paper, *The Israelite*), were these disheartening words:

> What is wrong with Orthodoxy in Cincinnati?…There is no unity in Orthodoxy anywhere and yet it manages to hold its own and even to thrive…. The Orthodox are divided into many elements, each intent upon its own little problems, ignoring entirely the sense of unity that should exist here.

In a subsequent issue in the same year:

> The manifold feelings of Cincinnati's Orthodox Jewry…[include] their failure in the support of their rabbis, their neglect of Jewish education, and their indifference to the needs of Palestine, all sins committed unknowingly through indifference and, therefore, likely to continue.

Rabbi Silver to the Rescue

This void was not filled until the coming of a person described as an irascible man, small in physical stature, with a heavy Yiddish accent: Rabbi Eliezer Silver. Despite his stature, he was a giant. He had received *smichah* (rabbinic ordination) from Reb Chaim Ozer Grodzinski in 1906, and traced his lineage back to King David. An expert in Jewish law, he was a dynamic, charismatic person with total fidelity to Torah Judaism, and sensitivity to Jewish suffering. His ceaseless activism, together with his cleverness, political sagacity, flair for the dramatic – and a considerable dose of chutzpah – led to numerous achievements on behalf of Orthodox Judaism in America and the world.

Invited by several congregations in Cincinnati to help resolve the lack of organization and unity, he became the president of the Union of Orthodox Rabbis. He created a Vaad Hoeir, an Orthodox city council, with all synagogues having equal representation, as well as a Vaad Hakashrut, to supervise kosher foods. Recognized for his leadership, he was offered a pulpit

12. Early photograph of Rabbi Eliezer Silver with his "box" or Litvisher *yarmulke*, c. 1920s

at Kneseth Israel in the fall of 1931, and moved in to Cincinnati, complete with his trademark top hat, *kapota* (long coat), and wispy beard, to a place he would stay until his death in 1968.

Rabbi Silver's activism and leadership of national organizations such as Agudath HaRabbonim, Ezras Torah, Vaad Hatzoloh (Rescue Committee), and Agudath Israel of America, propelled him to national and international prominence. He galvanized his following by demanding a kosher kitchen at the Jewish Hospital and outraged the city's Reform leaders by bringing an Agudath Israel convention to the very capital of Reform Jewry.

Rabbi Yaakov Lustig, who was the acting rabbi of Kneseth Israel after Rabbi Silver's passing, and an impressive, learned rabbi in his own right, told me that when Rabbi Silver planned to build a *mikveh* close to the Reform Rockdale Temple (formerly the original Bene Israel congregation of Joseph Jonas), they took him to court. It happened that the judge was blind. The temple's attorney, trying to portray Rabbi Silver

13. Rabbi Silver (1882–1968), with his trademark top hat, wispy beard, and *kapota* (long coat), changed the course of history in this city.

as backward, described the rabbi's attire. "Here is a man," he told the judge, "dressed in a long black caftan and a square box hat. I will show you that his mindset is as medieval as his clothing." Turning to Rabbi Silver, he said, "Do you believe everything in the Torah?" The rabbi answered, "Yes."

Citing the incident in Deuteronomy of Bilaam's donkey, he asked incredulously, "Do you believe that an ass can talk?"

"Of course," answered Rabbi Silver, "and now I see it with my own eyes!"

The judge and gallery erupted in laughter. The judge turned to Rabbi Silver and asked him if he would hold services in the *mikveh* (because that would be allowed by law). He answered "yes" and for the next few years, Minchah services were held at the *mikveh* once a month!

Elinor Ziv, longtime resident of Cincinnati's Jewish community and guide extraordinaire, told me of the time that Rabbi Silver's driver was stopped by a policeman for exceeding the speed limit. Pleading with the officer, the driver said, "Do you know who I have back there?" Pointing over his shoulder, he intoned gravely, "the president of the Union of Orthodox Rabbis..."

"I don't care if he's the president of the United States," the officer snapped. To the cop's surprise, Rabbi Silver squeaked from the back seat in his Yiddish accent, "*unt* Canada, too!"

14. Elinor Ziv, guide extraordinaire and fountain of information

In October of 1943, he helped organize and lead a mass rally of more than 400 Orthodox rabbis (the first of its kind) in Washington, DC, reciting Psalms on the Capitol steps, and pressing for decisive action to save European Jews from the Holocaust. While the rally failed in its objective to meet with President Roosevelt, it directly led to the formation of the War Refugee Board, opening the door that saved countless lives. He said, "We are prepared to violate many [American] laws to save lives. We are not mixing in war, not in politics. We are rescuing."

His greatest achievement, in fact, was to directly help save thousands of Jews in eastern Europe during the Holocaust. Under the auspices of the Vaad Hatzoloh formed in 1939, of which he was one of the founders and president, he rescued many, including numerous Torah scholars. He met with the political powers of many countries, and used his friendship with Senator Robert Taft, grandson of the former president William Howard Taft (with whom he was also friendly), to help reach his goals. He even negotiated with the German SS, using legal and not-so-legal means to free concentration camp prisoners by the thousands.

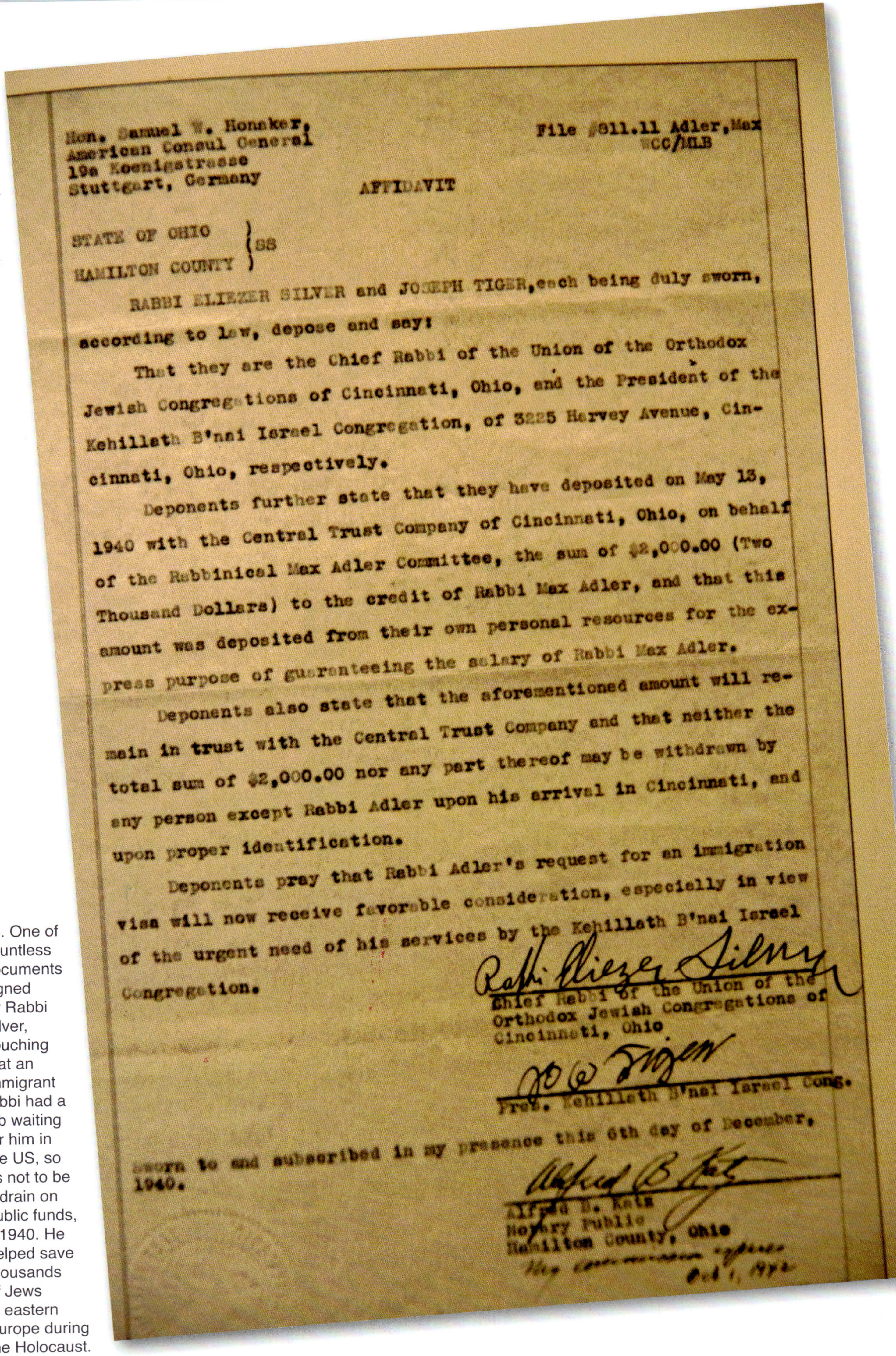

Hon. Samuel W. Honaker,
American Consul General
19a Koenigstrasse
Stuttgart, Germany

File #811.11 Adler,Max
WCC/MLB

AFFIDAVIT

STATE OF OHIO)
) ss
HAMILTON COUNTY)

RABBI ELIEZER SILVER and JOSEPH TIGER, each being duly sworn, according to law, depose and say:

That they are the Chief Rabbi of the Union of the Orthodox Jewish Congregations of Cincinnati, Ohio, and the President of the Kehillath B'nai Israel Congregation, of 3225 Harvey Avenue, Cincinnati, Ohio, respectively.

Deponents further state that they have deposited on May 13, 1940 with the Central Trust Company of Cincinnati, Ohio, on behalf of the Rabbinical Max Adler Committee, the sum of $2,000.00 (Two Thousand Dollars) to the credit of Rabbi Max Adler, and that this amount was deposited from their own personal resources for the express purpose of guaranteeing the salary of Rabbi Max Adler.

Deponents also state that the aforementioned amount will remain in trust with the Central Trust Company and that neither the total sum of $2,000.00 nor any part thereof may be withdrawn by any person except Rabbi Adler upon his arrival in Cincinnati, and upon proper identification.

Deponents pray that Rabbi Adler's request for an immigration visa will now receive favorable consideration, especially in view of the urgent need of his services by the Kehillath B'nai Israel Congregation.

Rabbi Eliezer Silver
Chief Rabbi of the Union of the
Orthodox Jewish Congregations of
Cincinnati, Ohio.

Joe Tiger
Pres. Kehillath B'nai Israel Cong.

Sworn to and subscribed in my presence this 6th day of December, 1940.

Alfred B. Katz
Alfred B. Katz
Notary Public
Hamilton County, Ohio
My commission expires
Oct 1, 1942.

15. One of countless documents signed by Rabbi Silver, vouching that an immigrant rabbi had a job waiting for him in the US, so as not to be a drain on public funds, c.1940. He helped save thousands of Jews in eastern Europe during the Holocaust.

Bess Paper, now a resident at the Cedar Village Senior Home, was Rabbi Silver's assistant for many years after the war. She told me that the rabbi went to the DP camps in his army captain (chaplain's) uniform with pockets full of money to help bring the refugees to the US. "You should see how much money he brought in. When he asked for money, you just couldn't refuse him. He was determined, aggressive, but with a certain sweetness."

On one trip, in 1946, he went to distribute funds and food as the destruction became clearer. Only five feet, five inches tall, he worked tirelessly day after day for weeks at a time, and lost 35 pounds in three months, going from 165 pounds to 130. Friends said he "lived on Torah rather than food. He lived and breathed *hatzoloh* – rescue." With his top hat and white beard, this small dynamo of a man became a cherished symbol of freedom to Jews worldwide.

An Unforgettable Lesson

Simon Wiesenthal, who later became the famous "Nazi hunter," described his encounter with Rabbi Silver in a DP camp. In Mauthausen death camp, Wiesenthal had seen one of the inmates lend a smuggled prayer book to many prisoners in return for a quarter of each person's daily soup ration. Later, when Rabbi Silver came to the DP camp with a Torah, Wiesenthal refused to participate in the dedication ceremony. He couldn't forget this man who greedily bargained faith for food, and felt he could no longer believe in a Torah that led to this kind of behavior. He told Silver of his anger at the man's hypocrisy. "*Du Dummer* [you silly man]," Silver chided him, "so you look only at the bad man who took something from the good ones?" He told him to look instead at the many good men who were willing to give up food for the chance to pray! Wiesenthal went to services the next day – and never forgot the incident.

Rabbi Silver's granddaughter, Judy (Silver) Shapiro, describes his moving visits to the church orphanages of Europe after the war, searching for Jewish children who had been hidden from the Nazis. The nuns would tell him that there were no Jewish children there. Nevertheless, he would gather all the children together and shout out the words of *Shema Yisrael* – the first prayer Jewish children are taught by their mothers – and invariably, a number of children would come out of the crowd and cling to him.

When Rabbi Silver ran out of rescue funds, he often used his own. He died penniless in 1968, but in the accounting ledger that matters most, Rabbi Eliezer Silver died one of the richest men in the world.

A Living Legacy of *Chesed*

The Jews of Cincinnati are rightfully proud of this gem who blessed their community with his presence. He exemplified *chesed*, the extreme loving-kindness of the Patriarch Abraham, which is a hallmark of the Jewish people.

And that *chesed* is alive and well to this day in Cincinnati. Rabbi Hanan Balk, the rabbi of the Golf Manor Synagogue for the past twenty years, told me that the *chesed* shown to those in need of food and housing is legendary. He said that one visitor, who had traveled widely, told him, "There are two places overflowing with *chesed*: Jerusalem and Cincinnati."

> "There are two places overflowing with *chesed*: Jerusalem and Cincinnati."

16. Rabbi Hanan Balk of the Golf Manor Synagogue looks over the massive quantity of food packages for his community's Ma'os Chittim (Passover food distribution) campaign to help the needy.

When I met the rabbi, he was preparing to sell his congregants' *chametz* before Passover. The history of his synagogue reflects beautifully the history of the Orthodox community in Cincinnati – and the movement of its people from downtown in the early 1800s to Avondale in the early twentieth century, and then to Roselawn and Amberly, where it is now. Rabbi Balk speaks with the exuberance and effervescence of a man proud of the accomplishments of his community. Most gratifying is the unity of the many different synagogues, organizations, and day schools. They have come a long way from the fractured divisiveness of the 1920s.

17. William Ziv appointing the rabbi as *shaliach* (legal representative) to sell his *chametz* as Alan Wolf looks on. The pen provides the needed object of value to exchange and complete the purchase.

Two women who experienced the growth of the Orthodox community from the beginning of the Silver era to the present are Esther Deutsch, whose family came in 1919, and Rae Levy, who had a great uncle in Cincinnati before the Civil War. "We lived *bamidbar* – in the wilderness – back in the 1930s," Rae said of Jewish life. "We went to public high school and an after-school Talmud Torah, run by a non-religious organization. That was all we had in Jewish education before Rabbi Silver came."*

18. Rae Levy (may her memory be blessed), left, and Esther Deutsch reviewing with enthusiasm the history of this incredible community. They have been no small part of its success.

Esther Deutsch brought me an article from the March 1928 edition of *Every Friday*. It was a marriage announcement that poignantly demonstrates the mindset of the isolated Orthodox community in the heartland of Reform Judaism:

19. A 1928 edition of the Jewish newspaper *Every Friday*

---

*   I must note with sadness that since my interview with her, Rae Levy has passed on. Her last words to me expressed her hope that she would live to see the book completed. May her memory be blessed.

Mrs. M'nucha Rubenstein has gone to Detroit to attend the wedding of her son, Shammai, to Gittle Peiman of Detroit. Gittle and Shammai! What a refreshing novelty in a land where Moses becomes Mortimer and Levy becomes Llewellyn…in a land where Jews are ashamed of the old Jewish names…making them known to all the world as Jews! All the respect to you, Mrs. Rubenstein.

The marriage announcement, by the way, was that of Esther Deutsch's parents!

20. Inspection card of M'nucha Rubenstein, c. 1921

…despite the setbacks, the seeds [Joseph Jonas] planted have borne fruit. With leaders such as Rabbis Illowy, Lesser, and Silver, the city now boasts day schools, a girl's Jewish high school, a Jewish hospital, kosher restaurants, many synagogues, and a sparkling reputation for doing *chesed* at every opportunity.

When Joseph Jonas struck the spark of the first Orthodox community west of the Alleghenies, he could not have foreseen all of the challenges that would arise in Cincinnati. But despite the setbacks, the seeds he planted have borne fruit. With leaders such as Rabbis Illowy, Lesser, and Silver, the city now

כֹּה אָמַר הי
זָכַרְתִּי לָךְ חֶסֶד
נְעוּרַיִךְ אַהֲבַת
כְּלוּלֹתָיִךְ לֶכְתֵּךְ
אַחֲרַי בַּמִּדְבָּר
בְּאֶרֶץ לֹא זְרוּעָה

ירמיהו ב:ב

boasts day schools, a girl's Jewish high school, a Jewish hospital, kosher restaurants, many synagogues, and a sparkling reputation for doing *chesed* at every opportunity.

Through the prophet Jeremiah, G-d praised the Children of Israel when they left Egypt on the very first Passover, more than 3,000 years ago: "I remember the kindness of your youth…following Me into the desert in a land not sown."

I feel sure that Joseph Jonas, too, would have been proud of his people who sojourned in this wilderness and, like their bold ancestors, never lost sight of G-d.

21. Students at the Cincinnati Hebrew Day School enjoying the "fruits" of their labor at Chabad's Model Matzoh Bakery

Life in the Queen City

22. The old Agudas Israel building, founded by immigrants from Poland and Romania in the early twentieth century. It eventually moved to Golf Manor in 1956.

24. The new Kneseth Israel – now Zichron Eliezer – building in progress, along with a *mikveh* in the rear

23. The interior of Golf Manor Synagogue today is designed in the shape of an ark. Just as the ark had to go through the turbulence and uncertainty of the flood, so, too, did this community – and came out of it strong.

25. The Jewish Home for the Aged and Infirm, 1889

26. You've come a long way! Cedar Village retirement home.

27. Mizrachi, a religious Zionist organization, was formed in the early twentieth century. Cincinnati served as host for the convention, demonstrating the significance of the city's Orthodox community, c. 1919.

29. Bernard Marks of Cincinnati was the Haganah captain of the historic ship the *Exodus* in 1947. He served on Merchant Marine ships during World War II, and wanted to help the Jews after hearing of the atrocities committed by the Germans. At that time the Haganah was a Zionist underground group working for the creation of the State of Israel.

28. Picketing the British consulate to protest the British policy in Palestine in 1946

32. Hirsch and Max Manischewitz, sent to study in Palestine

30. Early ad for Crisco; hydrogenated vegetable shortening was first introduced to the public in 1911 as a substitute for both butter and lard. It was an enormously successful product both for Jews (as a practical kosher product) and non-Jews alike, c. 1913.

33. Yiddish cookbook by Manischewitz, c. 1930s

31. John Marx, the bagel man, started his Hot Bagel store in 1969 after two years as a "bouncer" in a local bar. Immediately, a rabbi approached him asking if he wanted to be kosher. Now, he's been doing it for over 40 years. "This has always been a great meeting place for Jews and non-Jews alike," he told me.

A touch of Silver – education in Cincinatti

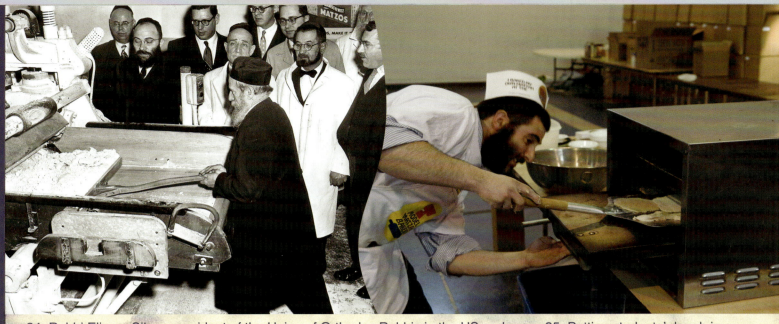

34. Rabbi Eliezer Silver, president of the Union of Orthodox Rabbis in the US and Canada, pushing unleavened dough for the opening of the matzoh-baking season at the state-of-the-art Manischewitz plant in Jersey City, NJ, c. 1953.

35. Putting students' dough in a demonstration oven at Cincinnati Hebrew Day School

36. Baking can be fun! Student joyfully puts her heart, soul, and hands into kneading the dough for the matzohs.

37. Rabbi Silver visits a classroom at Chofetz Chaim Day School, date unknown.

39. Rabbi Silver with the Lubavitcher Rebbe, Joseph Isaac Schneersohn, who was visiting Cincinnati, c. 1943

38. Cincinnati Hebrew Day School; a Chabad rabbi visited to teach about baking matzoh for Passover.

40. Midnight at the oasis! Always the traveler, Rabbi Silver visits Egypt in 1946.

The Seder

41. Rendition of Civil War Seder. The only conventional Seder items available to Jews of the 23rd Ohio Volunteer Regiment in West Virginia were matzohs and Haggadahs. They built a hut, obtained kegs of cider in place of wine, used peppery weed instead of traditional bitter herbs (*maror*), and set a brick on the table to represent *charoses* (usually a mixture of wine and nuts to represent the mortar used to build the bricks).

42. Seder in Paris during WWI. c. 1919

43. "We were slaves to Pharaoh in Egypt." It is traditional to act out the Seder as if you were there today. Students and seniors participate together in the model Seder at the Cedar Village retirement home. The residents loved it!

44. At the end of WWII, 1,300 Jewish soldiers took part in the 1945 Seder celebrating Israel's deliverance from bondage. This held particular significance on the eve of the liberation of the concentration camps.

45. Arts and crafts celebrating Passover at the Cincinnati Hebrew Day School

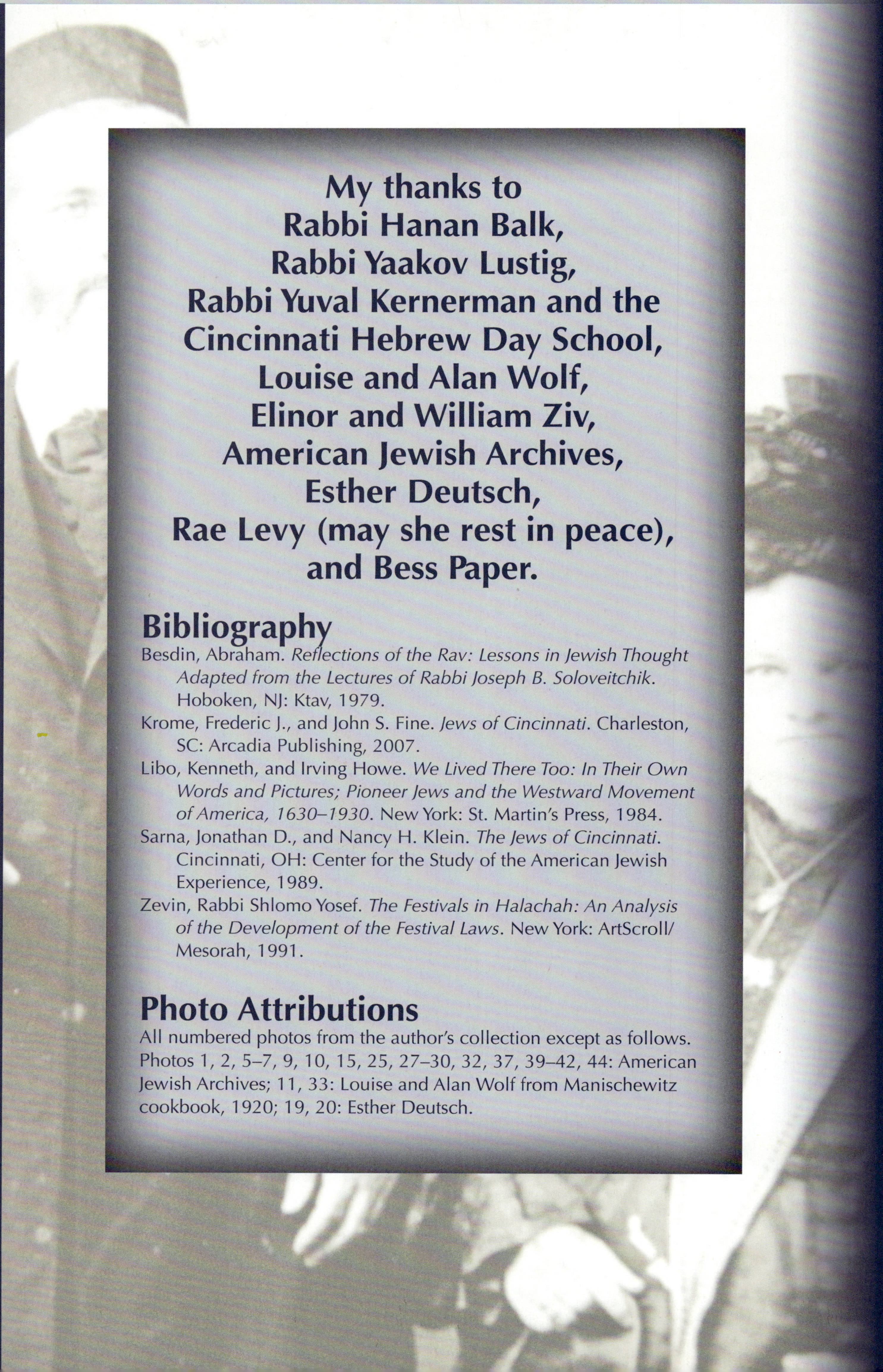

My thanks to
Rabbi Hanan Balk,
Rabbi Yaakov Lustig,
Rabbi Yuval Kernerman and the
Cincinnati Hebrew Day School,
Louise and Alan Wolf,
Elinor and William Ziv,
American Jewish Archives,
Esther Deutsch,
Rae Levy (may she rest in peace),
and Bess Paper.

Bibliography

Besdin, Abraham. *Reflections of the Rav: Lessons in Jewish Thought Adapted from the Lectures of Rabbi Joseph B. Soloveitchik.* Hoboken, NJ: Ktav, 1979.

Krome, Frederic J., and John S. Fine. *Jews of Cincinnati.* Charleston, SC: Arcadia Publishing, 2007.

Libo, Kenneth, and Irving Howe. *We Lived There Too: In Their Own Words and Pictures; Pioneer Jews and the Westward Movement of America, 1630–1930.* New York: St. Martin's Press, 1984.

Sarna, Jonathan D., and Nancy H. Klein. *The Jews of Cincinnati.* Cincinnati, OH: Center for the Study of the American Jewish Experience, 1989.

Zevin, Rabbi Shlomo Yosef. *The Festivals in Halachah: An Analysis of the Development of the Festival Laws.* New York: ArtScroll/ Mesorah, 1991.

Photo Attributions

All numbered photos from the author's collection except as follows. Photos 1, 2, 5–7, 9, 10, 15, 25, 27–30, 32, 37, 39–42, 44: American Jewish Archives; 11, 33: Louise and Alan Wolf from Manischewitz cookbook, 1920; 19, 20: Esther Deutsch.

THE
West

SEATTLE

Dedicated to our beloved brother

Dore Svei, a"h

דוב בן חנוך היינד

son of Henry and Beatrice Svei, a"h
1954–2010

"A man of integrity and a friend to all."

**Shelly Shalev and family
Michael and Cheryl Svei and family**

OAKLAND

In memory of my father-in-law,

Ernie Hollander, a"h,

whose dream was to "bring *Yiddishkeit* to the desert,"
and my husband,

Michael, a"h,

whose dream was to be like his father.

And in honor of my mother-in-law – my Naomi – *my "Immie,"*
a true *eshet chayil*, who has been my role model.

Kathy Hollander

‫»לֹא-יֵאָמֵר לָךְ עוֹד עֲזוּבָה; וּלְאַרְצֵךְ לֹא-יֵאָמֵר עוֹד שְׁמָמָה...‬
‫וּמְשׂוֹשׂ חָתָן עַל-כַּלָּה, יָשִׂישׂ עָלַיִךְ אֱלֹהָיִךְ.«‬

‫ישעיהו ס:ד, ה‬

"You shall no more be termed Forsaken;
neither shall your land be any more termed Desolate...
And as the bridegroom rejoices over the bride,
so shall thy G-d rejoice over you."

Isaiah 62:4, 5

Oakland/
San Francisco,
California

Adath Israel
Beth Jacob of Oakland
Chevra Thilim (San Francisco)
Lisa Kampner Hebrew Academy
Judah L. Magnes Museum
Fillmore District

Oakland/San Francisco, California

A Wedding, Tisha B'Av, and an Eruv!

1. Temple Emanu-El was gutted during the earthquake of 1906.

April 18, 1906, 5:12 AM: As most of the city slept, one family was about to experience the intense contradiction of new life in the midst of destruction. Mrs. Rebecca Dulberg was in her South of Market apartment giving birth to her baby when the big one hit. The earth-shattering process within her own body was matched outside by the worst earthquake in US history. When the ground stopped shaking, 25,000 buildings had fallen, 3,000 were dead, and 225,000 of the city's 400,000 residents were homeless. The downtown area where the Jews lived was totally destroyed by the earthquake; most of the nearly 30,000 Jews in the city lost their homes and businesses.

For more than a century and a half, San Francisco's Jews, and those of neighboring Oakland, have endured tumultuous and destructive times. How did they persevere, passing on their traditions in the ever-changing environment of the "Bay Area"?

To answer this question, let's travel back to 1859 and hear the thoughts of one "Benjamin the Traveler"; we'll share the story of the quake as told by the Jewish survivors, and listen to the Jewish leaders who experienced the revolutionary changes of the 1960s and beyond.

I am here in the Bay Area, appropriately enough on the week of Tisha B'Av, the saddest day of the Jewish year, commemorating the destruction of the Holy Temple of Jerusalem, as well as the many devastating events that have happened to the Jewish people around the world since that time. It is, however, also a time of hope, a time to celebrate survival and rebuilding. This is the story of communities whose people had the will and belief to survive, in spite of conditions that might have dictated otherwise. This is a story of Tisha B'Av, an *eruv*, and a wedding.

2. Tisha B'Av   3. Eruv   4. Wedding

Gold!

A unique and fascinating look at early American Jewish life comes from a largely unfamiliar and strange source: a multi-volume work called *Three Years in America 1859–1862* describes the extensive travels of Israel Ben Joseph, dubbed "Benjamin the Traveler." Born in 1818 in what is now Romania, the author appears to see himself as a reincarnation of the renowned medieval traveler Benjamin of Tudela, who trekked the whole known world of the twelfth century to seek out the scattered remnants of the tribes of Israel. We will soon see what this latter-day Benjamin found in California.

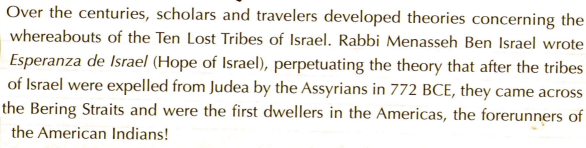

Seekers of the Lost Tribes

Over the centuries, scholars and travelers developed theories concerning the whereabouts of the Ten Lost Tribes of Israel. Rabbi Menasseh Ben Israel wrote *Esperanza de Israel* (Hope of Israel), perpetuating the theory that after the tribes of Israel were expelled from Judea by the Assyrians in 772 BCE, they came across the Bering Straits and were the first dwellers in the Americas, the forerunners of the American Indians!

5. Mordechai Manuel Noah (1818–1864) was a publisher, politician, and sheriff as well as a writer. He wrote, as did Menasseh Ben Israel before him, a discourse in 1827 on the possibilities that the American Indian emerged from the "Lost Tribes of Israel."

In 1846, Yerba Buena was a quiet Mexican village of 200 people. A year later, its name was changed to San Francisco, and the following year California was ceded to the United States.

With the cry of "Gold!" coming from Sutter's sawmill in Coloma, California, in 1848, San Francisco would never be the same, though it was over 130 miles from the site. The discovery sparked the largest mass movement of people in the Western Hemisphere: the famous Gold Rush of 1849.

Along with everyone else, Jews clamored to the West Coast to seek their fortunes. They came from the East Coast by wagon and from Europe by ship around Cape Horn at the southern tip of South America, or by passage across the Isthmus of Panama or Nicaragua. Jewish "'49ers" were pioneers among pioneers. While other prospectors could go back to their families in the East when their luck ran out, most Jews came from Europe, where political conditions made it impossible to return. If they didn't find gold, they made the best of the situation by becoming peddlers who supplied the prospectors with clothing, boots, hats, and tools. (Morphed by the passing of history, today "the 49ers" is a San Francisco football team.)

"Benjamin," our intrepid traveler, describes the famous San Francisco fog in biblical terms: "Towards seven o'clock, a monstrously great cloud like a mountain in the distance stood over the sea in bold relief. The ship sailed on and suddenly we were enveloped in clouds. All about us was dim and dark, just as the Bible describes the Egyptian darkness. The fog was so thick, it could almost be grasped."

And he has this to say about the excitement of the Gold Rush: "From all parts of the Earth…they felt themselves drawn to this great magnet…a general migration began as if a new Jerusalem was to be besieged." He continues, somewhat prophetically, describing the phenomena of mass migration "such as perhaps an earthquake… could produce."

"Benjamin" goes on to discuss his disappointment in the lack of tradition in the San Francisco Jewish community: "Of the conditions of Jews in this place… it is the least cheery. Matzoth for the Passover feast are baked with flour offered for sale in the market and a wedding was celebrated during the middle days of Passover [referring to *chol hamoed*], without regard to our custom not to do so." In a hopeful tone, he adds, "But this will also pass. For Israel, the threatening changes that frivolity conjures up will, fortunately not last and the day will dawn…we'll see Israel's loftiest goals [reached] in keeping G-d's laws."

6. Israel Ben Joseph (or Benjamin the Traveler or Benjamin II) modeled himself after the twelfth-century Jewish traveler Benjamin of Tudela. Benjamin the Second became a traveler with the express intention of seeking the lost Ten Tribes.

What became of the Jewish '49ers? One Jewish immigrant named Abrahamsohn was a baker who set up a canvas-roofed store in the long wharf where he sold his baked goods. But the lure of gold overcame him, and he too grabbed a spade, a pan, and warm clothing and joined in the digging a hundred miles away. After three months of intense work and sleepless nights (for thieves and murderers abounded at night), he counted in his swollen hands a net profit of only $40. In addition to being a baker, Abrahamsohn was a *mohel*, and when he received an offer of $60 plus expenses from a fellow Jew in Sacramento, he knew his gold-digging days were over. When he returned to San Francisco, he opened a boarding house. In 1852, due to one of the numerous fires that plagued the city, he was wiped out. He'd had enough! So Abrahamsohn picked up and moved to Australia – where he discovered gold and amassed a fortune!

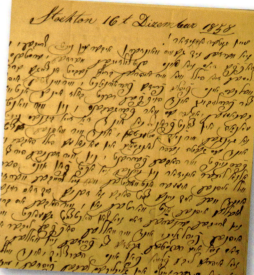

7. Gold rush letter written by a Jew in Stockton, California, in Yiddish, c. 1858: "…we went to San Francisco for two months…the business did not go well. My sister-in-law has been here for two years and does not like it…but one must get used to everything."

The world owes a debt of gratitude to another adventurous young Jew named Loeb Strauss. At the age of 18, Strauss came from Germany to California by way of the Panama route in 1853. He met a tailor named Jacob Dans, and together they improvised a way to make denim pants stronger by placing metal rivets at the pocket corners. It was just what the prospectors needed, as well as everyone else engaged in a rugged line of work. Loeb was now known as Levi Strauss, and his famous "Levi's Jeans" became an indispensable American article of clothing.

8. It's amazing what a few well-placed rivets can do! Jeans similar to those originated by Levi Strauss.

A *Shul* and a Breakaway

Was Jewish religious life as bad as Benjamin the Traveler depicted? Back in September of 1849, San Francisco was riddled with saloons, gambling, and crime – and there was some talk of building a *shul*. Thirty worshippers gathered in Lewis Franklin's tent store on Jackson Street to observe Rosh Hashanah. It was the first known Jewish public worship service held in the Far West. Those who responded to the newspaper ad announcing this service came from such diverse places as England, Australia, Poland, Russia, and Bavaria. Franklin spoke on the High Holy Days on the temptations of vice facing the people of the city, cautioning against the feverish love of gold. He pleaded with his fellow Jews to use the gift of freedom in America to renew their commitment to Jewish law.

When Henry Johnson, a Jew, died from eating a poisonous mushroom, the town's Jews got together for the first time to discuss the acquisition of a burial ground. The Hebrew Benevolent Society was formed to establish a cemetery, ritually prepare the dead for burial, and assist the sick and needy.

But founding a synagogue was a greater trial. At the initial meeting, a bitter quarrel erupted over the selection of a *shochet*. The Polish faction wanted their man, and the Germans wanted theirs. The Polish Jews left the meeting and founded Sherith Israel and the Orthodox Germans started Congregation Emanu-el. Upon hearing of the influx of Jews to San Francisco, Englishman Sir Moses Montefiore offered a gift of a Torah to the first congregation to be organized in the city. Although both were founded in the same year, Emanu-el was awarded the Torah in 1850.

9. Some of the oldest cemeteries can be found in Colma. Some call it "the city of the dead," because there are more graves than living inhabitants of the town. Many of the oldest Jewish headstones can be found here.

Benjamin had this to say about Sherith Israel: "The congregation has about 110 members...follow[ing] the correct Polish *minhag* (rite) and is strictly Orthodox.... Until the autumn of 1857, the congregation had no regular minister, and the *mohel* or *shochet* conducted religious services...in the true Jewish manner as our ancient ancestors used to conduct it.... In the autumn of 1857, the congregation elected the Rev. Dr. Henry of New York to preach and conduct the services.... He receives a salary of $1500...." Ironically, though Sherith Israel and Emanu-el had started out as two factions arguing with each other over religious standards, neither remained Orthodox for long.

Benjamin describes with "pleasant surprise" the large number of Jewish organizations founded since 1859: the Hebrew Benevolent society for the Polish, and the German Eureka Benevolent Association. He mentions B'nai B'rith as well, calling it a "secret society." Most interesting was Heftsi-Vah (My delight is in her), a Jewish school founded in 1854, of which he says: "Sixty children attend the school daily and are instructed in all branches usual at English and Jewish educational institutions."

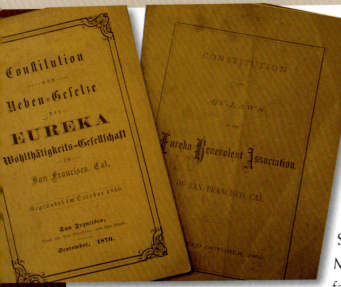

10. There were many Jewish charitable institutions formed from the 1850s on. The Eureka Benevolent Association was the German equivalent to the Polish Hebrew Benevolent Association. Here is the original constitution and bylaws written in English, c. 1850; the Yiddish version dates to 1870.

At the end of his stay in 1862, Benjamin describes the completion and presentation of a Torah by the "Hebra Bikur Holim" (society for visiting the sick) to Sherith Israel: "Upon invitation…[I] was a spectator at a scene the like of which I had not seen for many years. The presentation of a Holy Scroll of the Torah…. A beautiful detail…was the sale of the privilege of filling in the last words of the Holy Scroll…. The first word that was sold was *Umosheh* ("and Moses"). It was sold to Moses Morris, Esq., for $50…. I cannot fail to mention with thanks that the president of the congregation bought me a word for ten dollars."

And to think that a mere eight years earlier, this was a sleepy Mexican village of two hundred. By 1880, San Francisco had the second highest Jewish population in the United States, exceeded only by New York City.

In 1892, five men signed the articles of incorporation of "Congregation Chebra Thillim" (society for the recitation of Psalms), which stated its objectives as "to hold religious services in accordance with the Orthodox rites of the Jewish religion, for social intercourse between its members and also for charitable purposes and to buy and sell real estate." Today, 117 years later, it is the oldest surviving Orthodox synagogue in San Francisco.

The Hardiness of Oak

While our traveler was writing his diary of San Francisco, another Jewish community was quietly developing across the Bay. The city of Oakland was named for its abundance of oak trees, which have the uncanny ability to renew themselves even when cut down to the trunk. Its first Jewish settlers arrived in 1852, when the city's population was a mere 300. It was incorporated in 1854 following the inevitable influx of people seeking their fortune in the rush to gold.

The Jewish history of Oakland originates, as it has in many other communities, with the acquisition of a plot of ground consecrated as a cemetery. This cemetery, established by Rabbi Henry A. Henry, is now known as Home of Eternity.

From the original "First Hebrew Congregation" emerged the Chevra Kadisha Burial Society (1883) and two synagogues: Beth Jacob and Beth Abraham (1894). Beth Jacob remains today as a leading Orthodox congregation in the Bay Area.

With the growth of Oakland's shipping industry, combined with the devastation of the San Francisco earthquake of 1906, the population of Oakland increased to 5,000.

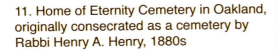

11. Home of Eternity Cemetery in Oakland, originally consecrated as a cemetery by Rabbi Henry A. Henry, 1880s

The Ground Quakes

1906

The tremors lasted for 47 seconds. Then the fires started. Mark Cohn watched the conflagration, and two days later gave the following account: "The fires are still raging and threaten the entire city. The whole business section [known as "South of Market"] is in ruins…Weinstock, Lubin and Co., Neiman and Levinson, Rosenthal, Rueful and Son. Everything that has wheels under it is in use to help carry some of the things people have to have to make out for the night. The oldest, wisest, and richest men are at a loss how to meet the calamity that befell the city."

The first landmark visible to ships, Temple Emanu-el's magnificent structure (completed in 1866), was gutted. The Torah scroll gifted to them by Moses Montefiore was in ashes.

Sherith Israel, only partially damaged, became the temporary home for the city courts for many years. Beth Israel, founded on the eve of the Civil War as an Orthodox synagogue, had erected a new building in 1905, only to see it totally destroyed. (It was rebuilt in 1910.)

The Jews set up a kosher kitchen in the "tent city" that was Golden Gate Park. When Rabbi Voorsanger of Emanu-el commandeered 35,000 loaves of bread to feed the "refugees," he referred to himself as the "biggest thief in the US." Tickets for the High Holy Day services in Golden Gate Park refugee camp were sold in the aftermath of the earthquake and fire.

The entire Jewish neighborhood was destroyed. Eventually, the community moved into the Fillmore District, which became a place of rich Jewish culture. Torah learning, kosher delicatessens, and Jewish music comprised the rhythm of daily life. This remained a key Jewish enclave into the 1960s.

12. The Lechner family camped in the tent city in Golden Gate Park after the 1906 earthquake and fire.

What about Rebecca Dulberg, who was giving birth during the quake? According to "The 1906 San Francisco Quake, the Fire and the Jews" by Dan Pine (*Jewish News Weekly of Northern California*, April 17, 2006):

Immediately after the 45-second temblor, her home demolished, Dulberg panicked. She was literally giving birth as the earth shook, but the terrified midwife quickly fled the apartment. Dulberg's husband and older daughter assisted in the delivery as best they could, while smoke and dust filled the building.

Two young men searching for survivors peered in the window and pulled the Dulbergs to safety, carrying Rebecca and her

Row............ No.....

RELIGIOUS SERVICES

will be held on

אש השנה ש״ט ויום כפור ת״רס״ו

September 20th, 21st 22nd and 29th, 1906

Camp No. 5   GOLDEN GATE PARK

Gentleman $1

13. Ticket for High Holy Day services in the Golden Gate Park refugee camp, after the earthquake

14. The Fillmore District became the new popular enclave for the Jewish population after the earthquake of 1906. There were kosher bakeries and restaurants, two *shul*s, and many Jewish-owned stores.

baby out on a mattress. They left the family on the sidewalk as throngs of frightened residents ran for their lives....

Meanwhile, in those early hours Dulberg and her baby lay on the street. Her husband had left in search of transportation, and soon returned with a horse-drawn wagon, taking the family to the only hospital that withstood the quake and fire: the Jewish-run Mount Zion Hospital.... Jewish doctors and nurses worked tirelessly in the days and weeks after the disaster.... One of those [helped] was Rebecca Dulberg who, along with her baby and family, survived.

Memories of the Early Twentieth Century

15. The Fillmore District today is a far cry from what it was in its heyday.

I had the opportunity to talk with Martin Sosnick, ex-president of Congregation Adath Israel in San Francisco, whose family has been active in this Jewish community for over a hundred years. "My grandfather came through Ellis Island in 1904 and worked in the sweatshops of New York City's Lower East Side," he told me. "He had been in the liquor business in Europe and was staked to a job in San Francisco in 1905." On the morning of the earthquake, "He was sleeping in a second-floor loft in South of Market, and when he woke up he was on the ground floor! He told me he was not awakened by the massive quake, and somehow he survived."

He went back into the liquor distribution business. When Prohibition took hold in 1920, the family opened a kosher market in Fillmore. After the Depression and World War II, they restarted wine and liquor distribution, and the family business continues to go strong.

Martin told me how his grandfather used to tell him that his good friend was Rabbi Mayer Zvi Hirsch, Chief Orthodox Rabbi of San Francisco, who produced kosher wine for Passover during Prohibition. "Kiddush wines in those days were port wines. There were no concord grape wines in California."

16. Rabbi Mayer Zvi Hirsch, Chief Orthodox Rabbi of San Francisco, supervised kosher sacramental wine for Passover during prohibition, c. 1920s.

A Resourceful Rabbi

Legend has it that in 1927, Oakland Congregation Beth Jacob was not able to pay their religious leader, Rabbi Paper. So the resourceful rabbi supplemented his income through the sale of "sacramental" wines for religious purposes. In the late 1940s, his family was the first to introduce Manischewitz wine, followed by matzoh, into northern California.

In the years after the earthquake, the Central Hebrew School of the Jewish Educational Society was founded. In 1926, Rabbi David Stolper, a native of Lithuania, became its superintendent and guided the program for more than twenty years. Accomplished in Hebrew and Yiddish, Rabbi Stolper wrote and directed numerous plays based on Jewish history. He also inaugurated the Yeshiva Ktano, a Hebrew high school to teach advanced courses in Hebrew and Talmud.

In 1948, Martin's parents moved to the Sunset District and started their own *minyan* in a house. Adath Israel grew quickly and moved to a storefront. It is now the largest Orthodox synagogue in San Francisco.

17. The Harvest Book Store (foreground), in the Sunset District, was the storefront location of Adath Israel before the present building was erected just blocks away.

18. Adath Israel today, just blocks from the storefront that housed its first building

Martin remembers the old neighborhood fondly, particularly at holiday time. "We grew up in a neighborhood that was 90 percent Jewish. Before Sukkos, we used to cut palm leaves for *s'chach* (natural covering for a *sukkah*). Cutting *s'chach* was a labor of love in those days. It was a matter of pride to have a *sukkah*. We had forty *sukkah*s in the neighborhood."

C'mon People Now – Smile on Your Brother!

Outside Adath Israel, I talked with Rabbi Jacob Traub, who was rabbi of this *shul* and a community activist for 40 years. He came here from Duluth, Minnesota, in 1966, just before San Francisco became infamous for the 1967 "Summer of Love." Women's lib, free love, Vietnam protests, and drugs were the order of the day. By the end of the decade, young people in the whole country were rocking to the strains of the quintessential hippie manifesto:

> C'mon people now, smile on your brother,
> Everybody get together,
> Try to love one another right now…

"The theme of this city was 'make love, not war,'" recalled Rabbi Traub, and he had come with the express intention of starting a Jewish day school in that environment! The school was to be under the auspices of the umbrella day school organization Torah Umesorah. He recalled meeting in the Sosnick house just as the Six-Day War broke out in Israel in 1967. The day school opened in 1968.

San Francisco, he told me, has always been an avant-garde city: they try everything here first. "Look," he said, "in the '60s, one percent of the total population here was Jewish. In Haight-Ashbury, the Mecca of the hippie generation, the Jewish population was ten percent! It was a tragic time for many families. It seemed like every day I would get a call from 'back East' that would go something like this: 'You're the rabbi in San Francisco? Please find my daughter, find my son!'

"'Where are they?' I would ask.

"'San Francisco – somewhere…' So my wife and I would walk along Haight Street, me wearing my *yarmulke,* and kids would come out of the woodwork – day school kids from the East, from Brooklyn and Queens – and I would give them dimes and tell them to go call their parents.

"Drugs abounded. There were even people who were encouraging me to try LSD!" He told me how he spoke about everything from the pulpit: gays, drugs, Vietnam. "My father used to say, 'Any fool can get up and say what the *parshah* [Torah portion of the week] says. The *chochmah* [wise usage] is to make the *parshah* say what you want it to say.'

"In forty years," he remarked thoughtfully, "you can really have an effect on a community. You're there for the complete life cycle of a person, or even a family. You can make a difference in their lives. This is the real 'outreach.'"

He told me of one of his proud moments, a quintessential San Francisco story. The first *mikveh* in "South of Market" was destroyed by the earthquake of 1906. The next one was located in what became a bad neighborhood, so the rabbi led the campaign to build a new one. "We enlisted the help of *the mikveh expert* in the country, the Helbitzer Rebbe, a Hungarian Rebbe who spoke only Yiddish. He went around the country building *mikvaos,* but he was always late. You see, if he was seated on a plane next to a woman, he would get off and wait for the next plane!

"So he came to us and we brought in two architects – both of whom happened to be good at their jobs and also happened to be gay. So here we are in San Francisco, with the Helbitzer Rebbe telling these two gay architects, in Yiddish, what they needed to do and me, in the center, interpreting the instructions in English!"

"You can really have an effect…. You can make a difference in their lives. This is the real 'outreach.'"

Reb Shlomo and the Holy Man Jam

At the height of the hippie era, the dynamic singer with a magnetic personality, Rabbi Shlomo Carlebach, made his way to Haight-Ashbury, hoping to attract lost souls to Judaism. He started the House of Love and Prayer (ultimately, at two locations) and kept it going from the mid-'60s to the mid-'70s. Every Friday night, hundreds of people would come, and many became his devoted followers.

An eyewitness told the following story of a particular event that was classic "Reb Shlomo."

"It was June of 1970, and a huge New Age 'happening' was about to start in Boulder, Colorado – the Holy Man Jam. Spiritual leaders of numerous religions, particularly Far Eastern Zen masters, gurus, and swamis of every type, were descending on the place. Reb Shlomo was invited to attend, to offer his brand of Jewish mystical experience to the thousands who would gather there.

"So Reb Shlomo got a bunch of us from the House of Love and Prayer into some vans and cars, and we made our way on down to Boulder. We found thousands of people spread like a colorful carpet over a huge campus. As the festival went on, everyone was getting higher and higher, and the speakers, singers, and chanters became more and more animated.

"Then it's Reb Shlomo's turn. He gets up on the stage with his guitar in hand and starts strumming very softly. He begins to tell an old Chassidic tale of Reb Nachman's called 'The Seven Beggars.' With his sweet, lilting voice, he begins to describe the beggars, each with a handicap – 'You see, the blind beggar, he wasn't really blind. He just couldn't bear to see the evil in the world; and the deaf beggar, he wasn't really deaf, but he couldn't stand to hear all of the terrible things people said about each other…' The audience is enraptured! Suddenly, a fellow in the middle of the huge multitude stands up with a flute in his hand, and he begins to accompany Reb Shlomo as he continues the story.

19. Shlomo Carlebach studied at Yeshiva Torah Vodaath and Yeshivas Chaim Berlin as well as Beth Medrash Govoha in Lakewood. He was recognized as a scholar by the *rosh yeshivah*, Rav Aharon Kotler, and by Rav Hutner, who gave him his *smichah* (ordination) and said that it was a loss to the Torah world that Carlebach chose a career in musical Jewish outreach over being a teacher.

"Then Reb Shlomo begins to sing one of his repetitive Hebrew compositions – they're mesmerizing, you know – softly, at first. Everyone is swaying, moving with the music. Some people have their eyes closed. Then he starts to sing louder, faster, with passion.

"At just the right second, he calls, 'Let's go!' He plays faster, and starts jumping up and down. Thousands of people are jumping up and down with him! He leaps off the stage and leads the whole crowd after him – singing, dancing, jumping, crying – all over the campus!

"They would have followed him anywhere. It was a scene none of us will ever forget!"

Encircling the Community

Originally from Miami, Rabbi Joshua Strulowitz came to Adath Israel as its rabbi in 2005. He was able to characterize the special character of the Bay Area Jewish community in just a few words.

"We have a very eclectic mix of people, from Holocaust survivors to young couples," he told me, as we sat in his office. "Its unique quality stems from the fact that this is a very open community – no preconceptions! Free thinkers abound."

Considering the fact that this is the fourth largest Jewish community in the country, the Orthodox population is small. Despite its size, I learned that in the past four years under his guidance, they've started a *kollel* (with Torah study groups for the public) and a Jewish preschool. What is more remarkable for a community of their size is that they just completed the first *eruv* in San Francisco!

20. Rabbi Joshua Strulowitz, the mastermind behind building the *eruv*, stands underneath the mass of wires that help constitute the San Francisco *eruv*.

An *eruv* is a symbolic enclosure, a device that expands the private domain and allows Jews to carry in public, within its boundaries, on the Sabbath – something that is otherwise not permitted. In a recent interview in the press, Rabbi Strulowitz explained the enormity of this accomplishment. "A community without an *eruv* often seems inhospitable to observant Jewish families," he said. "So an *eruv* is a statement, that this community is on the map and that it is actively together [united]." Rabbi Strulowitz and *shul* leaders worked on creating the *eruv* for two years. In total, they received the required approvals for the *eruv* from the San Francisco Department of Public Works, the California Public Utilities Commission, Pacific Gas and Electric Company (PG&E), the chief of police, and the city supervisor.

Why were all these approvals necessary? As opposed to many other *eruvim* in the country, this one required virtually no construction: most of the boundaries are drawn from the already existing complex of telephone poles and wires for which San Francisco is famous (for cable cars and electric buses). "In reality," the rabbi smiled, "San Francisco built us an *eruv* a long time ago. We just had to find it."

> "In reality," the rabbi smiled, "San Francisco built us an *eruv* a long time ago. We just had to find it."

Every week, the rabbi or a lay leader checks the perimeter of the *eruv* to make sure it's intact. That's when this ancient tradition gets high tech. Updates are posted by the rabbi on Twitter. The good part is that if a wire does go down, the city fixes it. It doesn't get any better.

bay area
License to carry: Eruv marks a San Francisco first

21. Read all about it: *eruv* makes headlines.

"Opting In"

In Oakland, Rabbi Judah Dardik has been the religious leader of Beth Jacob (founded in 1893) for the past eight years. It is a pleasure to talk to him. "When I first came here, this synagogue had a characteristic that intrigued me," he began. "Only one third of the membership was *shomer Shabbat* [Orthodox], but 85 percent were active in the *shul*!"

This inclusive spirit goes back to the history of the *shul* building. The property they had planned to build on turned out to be in the center of the future Route 580 – an eight-lane highway! So they convinced the government to pay them for the land immediately, so that they could build elsewhere. When they ran out of that money, they built the rest themselves, with their own hands.

"This is an 'opt-in' community," the rabbi explains. "People do *mitzvot* not because they are forced to, but because they want to. They wake up and say, 'Today I want to do this *mitzvah*.' Welcome to the Bay Area!"

Examples of the "opt-in" mentality?

"So we have had someone who shows up on Shabbat with a 'halachic belt' where his key is part of the belt, allowing him to carry it on Shabbat. (There is no *eruv* in Oakland). The key, however, is his car key!

"We have a member who is a committed vegetarian (not unusual here at all). He kept a shank bone in his freezer for years. He would put it on his Seder plate each Passover, and then put it right back in the freezer for the following year. He couldn't stand even buying the meat bone!"

22. Rabbi Judah Dardik: "This is an 'opt-in' community."

For Rabbi Dardik, the Oakland community presents a wonderful opportunity to do what he likes to do most: outreach.

Two of the most dedicated and giving people in Beth Jacob are also two of the most pleasant people I have met on my odyssey across the country – this, despite the fact that they have every right not to be. You see, Anna Hollander lost her husband seven years ago, and then her son just a few months ago. When she and her daughter-in-law Kathy agreed to be interviewed, I had no idea of the depth of their grief. This is the kind of people they are.

Anna Hollander, a Holocaust survivor, came here with her late husband, Ernie, also a Holocaust survivor. (Though they were both in Auschwitz, they never met there). They were married on a rooftop in Haifa, Israel, in 1947, on the day of the United Nations partition vote. As soon as Israel was voted a legal state, the Arabs attacked. All of the wedding guests had to stay in one small apartment. Ernie fought for the Irgun and in the War of Independence and was wounded three times.

Anna told me more about Ernie. He was born in 1925 in what was then Czechoslovakia. His family, whose original name was Albergezie, was Sephardic. They left Spain with the Expulsion of 1492. They migrated first to Holland – hence the origin of their present name. In every generation from the Expulsion to the Holocaust, his family continuously produced rabbis.

23. Beth Jacob in 1961. It was designed as a tent to symbolize the welcoming philosophy of our forefather, Abraham, who waited by his tent to welcome guests.

24. Unique way to spend a honeymoon! Ernie and Anna Hollander being married on a rooftop in Haifa, Israel, in 1947, on the day the United Nations voted in favor of partition. The Arabs attacked and Ernie fought with the Irgun. He was wounded three times.

He was sent to Auschwitz, where his father was shot before his eyes. He and his brother were the only two of 15 children to survive. Or so he thought.

After great contemplation and inner debate, Ernie decided to accept an invitation to go on *The Montel Williams Show* to debate a Holocaust denier. A Brooklyn man watching the show recognized his face as similar to that of a friend of his. That friend turned out to be Ernie's brother. All Ernie knew was that his brother had been hanged by the Nazis. Apparently, he was cut down before he expired. He played dead on the ground and escaped. Six hundred people attended the reunion of Ernie and his brother, hosted by Montel Williams!

Anna told me that Ernie refused to go to *shul* with her after Auschwitz. As a matter of fact, he would intentionally go the long way around to avoid passing a *shul*. "One time," she told me, "I faked being tired and hurt trying to go up the hill to *shul,* and I asked him to help me. He pushed me all the way there." And that's how she got him to enter a *shul* for the first time since the war.

Yet, I had been told that Ernie was the *gabbai* of the *shul* for 40 years and the most valuable member of this congregation. How did that happen? Anna explained his transformation: one day, he found a swastika painted on the roof of Beth Jacob. His anger flared up, and the spark was once again lit.

It was time to go home, back to *shul*, time to rebuild Judaism in defiance of the Nazis. "He wanted to bring *Yiddishkeit* to the desert," Anna said.

Kathy Hollander, who had just recently lost her husband (Anna's son), is the administrator of the *shul*. But she is what we would call a *kol bah* – one who does it all. She gets the *minyan* together every day, cooks breakfast for the Sunday *minyan* and Torah classes, organizes the Shabbat Kiddushes, and runs the *chevra kadisha*.

I asked Kathy about the unusually warm qualities of this *shul*. "We are always welcoming," she emphasized, "and so accepting of each other." The minute you walk in, you're family. This is everyone's home. The *shul* was built in 1950 in the shape of a tent to emulate Abraham's tent, and the welcoming atmosphere to strangers it represented.

No one knows this better than Kathy. She was born to devoutly Catholic parents. "I always wanted to be a Jewish nun, even as a child," she said with a laugh. "You see, a nun is the closest a female can get to God, and the Jews are the chosen people: it seemed the perfect combination!" Who knew?

"I studied many, many years to convert," she added seriously. Over the years, she grew and grew spiritually, a fact evident in her manner and genuine love for all Jews.

She embodies kindness, commitment, and dedication. How else do we, as Jews, survive after tragedy? Anna and Kathy taught me a deep lesson in

25. Ernie Hollander, Holocaust survivor, stands in front of the unique memorial with all the carved figures deformed in some way to make it halachically acceptable. No complete human form would be allowed in this *shul*, in deference to the prohibition on graven images.

26. *Hagbah* (raising of the Torah) is performed in this welcoming *shul* shaped like a tent.

27. Anna and Kathy Hollander reviewing images of the past in old photographs

perseverance, one that took on greater meaning as I contemplated the upcoming Tisha B'Av. I felt humbled in their presence.

So there I am – sitting on the floor on Tisha B'Av in Beth Jacob – and Rabbi Dardik is explaining some of the *kinos* (liturgical poems read on this day). The rabbi suddenly stops and starts describing questions that were asked during the Holocaust. These weren't just any questions; these were questions on *halachah* (Jewish law) asked by Jews of their rabbis as they were going to their deaths. The incredible commitment these Jews had in perpetuating the Torah, even in the face of death, brought us all to tears.

From the Greatest Sadness to the Greatest Joy

It is the Sunday after Tisha B'Av, the saddest day of the year, and I am at the wedding of a Beth Jacob member, Matt Zinn. In four days, to go from the emotionally intense fast day of Tisha B'Av to this event – where only joy abounds – means everything to me: the sequence of destruction to rebuilding fills me with hope.

The Talmud tells us that when three famous sages (Rabban Gamliel, R' Elazar Ben Azariah, and R' Yehoshua) came with the great Rabbi Akiva to the mount where the Holy Temple was destroyed, they saw a fox emerge from where the Holy of Holies used

28. Stained glass window found in Adath Israel memorializing Yom Hashoah and Tisha B'Av

to be. They started crying. But Rabbi Akiva laughed. In answer to their question of why, he answered that he was laughing because he realized that just as the prophecy of destruction was fulfilled, so is the fulfillment of the prophecy that "the streets of the city shall be full of boys and girls playing" closer at hand.

Benjamin the Traveler said of San Francisco in 1859: "All hearts were deeply touched by the swift progress…of the community. In a few years, plains and mountains had been converted into peaceful habitations. Out of a Sahara of the desert, they had come into a Canaan."

I have heard this area called a "*galus* within a *galus* – an exile within an exile." And yet, the Bay Area has afforded me a lesson in tragedy and hope, of building, suffering destruction, and rebuilding.

The wedding ceremony is about to conclude. As Rabbi Dardik sings "If I forget thee, O, Jerusalem," the groom shatters a glass. But this action is not only a reminder of the tragic destruction of the Temple: it is the also the signal to begin great rejoicing. As shouts of "*Mazal tov!*" fill the air, the vibrant hope of a united Jewish people rises again in this community that calls all who come to it "family."

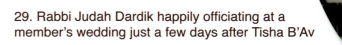

29. Rabbi Judah Dardik happily officiating at a member's wedding just a few days after Tisha B'Av

PROGRAM *at the* LAYING OF
THE CORNER STONE *of the*

Beth-Jacob Congregation

A. MERRILL BOWSER, ARCHITECT

Sunday, June 2nd   The 20th of Sivan
1907   5667

NINTH AND
CASTRO STS.

OAKLAND   CALIFORNIA

30. The original program for the laying of the cornerstone for the first Beth Jacob building in 1907

31. The original Beth Jacob building on 9th and Castro was dedicated over 100 years ago with a membership of 40 families. The annual income of the congregation was $100! When Rabbi Paper sold his "sacramental wine" during Prohibition, for religious purposes, Beth Jacob reaped a 12 percent profit on the $6.50 price of a gallon of wine.

32. On April 11, 1954, the groundbreaking was held for the present Beth Jacob. When they ran out of money in the middle of building, "We were there watering down the cement, pulling nails out of boards, and laying down the tile ourselves. With all of this, we made sure to build the *mikveh*." Photo shows Beth Jacob in 1961 with no *mechitzah* and rented folding chairs.

33. Some of the men who helped build the present *shul* when funds ran out, c. 1953–1954

34. Beth Jacob today: as welcoming as the tent it represents

35. The exterior of Beth Jacob today

36. A symbol for the ages: a trolley car in front of the new Temple Emanu-El, c. 1880

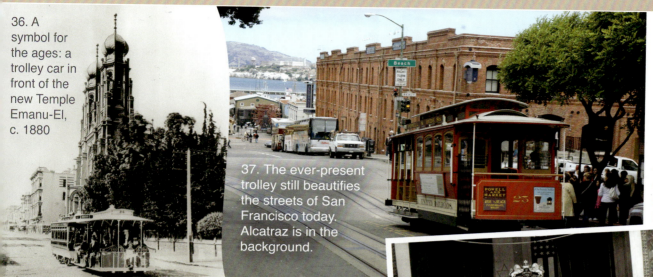

37. The ever-present trolley still beautifies the streets of San Francisco today. Alcatraz is in the background.

38. Temple Emanu-El was gutted in the earthquake of 1906, with only the towers of the domes and its stone walls remaining. The Torah sent by Moses Montefiore to the Jewish pioneers in 1851 was also destroyed.

39. After the quake, the Jewish community, without losing hope, left their destroyed homes and shops in South of Market and started anew in the Fillmore District. In the years following the quake, the Central Hebrew School was founded. In 1926, Rabbi David Stolper became its superintendent, and stayed on for 20 years. This is the Children's Synagogue in the Central Hebrew School, c. 1926.

40. The Hebrew Academy in San Francisco opened in 1968 thanks to the leadership of Rabbi Jacob Traub, spiritual leader of Congregation Adath Israel; he originally came here for the sole purpose of opening a day school.

43. Famous Diller's Delicatessen in the Fillmore District, c. 1940. A Jewish center from after the earthquake until the 1960s, the Fillmore had a wonderful array of food stores and dry goods.

42. As the *kallah* circles the *chassan* (from Beth Jacob) seven times, one can only think of building a true house amidst the family of Israel in a town that has seen its share of rebuilding.

44. Oakland Kosher Food and Deli has the look of Diller's and continues its tradition with a wonderful selection of food and wines.

41. Amidst the joy we remember the tragedies: this is one of the reasons for breaking the glass at the end of a wedding. This is an image of a wedding party in front of Temple Beth Israel in San Francisco, four years after the earthquake, c. 1910. Beth Israel was founded on the eve of the Civil War as an Orthodox synagogue. It had erected a new building in 1905, only to see it totally destroyed one year later. It was rebuilt in 1910.

45. Rabbi Joshua Strulowitz shows a piece of the *eruv* he masterminded; known as a *lechi*; this piece designates the pole as part of the *eruv*. The eruv expands the private domain and allows Jews to carry things within its boundaries, something that is otherwise forbidden. "An *eruv* is a statement, that this community… is actively together…growing…building an infrastructure for traditional Jewish life." As one member of his *shul*, Adath Israel said, "It's very exciting – we can all go as a family to *shul*."

46. The Rozen family. Left to right: Jason, Nana, Bruria, and Miriam (newborn). Rabbi Rozen teaches at the Oakland Hebrew Day School and the family are transplants from the East Coast (New Jersey). "Most people have no family here. In this community, we are family to each other. People are very appreciative of everything they get here in *Yiddishkeit.*" Three of their children were born during the time of the year when I visited, between Tammuz and Av, and one on Tu B'Av (the 15th of Av, a time the Talmud says will be the happiest day of the year when the *Moshiach* comes).

47. The *chevra kadisha* or Jewish burial society was organized in San Francisco in 1901. Its name was changed to Sinai Memorial Chapel in 1937 and it still retains that name today. Tradition has it that when Moses died, on the 7th day of the month of Adar, his burial needs were taken care of by a *chevra kadisha* under the direction of G-d. *Chevra kadisha*s around the world meet on this day to complete a tractate of Talmud or Mishnah. Here, the group meets with former Israeli prime minister David Ben-Gurion on the 7th of Adar, c. 1965.

48. In 1933, the first German Jews came to the Japanese-occupied Shanghai ghetto seeking asylum from the Nazis. From 1938 to 1942, thousands of refugees from Germany and eastern Europe converged on this small ghetto, including the 400 members of the Mir Yeshiva faculty, making the harsh conditions unbearable. The difficulty in finding asylum caused Chaim Weizman to say, "The world seemed to be divided into two parts: those places where the Jews could not live and those where they could not enter." The Germans demanded the return of all the Jews. The Japanese asked Reb Kalish, "Why do the Germans hate you?" He replied in Yiddish, "Because we are Oriental." The Jews were never handed over to the Germans. Some ended up in San Francisco and many in Israel. Here, a passport and armband for the fortunate few leaving Germany for Shanghai before 1942.

49–50. Rav Meir Tzvi Hirsch, who led San Francisco Jewry in the early twentieth century for 30 years, died on Shabbos Chazon before Tisha B'Av. This is a book containing many of the letters of consolation from virtually every Jewish organization: HIAS, B'nai B'rith, Hadassah, Mizrachi, Yeshiva Torah Vodaath, the Hebrew Free Loan Association, Yeshivas Chofetz Chaim, and (above) the Telshe Yeshiva of Cleveland.

51. Reciting *Eichah* at Beth Jacob

52. This custom is based on a story found in the Talmud. Mar the son of Ravina was giving a party the day of his son's wedding. When he looked around, he saw the scholars clowning around for too long. To put a stop to this frivolity, he took a glass and smashed it on the floor, attracting their attention and silence. Even in times of joy, he taught we should always remember our greatest loss: the destruction of the Temple.

53–54. Dancing a new Torah into the *shul* under the *chuppah*, 1997: one of the true occasions in Jewish life where unbounded joy fills the air. Just as the *chuppah* brings a couple into their *bayis ne'eman* (faithful home), so does the *chuppah* bring the people of Israel into their *bayis* as they escort the Torah.

Mei'afailah l'or gadol (from darkness to light)

My thanks to
Rabbi Judah Dardik,
Rabbi Jacob Traub,
Rabbi Joshua Strulowitz,
Kathy and Anna Hollander,
Jason and Bruria Rozen,
Martin Sosnick,
Lara Michels at the
Judah L. Magnes Museum,
and Gene Kaufman.

Bibliography

Besdin, Abraham, ed. *Man of Faith in the Modern World. Reflections of the Rav*, vol. 2. Adapted from the lectures of Rabbi Joseph B. Soloveitchik. Hoboken, NJ: Ktav, 1989.

Friedman, Lee M. *Jewish Pioneers and Patriots*. Philadelphia: Jewish Publication Society, 1942.

Libo, Kenneth, and Irving Howe. *We Lived There Too: In Their Own Words and Pictures; Pioneer Jews and the Westward Movement of America, 1630–1930*. New York: St. Martin's/Marek, 1984.

Rochlin, Harriet, and Fred Rochlin. *Pioneer Jews: A New Life in the Far West*. Boston: Houghton Mifflin, 1984.

Rosen, Dov. *Shema Yisrael*. Translated by Leonard Oschry. New York: Zion Talis, 1972.

Zerin, Edward. *Jewish San Francisco*. Images of America. Charleston, SC: Arcadia Publishing, 2006.

Photo Attributions

All numbered photos from the author's collection except as follows. Photos 7, 10, 12, 13, 16, 36, 38, 39, 41, 43, 48, 50: Judah L. Magnes Museum, Berkeley, California; 21, 23, 25, 30, 32, 33, 53: Beth Jacob Archives; 47: Sinai Memorial Chapel; 24: Kathy and Anna Hollander.

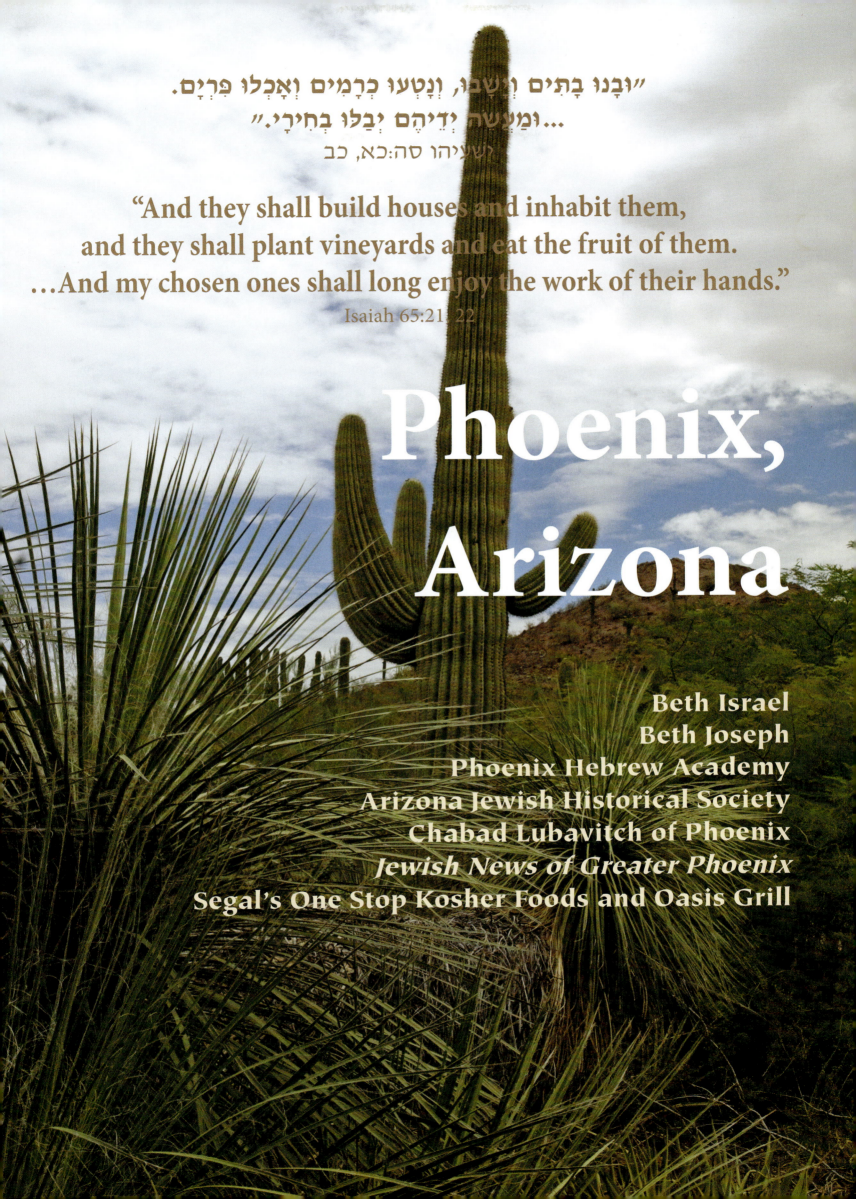

"וּבָנוּ בָתִּים וְיָשָׁבוּ, וְנָטְעוּ כְרָמִים וְאָכְלוּ פִּרְיָם.
...וּמַעֲשֵׂה יְדֵיהֶם יְבַלּוּ בְחִירָי."
ישעיהו סה:כא, כב

"And they shall build houses and inhabit them,
and they shall plant vineyards and eat the fruit of them.
...And my chosen ones shall long enjoy the work of their hands."
Isaiah 65:21, 22

Phoenix, Arizona

Beth Israel
Beth Joseph
Phoenix Hebrew Academy
Arizona Jewish Historical Society
Chabad Lubavitch of Phoenix
Jewish News of Greater Phoenix
Segal's One Stop Kosher Foods and Oasis Grill

Phoenix, Arizona

Tu B'Shevat at an Oasis in the Desert

There is a Talmudic story that is often told of a great and holy man, Choni Hamaa-gal, who was known to not only talk G-d into bringing rain, but also to tell Him how much! Choni is walking in the land of Israel and sees an old man planting a carob tree, which is known to take 70 years to bear its first fruit. Choni is mystified. The old man must know that he will never see the fruits of his labor. What's the point of planting this tree?

So he approaches the man and says, "Old man, why are you planting this tree? Even if you live a long life, you will never see this tree bear fruit! The old man smiles at Choni, spreads his arms wide as if to encircle all the carob trees around him, and replies, "When I came into this world, all these trees and their beautiful fruit were here to greet me with all their pleasure. They were planted for my enjoyment by people who would never see the fruit. I, too, am planting for future generations. My ancestors planted for me, and now I plant for my children."

I am on my way to Phoenix for one day and for one purpose: I have heard that this Jewish community spends considerable time and effort preparing for a full day's celebration of Tu B'Shevat – a Jewish holiday that is never mentioned in the Torah, and is alluded to only once in all of the Mishnah (tractate *Rosh Hashanah* 1:1). Why would they do this?

Known as the "New Year for trees," the holiday of Tu B'Shevat is named simply for the date when it occurs: annually on the fifteenth day of the Hebrew month of Shevat. It is customary to plant trees and eat of the fruits of the land of Israel on this day. In the mid-1500s, the students of the Ari, Rabbi Isaac Luria Ashkenazi, formulated a special Tu B'Shevat Seder set up along the lines of the Passover Seder; in 1753 it was published in a Tu B'Shevat "Haggadah," entitled *Pri Etz Hadar* (fruit of the beautiful tree). As a matter of fact, this is the first stage of the countdown to Passover, celebrating the birth of the Jewish nation, which is two months from Tu B'Shevat.

By far the youngest Jewish community that I have visited during my three-year odyssey of visiting Jewish cities across the USA, Phoenix is the perfect community in which to celebrate Tu B'Shevat. You'll soon see why.

1. *Mezuzah* depicting the seven species found in Israel and mentioned in the Torah. The fruits of Israel are celebrated on Tu B'Shevat.

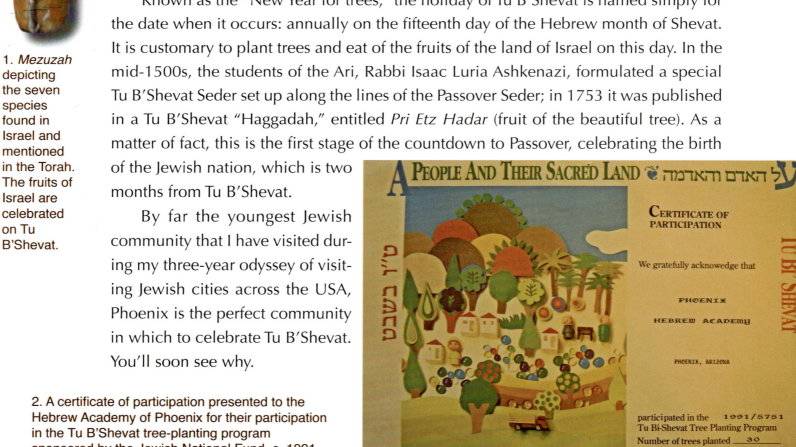

2. A certificate of participation presented to the Hebrew Academy of Phoenix for their participation in the Tu B'Shevat tree-planting program sponsored by the Jewish National Fund, c. 1991

That Pioneer Spirit

As early as the sixteenth century, Luis de Carvajal y de la Cueva, a *converso* ("convert," i.e., a secret Jew during the Inquisition era), explored New Mexico as part of a larger exploration of North America for Philip II of Spain. He settled over 100 "secret Jews" from 1579 to 1589. Most of them, unfortunately, were later executed in the Mexican Inquisition.

Modern Jewish beginnings date from 1846, with the arrival of Solomon Jacob Spiegelberg, who came with the American troops during the Mexican War. He brought family and friends to form what became the nucleus of Jewish communities in Albuquerque and Roswell.

In the days when Indian fights, drunken brawls, and cold-blooded murders were everyday occurrences, Jewish settlers generally stuck to their morality and traditions. Some even went back to Europe to find a Jewish wife. Spiegelberg brought his German-born Jewish wife, Flora, back with him, and she became friendly with the New Mexico territorial governor, Lew Wallace. After a long military career, Wallace became a famous novelist. He plied Flora with questions about Jewish customs, gratefully accepting her answers as he worked on his book set during the era of the Roman occupation of Judea. *Ben Hur* was published in 1880.

Louis Friedenthal's Divine Test

Religious Jews coming to New Mexico had to deal with the challenge of keeping kosher. For some, it was a serious test of their resolve to cling to the Judaism of their forefathers. Louis Friedenthal, who made his way as an entrepreneur to New Mexico in 1856, could cope with outlaws and Indians. Even the rough life of the frontier couldn't sap his strength nor weaken his resolve. What did weaken him, he thought, was a lack of meat protein. He would not eat meat that was not kosher, and he did not himself know how to slaughter animals according to Jewish law. But after three years of a meatless diet on the frontier, he made the desperate decision to slaughter a chicken any way he could.

It appears that a Higher Authority intervened. Just as he held his axe over the chicken, some vandals attempted to rob his store. Seeing him with the axe, they threw stones at him and ran away. For Louis, the stones were a direct sign from Heaven, punishment for the sin he was about to commit. So he put down the axe and satisfied his hunger by going fishing in the Rio Grande.

Another Jewish pioneer was Solomon Barth, an Indian trader. He purportedly swung a deal with the Navajo tribal chiefs that granted him much of the northern Arizona Territory, including the Grand Canyon! He was also a rider for the Pony Express, the relay mail service – a wonder of its time – that could get a letter from the Atlantic coast to the Pacific coast in just ten days. (It was not a long-lasting job, however. Most people don't know that the Pony Express ran for only 18 months, from April 1860 to October 1861, until it was replaced by the First Transcontinental Telegraph.)

Philip Drachman, along with his brother Samuel, was hidden in a cellar tunnel in Lodz, Poland, to escape conscription into the czar's army in 1852. Once in the US, he went west, and became a successful cattle rancher. When it came time for him to marry, he braved the long and arduous journey to New York to find a Jewish bride. The new couple went by ship to San Francisco, then journeyed overland to Tucson. Listen as Rosa Katzenstein Drachman describes the arduous trip:

> We started for Tucson on October 21, 1868. We traveled in a four-horse ambulance that was a relic of the Civil War. The first night we camped, I could not sleep on account of the howling of the coyotes. In the morning, I looked for my sunbonnet made of straw…and horses had eaten it. As we traveled, we passed many graves of poor people who had been murdered by the Indians or other desperate characters. There was nothing but cactus, sand and brush.

3. Philip and Rosa (Katzenstein) Drachman seen not long after their marriage in New York City, c. 1868

Philip's brother Samuel found his wife in San Bernadino. Together, the brothers founded the B'nai B'rith lodge in Tucson and the Jewish Cemetery Association. In 1910, they helped build Arizona's first synagogue, Temple Emanuel, in Tucson. A Purim ball, a popular fundraiser of the era, was held yearly by the Hebrew Ladies Benevolent Society to help raise support for the synagogue building.

Sam served as lay leader of Tucson Jewry from 1867 until his death in 1911, performing weddings and other Jewish ceremonies throughout the Arizona territory and Texas. It was said that for many members of the extended Jewish community, no wedding was official without "Uncle Sam."

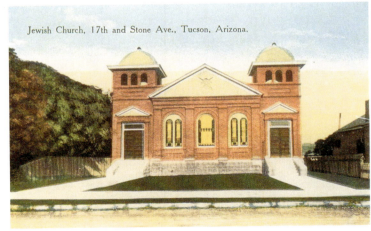

4. Original postcard showing "Jewish church on Stone Ave.," c. 1914. It was actually Temple Emanuel in Tucson, the first synagogue built in Arizona (1910).

Though not a rabbi, nor even the son of a rabbi, Sam Drachman made the Arizona desert bloom with *Yiddishkeit*.

In 1881, during the mining boom in Tombstone, the first Jewish organization in Arizona emerged – the Tombstone Hebrew Association – and held High Holy Days services that year. There is

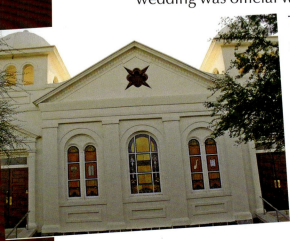

5. The original Emanuel building now serves as the Jewish History Museum of Tucson.

a Jewish cemetery in Tombstone, but not one Jewish person is buried there!

Unlike Louis Friedenthal, most Jewish pioneers in the Southwest did not share the stereotypical Jewish image of a storekeeper or a peddler laden with *pecklach* on his back. By 1885, the Jewish population included ranchers, miners, railroad builders, irrigation experts, soldiers, and traders. There was "Navajo Sam Dittenhoefer," who lived on an Indian reservation. Legend has it that he became a Jewish folk hero by outwitting Billy the Kid. When carrying $25,000 in coins to the Spiegelberg's main store, he hid them in flour barrels with false bottoms. When he was held up by "the Kid," all the robber took was flour!

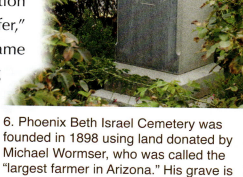

6. Phoenix Beth Israel Cemetery was founded in 1898 using land donated by Michael Wormser, who was called the "largest farmer in Arizona." His grave is in the forefront, c. 1898.

The leading farmer was Michael Wormser, known as Don Miguel El Judio by the Mexican sharecroppers. While he wasn't religious, he left land for what became the Phoenix Beth Israel Cemetery in 1898.

By the time Arizona became a state in 1912, there were 1,000 Jews living there, but it wasn't until ten years later that the first synagogue building in Phoenix, Congregation Beth Israel, was built. The architect's design was based on the style of the old missions. It is presently being restored by the Arizona Jewish Historical Society. There were times when services were cancelled due to excessive heat (120 degrees). As a matter of fact, the invention of air conditioning was the single most important reason for increase in the state's population.

7. Congregation Beth Israel, the first synagogue in Phoenix, was built in 1922. It was just restored and serves as the Arizona Jewish Historical Society.

A second congregation was started when the Orthodox *shochet*, Reverend Yehiel Dow, and other members broke away from Beth Israel to form Beth El. Dow was a *shochet*, *chazzan*, *mohel*, and teacher.

In the early 1940s, the kosher place to eat was May's. David Bloom, a member of a pioneer family, recalls, "When I was a kid, my parents took me to May's for dinner. At the entrance, there was a cup of water and a towel. I picked up the cup and drank the water. I didn't learn until later that the water was for the ritual washing of the hands!"

You can see the exponential growth of the Jewish population throughout the 1950s: in 1948, there were 3,500 Jews in Phoenix; by 1960, there were 8,000! A group of older Phoenix residents and Holocaust survivors joined together to found Phoenix's first Traditional

8. Reverend Yehiel (Ydel) Dow and family. He was one of Arizona's early religious leaders. He came to Tucson in 1925 and was a *shochet* while his wife, Bessie, ran a delicatessen on Stone Ave. He moved on to Phoenix in 1927 and was that community's first *shochet*; he also served as a *chazzan*, *mohel*, and teacher.

9. Beth Hebrew Congregation, the first traditional congregation in downtown Phoenix (1950). The exterior was shaped like Noah's ark.

synagogue in the downtown area in 1950, Beth Hebrew Congregation. It was built in the shape of Noah's ark. There was another small Orthodox synagogue downtown holding Shabbos services in the late '50s called Tiphereth Israel.

By the early '60s, the Jewish population in Phoenix had exploded to 10,000. It had been more than 100 years since the arrival of the first Jew and a long, arduous process had prepared the ground for a stable, truly Jewish community. But who would plant that first seed?

Planting the Seed

Hailing from Sale, Morocco, Rabbi David Rebibo has been rabbi of this community since 1965. Who better to talk to about planting seeds than the "farmer" himself?

"In Sale," he told me, "everyone was Orthodox. It was a total Torah environment, the Meah Shearim of Morocco." After learning with Rabbi Yitzchak Chaikin, a student of the Chofetz Chaim, and also in France, he continued his studies at the Slobodka Yeshiva in Bnei Brak, Israel. On what was to become one of the most fateful days of Rabbi Rebibo's life, Dr. Joseph Kaminetsky, the founding director of Torah Umesorah National Society for Hebrew Day Schools in America, walked into the yeshivah. Dr. Kaminetsky told Rabbi Rebibo to look him up in New York when he returned to America. There, "he showed me a map with pins in every community of over 10,000 Jews. Then he pointed out the only one without a Jewish day school."

10. Rabbi Yitzchak Chaikin, the *rebbe* of Rabbi Rebibo, was a student of the Chofetz Chaim.

At the time, Rabbi Rebibo was planning to open a high school in Memphis, a more developed community, with the funds already in place. "Dr. Kaminetsky told me that in the wasteland that was Phoenix, there was no *shul*, no school, no *mikveh*, no food, no money. His eyes glowing, he asked me, 'Where are you going to find an opportunity like this to start all these things?'"

Odette, the good rabbi's wife, came into the room as I interviewed him. Upon overhearing the story of their decision to come to Phoenix, she smiled and said, "We were young and stupid!"

11. Rabbi David Rebibo standing in front of the yeshivah in France where he was a student, c. 1950s

12. Rabbi David and wife, Odette, pioneers in the "Wild West" since 1965

Pointing to her husband, she respectfully corrected herself: "We were young and idealistic!"

Odette grew up in Nazi-occupied Paris, and remembers the yellow star Jews were required to wear. They lived in fear of an officer coming over and seeing if he could put a pencil point between the stitches. If he could, the penalty was deportation.

Taking up Dr. Kaminetsky's challenge, they came to Phoenix in 1965 – and found even less than they expected. Beth Hebrew was not strictly Orthodox and Tiphereth had trouble getting a *minyan* on Shabbos. "The only kosher meat available was the Queen Esther brand chicken from St. Louis," Odette told me. "My kids said, 'If we eat one more chicken, we're all going to lay eggs!'"

"Odette had to bake bread every day," Rabbi Rebibo added. "To tell you the honest truth, it was the Wild West – I called it *Tohu vavohu*! [As at the start of Creation, complete nothingness.]

"I found myself dealing with two constituencies: the people who had children and needed a day school had no money; and the people who had money had no children and had no need for a school. But they wanted a *shul*! So I told them, 'Give me money for the school and I'll build you a *shul*.'" Moreover, the school had support from some non-Orthodox parents as well. "A Reform rabbi bluntly told me, 'We need a day school, and the record shows that the Orthodox are the only ones successful at this. If you open, I'll put my kids in.'"

As a result, Phoenix Hebrew Academy opened in 1965, and the *shul*, Beth Joseph, opened two years later. They are physically connected on the same property and the spiritual bond between them is strong. Prior to its building, the first *minyan* was in the house behind the school, which also housed the first and only *mikveh* in Phoenix at that time.

Odette clearly remembers asking Dr. Kaminetsky about a *mikveh*, and she was assured it was "pretty close, in Tucson." She laughs at her recollection. "I guess, to him, 115 miles on a map looked short. But in those days, there were no highways: it took three hours to get there, three hours back, and an hour in between!" She added, "Between the total populations of Tucson and Phoenix, two people used that *mikveh* – one woman in Tucson and me! Every time I went there, I thought of Dr. Kaminetsky telling me how close it was!"

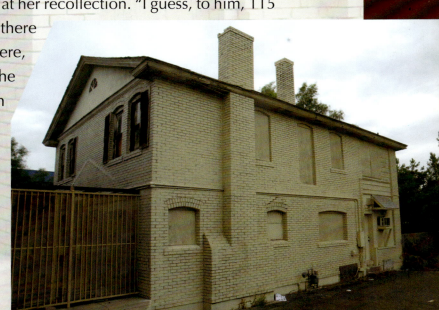

13. This building housed the first *minyan* and the *mikveh*.

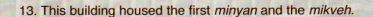

They finally built a *mikveh* in Phoenix in the early '70s. But they had one major problem: no rain. There had been a long drought in this desert location, and rainwater was necessary to fill the *mikveh* according to Jewish law. So they called up Rabbi Moshe Feinstein, the halachic expert of the day, who gave them the solution: go to Flagstaff (two hours away) and bring back a truckload of snow! They arranged to buy the snow and have a special freezer truck transport it. The night before the truck was supposed to leave to pick up the snow, the heavens opened up and there was so much rain in the next three days that it filled the *mikveh*! Choni Hamaagal would have been proud!

"We were pioneers," says Rabbi Rebibo wryly, "in every sense of the word."

Abundant Fruits

The Rebibos came to Phoenix to plant the seed of *Yiddishkeit* in a community parched for Torah, and the beautiful fruits are apparent. A Jewish community of barely 10,000 Jews in 1965 has grown into a vibrant community of 100,000, and is one of the fastest growing Jewish communities in the United States.

14. The *kollel* houses the second largest Bucharian *shul* outside of New York, servicing 600 families from Uzbekistan. Rabbi Baruch Cohen brought over 100 families himself. He has kashered over 200 kitchens.

"Once you start a project, it really has a hold on you," the rabbi says modestly. Let's look at the score sheet: aside from the school they now have multiple *shul*s, including a Bucharian synagogue to service the large influx of Jews from Uzbekistan. (It's the second largest Bucharian population in the country outside New York.) They have brought in a *kollel*, a girl's high school, six kosher restaurants, three *mikvaos*, an *eruv*, and many Chabad branches. Rabbi Rebibo also founded the Vaad Hakashruth to provide kosher supervision, even for the hotels on Passover.

Because the Jewish community now seems so well established, it's hard for some people to envision it otherwise. They are unaware of the challenges that existed here until relatively recently. "People don't realize that this was really a *midbar*, a desert," Odette commented. "My children learned that if you don't have something, you don't compromise your principles or beliefs."

15. Rabbi Zvi Holland, *rosh yeshivah* (dean) of the Phoenix Community Kollel, stands next to the *aron* in the *kollel shul* that was made by Yossi Gagliano, descended from Italian master carpenters.

Because the Jewish community now seems so well established, it's hard for some people to envision it otherwise. They are unaware of the challenges that existed here until relatively recently.

A favorite story depicts the wonderful success of their outreach. There was a family that was not religious, but the four children were sent to the Hebrew Academy. When they graduated, their father, a physician, took a job offer in a mining town near Nogales, Arizona, on the Mexican border. On the first morning after they moved, the principle of the Hebrew Academy got a surprise call from one of the boys. Their question? "Can you tell us which way is *mizrach*?" (east – the direction observant Jews face for prayers). He was delighted!

Torah in the Desert:
A Story of Southwestern Jewish Unity

When I was researching my chapter on Denver, Colorado, I met an amazing pioneer in his own right, Rabbi Hillel Goldberg. A versatile scholar and gifted writer, he is the editor of the *Intermountain Jewish News* and wrote a magnificent supercommentary on the commentary of the Vilna Gaon on the laws of the *mikveh*, called *Hallel Hacohen*.

He is also a founder of Torah Bamidbar (Torah in the Desert), a Jewish creation flowering remarkably in this environment.

Santa Fe, the capital of New Mexico, had 1,200 Jews in 1981, serviced by a Reform congregation. The rabbi of Temple Beth Shalom suggested that the Temple start a Traditional *minyan* to satisfy the needs of the entire community. He contacted Rabbi Goldberg, as well as other shakers and movers, who began to work with him on a new idea, albeit from nearly 400 miles away.

16. Hillel Goldberg, editor of the *Intermountain Jewish News* in Denver and founder of Torah Bamidbar

Courses in diverse Jewish topics, taught by Orthodox rabbis, were made available via telephone. One woman, a member of the Temple, became sincerely committed to a Jewish lifestyle through these courses, and expressed an interest in using a *mikveh*. Because there was none in Santa Fe, she would walk a mile from the nearest road to use the Pecos River, an acceptable alternative. She persevered, though sometimes she had to walk through snow and ice. (Yes, Santa Fe averages 32 inches of snow per year!) Although no one else was interested, it pained her friends to see her struggle, so they committed to building a *mikveh* within the orbit of the Reform Temple.

The Temple then gave their old building to the Traditional congregation and even helped build their *mechitzah*!

Torah Bamidbar Academy of New Mexico, a full-time Hebrew day school, started as a one-room schoolhouse with nine students spread over eight grades! The community now has a *chevra kadisha*, a *shul*, a *mikveh*, and a day school.

Looking Back at the Struggle

I had a wonderful conversation with a person who opened the gates wide to kosher food availability in Phoenix in the 1960s. Zalman Segal was born in Tel Aviv in 1929, and learned *shechitah* in Baltimore, getting his license at the age of 18.

BEN'S
WISHES ALL
A HAPPY NEW YEAR
STRICTLY KOSHER
MEAT, POULTRY AND
DELICATESSEN MARKET
— Under supervision of Phoenix Vaad Hakashruth —
EXCLUSIVELY at Ben's can you get turkeys, chickens, fryers and all meats FRESH KILLED DAILY ON OUR OWN PREMISES
ON OUR OWN PREMISES
ORDER YOUR POULTRY AND TURKEY EARLY
AL 8-1298   512 E. Washington
Open Sunday till I p.m.—Free Delivery

17. Ad for Ben's Kosher Market, 1950s and '60s: "All meats fresh killed on the premises."

"I was a *shochet* in the packing houses of Chicago, and then in Nebraska where it was, at times, 15 below zero! Then Rabbi Rebibo calls me in 1967 and asks me if I want to buy Ben's Kosher Market, which was closing. He said they needed a kosher meat market, and he really did a good job of convincing me to come."

Zalman showed up in Phoenix ready to take on the challenge – but was unprepared for the lack of everything Jewish there in the mid-'60s. "There was nothing here! Even Rabbi Rebibo went to Tucson for Rosh Hashanah and Yom Kippur!"

Yet the rabbi was so anxious for Zalman to stay that he organized a Melaveh Malkah get-together to welcome Zalman and his wife, Pearl. "They mustered up every living, breathing guy – Orthodox, not Orthodox – and filled up the house. At the time, I thought it was a fraction of the community!

"Two men from New York came to the store when I first opened and asked for two Shabbos meals. I told them I don't have the equipment to prepare meals. They were expecting a New York–type takeout.

"So they say to me, 'Do you eat on Shabbos?' I laughed and said, 'Of course.' 'Well, who does your cooking?' they asked. 'My wife,' I answered.

"They kind of looked at me. 'So couldn't she cook a little more?' Of course! So they ate at our house on Shabbos. After Shabbos, they wanted to pay me. I told them to give a donation to the school instead. They gave $750! That's the most money I ever got for a couple of chickens!"

Proud of the community's recent progress, Zalman told me that when he first came he would get a call in the middle of the day to fill in at a *beis din* – Jewish tribunal – which requires Orthodox Jews. They could barely find the required three people. "Today," he sighs, "they don't need me anymore," but he's glad!

18. Zalman and Pearl Segal reminiscing about their landmark restaurant in Phoenix. For decades, it was the meeting place for visitors all over the world.

Irwin Sheinbein's family came from Washington, DC, in 1959, and his father, Jack, played a pivotal role in the founding of the Phoenix day school. At that time it was not a popular move, for a Jewish school was considered exclusionary and un-American. Jack was one of the few to back Rabbi Rebibo.

"We had great Jewish education in DC, so it was hard to adjust to a Talmud Torah after public school," Irwin said. "The [Reform] Beth Israel played a big role [in getting the day school started]. Rabbi Rebibo was always looking for the next need – a school, *shul, mikveh, vaad*…"

19–21. Irwin Sheinbein's father came from Poland to Palestine, a British colony at the time, in 1938. The Polish stamp for the Jew was in the shape of the tablets of the Ten Commandments. The inside of the British passport for Palestine was in Arabic and Hebrew.

Carol Goldstein's father was here in Phoenix before Arizona became a state. She and her husband, David, talked to me about the effect the Orthodox community has had on them. David volunteered a warm recollection: "My mother remembers Rabbi Rebibo going house to house, door to door, collecting money for the day school – and giving out Kiddush wine for Shabbos." The rabbi's earnest efforts obviously had a positive effect on David, because he became a leader in the community and was involved in constructing the *eruv*.

"It seems I was disconnected from my people and now we've been put back together, again, thank G-d."

Carol's story is fascinating. Years back, she converted to Judaism, but well before that, there was a tradition in her family that they were descended from a major Spanish Jewish scholar. It gets better. "I've been told that in the early to mid-1800s, I had relatives who were hidden in a convent in New Mexico, but we can't be sure. It seems I was disconnected from my people and now we've been put back together, again, thank G-d." David's grandfather was a *shochet* in Morocco, so there is Sephardic blood on his side as well.

Their cooking is a reflection of many influences. Carol uses a cookbook of *converso* recipes from the time of the Inquisition, called *A Drizzle of Honey*. On many a Shabbos, they would eat a type of Mexican chili instead of cholent. "And we have our own southwestern 'gefilte fish,'" David smiled. "It's called *cerviche*. We use cod, flounder, or tilapia cut into cubes, put it in lime juice for half a day so that it pickles, put salsa on it, and eat it cold."

"Once we found a kosher symbol that we couldn't identify on some hot sauces," said Carol, "so we brought it to Rabbi Rebibo. He identified the symbol as the Beis Din of Mexico City (KMD) – and quickly asked if he could use some for himself before returning it!"

22. Hot sauce from Mexico joins traditional Jewish ingredients in the Goldsteins' cooking.

The rabbi's warm relationship with the Goldsteins, as well as with so many in the community over 50 years, is well reflected in the products of his labors – both physical and spiritual.

A great sage, the Alter of Novardok, once said, "When it is necessary to send a letter, I send a telegram; when it is necessary to send a telegram, I send an emissary; and when it is necessary to send an emissary, I go myself."

Rabbi Rebibo went himself. His legacy will last for generations.

What a Harvest!

It's no wonder that Tu B'Shevat is meaningful here in Phoenix – a city literally set in the desert where produce would not naturally grow. Even in fertile soil, the act of planting, itself, is an act of faith. A seed is buried. There is no way to track its progress, and the farmer has few means of control. There are so many things that could go wrong: too little rain, too much rain, chemical imbalance in the soil, disease – it's nothing short of a miracle that a seed nearly rots in the ground, then takes root and produces a lush harvest.

The ground here was prepared so long ago by Jews like Sam Drachman and Yehiel Dow, but the success of those first seeds can only be seen by their fruit many years later. To kabbalists, an abundance of fruit represents the effect a person has on his family and on his community. Rabbi Rebibo, and those who joined him in painstakingly building this community, have nurtured those seeds and reaped fruit beyond all expectations.

The story of Phoenix is the story told of all communities striving to be successful centers of Torah Judaism. "My ancestors planted for me, and now I plant for my children."

The roots are firmly in place and the first fruits look great, on this Tu B'Shevat.

23. Rabbi Ariel Shoshan and daughters enjoying the fruits of Tu B'Shevat. "Tu B'Shevat," he told me, "is a testament to the enduring truth of the Oral Torah as expressed in the Mishnah. Who would have believed in 1920…that Jews from every walk of life would honor and celebrate a day mentioned only once [in Jewish Scripture] – in the *Mishnah Rosh Hashanah*." Rabbi Shoshan is the head rabbi at Ahavas Torah – The Scottsdale Torah Center.

Life in the Southwest

Congress Street, Tucson, Ariz.

24. Postcard depicting early Tucson, where Jewish life started in the Southwest, c. 1880s–'90s

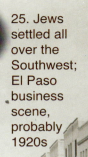

25. Jews settled all over the Southwest; El Paso business scene, probably 1920s

26. Sam Korrick's New York Store, as it looked when it opened in Phoenix, c. 1895. It advertised itself as "The cheapest Place in the City." There was so little money that his display cases were made of boards laid across packing crates.

27. Phoenix area downtown where Jewish life began from 1880 to 1920

28. It was the "Wild West" for Charles Strauss (with unidentified boy), who was elected mayor of Tucson in 1883, the first Jewish mayor in the Arizona Territory. He opposed the election of Ulysses Grant for president because of Grant's anti-Semitic General Order No. 11, expelling Jews from the South; the order was quickly rescinded by Lincoln. Strauss was there for the pow wow and surrender of Geronimo, chief of the Apaches, c. 1883.

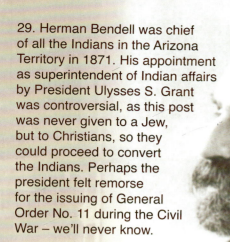

29. Herman Bendell was chief of all the Indians in the Arizona Territory in 1871. His appointment as superintendent of Indian affairs by President Ulysses S. Grant was controversial, as this post was never given to a Jew, but to Christians, so they could proceed to convert the Indians. Perhaps the president felt remorse for the issuing of General Order No. 11 during the Civil War – we'll never know.

30. Katz's Butcher Shop in the early '60s

STRICTLY KOSHER MEAT & POULTRY

We do not charge for killing and cleaning

Delicatessen and Groceries

A. Katz

512 E. Washington   Phone 3-8685

31. Longing for the old days at Katz's: "We do not charge for killing and cleaning."

32. The "must" stop before the Canyon!

33. Rabbi Rebibo and family in the early days of the Hebrew Academy and Beth Joseph, c. 1960s–'70s

34. A historic moment recounted in the *Jewish News of Greater Phoenix*: President Truman signing a proclamation at the de jure recognition of Israel in 1949

De Jure Recognition

Prayer and study

35. Interior of the original synagogue, Beth Israel, being renovated as the architects keep an enlarged photo of this interior as it was 80 years ago, to duplicate it

Passover Seder

36. Cornerstone of the synagogue Beth Hebrew showing the Hebrew name as Kahal Kodosh Ein Yaakov, 1955

37. The original Phoenix Hebrew Academy on the same site as the present one. The old building, on the left, is still there, serving as offices.

38. The Phoenix Hebrew Academy with Congregation Beth Joseph connected to the right. Both are the brainchildren of Rabbi Rebibo.

39. The Chabad Lubavitch center, with a wonderful variety of learning opportunities for all, is headed by Rabbi Zalman Levertov; another center is led by Rabbi Mendy Levertov, with whom I had the pleasure to talk. This building was scheduled to be a church, he told me, but the state had to take it over for financial reasons, so Chabad got lucky. Among their impressive activities, they organized "The Friendship Circle" to help children with special needs; through this they teach their own teens that it is better to give than to take.

40. This community has redefined the word *achdus* (unity). All spiritual leaders are always working together. The community uses plastic sheathing for part of their *eruv* (a device to allow carrying on Shabbat). Rabbis get together at a moment's notice on Friday with the electric company to fix a loose tube on the pole. Left to right: representative of the electric company, Rabbi Gross of the Young Israel of Phoenix, Rabbi Zvi Holland of the Phoenix Kollel, and Rabbi Yudi Moskowitz, in charge of *kiruv* (bringing Jews closer to their religion) on university campuses.

Tu B'Shevat

picture of a great event!

41. Happy third anniversary! An ad by the United Jewish Appeal encouraging planting trees in Israel, c. 1951.

WHAT IS SO REMARKABLE, you ask, about a father helping his son plant a seedling tree?

This is what is remarkable: it is happening in Israel — today, on Israel's third anniversary of Statehood. And the odds were — overwhelmingly — that it could never happen at all.

The odds were that the father would die in Europe as six million other Jews died under Hitler. Yet he got through to the new, shining land. The odds were that the desert soil of Israel could not be made to flourish. But the father, and tens of thousands like him, brought more to the task than hoes and harrows . . .

Now you see the roots going down. Not just the roots of the seedling . . . human roots, too. The tree, the boy and Israel will all grow together. And along with them will grow and flourish the world's most precious way of life — democracy.

In just three years you have helped transplant 500,000 homeless refugees to Israel, have given them the chance to begin a new and hopeful life. But the work is only half done. Your help—through the United Jewish Appeal is needed still to bring 200,000 more this year, to reclaim land, plant forests, build settlements and homes so that these newcomers, too, can sink firm roots in Israel's soil. Give now, while there is time.

Cash—Your Birthday Gift to Israel

Let Israel's Third Birthday be the occasion for a birthday gift— a birthday gift that you can give today. You can give it by paying your pledge — the pledge you made to our community campaign on behalf of the United Jewish Appeal. Pay your pledge today— and thereby give the UJA the cash it must have for great events like the one shown here. Today, more than ever before, cash means life. Cash today for UJA means that Jews who are now in lands of darkness will celebrate Israel's fourth birthday—in Israel.

If you have not already made your contribution please call or write.

UNITED JEWISH WELFARE FUND
Headquarters 915 North 4th Street
Phone 4-5573
GOAL: $175,000 IN 1951

United Jewish Appeal

on behalf of Joint Distribution Committee · United Palestine Appeal · United Service for New Americans

We salute the State of Israel on the Third Anniversary of its Independence

42. The custom continues as children at the Chabad center plant trees in their own way on Tu B'Shevat.

Tu B'Sheva

This Tu B'Shevat you could make a difference. Plant a tree in the Negev.

43. A more recent ad talks about planting in the Negev and the possibilities. It could have been talking about the desert of Arizona as well!

To plant trees, call
1-800-254-8733

VOL. IX   Phone ALpine 4-7494   Phoenix, Ariz., February 10, 1956

Children Observe Jewish Arbor Day

45. You never thought shoveling dirt could be this much fun – except when you are planting a tree with friends on Tu B'Shevat.

44. Planting on "Jewish Arbor Day," a name given by some to Tu B'Shevat, c. 1956

46. The Annual Phoenix Tu B'Shevat Extravaganza celebrates a sometimes forgotten holiday. The crowds are enormous and there are booths set up for food, a Seder, arts and crafts, Judaica and just plain fun.

47. Mayor of Phoenix wearing the perfect yarmulke to observe the Tu B'Shevat celebration. Note the old-style Keren Kayemet-JNF *tzedakah* box.

49. Girl with a balloon palm tree – her way of celebrating at the Tu B'Shevat Seder.

48. Smokey Bear and Tu B'Shevat? Who would've thought?

50. In the mid 1500s, the students of Rabbi Isaac Luria, or the Ari, formulated a special Tu B'Shevat Seder set up along the lines of the Passover Seder, which comes only 60 days later. There are four cups of wine and the fruits of Israel. The first cup is all white wine representing the winter. The second cup is filled with ¾ white and ¼ red, the coming of spring. The third cup is filled with ½ red and ½ white, the start of summer. The fourth cup is filled with ¾ red and ¼ white, representing the ripening of the fruits, and a touch of winter. Everyone pours for each other, and drinks reclining as on Passover. A festive meal follows. It is customary to pray for your *esrog* (citron fruit used during the holiday of Sukkos) and imagine its color, shape, and size. The rest of the day is spent singing, dancing, and learning Torah.

51. Seders of the past – Seder held in the "sukkah" of the Phoenix Hebrew Academy, date unknown

My thanks to
Rabbi Daniel and Odette Rebibo,
Fred Zeidman, Zalman and Pearl Segal,
Rabbi Zvi Holland,
Rabbi Mendy Levertov, Larry Bell,
Leisah Woldoff and the *Jewish News of Greater Phoenix*,
Rabbi Harris Cooperman,
Irwin Scheinbein,
David and Carol Goldstein,
Rabbi Ariel Shoshan, Eileen Warshaw,
and Vivian and Seymour Salit, *a"h.*

Bibliography

Chanin, Abraham S. *Cholent and Chorizo: Great Adventures of Pioneer Jews on the Arizona Frontier*. Tucson, AZ: Midbar Press, 1995.

Epstein, Morris. *All about Jewish Holidays and Customs*. New York: Ktav, 1959.

Feldberg, Michael, Ph.D. *Chapters in American Jewish History*. Chapter 21, "Staying Jewish on the Arizona Frontier." New York: American Jewish Historical Society, 2002.

Fischer, Ron W. *The Jewish Pioneers of Tombstone and Arizona Territory*. Tombstone, AZ: Ron Fischer Enterprises, 2002.

Libo, Kenneth, and Irving Howe. *We Lived There Too: In Their Own Words and Pictures; Pioneer Jews and the Westward Movement of America, 1630–1930*. New York: St. Martin's/Marek, 1984.

Tobias, Henry J. *A History of the Jews in New Mexico*. Albuquerque: University of New Mexico Press, 1990.

Photo Attributions

All numbered photos from the author's collection except as follows. Photos 2, 51: Phoenix Hebrew Academy; 3, 26, 28, 29, 30, 45: Arizona Jewish Historic Society; 4, 5, 24, 25: Jewish History Museum, Tucson, Arizona; 17, 34, 41, 43, 44: *Jewish News of Greater Phoenix*; 10, 11, 33: Archives of Rabbi David and Odette Rebibo; 16: *Intermountain Jewish News*; 19, 20, 21: Irwin Scheinbein collection.

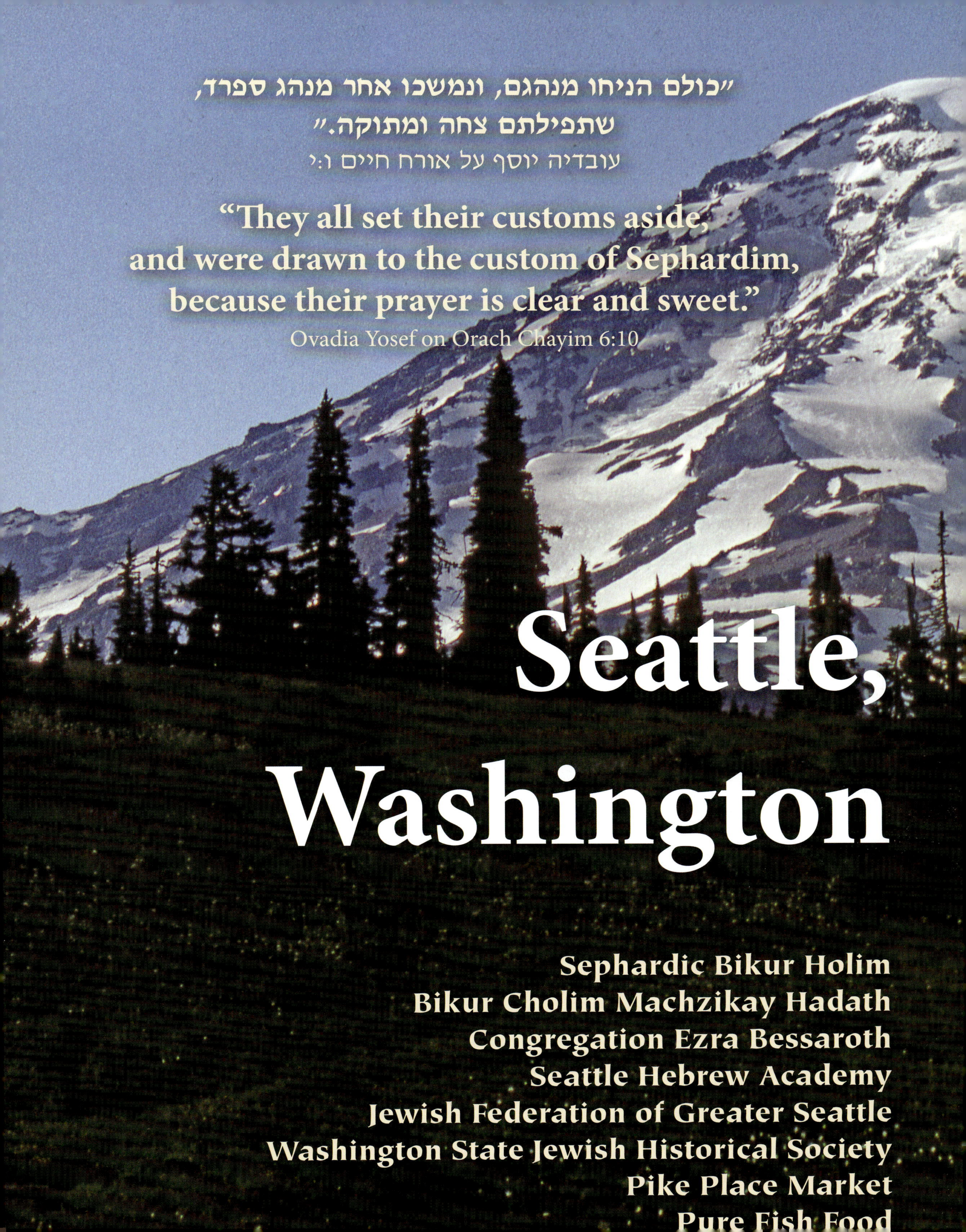

"כולם הניחו מנהגם, ונמשכו אחר מנהג ספרד,
שתפילתם צחה ומתוקה."
עובדיה יוסף על אורח חיים ו:י

"They all set their customs aside,
and were drawn to the custom of Sephardim,
because their prayer is clear and sweet."
Ovadia Yosef on Orach Chayim 6:10

Seattle, Washington

Sephardic Bikur Holim
Bikur Cholim Machzikay Hadath
Congregation Ezra Bessaroth
Seattle Hebrew Academy
Jewish Federation of Greater Seattle
Washington State Jewish Historical Society
Pike Place Market
Pure Fish Food

A Hidden Treasure in the Pacific Northwest

March 31, 1492: "Convert or leave." Over 500 years have passed since this cruel ultimatum was decreed in the form of an edict to the Jews of Spain by King Ferdinand and Queen Isabella.

1. Edict of Ferdinand and Isabella expelling the Jews from Spain, March 31, 1492. Royal seal and signatures.

The expulsion of the Jews from Spain ended the longest continuous recorded history in the diaspora: they had been living on Spanish soil for nearly 2,000 years. During that time, they had experienced a "Golden Age" under Moorish rule (approximately eighth century to twelfth century) and later (through the fifteenth century) from which Jews the world over still benefit today. The Jews of Spain (called Sephardim because Spain in Hebrew is *Sepharad*) produced such luminaries as Moses Maimonides (Rambam), philosopher, physician, and codifier of Jewish law; poet Judah HaLevi; poet and statesman Shmuel HaNagid; scholars, thinkers, and poets Abraham Ibn Ezra, Nachmanides (Ramban), Solomon Ibn Gabirol, Dunash Ibn Labrat, Rabbeinu Bahya Ibn Paquda, Don Isaac Abarbanel, and many more. Anyone who cherishes biblical commentary – in fact, anyone who sings *zemiros* on Shabbos – owes a world of gratitude to these Sephardim who so greatly enriched these legacies.

The tragic Edict of Expulsion meant the broad proliferation of Spanish-Jewish culture in other parts of the world, for the Jews were rich in language, art, and science as well. When Jews from Spain started arriving in Turkey, the Turkish sultan sent a letter to the Spanish king and queen saying, "You fools, you gave us your riches and kept the poor!" Like him, there are many who consider the departure of the Jews in 1492 to have been the prime factor in the later decline of Spain as a world power.

Distinguished Sephardim who thrived in other lands in the many years since the expulsion include such diverse personages as the scholar and codifier of the *Shulchan Aruch* (handbook of Jewish law) Rabbi Joseph Caro, British prime minister Benjamin Disraeli, and chief justice of the US Supreme Court Benjamin Cardozo.

Two great traditions were created by the Sephardim in their exile, developing along geographic lines. One developed in the Mediterranean Basin – Turkey, Greece, and Morocco – while the second evolved in the "Atlantic community" of Holland, England, the Caribbean, and the United States. Both of these traditions reflect a powerful ability to adapt to changing times and difficult conditions.

What does this Jewish history lesson have to do with Seattle? The fact is that Seattle has been the home of a huge contingent of Sephardic Jews – inheritors of this proud legacy – for many years. But I'm getting ahead of myself. As it happens, the very first Jew to set foot in the Washington Territory was not Sephardic.

He was a single adventurer, a 24-year-old Latvian native named Adolph Friedman. He came to the region around 1845 and made it into the record of Jewish "firsts" by becoming the first merchant in the area of present-day Tacoma to supply goods for fishermen. He settled in the area, married a relative from nearby Vancouver, and died at the age of 90 in 1911.

He was surely aware of the first trickle of Jewish immigrants to Seattle during the mid-nineteenth century, followed by much larger migrations later on. First came the German-speaking Jews from central Europe, then the Yiddish-speaking Jews from eastern Europe, followed by Ladino-speaking Sephardic Jews from Turkey and Rhodes. Ladino can best be called Judaeo-Spanish, the Sephardic equivalent of Yiddish, for it incorporates languages picked up through diaspora travels: today it is a mixture of Old Spanish, Hebrew, Aramaic, Arabic, Turkish, and Greek. Jews in this remote end of the country were not only isolated from the larger centers of American Jewish life; each group had little in common with the other – except that they all identified as Jews, and many were merchants in one fashion or another.

Jennie Schermer, whose Seattle family dates back to the mid-nineteenth century, describes her father's work in the early days. "He had a pack train in Victoria, British Columbia...and would go up to the Indians who would buy rifles from him. They would take a shotgun to measure height, and pile up furs until they got to the top. That was the way they paid for the shotguns."

Expecting a major influx of people due to a planned railroad hub in Seattle, three enterprising Jewish brothers from Germany, the Schwabachers, opened a major store in 1869 that would provide everything "from a needle to an anchor," both wholesale and retail. It was a huge success. The Schwabachers went on to build Seattle's first brick building, at the corner of Front Street and Yesler Way, in 1872. By 1875, the manager of the store, Bailey Gatzert, was so trusted and renowned that he was elected the first (and only) Jewish mayor of Seattle. He's been celebrated

> Jews in this remote end of the country... had little in common with the other – except that they all identified as Jews...

2. Bailey Gatzert, the only Jewish mayor in Seattle, c. 1880s. He was the founder of the Seattle Chamber of Commerce and founding member of the first synagogue, Ohaveth Sholum. Steamers and schools were named after him.

on a postage stamp, had his name placed on ships and schools, and hosted the first American president to travel west of the Rockies (Rutherford B. Hayes). He was also the founding member of the state's first Jewish house of worship, Ohaveth Sholum.

The discovery of gold in Alaska and the Canadian Yukon in 1897 put Seattle on the world map, setting off two decades of unprecedented growth. Seattle became the "Gateway to the Klondike," and Jews were on hand to help: Cooper & Levy was one of many Jewish-owned companies that outfitted the prospectors.

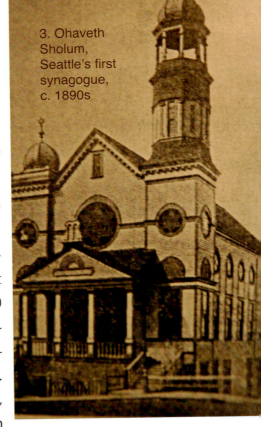

3. Ohaveth Sholum, Seattle's first synagogue, c. 1890s

Seattle received its first charter in 1880 and its first railway connection in 1884. (Abe Brenner, unhappy with his life on the East Coast, went to a train station in Virginia and asked for a ticket that would take him "as far away as I could get." The ticket brought him to Seattle!) Yet as early as ten years before that, there were *minyan* gatherings in homes and stores. A handful of Jews met in Red Man's Hall, downtown, for

4. Gold! Supplies for prospectors on their way to the Yukon overflow onto Yessler Way, in front of the Cooper & Levy store.

the High Holy Day services. By 1888, the *Jewish Messenger* of New York estimated that 20 Jewish families resided in Seattle, the largest concentration in the Washington territory, though miniscule compared to the general population of about 42,000. In 1892, the group became known as Congregation Chevra Bikur Cholim (society for visiting the sick), located itself in rented rooms on 13th and Washington Street, and also acquired property for a cemetery.

A founding member, Frank Antel, recalls that one year, "during Yom Kippur services, the doors opened suddenly and the members of a black dance band entered and began to set up their instruments. I took the *sefer Torah* and everyone ran out of there…the landlord had inadvertently rented the hall for a dance that night!"

5. Chevra Bikur Cholim, the first Orthodox congregation in Seattle, incorporated 1891

The Blessing of Rain

Not everyone living in eternally damp Seattle would agree that its notoriously high rate of precipitation is a blessing. But Jacob Radinsky's family came to Seattle in 1916 from an agricultural village in Russia where "If you don't have rain, you starve."

"We arrived on a typical November day in Seattle," he recalls, "dark, grey, and rainy. So my mother looks at the Seattle rain and almost in rapture, she says in Yiddish, 'We've landed in a *mazeldike shaah* [a lucky hour].' My father, who had come there before us and met us at the ship, replied curtly, 'Every hour in Seattle is a *mazeldike shaah!*' Ironically, for those immigrants, it was *rain* that made Seattle a *goldene medinah* – not gold!

Initially, the Jews in the remote Pacific Northwest relied on the established Jewish community in Victoria for rabbinic authorities. With the establishment of the first Orthodox synagogues such as Bikur Cholim (1889), eastern European Jews in Seattle were able to look to their own rabbi – Rabbi Hirsch Genss – for savvy leadership. Before marrying any young Jewish immigrant to the girl of his choice, Rabbi Genss insisted that a letter be written back to the old country first – to ensure that the prospective groom was not already married!

Rabbi Genss was the *shochet* for the Seattle Jews in the 1890s and, appropriately enough, also operated the meat market. By 1910, the Jewish population grew large enough to sustain kosher restaurants, butcher shops, and bakeries.

6. Rabbi Hirsch Genss, early pioneer in helping immigrants in an unfamiliar society, was a grocer, *shochet*, and *mohel*. He gave Bikur Cholim its first Torah in 1893 and served as its first rabbi without being officially elected, c. 1890s.

"Yehudi! Yehudi!" Sephardim Arrive in Seattle

The first Sephardim to come to Seattle were two young men who arrived almost by chance in June of 1902. Wearing *tzitzit* and carrying their prayer shawls and *tefillin*, Solomon Calvo and Jacob Policar came from the Turkish island of Marmara. Unable to speak English and eager to find other Jews, they stood on the waterfront street calling out, "*Yehudi, Yehudi!*" ("Jew, Jew!") The strategy worked. When a curious crowd gathered around them, 13-year-old Jacob Kaplan came over to say he was a Jew, too. He took them to Rabbi Genss, who introduced them to his congregants.

7. The first Sephardic Jews to settle in Washington. Standing: Mushon Eskenazi, Jacob Policar, Moshon Adatto; seated: Solomon Calvo and unidentified man, c. 1900–1910.

They were not like any Jews the *shul* members had ever seen. Their Ladino language was strange. When asked for proof that they were Jews, they read from a Hebrew prayer book, but their pronunciation was so incomprehensible that no one was at all convinced that they were Jewish! A letter to New York leaders cleared up the mystery. Unlike Caribbean Jews who had come to the area a century earlier, these Turkish Jews had different customs.

The two Sephardic pioneers were followed by others, and soon prominent Sephardic families with names that included Alhadeff, Calvo, Policar, Hazan, Eskenazi, and Benezra (among many others) formed the nucleus of Seattle's Sephardic community. Once they established themselves, a good number of Sephardim arriving at Ellis Island chose to make the trip to Seattle to join them.

The Ashkenazim didn't know what to do with these exotic Jews! They had never encountered Jews who smoked water pipes and drank Turkish coffee. Why, on Chanukah, they didn't even eat proper latkes – preferring *buñuelos*, a donut dipped in oil, fried, and served with sugar and honey! Yet Rabbi Genss was impressed. He told his people that these *Turkeshe Yidden* (Turkish Jews) were more religious than the Ashkenazim.

Apparently, they were also truer to their Spanish heritage than others descended from Iberian ancestors. Historian Albert Adatto (from a well-known Sephardic family) wrote in his master's thesis, "If Columbus were to return to life…[he] would find…a greater…affinity with these Sephardim than any group of modern Spaniards."

8. Early Sephardim with customs unfamiliar to the Ashkenazic Jews, c. 1910–1915

Due to their substantial differences in customs and prayers, the Sephardim did have to separate themselves from Ashkenazic synagogues, renting their first location near 10th and Yesler Way. The Marmaralis (Turkish Sephardim from Marmara) built new synagogues such as the Sephardic Bikur Holim and Ahavath Achim (which merged in 1914), and the Rhodeslis (Jews from Rhodes) built their synagogue, Ezra Bessaroth. These synagogues have emerged among the premier Sephardic congregations in the country.

"We didn't know how to welcome the Sephardim and vice versa. They were poor, but cultured and artistic," affirms Lillian Radinsky, who was born in Seattle in 1915. When she was a child, the area of Yesler Way and Cherry Street was the distinctly Jewish neighborhood, with synagogues within blocks of each other. The neighborhood was dotted with Jewish-owned bakeries, butcher shops, and groceries as well as dry goods stores.

What was life was like in the 1920s and '30s on Yesler Way? "My family," Lillian reports proudly, "came here in the gold rush days and outfitted the prospectors. My father found property for the cemetery. Ah, and I remember that *yom tov* [Jewish holidays] – and especially Yom Kippur – was a meeting time for the teenagers. We paraded on Yesler Way: it was a never-ending procession from *shul* to *shul*.

9. One of many kosher butcher shops on Yesler Way

"We had Brenner Brothers Bakery and Ziegman, the butcher. Before every Yom Kippur, I was sent to choose a live chicken, feel it for its fat, and stand on line to have it slaughtered. I can still recall watching so many chickens running around the sawdust-covered wooden floors without their heads! I didn't want to eat meat for a long time! But I do remember the excitement we had when we found eggs inside the chicken [a real delicacy]."

10. Lillian Radinsky: her husband was active in the key Ashkenazi *shul*, Bikur Cholim Machzikay Hadas, her father found the property for the cemetery, and her grandparents came here to outfit the gold prospectors in 1902.

The New Pike Place Market (a must-see for visitors, even today) offered the right ambience and camaraderie for the new Sephardic immigrants from Turkey and Greece. At first, they sold fish out of a basket on the street corner, then graduated to a pushcart, and soon were opening stores. "Pure Food Fish" is a Sephardic-owned store that is still going strong 100 years after its founding.

11. Contemporary view of the Yesler-Cherry St. neighborhood, which featured stores such as Brenner Brothers Bakery

The Maimons Come to Town

In 1924, Sephardic Bikur Holim brought Chacham (rabbi/scholar) Abraham Maimon from Turkey to be their spiritual leader. I had the incredible privilege of speaking with his son, the legendary leader of the present Sephardic community, Rabbi Solomon Maimon.

12. Pure Food Fish is the only remaining Sephardic-owned fish establishment in Pike Place Market.

I was fortunate to meet him as he was celebrating his ninetieth birthday, an event that coincided with a Maimon family reunion (with hundreds of family members from across the country), which occurs every five years.

He was born in Tekirdağ, Turkey, on the Sea of Marmara, 70 miles south of Istanbul. The story goes that less than an hour after his mother gave birth to him, she was up, cooking, and preparing for the Sephardic custom of visiting the sick, which includes women who have just given birth. She expected quite a crowd, so she cooked a lot. After she finished, she jumped back into bed, folded her arms, and waited to receive the people who would visit her. Rabbi Maimon laughs at his own stories so robustly, you can't help laughing with him.

When he was five years old, he and his five siblings were on the boat with their parents going from Turkey to America. There was a tremendous storm and it looked like the ship might go down. His father gathered the family together and made them take an oath that if they survived they would always remain Sabbath observers. It was a powerful lesson.

"We arrived at Ellis Island in 1924, just before Rosh Hashanah," he recalls. "The Sephardic community in New York brought a Torah, a shofar, and enough men for a *minyan* so we could have Rosh Hashanah right there on Ellis Island!

"On the way to Seattle from New York, the train stopped in Chicago's Union Station. My mother had never experienced hot water from a faucet nor seen a soap dispenser. She was so excited! She runs out of the public bathroom, calls the family together, and tells us all to go back into the train, take our clothes off, and give them to her – and she does a wash right there!"

When they reached Seattle, his father saw that his work was cut out for him. Many members of the Jewish community were not Sabbath observant and they knew little about their heritage. "My father did *kiruv* [outreach] 80 years before it was popular to do so. He would invite himself to someone's house on Shabbat and relate stories from the Talmud. With his expertise in *Ein Yaakov*, this was not difficult for him. He would keep them intrigued all day, so they wouldn't go to work. That's *kiruv*!"

13. Chacham (Rabbi) Abraham Maimon came from Tekirdağ, Turkey, in 1924, to lead Sephardic Bikur Holim.

In those early days, the pledges from these poor people for an *aliyah* (being called up to the Torah) would be a box of apples or sack of potatoes! And, of course, these were graciously accepted.

In the 1930s, Rabbi Maimon went to public school, worked in the family fruit market, and attended the Seattle Talmud Torah. "We learned very little Talmud, so when I took the exam to get into Yeshiva University, I failed miserably." Only 17 at the time, he absorbed this temporary setback, for the college ultimately decided to accept him despite

14. Rodosto Synagogue in Tekirdağ, Turkey, birthplace of Rabbi Solomon Maimon

the exam. "I think that they were intrigued by the idea of having the first Sephardi at their school to possibly receive *smichah* [rabbinic ordination]," he surmises. "And, in fact, I was the first American-trained Sephardic rabbi, in 1944."

And how is it that a Turkish Sephardi, who speaks a fluid Ladino, also speaks fluent Yiddish? "Ah – that's because my teacher in YU, Rabbi Steinberg, spoke only Yiddish. So I grabbed some guys and said, 'Teach me Yiddish.' I learned briefly under Rabbi Moshe Soloveitchik, and then under Rabbi

Yosef Ber Soloveitchik. They were tough on us – lifting us up high and letting us down with a parachute. Rav Moshe once gave us an assignment and I raised my hand and recited in my jerky Yiddish. So he stops me and says, 'You're *ploidering* [speaking incoherently] like a Turk!' Everyone laughed because they knew that I *was* a Turk!"

Coming home from New York, Rabbi Maimon took his father's place as the rabbi of the Sephardic Bikur Holim. It was 1944 and World War II was still raging. He made sure to correspond with congregation members fighting in the war, keeping their spirits up. In turn, he was inspired by their devotion to Judaism. "I know that many of them used their helmets as pots and pans just to keep kosher."

The rabbi's main concern has always been the children; and in the 1940s, Jewish education in Seattle was deficient. He had to do something to steer the next generation away from the inevitable assimilation and intermarriage that would be wrought by ignorance. Along with Ashkenazic rabbi Solomon Wohgelernter, he started a Jewish day school in 1947. He repelled the usual complaints of this era – that the initiative was un-patriotic and un-American – and ploughed on.

15. Eli Genauer, historian and wonderful guide, shows author's wife, Marlene, the old site of the Seattle Talmud Torah. Rabbi Maimon went to the original Talmud Torah.

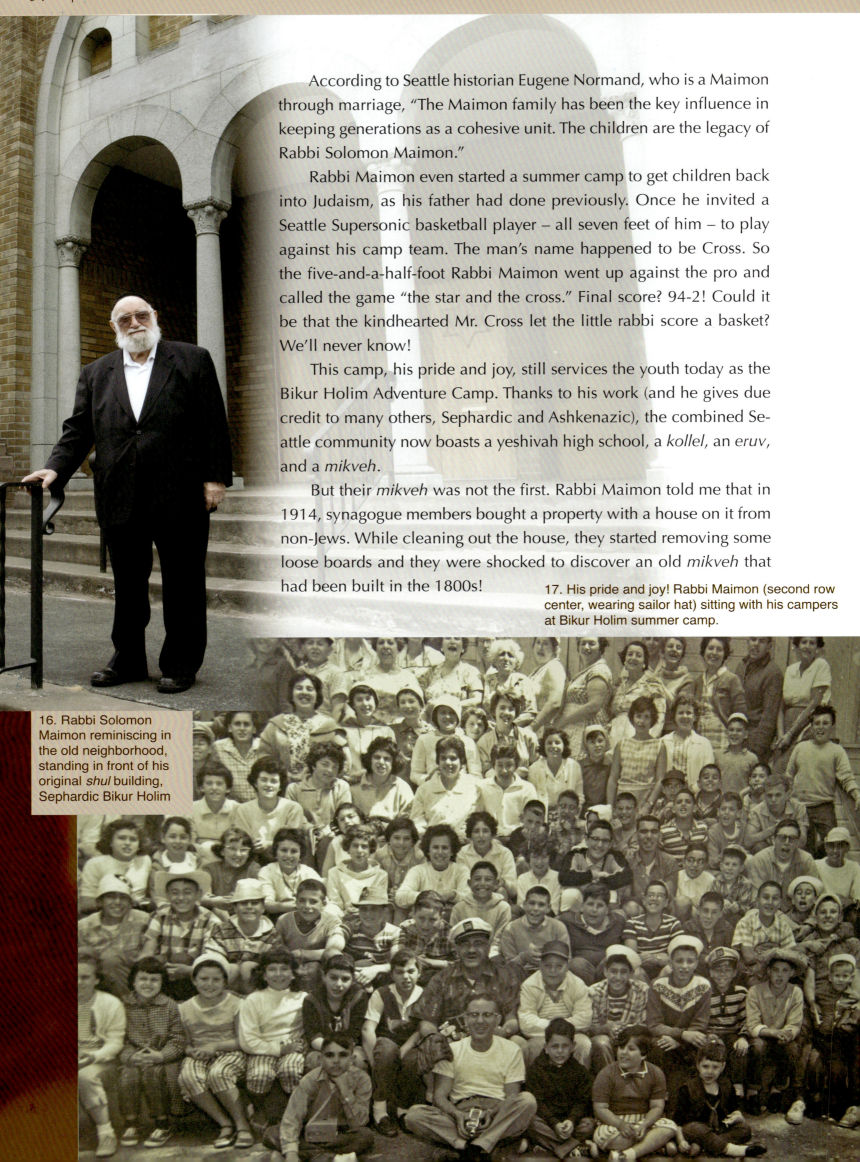

According to Seattle historian Eugene Normand, who is a Maimon through marriage, "The Maimon family has been the key influence in keeping generations as a cohesive unit. The children are the legacy of Rabbi Solomon Maimon."

Rabbi Maimon even started a summer camp to get children back into Judaism, as his father had done previously. Once he invited a Seattle Supersonic basketball player – all seven feet of him – to play against his camp team. The man's name happened to be Cross. So the five-and-a-half-foot Rabbi Maimon went up against the pro and called the game "the star and the cross." Final score? 94-2! Could it be that the kindhearted Mr. Cross let the little rabbi score a basket? We'll never know!

This camp, his pride and joy, still services the youth today as the Bikur Holim Adventure Camp. Thanks to his work (and he gives due credit to many others, Sephardic and Ashkenazic), the combined Seattle community now boasts a yeshivah high school, a *kollel*, an *eruv*, and a *mikveh*.

But their *mikveh* was not the first. Rabbi Maimon told me that in 1914, synagogue members bought a property with a house on it from non-Jews. While cleaning out the house, they started removing some loose boards and they were shocked to discover an old *mikveh* that had been built in the 1800s!

17. His pride and joy! Rabbi Maimon (second row center, wearing sailor hat) sitting with his campers at Bikur Holim summer camp.

16. Rabbi Solomon Maimon reminiscing in the old neighborhood, standing in front of his original *shul* building, Sephardic Bikur Holim

Enriched by Age-Old Customs

I asked Rabbi Maimon if he has a favorite Sephardic custom. "We have a beautiful custom for a new groom, the Sabbath after his marriage," he answered. "It is called *Shabbat de Avraham Siv.* He went on to explain that on this day, after the weekly Torah portion is read, another Torah is brought out for the *novyo* (groom), to the delight of friends and family. The reader chants the portion describing Abraham selecting a bride for Isaac, while someone else chants each verse in Aramaic. "This *zivug* [marriage] of Isaac was successful," he explained, "and we are wishing the same success to this groom and bride. We sing to the groom coming up for the honor and upon his completion. This is a very old, emotional, and beautiful custom." Rabbi Solomon Maimon is one beautiful man.

Since I arrived in Seattle the week after Tisha B'Av, I asked Rabbi Simon Benzaquen, the rabbi who followed Rabbi Maimon as rabbi of Sephardic Bikur Holim 25 years ago, about the Sephardic customs for this sad day. He told me of a very old and interesting *minhag* (custom) that has been handed down for hundreds of years through many generations. "Our tradition is that the destruction of the Second Holy Temple by the Romans took place in the year equaling the *gematria* [numerical equivalent] of the word *chayim*, or life, which would be 68 CE, as opposed to the more common belief that it happened in the year 70. We keep this memory alive by starting off Tisha B'Av asking, 'How many years since the destruction?' And this year we answered, '1,941 years.' After reading the *kinot* and prayers in the synagogue, we go to someone's house (usually Rabbi Maimon's) and read the *Haftorah* [portion of the prophets] again, with the *midrash* of each line read in Ladino."

I had the pleasure and unique experience of staying in the home of Lucy and Isaac Varon, another of the prominent Sephardic names in the community. For the Shabbat meal, Eli, one of their sons, who is very active in the synagogue and a great cook, prepared the Turkish dish *Cebollas de Carne*, onion-stuffed chopped meat and rice, filled with tomato sauce, topped off with Moroccan tea. (What else?) Soul food, he calls it.

The synagogue was equally as interesting. The *chazzan* reads every word of the prayers out loud with everybody joining in. Everyone knew all the words by heart, and there was hardly any silence. There is always singing, and the haunting Sephardic melodies can be quite complex. An expert leader learns fifty ways to chant!

18. All the trimmings: *Cebollas de Carne*, an Eli Varon special, with Moroccan tea and two bottles of wine; one from Spain and one from Portugal (coincidently, two countries to have expelled the Jews!)

As in some Ashkenazic synagogues, honors related to the Torah reading are auctioned off: but here, the bids are in pennies and the winner is announced in Hebrew and Ladino. When one of the winning bids was given to me to hold the Torah, I, too, gave a donation and, to my joy, it was announced in Ladino! When someone is called up to the Torah, everyone shouts out, "*Kavod*" (honor!) and when he is finished, the warm greetings are "*Chazak u'baruch*" (strength and blessing).

Even during my short stay in Seattle, it became clear to me that this group of Sephardim – whose ancestors endured the Spanish Expulsion of 1492 – possess enormous strength, reflected in their consistently positive outlook. I understand now what Rabbi Maimon meant when he said, "Throughout history, we've always looked at the bright side of the moon." To this spiritual leader, a half cup of water is never half-empty, but always half-full. His contagious laugh and bubbly attitude almost demand a sunny outlook from all who meet him.

> "Throughout history, we've always looked at the bright side of the moon."

19. Seattle's pride and joy! Rabbi Solomon Maimon celebrating his 90th birthday, attracting hundreds of relatives from across the country.

Shabbat at Sephardic Bikur Holim was dedicated to Rabbi Maimon's ninetieth birthday and the family reunion. An analogy drawn from books of Mussar explains that the life of a community can be likened to a boat in a moving body of water: unless great efforts are made to battle the current, the boat will not remain stationary, but will even move backward. In Seattle, that boat has stayed its course through attention to prayer, family, and education over the long pull of many years, making it one of the largest and most successful Sephardic communities in the United States, in the most unlikely of places – a true treasure. And Rabbi Maimon was a key individual in that story.

During the Shabbat birthday festivities, while I held the Torah, Rabbi Maimon's son from Monsey, New York, Rabbi Abraham Maimon, spoke of the difficulty of keeping the *mitzvot* in the diaspora, so far from the palpable Presence of G-d. So how do Jews survive? By having a leader who is so devoted to the Torah and *mitzvot* that he brings G-d closer to the Jews. And this is precisely what Rabbi Solomon Maimon has done: by bringing G-d closer, by forging a deeper connection between the Divine and Seattle's Jews, he has enabled them to survive and flourish, even in this isolated part of the country.

There is a saying in Ladino: "*Esta en sus treje*," which means, "He's standing on his thirteen." This puzzling expression goes back to the early days of the Inquisition, when priests tried to force Jews to abandon Judaism under torture, and subsequently failed in their efforts. The priests would utter this saying, reporting that the Jew wouldn't budge from his belief in the Thirteen Fundamental Principles of Judaism. Their spirit lives on!

Esta en sus treje

Life-Cycle Events in the Sephardic Community

The family and synagogue are the essence of Sephardic life. These beautiful customs have endured for centuries and are still lovingly performed to this day.

Soon after a future mother notifies both families that she is expecting, the families set a date to invite all female friends and relatives to a gathering called the *corte de fashadura* – that is the "cutting, measuring, and sewing" of the baby clothes.

In keeping with the traditional belief that the prophet Elijah attends all circumcision ceremonies, someone is designated as *kitado* (godfather, similar to the *sandek* in Ashkenazic custom), who sits in *la siya de Eliyahu Hanavi* (the chair of the prophet Elijah).

After the *brit* and the blessing on the wine, a blessing on lemon or rosemary is recited, thanking G-d for our sense of smell, the symbol of the *neshamah* (soul).

The Sephardic name for bar mitzvah is *cumplir minyan* (completing the quorum of ten). The bar mitzvah boy's *aliyah* is next to the last, *samuh*. The bar mitzvah does not read the *Haftorah*, but he does read the Torah.

The night before her wedding, the bride invites her close friends to her house for *noche de alhenya*. One of her friends applies *al-henya* (henna) as rouge or on her nails. It's a high-spirited evening, with singing and dancing.

20. Blessing from grandfather: Sephardic bar mitzvah at the Kotel, Jerusalem, Israel

All Jews are married under a *chuppah* or canopy, but Spanish Sephardim practice an additional custom of *echar taleth* (spreading of the *tallit*). The bride's parents on one side, and the groom's on the other, hold onto the fringes while the *tallit* is placed on the head of the *novyo* (groom) and *novya* (bride). This very old custom signifies the groom saying to the bride, "From now on, you're under my shelter and protection" as they are sanctified as one unit. This is the origin of the solemn oath of the parents of a growing boy: "*Asi ke mos ayegue el Dio echar taleth a mi ijo*" (May G-d help us be able to spread the *tallit* over my son).

21. Sephardic bride visits the Kotel before the *chuppah*, Jerusalem, Israel

22. Memories: Rabbi Simon Benzaquen, who succeeded the legendary Rabbi Maimon, joins the rabbi as they examine images from the archives of Sephardic Bikur Holim.

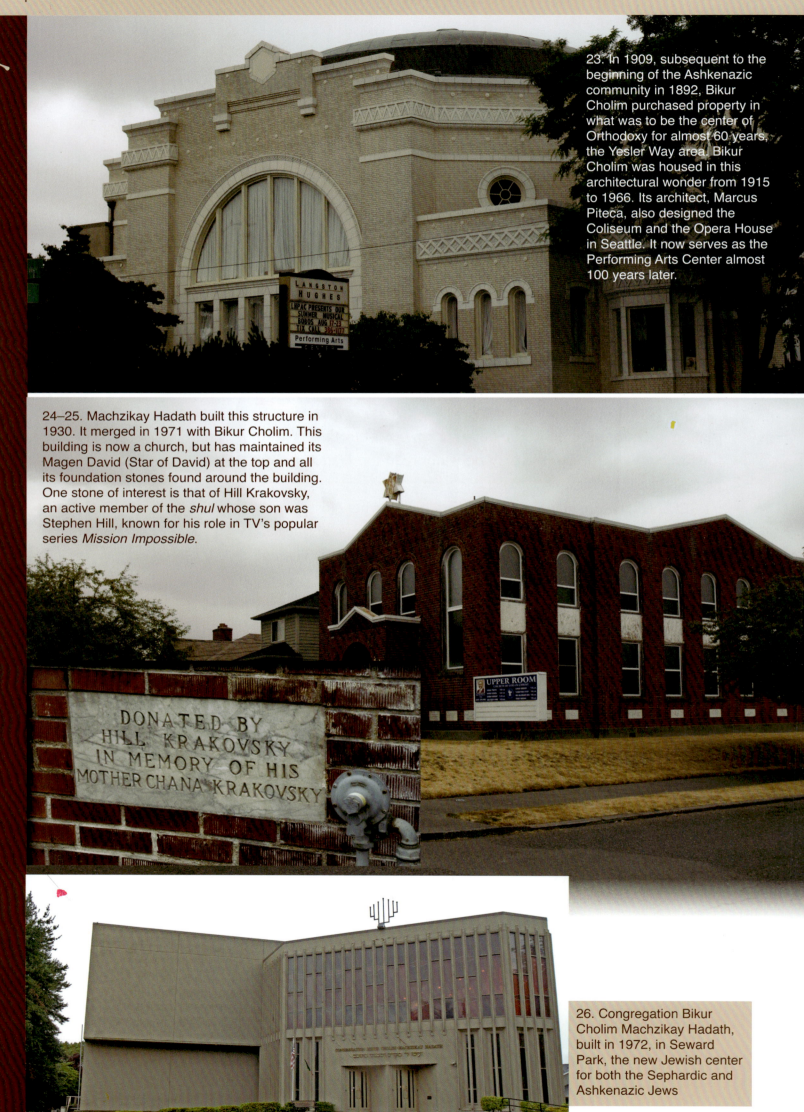

Evolution and the Ashkenazic community

23. In 1909, subsequent to the beginning of the Ashkenazic community in 1892, Bikur Cholim purchased property in what was to be the center of Orthodoxy for almost 60 years, the Yesler Way area. Bikur Cholim was housed in this architectural wonder from 1915 to 1966. Its architect, Marcus Piteca, also designed the Coliseum and the Opera House in Seattle. It now serves as the Performing Arts Center almost 100 years later.

24–25. Machzikay Hadath built this structure in 1930. It merged in 1971 with Bikur Cholim. This building is now a church, but has maintained its Magen David (Star of David) at the top and all its foundation stones found around the building. One stone of interest is that of Hill Krakovsky, an active member of the *shul* whose son was Stephen Hill, known for his role in TV's popular series *Mission Impossible*.

DONATED BY HILL KRAKOVSKY IN MEMORY OF HIS MOTHER CHANA KRAKOVSKY

26. Congregation Bikur Cholim Machzikay Hadath, built in 1972, in Seward Park, the new Jewish center for both the Sephardic and Ashkenazic Jews

27–28. The beautiful *aron* (ark) in Bikur Cholim on Yesler Way was designed in 1915 using tens of thousands of tiles.

When it closed down in 1966, its tiles were removed, one by one; each tile was marked and brought to the new Seward

Park *shul* and, painstakingly, put back together like a puzzle, as it was originally in 1915. At right, the *aron* today.

29. Close-up of *Aron* today

30. Interior today with *ezras nashim* (women's section) above

31. *Taharah* facility in Seattle, where the rite of ritual washing of the corpse before burial occurs. This rite is derived from the biblical injunction "As he came so shall he go" (Ecclesiastes 5:15). When a man is born, he is washed, and when he dies he is washed. The association that performs this service is named the *chevra kadisha* (the holy society, or Jewish burial society). Rabbi Eliezer Askenazi laid the foundation and model of an efficient burial society, in Prague, in 1564. To assist in the preparation and burial of the dead is considered one of the greatest mitzvos of the Jewish faith.

כל עמת שבא כן ילך

MEL WOLF
MEMORIAL
TAHARA FACILITY
DEDICATED JUNE 2001
תמוז תשס"א

32. Old Sephardic cemetery, 1906

PHARDIC • CEMETERY
IED 1906

CEMETERY PRAYER

ברוך אתה יי, אלהינו מלך העולם.
אשר יצר אתכם בדין. וההיה אתכם
בדין, וזן אתכם בדין. דיודע מספר
כלכם בדיך. והוא עתיד להחיותכם
ולהקימכם בדין. ברוך אתה יי.
מחיה המתים:

33. The burial place of Rabbi Abraham Maimon, leader of the Sephardic synagogue, Bikur Holim

REV. ABRAHAM MAIMON
BORN 1874   DIED 1931

5694
VICTOR SADES
DIED MARCH 21 1937

34. Pine needles fill in weather-worn lettering on an old Sephardi monument.

THE SEATTLE MIKVAH
THE RIVKA GAMEL BUILDING

35. The Seattle *mikveh*. The *mikveh* is a ritual bath, with sources from the Torah, for the purpose of ritual immersion; the waters of the *mikveh* always remain in contact with a natural source of water (such as naturally collected rain water). Halachic sources tell us that this *mitzvah* is so important that an Orthodox community must build a *mikveh* before building a synagogue.

36. Yeshivas Rabbeinu Chaim Ozer provided higher education in 1938.

37. Rabbi Maimon studying with the pre-minyan study group

38. Rabbi Maimon at Shacharit (morning) services

39. Seattle Hebrew Academy (1969): Jewish education has progressed from the first single-room *cheder* in 1898 to this beautiful complex.

40. First Bikur Cholim religious school, c. 1915–1925

41. Affixing the *mezuzah* at the dedication of the educational center

Making a living

42. The 24th Ave. Market on Yesler was owned by Sam Maimon. On the far right is a young Solomon Maimon, c. 1934; he later became the charismatic leader of Sephardic Bikur Holim.

43. King's Deli on Yesler used to be the famous kosher bakery Brenner's in the old neighborhood.

44. Large kosher bakery found in local supermarket today

45. Pike Place Market as it looked when it first opened in 1907. Many of the food concessions, especially those selling fish, were owned and run by the new Sephardic immigrants.

46. Pike Place Market today is one of the oldest continuous running markets in the US. The only remaining fish concession run by Sephardim is Pure Food Fish, owned by the Amon family.

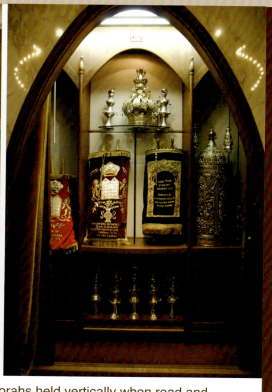

Sephardic traditions

47. Sephardic Bikur Holim, whose immigrants came from Marmara and Turkey

48. Beautiful *aron* showing Torahs held vertically when read and Torahs read flat on the table, which are the ones used in this *shul*

49. The silver shovel ceremony and *kaporah*. There is a Sephardic custom when putting up a new structure. Before digging the first hole, everyone asks for forgiveness, as we do before Yom Kippur, by saying *kapores* with a chicken (many now use money) and then *shechting* it. Some eyes are on the shovel and some on the chicken, at groundbreaking for the new Bikur Holim as the *shochet* stands by, c. 1964.

50. Rabbi Simon Benzaquen was born in Spanish Morocco, and became rabbi of Sephardic Bikur Holim in 1984 upon the retirement of Rabbi Solomon Maimon. He is also a *sofer* who writes *sifrei Torah*, *tefillin*, and *mezuzos*, as well as being a *mohel*, performing ritual circumcisions. (As it says on his card, "Fastest *mohel* in the West!") He is also a *dayan* (judge) for divorces. Above, putting the final touches on a *sefer Torah*.

51. Sephardic Jews carrying Torah scrolls in Rhodes, c. 1936. Today, Sephardim from Rhodes are represented in Congregation Ezra Bessaroth.

52. Congregation Ezra Bessaroth

My thanks to
Rabbi Solomon Maimon,
Rabbi Simon Benzaquen,
Eugene Normand,
Jerry and Larry Adatto,
the wonderful cooperation
at the Washington State
Jewish Historical Society,
Isaac Azose,
Isaac and Lucy Varon,
Rabbi Moshe Kletenik,
Eli Genauer,
and Lillian Radinsky.

Bibliography

Adatto, Albert. "Sephardim and the Seattle Sephardic community." MA thesis. Seattle: University of Washington, 1939.

Cone, Molly, Howard Droker, and Jacqueline Williams. *Family of Strangers: Building a Jewish Community in Washington State*. Seattle: University of Washington Press, 2003.

The Jewish Experience in Washington State: A Chronology, 1845–2005. Seattle: Washington State Jewish Historical Society, 2006.

Maimon, Sam Bension. *The Beauty of Sephardic Life: Scholarly, Humorous, and Personal Reflections*. Seattle: Maimon Ideas Publications, 1993.

Rochlin, Harriet, and Fred Rochlin. *Pioneer Jews: A New Life in the Far West*. Boston: Houghton Mifflin, 1984.

"Scenes of Sephardic Life." Seattle: Washington State Jewish Historical Society, 1992.

Photo Attributions

All numbered photos from the author's collection except as follows. Photos 2 (1379), 3 (1105), 4 (130), 5 (26513), 6 (neg. 1097), 7 (neg. 1084), 8 (neg. 15643), 9 (neg. 1447), 14, 45, 51: University of Washington Libraries, Special Collections; 17, 27, 36, 40, 41, 42, 49: Bikur Holim archives.

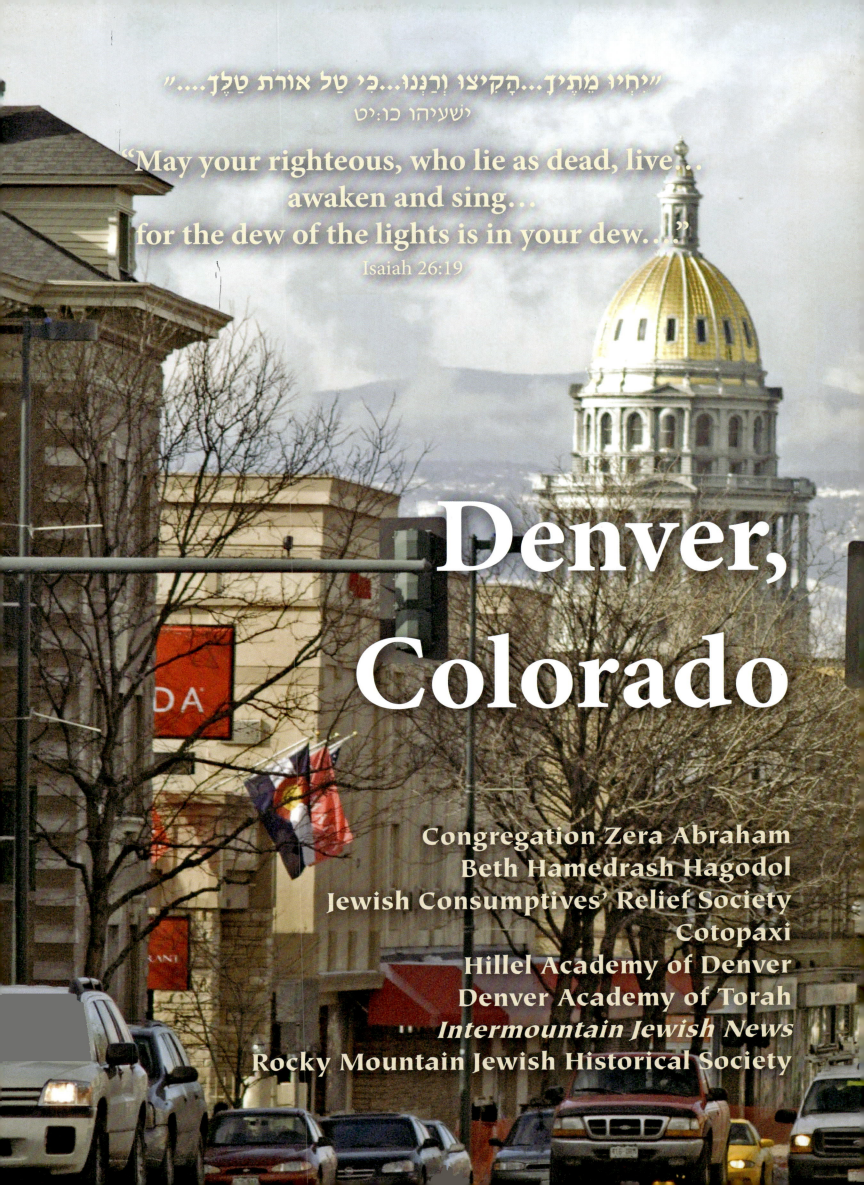

"יִחְיוּ מֵתֶיךָ...הָקִיצוּ וְרַנְּנוּ...כִּי טַל אוֹרֹת טַלֶּךָ...."

ישעיהו כו:יט

"May your righteous, who lie as dead, live…
awaken and sing…
for the dew of the lights is in your dew…."

Isaiah 26:19

Denver, Colorado

Congregation Zera Abraham
Beth Hamedrash Hagodol
Jewish Consumptives' Relief Society
Cotopaxi
Hillel Academy of Denver
Denver Academy of Torah
Intermountain Jewish News
Rocky Mountain Jewish Historical Society

Denver, Colorado

Chanukah and the Chuppah
in the Wild West

In an empty room in Southeast Denver's Aish Denver (formerly Ahavas Yisroel), I stand alone, save for a few members of a family about to have a wedding. The scene is incredibly beautiful on many levels. It is the third night of Chanukah and we watch as the bride, dressed in her wedding gown, lights the Chanukah candles. Now she is reciting the prayer "*Haneiros Hallalu* – We light these lights… to praise Your great Name for Your miracles, Your wonders, and Your triumphs…"

1. Candle lighting before the *chuppah*: Is this heaven?

There are half a dozen menorahs on the table, but the large picture window reflects an endless array of light, just as the glow from all the candles reflects the boundless joy, anticipation, and gratitude on the bride's face. As the family sings "Ma'oz Tzur," a hymn full of hope for the future rebuilding of the Holy Temple, the energy and poignancy of the moment takes my breath away.

It's hard to believe that this thriving Jewish community is rooted in the Wild West that emerged here more than 100 years ago. Denver represents just about everything we envision of those days: the Rocky Mountains, the Pike's Peak Gold Rush of 1859, cattle ranchers, saloons, gun battles, the Comanches, Arapahoes, Utes, Sioux, and the Cheyenne.

2. Endless array of light

Colorado is Spanish for "colored red," for the Colorado River runs through red canyons. The state joined the union in 1876, the centennial of the founding of the USA – which is why it's called the Centennial State. By then, synagogues and Jewish organizations had long been in place! Why would Jews take all the obvious risks to come here? Was this a place to start a nice Jewish family?

Die Goldene Medinah – Literally

The answer is that Colorado was the ultimate *goldene medinah*. In 1858, prospectors found gold along Cherry Creek near present-day Denver. Manifest Destiny was in the air and newspaperman Horace Greeley popularized the phrase "Go west, young man."*

And they did.

---

*   The phrase was actually coined by Indiana journalist John B.L. Soule; Greeley reprinted Soule's editorial in his *New York Tribune*, and although he credited Soule, the phrase stuck to the better-known Greeley.

In one year, 100,000 people – known as the '59ers – reached the area in search of wealth and adventure. "Pikes Peak or bust!" was the pioneers' slogan scrawled on one covered wagon after another.

A dozen Jews from Germany and central Europe were among them. The three Solomon brothers, all with the middle name of Zadok (righteous person), came from the East Coast by covered wagon as merchants. The Myers family came and opened a hotel in Colorado Springs, described by Burton Myers's wife as "a typical wild west hostelry where liquor was sold and card games ran all night." Gold dust was used as currency in exchange for merchandise.

3.
Gold
pan and
brochure instructions

The first Jewish religious service in Denver was either for Rosh Hashanah or a bar mitzvah (records are unclear) in 1859. Just one year later, the Hebrew Burial and Prayer Society was founded. Recognition of the Jewish presence soon translated into a resolution by the Denver Town Company which read, "That the trustees of the Hebrew synagogue be donated ten lots… providing they build a house of worship… within eight months, said house to cost not less than $700."

4. Leopold Mayer established a bank and store after traveling 600 miles by foot in 1859, to what was to become Denver.

5.
Clara
Goldsmith,
whose
parents migrated to Denver by covered wagon in 1859, was the first Jewish female born in Denver. The death of her mother in childbirth (to Clara) was the impetus behind the organization of Denver's first Jewish burial society.

More than 100 pioneer Jews arrived by 1866. Some were miners, literally out to partake in the gold rush, but most came to this untamed wilderness to provide the miners with the necessities of life. The first Jewish physician was Dr. John Elsner, who arrived at the head of a 27-strong wagon train in 1866. What he found was truly the Wild West. When he arrived from the East wearing his high hat, it was promptly shot off!

Changing his style of dress, he faithfully ministered to white and Indian alike, putting into practice all of his medical and surgical knowledge. And he had to be on his toes too – someone was shot almost every night! As *mohel* for the entire Colorado territory, Dr. Elsner officiated at the *brisim* of infant boys, who might be several months old by the time weather permitted the trip. Aside from his duties as doctor and *mohel*, Dr. Elsner was a member of the first *minyan*, a committee member of the first Hebrew school, and a member of the early B'nai B'rith.

The *Rocky Mountain News* reported Jewish services on the holidays of "Yom Kippur, Tsukes and Simhas Tore." And it was not only the men who demonstrated their pioneering spirit. For women to get to the mineral springs then used as their monthly *mikveh* (ritual bath), they had to traverse a 15-mile trip from the mining camp over a dangerously narrow precipice on the sidewall of a mountain!

Congregation Zera Abraham, the first permanent Orthodox *minyan*, was organized by Chassidim in 1877 and is still very active today. But this was just the beginning. By 1879, the YMHA (Young Men's Hebrew Association, the Jewish counterpart of the YMCA) felt it had enough of a following to hold its first social venture, a Purim Ball.

6. Congregation Zera Abraham, oldest extant congregation on the West Side, organized in 1887 as a Chassidic congregation. This was its second home.

Wealth and Health

On the heels of the gold seekers came the health seekers. The climate and invigorating clean air of Denver (called the Mile High City because of its mile-high altitude) became known throughout the country as favorable for curing respiratory diseases, especially the dreaded tuberculosis, or "consumption," as it was more commonly known. Colorado became known as the "world's sanatorium" (the old term for hospital).

I visited with the resident authority on Colorado Jewish history, Dr. Jeanne Abrams. Originally from upstate New York, she later came to Denver, planning to move on to Tucson, Arizona. But she loved Denver so much that she and her family have stayed for 37 years. She concentrated on the American colonial experience, but wrote her doctorate on the JCRS, the Jewish Consumptives' Relief Society of Denver – and from then on, she was hooked on this branch of history. Today, through her numerous books, she is putting Colorado Jewish history on the map.

"More people came in search of health than in search of wealth," she told me. "The Denver Jewish community is unique because it survived early on when other Jewish communities in the United States stagnated." The eastern European Orthodox Jews, among others, who came here for health reasons, at first came to the National Jewish Hospital for Consumptives, founded and run by the German Jews. This hospital was for

7. Jewish Consumptives' Relief Society (JCRS), founded in 1903 by Jewish working-class immigrants, who launched the institution by raising $1.10! This photograph, c. 1907, shows the early buildings and the tent cottages built to give tuberculosis patients the maximum exposure to fresh air.

incipient, curable cases only, and had no kosher facilities. Then Dr. Charles Spivak, a physician from Jefferson Medical College in Philadelphia who had fled the pogroms of Russia in 1881, came to Denver in 1886. Known as the "guiding genius" of the JCRS, he helped found the largest institution of its kind in the US along with Rabbi Elias Hillkowitz, considered the dean of Denver's early West Side Orthodox rabbis; his son, Dr. Philip Hillkowitz; and Rabbi Charles Eliezer Hillel Kauvar, the first rabbi of the Beth HaMedrosh Hagodol (1901).

8. Dr. Charles Spivak, known as the "guiding genius" of the JCRS, c. 1920

"It was Rabbi Hillkowitz," Dr. Abrams added, "who suggested the JCRS motto from the Talmud: 'He who saves one life saves the world.'" The JCRS, with its kosher kitchen and synagogue, was clearly attuned to the needs of the Orthodox community.

Denver's reputation as a health-restoring city grew and endures to this day. Jeanne remarked, "I have a neighbor who moved here in the 1970s and went back to New York's Lower East Side for a visit. When he met an old friend, he told him that he had moved to Denver. The friend looked him up and down and said, 'You don't look sick!'

"In a way, this was an early stereotype of Denver. But, the wide-open territory offered a wonderful opportunity for economic success as well. For example, the Shwayder family, of Samsonite luggage fame, was an Orthodox family. One of the children, the story goes, received an important letter from a close relative in Europe on Shabbos – but he wouldn't open it until after Shabbos, much to the chagrin of the curious people around him! Also the May Company opened a number of stores and eventually evolved into Macy's."

10. Goldenhill Cemetery; one of the oldest Jewish cemeteries in Denver (1908). This is a section for the JCRS patients with the Rockies in the background. Dr. Spivak is buried here as well.

11. The five Shwayder brothers standing on a board to demonstrate the strength of their suitcase, c. 1910. They eventually opened a small suitcase factory that turned into one of the largest in the business, the Samsonite corporation.

9. Rabbi Elias Hillkowitz, dean of Denver's early West Side Orthodoxy. A supporter of JCRS, he suggested the motto from the Talmud: "He who saves one life is considered as if he had preserved the whole world."

A Thriving Community Emerges from a Failure

In 1881, a group of Orthodox Jews from Russia trekked by wagon train from New York to Cotopaxi, Colorado (a day's ride out of Denver) to mine for silver. They had been assured they would be provided with homes and supplies, but after a year of broken promises and great suffering, they were rescued by HIAS (Hebrew Immigrant Aid Society) and B'nai B'rith. They came down from the mountain and settled in the West Colfax area of Denver, where they formed the Orthodox nucleus of the present-day community. The Cotopaxi group and their descendants became a contributing force in all aspects of Denver life. The failure of the Cotopaxi Colony helped to seed the West Denver Orthodox community. Meanwhile, the German, Reform Jews strengthened the East Side. It would be some time before the German and Russian Jewish factions would meld into a cohesive community.

12. Channah Milstein, former colonist in the failed Cotopaxi Jewish colony, became a fixture in Denver's eastern European West Side community collecting for the needy.

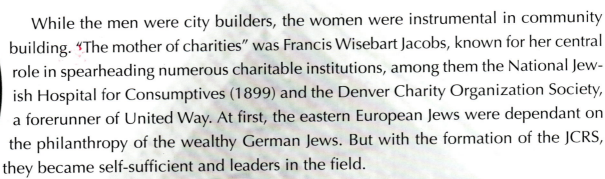

While the men were city builders, the women were instrumental in community building. "The mother of charities" was Francis Wisebart Jacobs, known for her central role in spearheading numerous charitable institutions, among them the National Jewish Hospital for Consumptives (1899) and the Denver Charity Organization Society, a forerunner of United Way. At first, the eastern European Jews were dependant on the philanthropy of the wealthy German Jews. But with the formation of the JCRS, they became self-sufficient and leaders in the field.

By 1907, there were 5,000 Jews in Denver; in West Colfax, there was never a shortage of *shul*s or rabbis. Many have compared this area to New York's Lower East Side, with the synagogues named after the streets on which they stood, no matter what their official names were. There was the "Hooker Street *shul*" or the "Tenth Street *shul*" as well as those named after people – the "Plonsky Congregation" or "Chotsky's Synagogue."

And some of these congregations faced harrowing experiences to stay alive. Israel Chatz was so anxious to keep his *shul* going that he bribed his neighbors with whiskey to get them to attend. Then there was the Mogen David Synagogue (founded 1885). During the flood of 1909, it was left standing in eight feet of water, but that didn't stop the congregation. Some of the worshippers paddled over in canoes and managed to climb inside the building to *daven*!

14. Mogen David Synagogue (1885), also known as the "Glazerlach *shul*"

"Our Jewish Heritage Was Worth Keeping…"

If you really want to know about Orthodox Denver's West Side in the early twentieth century, just speak to charming and effervescent Frieda Shames-Makovsky. "I'm 92," she told me as we sat in her living room, "and my father was born in Denver in 1885. His parents and their large family lived in Russia at the time of the pogroms. My grandparents and extended family, all Orthodox, came to the New York harbor. They were coaxed immediately to come to Cotopaxi by a swindler named Saltiel to work his mines. They somehow retained their Jewish traditions through all their suffering until, after an investigation by HIAS revealed the hoax, they were brought to West Colfax in Denver.

"My family started out as farmers – about where the Denver airport is now – and they built the Orthodox community. Their dream was to be successful farmers, but the land was rocky and not conducive to farming. Although agriculture seemed destined to failure, the religious aspects of their lives flourished. Their first request to the New York HIAS was for a Torah scroll and matzoh for Passover.

"There was no shortage of *shochtim*, butchers, bakers, and, of course, *shul*s in the early 1900s. My mother milked the cows and we children would bring the full containers of milk down the hill and sell quarts of milk for a dime each. But we were too young to be trusted with the money, so we would take the caps home

15. Frieda Shames-Makovsky and son Evan. Parents and grandparents started in Cotopaxi Colony.

16. Hebrew school students and *rebbe* on steps of Yeshiva Etz Chaim building, c. 1913

and a record would be kept. I suppose the adults collected the money later.

"It was clear to us that our Jewish heritage was worth keeping. All the boys went to Talmud Torah after school, and the *rebbe* was always nearby to keep an eye on them."

In fact, by 1915, there were three types of Hebrew schools in Denver: secular Yiddish, Zionist, and Orthodox. One of the foremost Orthodox lay leaders of this country and supporter of Torah-based Jewish education was Sheldon K. Beren (1922–1996). A wealthy Denver oilman, he was the founder of Denver's Yeshiva Toras Chaim in 1966 and Beth Jacob High School in 1967. He also served as national president of Torah Umesorah National Society for Hebrew Day Schools in America, and provided much of the funding for the building of the Hillel Academy of Denver.

What was Shabbos like in the early twentieth century? "I remember," Frieda said with a smile, "that my grandmother used to make a cholent [stew] before Shabbos and there was a bakery two blocks away. All the children would bring their family's cholent over to the bakery to put in the oven to keep warm; then we'd pick it up after *shul* on Shabbos. [This was also commonly done in Europe.] My other job was to bring a live chicken to the *shochet* and bring it back after the deed was done. We bought live fish for Shabbos. It would swim around in the bathtub until my mother was ready to prepare it. It was important to have cordial relations with the non-Jews in the area, for we depended on them to come light our wood furnaces on Shabbos – otherwise we'd freeze!"

17. Sheldon K. Beren (1922–1996), one of the major supporters of Torah-based Jewish education in this country

Fortunately, anti-Semitism was generally minimal, but there were reminders that the Jews were not entirely welcome. Frieda recalled the stormy days of 1925, when the Ku Klux Klan controlled the government and tried to take over West Colfax. "They were voted out of office one year later, but it was nervous times.

"When Pearl Harbor was attacked," she said with pride, "my father said to my brothers, 'You're Americans and you're observant Jews: you must serve in the army. Do what you have to do and when you come back, remember your traditions.'" Her four brothers served in the US army at the same time.

18. Shames family in uniform

Another "Denver boy" who served as a US soldier during World War II was Ivan Goldstein, who was wounded and taken prisoner by the Germans during the Battle of the Bulge. I talked with his son, Dan Goldstein, about his extraordinary family. Dan's great-great-grandparents came to Denver in 1870 by covered wagon. His father presently lives in Jerusalem, and wrote a book of his memoirs about growing up Jewish in Denver and his war experiences. Ivan recounted how, as a child in the 1930s, he would help out his mother in the family's jewelry store. A Sioux Indian chief, who brought his tribes' homemade items to sell at the store, would swap stories with his mom about Indian and Jewish culture and history. The chief always said with a wink, "We're so much alike; the Sioux must be one of the Lost Tribes of Israel!" And Ivan would tell of his grandfather's horse, Jack, who seemingly sensed the coming of Shabbos, and would gallop home extra fast on Friday afternoons.

At the turn of the century, Ivan recalled, there was a *shvitz,* a steam bath that was sacred territory on the West Side for three generations of Jewish men. Today, the Denver Broncos football team plays in the stadium built on that site. Could it be that some places are forever destined for sweat?

Though his formal Jewish education consisted of afternoon Hebrew school, Ivan was taught by his mother about trusting in G-d at all times. The day he was leaving Denver for army basic training, his mother reminded him to take along his *tefillin.* When he protested that he wouldn't have time to pray during battle, his mother replied that there would come "a special time." That day came on his first day in the Battle of the Bulge when he left his tank and put on his *tefillin* in the darkness of the freezing cold early morning. That day, his tank was blown up and he was taken prisoner. His pockets were emptied by the Germans, who picked up a letter from his mother that had fallen to the floor. "Ivan," it read, "I hope you received the package I sent you for Chanukah." That sealed his fate.

The German major ordered that the Jew be taken out and shot in the morning. But before the order could be carried out, a major American offensive started and the Germans and their prisoners had to run. Ivan's *tefillin* were lost, but Ivan recalled, "I vowed I would never forget G-d's presence in my life." For the next four months, Ivan was saved miraculously from one certain death after another, surviving German prison camps and deadly disease.

After the war, he kept his vow, and became an active member of the Denver Orthodox community and president of the Hillel Academy. Interestingly enough, one of Ivan's best friends was David Spivak, the grandson of Dr. Charles Spivak, who founded the JCRS in 1904.

19. Ivan Goldstein, a Jewish survival story: he fought in the Battle of the Bulge, became president of Hillel Academy.

Ivan was taught by his mother about trusting in G-d at all times.... "I vowed I would never forget G-d's presence in my life." ...He kept his vow...

Surrounded by G-d's Magnificent Creation

I asked Dan Goldstein about the uniqueness of Denver Jews. He said there is a special connection between Denver Jews and nature. "My great-grandmother, I'm told, saw beauty in everything. I'm sure she felt, as we do, that nature adds to religion. It's an instant connection to G-d."

Frieda's son, Evan, echoed that sentiment. "For one thing," he said, "we are surrounded by nature and we really appreciate it. You can go to the Rockies for Shavuot with a *minyan* and really picture receiving the Torah on Mount Sinai. Isn't that more moving than in a *shul*?"

And like Dan Goldstein, he is well aware of his family's history. "Perseverance," he said. "Perseverance was the key. They lived through the hardships in the mountains of Cotopaxi with no kosher food, no stores, no schools – and were still able to retain Jewish tradition. The link in the Orthodox chain never broke: an amazing phenomenon!

"What's different about Denver?" he mused. "First of all, this is not so large a community that you get lost. Everyone must participate to survive. Secondly, the Denver Jew is uniquely independent."

The editor of the *Intermountain Jewish News*, Rabbi Hillel Goldberg, agrees. "You don't come to Colorado if you don't have an interest in the outdoors, an appreciation of the beauty of G-d's world…. And yes, this is a highly independent group of people," he chuckled. Rabbi Goldberg's great-grandparents on his mother's side came to Denver before the Civil War. His father, Max Goldberg, was a key figure who brought Denver to national attention. In 1943 he became editor of the *Intermountain Jewish News*, founded as the *Jewish News* in 1913, and the Goldberg family has been at the helm ever since, with his wife, Miriam, and son Hillel publishing it to this day. Max was a community leader as well as a media pioneer, bringing television to Denver in 1952. He pioneered both the TV telethon to help conquer polio, and the television "talk show" genre. The founder of the Rose Memorial Hospital, Max brought countless celebrities – among them Jerry Lewis, Al Jolson, Danny Kaye, Jack Benny, and Jane Russell – to help build the hospital.

20. Rabbi Hillel Goldberg; author, editor of the *Intermountain Jewish News*

That characteristic independent streak and pride in his Jewish heritage sustained Hillel Goldberg in college. "I lived in Berkeley, California, during the '60s, when there were three *shomer Shabbos* students out of 27,000 students!"

21. Max Goldberg, media pioneer and community leader, shown here with then senator John F. Kennedy in 1959

A City of Independent Spirits

"You have a certain independence of mind here," he commented. In 1986, Goldberg founded an Orthodox community in a Reform temple in Santa Fe, New Mexico, and there is a tremendous interaction between the communities of Denver and Santa Fe. "This could never have happened without the independence of mind found in Denver."

He maintains that this sort of pluck made it possible for traditional Jews to survive in West Colfax early in the twentieth century – heroic Jews who refused to succumb to the temptation of assimilation, and refused to open their stores on Shabbos. Denver's reputation as a city of religious Jews spread. "In 1921," Goldberg pointed out, "Rabbi Kook, Rabbi Moshe Mordechai Epstein, and the Kovner Rov were all in Denver on the same day. So there were clearly some religiously substantial Jews in Denver in those days. You have a Rabbi Yehudah Leib Ginsburg, who published many *seforim* [books on Torah topics] in Denver. He could have published anywhere, but there is such a thing as needing solitude for scholarship."

Rabbi Daniel Alter, head of the Denver Academy of Torah (DAT) elementary school, has been in Denver for nine years. "People see themselves, here, as 'out of the box,'" he says, "with less judgmentalism. We have a daily and Shabbos *minyan* here at DAT and someone once called our diverse membership the 'sweaters, sandals, *shtreimel*s and suits.'" He noted that in addition to Rabbi Yehuda Leib Ginsburg, another rabbi who had a huge impact on Denver was the Hornosteipler Rebbe, Rabbi B.C. Shloime Twerski. A direct descendant of the Baal Shem Tov, Reb Zusia of Annipoli, and the Meor Einayim, among others (and oldest of a group of brothers that includes Rabbi Michel Twerski of Milwaukee and the noted psychologist Rabbi Dr. Abraham Twerski), he was the rabbinic leader of the historic Zera Abraham Synagogue. His *talmidim* started Chassidic *shul*s in Baltimore and Jerusalem, and his son carries on the tradition in Flatbush today.

I asked Rabbi Alter what this city, so close to the impressive Rocky Mountains, has done for him, and his response was classic Denver: "Look," he answered, "I come from Toronto and West Orange, New Jersey, and was never very athletic. But something came over me here. On I whim, I bought a bicycle and have been biking to my yeshivah ever since. When my sister in New Jersey found out, she chided me, 'Heads of yeshivos don't bike!' Well, I guess this one does!"

22. Rabbi Yehudah Leib Ginsburg (1888–1946), a key religious leader in Denver, wrote many *seforim* (books on Jewish topics).

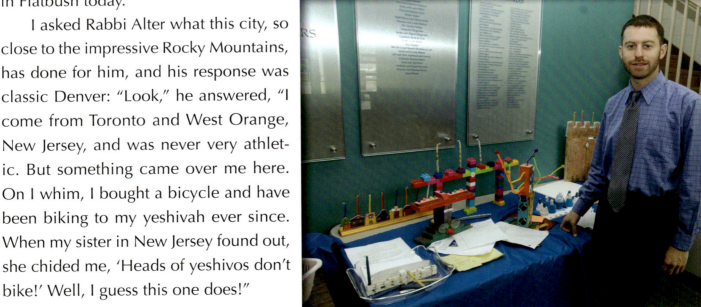

23. Rabbi Daniel Alter, head of the Denver Academy of Torah (DAT) elementary school, shown here with students' art designs for Chanukah

Keeping the Flame Burning

Yes, there is something different, almost magical, about this place. As I watch the bride and the groom take their places under the protection of the *chuppah*, my mind goes back to their ancestors and fellow Jews of the Wild West: those hopeful pioneers who came by wagon train, stagecoach, ox-drawn carts, horseback, even on foot. They came by boat through the Isthmus of Panama, later by Ellis Island or through Galveston, Texas, the "Ellis Island of the West." The promise of religious freedom, economic success, good health, and hardy adventure drew them here, and Denver welcomed them – for they were a stabilizing influence to help uphold morality and order in this rough frontier town.

It's been said that the Jews can be compared to the olive oil of the Chanukah menorah. While all liquids mingle with one another, oil stays separate. When Jews do *mitzvos*, they, too, maintain their distinction from other groups. The independence of Denver's Jews has certainly kept the flame burning for 150 years.

As the wedding ceremony concludes, the groom readies himself to break the glass in remembrance of the Temple, and the vow *"Im eshkachech Yerushalayim* – if I forget you, Jerusalem" rings in the air. It proclaims our eternal faith in the rebuilding of our House of G-d. How appropriate this is, I think, at the same time that the bride and groom are pledging to build a true Jewish home in the nation of Israel.

Pledging their commitment to fortifying the Jewish nation, this young couple epitomizes the continuity and perseverance that is Denver. The *Intermountain Jewish News* wrote in a memorial to Shearith Israel, one of the oldest remaining synagogue structures surviving in the city: "There it stands today – abandoned – alone – forgotten. [But] Shearith Israel is not dead and will never die. Its children and grandchildren have been instilled with a belief in G-d that will continue unto generations yet unborn."

24. Breaking the glass to remind us of the incompleteness of all rejoicing as long as the Temple is in ruins

A Bubbie's Chanukah Blessing

Frieda Shames-Makovsky and her son Evan have fond memories of Bubbie Shames, Frieda's mother, who always gave all the grandchildren silver dollars as Chanukah *gelt*. This was the real thing, back in the days when a silver dollar was a silver dollar – not chocolate!

The last time she lovingly gave to Evan his Chanukah *gelt* was in 1961, the year of her passing. He carried it with him in his pocket at all times. In 1969, when he met his wife-to-be, he wanted to give her a gift for their engagement. He had nothing to give her at the time, but he reached in his pocket and excitedly pulled out his Bubbie's Chanukah *gelt*. She was visibly moved. "At the wedding," Frieda beamed, "the bride presented Bubbie's silver dollar to him as a gift. They had it framed and it has been hanging in their home ever since." The legacy of Bubbie Shames lives on!

25. Wedding of Evelyn and Evan Makovsky; the legend of Bubbe Shames lives on!

26. "We light these lights… to praise Your great name for Your miracles, Your wonders, and Your triumphs…"

Early life in the Rockies

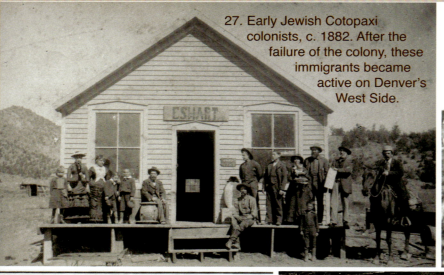

27. Early Jewish Cotopaxi colonists, c. 1882. After the failure of the colony, these immigrants became active on Denver's West Side.

28. Founding women of the Denver Sheltering Home for Jewish Children, c. 1907

29. Entrance at Texas building of the JCRS, c. 1930s

30. Tuberculosis patients' beds moved out onto porches for heliotherapy – maximum exposure to the sun

31. National Jewish Hospital (1899). Motto: "None may enter who can pay – none can pay who enter." National Jewish kashered its kitchen only in 1925; the Jewish Consumptives' Relief Society opened in 1904 in part to address this need.

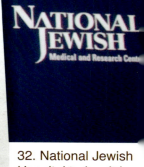

32. National Jewish Hospital today. It is no surprise that it is the top respiratory hospital in the US.

33. This tent served as a synagogue at the JCRS before a permanent building was erected in 1911.

34. The old building of the Beth Hamedrosh Hagodol Synagogue. Rabbi Charles Eliezer Hillel Kauvar, Zionist and ardent supporter of the JCRS, was its first rabbi in 1901 and served for 50 years.

35. Old Zera Abraham Synagogue still standing

36. Zera Abraham Synagogue today. It was founded in 1877 as a Chassidic congregation, and still retains *Nusach Sephard* customs.

37. Denver Academy of Torah (DAT)

38. Hillel Academy

39. We're going on a kosher picnic! The Denver section of the National Council of Jewish Women (NCJW), founded in 1893. The sign being held up in the horse-drawn wagon advertises a kosher picnic in 1895.

Making a living

40. Otto Mears (second row, first person on the left), pioneer, road builder and Indian mediator, shown here negotiating a treaty with Ouray tribal chieftains in 1874.

41. Shul Baer Milstein, a kosher butcher in Denver in the late 1800s, was one of the Cotopaxi colonists in the 1880s and took a leadership role at Zera Abraham Congregation.

42. Phil Brown in his kosher butcher shop in 1921

43. All your kosher needs! The East Side Kosher Deli has meat, groceries, and a restaurant. Phil Brown would be proud!

44. Star Bakery delivery horse-drawn wagon, c. 1915. Note the Magen David above the rye bread sign.

46. Ida Mosko, wife of a blacksmith, and family, c. 1918. The small girl dressed in a nurse's uniform, Ruth, later with her husband founded the enormously successful Mattel toy company. Ruth created the famous Barbie doll.

45. Play ball! Harry and Ida Cook opened Cook's Russian Baths in Denver, which served both as a *mikveh* (ritual bath) operated at night by Ida and as a steam bath during the day, complete with kosher meals. Shown here is the business's baseball team, c. 1918.

48. Max Stein, pictured in 1910 as a mounted policeman

47. The East Side Kosher Deli

49. Robert Lazar Miller, a rancher and meat dealer who arrived in Denver in 1881, at the Denver stockyards with his grandson in 1932

50. Boy lighting Chanukah candles in Denver, 1968

51. Lighting with deep concentration, 2007

52. Gratitude for the miracles all over the world: soldier lighting Chanukah candles, 1956

53. "For these miracles we do light." Israeli soldier praying at the Wall after capture of the Old City of Jerusalem in 1967 (left). Family playing dreidel together after lighting the candles, 1969.

54–55. "*Sevivon, sof, sof, sof…*" Popular children's song about the spinning dreidel as depicted in this hanging artwork joining the other Chanukah art at the Denver Academy of Torah.

FREEDOM

SPIRIT OF THE MACCABEES

A JEWISH HOMELAND

FREEDOM FROM DISCRIMINATION

CHANUKAH INSPIRATION.

56. Chanukah inspiration in December 1947, only a few months from the reestablishment of a Jewish homeland.

57. Is it real? All of it! A gingerbread dreidel decorates the counter at the East Side Kosher Deli. Hard to just take a picture!

58. Painting of candles lit on the second day of Chanukah hanging in the East Denver Orthodox Synagogue (EDOS). Appropriately enough, I was there on the second day!

59–60. Sumptuous Chanukah food hosted by Denver's Chabad. Latkes (potato pancakes) and donuts are traditional Chanukah foods because they are made with oil, reminding us of the miracle of the oil that lasted for eight days.

61–62. Chanukah extravaganza on ice! All were invited to skate around the menorah in the center, after which the candles were lit and food was served, compliments of Denver's Chabad.

"*Haneiros hallalu…we light these lights*"

Chanukah and *chuppah*

63. Before the *chuppah* at Aish Denver, the kallah (bride), Leah, has just lit the Chanukah candles as all the family sings "Haneiros Hallalu" (these lights).

64. The miracle celebrated in an extraordinary way!

65. The *tisch* or table. With the Chanukah menorah lit in the background, the men – friends and family – gather with the groom, Eli, to sing and drink and hear the reading of the *tannaim* (betrothal document) in front of the witnesses.

66. The signing of the *tannaim* with parents and groom looking on with interest

67. Eli handing over a pen for the signing of the *kesubah* (marriage contract), which he must hand over to the bride under the *chuppah* after he gives her the ring

68. The *bedeken* (veiling): the groom looks on as the father of the bride bestows on his daughter his blessings. The bride then wears the veil to recall Rebecca's gesture of modesty when she first saw her husband.

69. The *chuppah*: the term originally refers to the bridal canopy but has now taken on the meaning of the wedding ceremony itself. The canopy represents the home that the bride and groom will make for each other. The number seven is important in the marriage ceremony. Here, the bride makes seven circuits around the groom and seven marriage blessings are recited. The circuits represent the bride's acceptance of the groom as the "center of her universe." The groom wears a *kittel* (white robe), as is worn on Yom Kippur, to symbolize that all sins of the bride and groom are forgiven on this day.

70. Sam and Anna Grimes were one of the early eastern European Jewish couples to be married in Denver. This wedding picture was taken in 1892.

71–72. The joy of the *chuppah* and the miracle of Chanukah!

My thanks to Rabbi Hillel Goldberg, Dr. Jeanne Abrams, Rabbi Daniel Alter, Frieda Shames-Makovsky, Evan Makovsky, Sheldon and Anne Ciner, and Dan Goldstein.

Bibliography

Abrams, Jeanne E. *Historic Jewish Denver*. Denver: Rocky Mountain Jewish Historical Society, 1982.

——. *Jewish Denver, 1859–1940*. Images of America. Charleston, SC: Arcadia Publishing, 2007.

——. *Jewish Women Pioneering the Frontier Trail: A History in the American West*. New York and London: NYU Press, 2006.

Goldstein, Ivan. *Hard to Forget, Harder to Remember: A Soldier's Tale of Faith and Survival*. Jerusalem: privately published, 2008.

Libo, Kenneth, and Irving Howe. *We Lived There Too: In Their Own Words and Pictures; Pioneer Jews and the Westward Movement of America, 1630–1930*. New York: St. Martin's/Marek, 1984.

Rochlin, Harriet, and Fred Rochlin. *Pioneer Jews: A New Life in the Far West*. Boston: Houghton Mifflin, 1984.

Scherman, Rabbi Nosson, and Rabbi Meir Zlotowitz, eds. *Chanukah*. New York: ArtScroll/Mesorah, 1981.

Uchill, Ida Libert. *Pioneers, Peddlers, and Tsadikim: The Story of the Jews in Colorado*. Denver: Sage Books, 1957.

Photo Attributions

All numbered photos from the author's collection except as follows. Photos 3–5, 7–9, 11–13, 16, 28–31, 33, 39, 41, 42, 44–46, 48, 49, 70: Courtesy Rocky Mountain Jewish Historical Society and Beck Archives, CJS and Penrose Library Special Collections, University of Denver; 14 (dated 7/01/03), 17 (2/16/96), 18 (7/7/08), 21 (12/13/68), 22 (6/30/98), 50, 52 (12/7/56), 53 (12/13/69), 56 (12/11/47): copyright and reprinted by permission of the *Intermountain Jewish News*; 19: archives of Ivan Goldstein; 25: archives of Evelyn and Evan Makovsky; 27: American Jewish Historical Society; 40: Colorado Historical Society; 72: Saul Landa and Ariana Dennenberg.

Afterword

History has long ago taught us the undeniable truth: to understand a people today, you must first understand its past. Or, as Walter Ehrlich put it in his book *Zion in the Valley*, "If you don't know where you've been, you won't know where you're going."[*] For me the last four years have been a hands-on demonstration of this principle.

Before I started this odyssey, I asked myself the fundamental question: How have the Jewish people been able to persevere and maintain their devotion to the Torah for over 350 years in a country replete with unparalleled freedom, but (not uncoincidentally) equally replete with the most challenging of tests? What makes this people "timeless"?

Well, now we have traveled together on this journey. If we allow ourselves to be illuminated by the rabbis who say that the totality of experience of all Jews who preceded us is implanted in our very souls, then the answer begins to become clear to us.

Despite the passage of time since I began my travels, the vision of diversity of both the people and their stories of survival remains as transparent as a cloudless day.

There are the Sephardi Jews from Turkish Marmara, whose customs were unrecognizable to the European Ashkenazim; the Jew from the deep South or Southwest whose method of food preparation and cooking differs from those Midwest and North. From the eclectic, free-thinking, "opt-in" community of San Francisco to the intense Chassidic community of Milwaukee, Jews in America come in every style and form.

Yet despite this wondrous diversity there is, I realize, a common bond that binds us together.

A Jewish Confederate soldier, fatigued from so much death and devastation in his years battling the North in the Civil War, accepts an invitation from a Jewish "Yankee" family he passes, to enjoy a Passover Seder together.

A Holocaust survivor, just a few years removed from the unspeakable horrors, has the pluck to bring a live chicken into the maternity ward of a Washington, DC, hospital to perform the tradition of *kapores* for her daughter and newborn grandson before Yom Kippur.

New Orleans Jews open their doors to the Jews of Memphis fleeing a Yellow Fever epidemic in the 1870s and then, over 100 years later, the Jews from Memphis open *their* doors to the New Orleans victims of Hurricane Katrina.

Yes, this is a passionately committed people. Look at the faces of the people in this book. Look into their eyes. These are people who, through hundreds of years on American soil, have fought through incredible trials to maintain their traditions.

---

[*] Walter Ehrlich, *Zion in the Valley: The Jewish Community of St. Louis*, vol. 2, *The Twentieth Century* (Columbia, MO: University of Missouri Press, 2002), xiii.

Do they seem familiar to you? They should: they are our parents, *bubbes*, *zeides*. They are, indeed, you and me. They are people, prime movers, who have kept their communities strong in Torah tradition throughout the years. While they might not necessarily be the "rich and famous," there is nothing "common" about them.

Many chapters in the Torah were written about our forefathers Abraham and Jacob. However, few verses were devoted to the forefather in the middle, Isaac. Our rabbis tell us that, in reality, his role was the most crucial: to be the link in the chain to connect the beginnings of our religion to the next generation, that of Jacob (whose children would become the twelve tribes of Israel). Without this link, our world would be lost. In the "wilderness" of the American diaspora, this has been the role of all those you see in this book.

They are a diverse people indeed, but the commonality of purpose and devotion to the Torah and to each other has never changed. This is indeed a timeless people.

Visiting our people in these communities, learning of their travels, and listening to their stories, has given me (and I hope you) incredible *chizuk*, strength. I realize (as I am told vehemently quite often) that there are many other communities quite worthy of being profiled. With your help and guidance, this certainly can become a reality.

We have seen but a small glimpse of the road our people have traveled in this country from past to present and stretching out to the future: life-cycle events and the emotions they evoke, holidays with their particular observances, customs, and traditions. From the sad contemplation of Tisha B'Av to the joy of a wedding, from Yom Hashoah to Yom Ha'atzmaut, from the freedom of Passover to the redemption of Shavuos, we have seen the past and the future together. I hope you feel my joy!

I invite you to contact me about this book or to tell me about *your* community! Please write me at atimelesspeople@gmail.com.

I invite you to contact me about this book or to tell me about *your* community! Please write me at atimelesspeople@gmail.com.